Innovative Policy Making for the Shift to Circular Economy

Mohamad Saad El Dine Knio
Lebanese International University, Lebanon

Najib Bou Zakhem
Lebanese International University, Lebanon

IGI Global
Scientific Publishing
Publishing Tomorrow's Research Today

Vice President of Editorial	Melissa Wagner
Director of Acquisitions	Mikaela Felty
Director of Book Development	Jocelynn Hessler
Production Manager	Mike Brehm
Cover Design	Jose Rosado

Published in the United States of America by
IGI Global Scientific Publishing
701 East Chocolate Avenue
Hershey, PA, 17033, USA
Tel: 717-533-8845 | Fax: 717-533-7115
Website: https://www.igi-global.com E-mail: cust@igi-global.com

Library of Congress Cataloging-in-Publication Data

LCCN: 2025028184 (CIP Data Pending)
ISBN13: 9798337338521
Isbn13Softcover: 9798337338538
EISBN13: 9798337338545

British Cataloguing in Publication Data
A Cataloguing in Publication record for this book is available from the British Library.

Table of Contents

Detailed Table of Contents

This theoretical study explores how innovative circular economy (CE) policies can redefine standards of living beyond traditional GDP metrics. Grounded in ecological economics and human development theory, the research critically assesses the inadequacies of GDP as a measure of well-being and highlights the necessity for alternative frameworks that integrate environmental, social, and qualitative dimensions of prosperity. By drawing on concepts such as the capabilities approach, the Doughnut Economics model, and well-being budget practices, the paper illustrates how circular economy principles can serve as a foundation for post-GDP policy making. Through the adoption of metrics that prioritize resource efficiency, environmental regeneration, social inclusion, and quality of life, circular economy policies can realign societal goals toward long-term sustainability and equitable well-being. The study contributes to the theoretical discourse on sustainability by arguing for a multidimensional understanding of prosperity that is consistent with circularity, sufficiency, and resilience.

This chapter examines how the financial sector is changing to promote economic circularity. It shows how green capital—sustainable financing and investments—can enable the transformation from linear "take-make-waste" to circular business models. Finance may assist in achieving circular economy goals, managing risk, and providing competitive investor returns. Recent studies show that circular economy solutions reduce investment payback default risk and improve risk-adjusted performance, indicating comprehensive risk management and future market growth. It will discuss green bonds, ESG-focused mutual funds, and sustainability-linked loans that support circular innovations as part of the circular economy transformation. It will provide global case examples of how banks, investors, and policymakers are using green capital to support circular solutions and offer recommendations and policy frameworks for finance, policy, and sustainability professionals to integrate circular economy aspects into their financial systems.

The chapter explores the critical role of green investors in promoting and scaling the circular economy, a regenerative economic model designed to eliminate waste, maximize resource efficiency, and create long-term sustainability. It examines how investment strategies aligned with environmental, social, and governance (ESG) principles can support circular business models, and how financial markets are evolving to meet the demands of sustainability-focused stakeholders. Through a blend of theoretical perspectives, case studies, and policy analysis, the chapter identifies key investment trends, actors, challenges, and enabling mechanisms that link capital markets with circular economy transitions. It also discusses how financial innovation, impact measurement tools, and regulatory frameworks are shaping the behavior of green investors.

This study has underscored the strategic convergence between Corporate Social Responsibility (CSR) and the circular economy (CE), emphasizing that CSR communication serves as a powerful enabler for innovative policy development. Through a thorough theoretical investigation, it has been demonstrated that CSR communication does more than inform stakeholders, it strategically frames sustainability narratives, fosters trust, and mobilizes diverse stakeholder groups to support and co-develop circular initiatives. CSR and CE together constitute a synergistic pathway where ethical responsibility and operational sustainability reinforce one another. Crucially, the study shows that transparent and credible CSR communication can build the legitimacy required to introduce systemic shifts and that stakeholder engagement facilitated through communication is not only a governance tool but a catalyst for transformative change.

This theoretical study examines the transition to a circular economy (CE) through the lens of political economy, emphasizing that circularity is not merely a technical or managerial challenge, but a fundamentally political and institutional transformation. Drawing on classical and contemporary political economy frameworks including Sector Governance Analysis, Power Analysis, Drivers of Change, and the CAR and CEL models, the study explores how power asymmetries, vested interests, institutional path dependencies, and ideological narratives shape the design and implementation of CE policies. By analysing how governance quality, stakeholder dynamics, and socio-political contexts influence reform feasibility, the research highlights the limitations of conventional economic models that ignore the politics of change. Instead, it argues for an integrated and anticipatory approach to CE policy-making, one that addresses not only the "what" but also the "how" of transition.

This thematic paper addresses the growing challenge of information pollution, or "infollution," characterized by the overproduction, duplication, and inaccuracy of digital content that impairs decision-making, affects trust, and burdens technology infrastructure. The circular economy (CE) has traditionally focused on the responsible management of physical resources, yet its principles can be adapted to address the challenges posed by infollution. This study suggests a framework that applies CE strategies, like data minimization, reuse, recycling, sharing, and quality enhancement as effective mitigation strategies to the information ecosystem. By recognizing data as a resource with value across its lifecycle, organizations may boost knowledge flows, decrease redundancy, and improve information quality. The integration of CE principles into data management leads to cleaner digital environments, enhanced operational efficiency, and more sustainable knowledge practices. This strategy not only minimizes the detrimental consequences of infollution but also supports global sustainability goals for the digital era.

This chapter explores the role of corporate finance in enabling the circular economy (CE), positioning financial decision-making as key to long-term transformation. It examines how capital budgeting, risk management, and investment strategies can either advance or hinder circular practices. Grounded in stakeholder, resource-based, and institutional theories, the chapter assesses how finance can internalize environmental externalities, value intangibles, and support uncertain long-term investments. Using a qualitative approach, it draws on academic literature, sustainability reports, and case studies (e.g., Philips, Schneider Electric, Interface Inc.) to show real-world applications. It highlights tools like green bonds, lifecycle costing, and performance-based financing, while noting structural barriers. Adapting finance to CE requires shifting financial logic, adopting new metrics (e.g., Total Cost of Ownership, Environmental P&L), and supportive policies. The chapter contributes to academic and managerial understanding of finance's role in circular value creation.

This study examines the strategic role of neuroscience in developing strong and sustainable brands through implementing cognitive, emotional and sensory insights into marketing strategies. Based on this, this study focuses as well as investigates how neuromarketing methods such as EEG, fMRI, GSR, eye tracking and facial coding enable the scientific measurement of unconscious consumer responses and how these responses turn into a marketing strategies to achieve sustainable brand loyalty among the consumers. In order to achieve this aim, in this study, first of all theoretical background will be formed. Accordingly, Kahneman's System 1 and System 2 framework and Krishna's sensory marketing approach will be touched upon to understand how consumers behave and their decision making processes work. Following to this, in this study, the theoretical discussion will be supported by the Hayat Kimya's Molfix brand' case study. Analyzes showed that eye-tracking and EEG analyzes revealed critical insights about attention, emotional activation, comprehension and memory retention. Based on the findings revisions made by the company and accordingly, significant improvements were achieved in brand loyalty among the consumers. The results demonstrate that neuroscience supported marketing strategies develop better communication with the consumers and contributes to significant improvements in long-term consumer loyalty. Such approaches also support the long-term sustainability of brands in competitive markets.

Preface

The global shift toward a circular economy represents a transformative approach to addressing pressing environmental, economic, and social challenges. By moving away from the traditional linear "take-make-dispose" model, the circular economy emphasizes resource efficiency, waste reduction, and regenerative systems that foster sustainability and resilience. *Innovative Policy Making for the Shift to Circular Economy* brings together diverse perspectives from academia, industry, and policy to explore how innovative frameworks, financial mechanisms, leadership strategies, and interdisciplinary insights can drive this transition. This edited volume offers a comprehensive examination of the policies, practices, and paradigms necessary to reimagine economic systems in alignment with circular principles, drawing on global case studies and theoretical advancements to chart a path toward a sustainable future.

CHAPTER OVERVIEW

Chapter 1 explores how circular economy policies can redefine well-being beyond GDP, using ecological economics and human development theory. It critiques GDP's limitations and proposes alternative metrics based on the capabilities approach, Doughnut Economics, and well-being budgets to promote resource efficiency, environmental regeneration, and equitable prosperity.

Chapter 2 examines the financial sector's role in transitioning to circular economies through green capital. It highlights how sustainable financing, including green bonds and ESG-focused funds, supports circular business models, reduces investment risks, and drives market growth, with global case studies and policy recommendations.

Chapter 3 focuses on green investors' role in scaling circular economies through ESG-aligned strategies. It analyzes investment trends, financial innovations, and regulatory frameworks that support circular business models, using case studies and policy analysis to highlight challenges and enabling mechanisms.

Chapter 4 investigates the synergy between Corporate Social Responsibility (CSR) and circular economy, emphasizing CSR communication's role in framing sustainability narratives, building trust, and mobilizing stakeholders to drive innovative policy development and systemic change.

Chapter 5 analyzes the transition to a circular economy through a political economy lens, exploring how power dynamics, vested interests, and institutional factors shape policy design. It advocates for an integrated approach to address governance, stakeholder dynamics, and socio-political barriers.

Chapter 6 addresses information pollution as an overlooked form of waste in digital ecosystems. It examines its impacts on sustainability and proposes technological and behavioral interventions, such as media literacy and global legislation, to foster resilient digital environments.

Chapter 7 explores how corporate finance influences circular economy adoption through capital budgeting and risk management. It discusses tools like green bonds and lifecycle costing, drawing on case studies to highlight barriers and propose new financial metrics for circular value creation.

Chapter 8 examines how neuroscience and neuromarketing tools (e.g., EEG, fMRI) enhance sustainable branding by understanding consumer emotions and sensory responses. It includes a case study of Molfix to illustrate how these insights boost brand loyalty and cultural relevance.

This volume synthesizes cutting edge research and practical insights to provide a roadmap for policymakers, business leaders, and scholars committed to advancing the circular economy. By addressing diverse dimensions from policy frameworks and financial systems to leadership and neuroscience, this volume underscores the interdisciplinary nature of the transition. We hope this collection inspires innovative solutions and collaborative action to build a regenerative, equitable, and sustainable future.

Mohamad Knio
Lebanese International University, Lebanon

Najib Bou Zakhem
Lebanese International University, Lebanon

Chapter 1
Beyond GDP:
Innovative Circular Economy Policies for Rethinking Standards of Living

Fatih Ölçekciler
https://orcid.org/0009-0007-4743-0867
Independent Researcher, Turkey

Mohamad Saad El Dine Knio
https://orcid.org/0000-0001-9074-8618
Lebanese International University, Lebanon

Gaby Badih Khoury
Lebanese International University, Lebanon

Bassam Mahmoud Tarhini
Lebanese International University, Lebanon

Nadine Hassan Abdelrahman
Lebanese International University, Lebanon

Suha Ali Tahan
Lebanese International University, Lebanon

Hassan Ahmad Houmani
https://orcid.org/0000-0002-9777-5237
Lebanese International University, Lebanon

Batoul Younes Jaafar
https://orcid.org/0000-0002-9949-6741
University of Balamand, Lebanon

ABSTRACT

This theoretical study explores how innovative circular economy (CE) policies can redefine standards of living beyond traditional GDP metrics. Grounded in ecological economics and human development theory, the research critically assesses the inadequacies of GDP as a measure of well-being and highlights the necessity for alternative frameworks that integrate environmental, social, and qualitative dimensions of prosperity. By drawing on concepts such as the capabilities approach, the Doughnut Economics model, and well-being budget practices, the paper illus-

DOI: 10.4018/979-8-3373-3852-1.ch001

trates how circular economy principles can serve as a foundation for post-GDP policy making. Through the adoption of metrics that prioritize resource efficiency, environmental regeneration, social inclusion, and quality of life, circular economy policies can realign societal goals toward long-term sustainability and equitable well-being. The study contributes to the theoretical discourse on sustainability by arguing for a multidimensional understanding of prosperity that is consistent with circularity, sufficiency, and resilience.

INTRODUCTION

Gross Domestic Product (GDP) has long been the dominant metric for gauging economic success and, by extension, the standard of living in a country (Reike, 2024). Policymakers and the public alike have often equated rising GDP per capita with improvements in welfare and quality of life. However, growing theoretical and empirical evidence suggests that GDP is an inadequate proxy for true prosperity, especially in an era of environmental limits and social complexity. As Simon Kuznets, the economist who pioneered national income accounting, warned as early as 1934, "the welfare of a nation can scarcely be inferred from a measure of national income" (Vanham, 2025). GDP measures the aggregate value of goods and services produced, yet it says nothing about how equitably that value is distributed or whether it translates into well-being. It ignores vital elements of human development and environmental sustainability: a nation can achieve GDP growth through overexploiting natural resources, polluting ecosystems, or concentrating wealth in few hands, outcomes that may undermine long-term living standards even as output rises (Vanham, 2025). These shortcomings have become more pronounced as the world faces sustainability challenges such as climate change, resource depletion, and social inequalities (Raworth, 2017).

In response to the accepted limits of GDP, scholars and international organizations have called for a redefinition of how "standards of living" are understood and measured (Vanham, 2025). This study explores a theoretical rethinking of standards of living "beyond GDP", grounded in the literature on alternative welfare indicators and the circular economy. The concept of a circular economy, an economic model aimed at eliminating waste and continually reusing resources, provides a compelling framework for this rethinking (Preston, 2007). A circular economy stands in contrast to the traditional linear "take-make-dispose" model of growth and offers a vision of prosperity that is not predicated on ever-increasing material throughput. By focusing on resource efficiency, regeneration of natural systems, and long-lasting product use, the circular economy promises to decouple high living standards from environmental destruction. This study examines how moving beyond GDP as the measure of progress aligns with circular economy principles to foster sustainable well-being.

THEORETICAL BACKGROUND

Origins and Criticisms of GDP

Modern national accounting and the GDP metric trace back to the mid-20th century, arising from a practical need to measure economic activity during the Great Depression and World War II. Pioneered by Simon Kuznets and others, Gross Domestic Product was designed to summarize in one number the total output of an economy, essentially the sum of all final goods and services produced within a country's borders in a given period (Parkin, 2003). GDP provided a crucial tool for policymakers of the time, enabling them to gauge the scale of the economic collapse in the 1930s and later to plan wartime production and post-war reconstruction (Nielsen & Hakala, 2022). By the Bretton Woods conference of 1944, GDP had been internationally accepted as the standard measure of economic performance. In the ensuing decades, the "Golden Age" of post-war growth, rising GDP became almost synonymous with progress. High growth rates in the 1950s and 1960s coincided with employment gains and poverty reduction in many Western countries, reinforcing the metric's primacy in economic discourse (Vanham, 2025).

Yet from the very inception of national income accounting, economists cautioned against conflating GDP with overall welfare. Kuznets himself was acutely aware of GDP's limitations as a measure of societal well-being. In his 1934 report to the U.S. Congress, Kuznets famously noted that "the welfare of a nation can scarcely be inferred from a measure of national income" (Vanham, 2025). This early warning highlighted that GDP is a measure of market activity, not a comprehensive gauge of living standards (Rockström et al., 2009).

GDP tallies economic transactions regardless of their nature, it counts money spent on cigarettes or oil spills cleanup just as readily as money spent on education or healthy food. It does not distinguish welfare enhancing activities from those that may be detrimental. As the World Economic Forum's retrospective on GDP observes, Kuznets' prescient critique was that GDP "tells us about aggregate consumption, but it does not tell us about personal well-being… It tells us about production, but not about the pollution that comes with it, or the depletion of natural resources it requires" (Vanham, 2025). In other words, GDP is blind to many qualitative aspects of growth such as environmental externalities, social costs, income distribution, and nonmarket work are all left out of its scope. Subsequent critiques in the economic literature have expanded on these issues. Economists and social scientists note several key problems with relying on GDP as the sole or primary measure of a country's standard of living (Vanham, 2025):

- **Exclusion of Non-Market Activities:** GDP only measures monetized activity, omitting unpaid work such as child-rearing, elder care, or volunteerism, which are vital to social welfare. It similarly ignores subsistence agriculture and household production. Because these activities have no market price, they contribute nothing to GDP, even though they clearly enhance wellbeing (Meredith, 2023). This omission has gendered implications too, since much unpaid care work is done by women. In short, GDP undervalues the "care economy" and other non-market contributions to quality of life (Schröder & Barrie, 2024).
- **No Account of Distribution:** GDP per capita is an average that says nothing about how income is distributed among a population. A high GDP per person can mask extreme inequality, a situation where an affluent minority enjoys enormous wealth while a large segment of the population remains in poverty. In such cases, the average output might be high, but the typical person's standard of living could be much lower. Countries can have similar GDP per capita but vastly different income distributions, resulting in different lived experiences for their citizens. For example, some oil-rich countries in the Middle East exhibit high GDP per capita comparable to Western nations, yet much of the wealth accrues to a narrow elite, with limited improvements in broader population welfare. GDP figures alone gloss over these disparities (Meredith, 2023).
- **Counting Costs as Gains:** GDP conflates costs and benefits. Expenditures on pollution cleanup, natural disaster recovery, medical treatments for stress-related illnesses, or building prisons all increase GDP, but they often represent defensive or regrettable expenditures rather than improvements in societal well-being. In the GDP framework, there is no subtraction for "bads" money spent due to negative outcomes. Thus, an economy can boost its GDP by overusing natural resources and then spending on environmental restoration, even though a preferable outcome would have been to avoid the damage in the first place. As Kuznets' insight implies, GDP would count the value of timber extracted from a forest but places zero value on the intact forest ecosystem services lost in the process. The destruction of natural capital is not registered as a decline in wealth (Nielsen & Hakala, 2022).
- **Neglect of Intangibles and Quality:** GDP emphasizes quantity of output over quality. It does not capture improvements (or deteriorations) in the quality of goods and services, nor does it measure qualitative aspects of societal progress such as health, education quality, trust, security, or happiness (Sen,

1987). A society could achieve a higher GDP by producing more goods, but if those goods have diminishing marginal utility or if people have less leisure time and worse health in the process, it is questionable whether real living standards improved. Critics argue that "personal well-being" and "quality of life" depend on far more than the volume of market consumption (Martin, 2018).

- **Short-Term Focus and Externalities:** As an aggregate flow measure, GDP does not directly consider sustainability or future impacts. An economy may boost short-term GDP through practices that erode long-term productive capacity, for example, overfishing the oceans or depleting soil fertility will raise output today but compromise future output and welfare (Korhonen, Honkasalo, & Seppälä, 2018). Such externalities and long-run considerations lie outside GDP's scope. The concept of "ecological deficit" has been used to describe how GDP growth can coincide with exceeding environmental limits. In the 1970s, it became evident that alongside GDP growth, indicators like the ecological footprint were also growing, signaling unsustainable resource use that GDP figures alone did not flag (Korhonen, Honkasalo, & Seppälä, 2018).

Over the decades, numerous thinkers have echoed these points. For instance, Nobel laureate economist Joseph Stiglitz and colleagues Amartya Sen and Jean-Paul Fitoussi led a 2009 commission which famously articulated the "limits of GDP as an indicator of economic performance and social progress" and called for a shift toward metrics that encompass well-being and sustainability (Stiglitz, Sen & Fitoussi, 2009). Their report argued that GDP should be complemented by measures that include environmental quality, health and education outcomes, and subjective life satisfaction, among others (Stiglitz, Sen, & Fitoussi, 2009). As they succinctly put it, "what we measure affects what we do," and relying narrowly on GDP can lead to policy distortion, prioritizing output growth at the expense of other goals (Stiglitz et al., 2009). These concerns tie into the notion of "Kuznets' Curse", which suggests that decades of single-minded focus on GDP growth have contributed to pressing problems like inequality and environmental degradation.

Defining Standards of Living

The term "standard of living" generally refers to the level of wealth, comfort, material goods, and necessities available to a certain socioeconomic class or geographic area (Kirchherr, Reike, & Hekkert, 2017). Traditionally, economists often used real GDP per capita as a proxy for standard of living, under the assumption that higher income allows individuals to consume more goods and services and thus achieve greater well-being (Easterlin, 2000). This view aligns with classical and neoclassical economic thought, in which per-capita output and income are core indicators of development (Vanham, 2025). Indeed, for much of the 20th century, many policy analyses implicitly treated increases in output (and income) as synonymous with improvements in living standards. Higher income was presumed to enable better access to goods that improve life, from basic needs like food and shelter to amenities like appliances, automobiles, and entertainment (Kakwani, 1993).

However, defining the standard of living solely by income or consumption has always been an oversimplification (Ison & Wall, 2007). There is no single agreed-upon definition of a "good" standard of living because it encompasses multiple dimensions economic, social, and even subjective. Several theoretical developments in the late 20th century expanded the concept:

- **Basic Needs and Physical Quality of Life:** In development economics, the "basic needs" approach emerged in the 1970s, arguing that progress should be measured by the extent to which basic human needs (nutrition, shelter, health, education) are met, rather than by aggregate income.

This led to composite indicators like the Physical Quality of Life Index (PQLI) and later the Human Development Index (HDI). The HDI, introduced by the United Nations Development Programme in 1990, incorporates three components: income per capita, life expectancy, and education (literacy and enrollment) (Finlayson, 2002). HDI emphasized that development is about enlarging people's choices and capabilities, not just raising incomes. The HDI thus operationalized a broader definition of living standards. It can be defined as "a way to measure the average level human beings can reach in using their basic capabilities, with three pillars: indicators of how long people live, how educated they are, and whether their living standards are adequate". This formulation explicitly includes health and education alongside material living standards (Easterlin, 1995).

- **The Capabilities Approach:** Economist-philosopher Amartya Sen profoundly influenced the conceptualization of living standards with his capabilities approach (Sen, 1987). Sen (1987) argue that standard of living should be thought of in terms of people's functioning and capabilities. Functioning are the beings and doings that people have reason to value, such as being healthy, being educated, being able to participate in community life. Capabilities refer to the freedoms or opportunities to achieve those functioning. In Sen's (1987) view, income is merely a means to expanding capabilities, not an end in itself. A person's living standard is better reflected by the substantive freedoms they enjoy than by their income level per se. This approach highlights that two individuals with the same income can have very different standards of living if one is in poor health and the other is well, or if one lives in a society with public services versus one without. Sen's framework was revolutionary in shifting focus from commodities and income to what people are actually able to be and do. As he famously stated, "commodities and income have no intrinsic value; their value derives from what they enable people to achieve". Thus, a high GDP per capita is of limited value if it does not translate into expanded capabilities for the population (e.g., if income is unevenly distributed or spent in ways that do not enhance human development) (Boulding, 1966). The capabilities approach underpins the human development perspective and has been influential in rethinking living standards beyond GDP (Easterlin, 2000).

- **Social Indicators and Quality of Life Research:** From the 1970s onward, a "social indicators" movement developed, integrating sociological and psychological measures into assessments of societal progress. Researchers began systematically tracking indicators such as literacy rates, infant mortality, access to sanitation, crime rates, and even self-reported life satisfaction. The aim was to construct a multidimensional picture of living standards. For example, Dasgupta and Weale (1992) in "On Measuring the Quality of Life" argued for considering health, education, distribution, and environmental quality when assessing social performance, noting that GDP growth can co-exist with quality of life stagnation or decline if those other factors are neglected. The rise of subjective well-being research further broadened the concept. Surveys like the World Values Survey and Gallup World Poll ask people to evaluate their life satisfaction and daily emotional experiences. Interestingly, these subjective measures often reveal diminishing returns to income. While very poor countries see happiness rise as GDP increases because basic needs are met, beyond a certain threshold the correlation flattens, a phenomenon known as the Easterlin Paradox (Easterlin, 1974). Richard Easterlin (1974) observed that within a society at a given time, richer individuals report higher happiness than poorer ones, but over time as a whole society grows richer, average happiness does not necessarily increase. One interpretation is that once basic material needs are satisfied, relative income and nonmaterial factors such as family, community, work-life balance, health play a larger role in determining well-being (Desrochers, 2004). This insight again underscores that "standard of living" cannot be equated in a linear way with GDP, cultural, relational, and psychological dimensions matter.
- **Welfare Economics and Multi-criteria Assessment:** Theoretical welfare economics has long distinguished between GDP and utility or welfare. Concepts like GDP per capita are at best an indirect proxy for welfare they

need adjustment for leisure time, life expectancy, inequality, and externalities. William Nordhaus and James Tobin's work in the 1970s on "Measuring Economic Welfare" adjusted GNP by subtracting "regrettables" and adding values for leisure and household work, producing a Measure of Economic Welfare (MEW) (Blomsma & Brennan, 2017). Similar efforts include the Index of Sustainable Economic Welfare (ISEW) and the Genuine Progress Indicator (GPI), which attempt to adjust national consumption for factors like income distribution, environmental degradation, and changes in capital stock (Alberich et al., 2023).

These endeavors reflect a theoretical recognition that living standards have environmental and social components that raw GDP ignores. The creation of the GPI, for instance, "was motivated by the lack of comprehensiveness of GDP, and the need to create metrics broader than GDP that put economic, environmental, and social factors together" (Alberich et al., 2023). While these composite indicators have not displaced GDP in official use, they contribute to a richer theoretical construct of what living standard entails.

In light of these developments, it can be defined "standard of living" in a circular and sustainability context as a multidimensional construct (Blomsma & Brennan, 2017). "Standard of living" encompasses not only the quantity of goods and services consumed, but the quality of life afforded by one's economic and natural environment. It includes access to clean air and water, health and longevity, education and culture, safety and security, the equity of opportunities, and the freedom to pursue one's goals. As Easterlin have shown, past a point, more goods do not equate to more happiness or life satisfaction (Easterlin, 1974). Therefore, a high standard of living in a wealthy society might involve shorter working hours, greater leisure and community engagement, and a clean environment, even if that means slightly lower measured output. Conversely, an adequate standard of living in poorer societies may rightly focus on increasing material consumption to meet basic needs, but in a way that builds human capabilities and avoids long-term resource traps (Barro & Sala-i-Martin, 2004).

Table 1. Comparison of GDP and Alternative Well-being Indicators

Indicator	Focus	Strengths	Limitations
GDP	Output of goods & services	Simple, widely used, historical benchmark	Ignores distribution, environment, quality of life
HDI	Income, education, life expectancy	Multidimensional, human-centered	Limited scope, no ecological balance
GPI	Adjusted consumption (adds leisure, subtracts pollution etc.)	Captures environmental & social costs	Complex, less common in policy use
Doughnut Economics	Social foundation & ecological ceiling	Integrates planetary boundaries	Normative, still experimental

Conceptual Foundations of the Circular Economy

The circular economy (CE) is a sustainability-oriented concept that has gained prominence as an alternative paradigm to the traditional linear economic model. In a linear economy, resources are extracted, turned into products, used, and ultimately disposed of as waste ("take-make-use-dispose"). By contrast, a circular economy is designed to be regenerative by intention and by design. It aims to keep products, components, and materials in circulation at their highest utility and value for as long as possible, thus minimizing both resource input and waste output. The underlying idea is often summarized by the "3Rs" or "4Rs": reduce, reuse, recycle (and recover) (Kirchherr, Reike & Hekkert, 2017). More expansive versions include up to 9R or 10R frameworks (refuse, reduce, reuse, repair, refurbish, remanufacture, repurpose, recycle, recover, etc.) which detail strategies for retaining value in material loops (Reike, 2024).

Although the term "circular economy" itself rose to prominence in the late 20th and early 21st centuries, the conceptual roots are much older (Barro & Sala-i-Martin, 2004). Historically, industrial societies have practiced forms of resource recovery and recycling, for example, scrap metal reuse or the use of industrial by-products whenever economic incentives favored it. In the 19th century, writers like Peter Lund Simmonds documented how one industry's waste could become another's input e.g. using cotton waste or leather scraps, driven by the profit motive to "convert useless products into those possessed of commercial value" (Desrochers, 2004). However, these practices were not motivated by environmental concern but by efficiency and cost-saving. Widespread environmental awareness informing economic models only began to crystallize in the mid-20th century. Key intellectual milestones in the development of circular economy thinking include:

- **Kenneth Boulding's "Spaceship Earth" (1966):** economist Kenneth E. Boulding introduced the metaphor of "Spaceship Earth" to contrast two distinct economic mindsets. He distinguished the "cowboy economy," characterized by an open-frontier, extractive orientation, from the "spaceman economy," which views the Earth as a closed system with finite resources and limited capacity to absorb waste. Boulding (1966) argued that humanity must move from the reckless consumption model to a cyclical, regenerative model. In his seminal essay "The Economics of the Coming Spaceship Earth", Boulding (1966) wrote that in a closed economy, success should be measured by the quality and stock of capital including natural and human capital, not by the flow of production and consumption. He famously stated that efficiency, the rate of extraction and disposal, should be minimized and that "the nature, quality, and complexity of the total capital stock, including the condition of human bodies and minds" should be preserved as the measure of progress. This early statement essentially called for something that was now thought of beyond GDP measures, focusing on sustainable well-being rather than the volume of economic activity. Boulding's (1966) work is often cited as an intellectual foundation for the circular economy concept because it underscored the need for closed-loop processes and recognition of ecological limits.
- **Walter Stahel and the Loop Economy (1970s - 1980s):** Swiss architect and economist Walter R. Stahel is widely regarded as a founding figure of circular economy ideas. In a 1976 report to the European Commission, Stahel sketched a vision of an economy in loops, emphasizing activities like reuse, repair, remanufacturing, and longer product lifetimes. This work, later published as "Jobs for Tomorrow: The Potential for Substituting Manpower for Energy" (1981), demonstrated that extending the life of products through maintenance, reuse, refurbishment not only conserves resources and reduces waste, but also creates jobs in labor-intensive restoration activities (Stahel & Reday-Mulvey, 1981). Stahel showed that a shift from manufacturing new goods to circular activities would likely require more skilled human labor for repair and maintenance while consuming less energy and materials, thus potentially addressing unemployment and resource depletion together. He even quantified how reconditioning goods at local "repair workshops" could boost local employment. This was a compelling argument that a circular economy could have positive social impacts in job creation along with environmental benefits. Stahel's later work introduced terms like the "performance economy" and he advocated for service-life extension, product-as-service models, and internalizing the costs of disposal. His insights laid early groundwork for what the Ellen MacArthur Foundation and others popularized decades later. Notably, Stahel's vision connected circularity with economic compet-

itiveness and resilience, proposing that economies that use resources more efficiently would have an edge, and that local repair jobs would strengthen communities (Stahel & Reday-Mulvey, 1981).

- **Industrial Ecology and Cradle-to-Cradle:** From the 1980s through 2000s, fields like industrial ecology emerged, examining material and energy flows in industrial systems and modeling them after ecological cycles (Anderton, 2006). Pioneers of industrial ecology promoted the idea of "industrial symbiosis", where clusters of industries arrange that each other's wastes become raw materials, mimicking a food web. A famous example is Kalundborg, Denmark, where a power plant, oil refinery, gypsum board facility, and others exchange by-products in a closed network. The "cradle-to-cradle" design philosophy, articulated by Michael Braungart and William McDonough in the early 2000s, further reinforced circular economy principles. They argued products should be designed from the outset either to be biological nutrients or technical nutrients, eliminating the very concept of waste.

These schools of thought contributed to the conceptual toolkit of the circular economy, emphasizing design for disassembly, material purity for recyclability, renewable energy use, and systems thinking (Alberich et al., 2023).

- **Emergence of the Term "Circular Economy":** The phrase "circular economy" itself began to appear in Chinese policy circles in the 1990s and early 2000s, influenced by both domestic issues such as pollution, resource scarcity and international ideas. China incorporated the concept into its national strategy with the Circular Economy Promotion Law (2008) and successive Five-Year Plans. This law explicitly aimed to improve resource efficiency, encourage recycling, and reduce waste, reflecting a government-led adoption of CE principles in practice. The Chinese approach viewed circular economy as an avenue for sustainable development and often focused on eco-industrial parks, cleaner production, and resource recovery systems, essentially operationalizing CE at firm and regional levels. Meanwhile, in Europe, the concept was popularized and advanced by organizations like the Ellen MacArthur Foundation (EMF) in the 2010s. EMF's influential reports e.g., "Towards the Circular Economy" series from 2012 onwards, synthesized many of the earlier ideas and presented economic evidence such as market opportunities, savings, innovation potential for transitioning to a circular model. EMF defined the circular economy as "an industrial system that is restorative or regenerative by intention and design", highlighting principles of designing out waste, keeping materials in use, and regenerating natural systems. This helped bring the concept into mainstream business and policy discourse in the West.

From a theoretical standpoint, the circular economy draws on systems theory and ecological economics (Alberich et al., 2023). It recognizes the economy as a subsystem of the environment, a view stressed by Herman Daly and other ecological economists who long argued that infinite growth is impossible on a finite planet. The CE concept is essentially a practical framing of how to implement the idea of a steady-state or at least a resource-efficient economy without sacrificing human well-being. It challenges the classic take-make-waste trajectory and instead posits a continuous cycle: resources flow in loops and waste from one process becomes input for another.

A widely cited definition by Kirchherr et al. (2017) encapsulates the concept as follows: "A circular economy is an economic system that replaces the 'end-of-life' concept with reducing, alternatively reusing, recycling and recovering materials in production/distribution and consumption processes. It operates at the micro individual firms, consumers, meso eco-industrial parks, and macro city, region, nation levels, with the aim of accomplishing sustainable development, thus simultaneously creating environmental quality, economic prosperity and social equity for the benefit of current and future generations". This definition highlights several important aspects: (1) elimination of the end-of-life notion, products are designed and managed for continuous recovery; (2) multi-scale implementation it's not just a firm level practice but can reorganize whole industrial ecosystems and economies and (3) the ultimate aims align with sustainable development, balancing environmental, economic, and social goals. Key principles or components of a circular economy, drawn from various frameworks include:

- **Design for Circularity:** Designing products for durability, reparability, upgradability, and recyclability. This may involve modular design, standardized components, and avoiding toxic materials so that products can be safely cycled. For example, eco-design in appliances might allow easy replacement of parts and use of recycled inputs. Upfront design decisions heavily influence whether a product will end up as waste or resource.
- **New Business Models:** Shifting from ownership models to service models e.g., product-as-a-service or leasing, which incentivize producers to create longer-lasting products and maintain responsibility for them through end-of-life. Sharing economy platforms also fall here, increasing utilization rates of products such as cars, tools, etc.. Business model innovation is crucial. For instance, selling light as a service instead of selling lightbulbs motivates manufacturers to produce long-lasting, energy-efficient bulbs since they retain ownership.
- **Resource Loops (Reuse, Remanufacturing, Recycling):** Developing systems to loop materials back into production. Reverse logistics and take-back

programs are needed for collecting end-of-use products. Remanufacturing, restoring used products to like-new condition, saves material and energy compared to new production. Recycling is a lower priority loop since it often downcycles material quality, but still important to recover materials that cannot be directly reused or remanufactured. Advanced recycling and recovery technologies, including chemical recycling for plastics or nutrient recovery in agriculture, expand what can be looped.

- **Cascade and Cross-industry Synergies:** Using resources in cascading ways across industries for example, waste from agriculture like rice husks or manure can be inputs for energy generation or industrial processes, and waste heat from one plant can be used in neighboring facilities. Industrial symbiosis exemplifies this, connecting disparate industries into a network that mimics an ecosystem where waste is food.
- **Renewable Energy:** Powering the economy with renewable energy is often considered part of circular principles, because an infinite loop of materials still requires energy inputs at each cycle. To be sustainable, those energy inputs should ideally be renewable such as solar, wind, etc. so as not to deplete resources or cause pollution.
- **Socio-cultural Change:** Though sometimes less emphasized in technical definitions, a circular economy also implies a cultural shift in consumption patterns, valuing access over ownership, embracing product longevity, and seeing waste as anathema. Education and consumer engagement for instance, encouraging return of used products, or willingness to buy refurbished goods are part of the ecosystem enabling circularity.

Importantly, the circular economy is not merely an environmental strategy. It is often presented as a positive economic opportunity (Aghion & Howitt, 1992). Proponents argue it can stimulate innovation, create jobs in new sectors such as recycling, remanufacturing, maintenance, resource recovery, and reduce dependence on scarce raw materials, thereby increasing economic resilience. For example, the EU's Circular Economy Action Plan (2020) is as much about industrial competitiveness and innovation as it is about waste reduction. Similarly, research suggests circular strategies could yield trillions in economic benefits globally through material savings and new markets (EMF, 2015). This win-win narrative has helped circular economy principles gain traction among businesses and policymakers. However, it's worth noting that academically the concept is still being refined. Scholars point out that the circular economy, as popularized, is somewhat "a melting pot of concepts" with varying definitions and scope (Alberich et al., 2023). It is essentially contested, lacking a singular theory, and spans fields from engineering and design to economics and management (Korhonen et al., 2018; Blomsma & Brennan, 2017). For some, it is primarily about waste management and recycling; for others, it implies a deeper transformation of production-consumption systems and even a critique of the growth paradigm. Critics also warn that a purely technical or market-driven implementation of circular economy, an "apolitical and technocratic" approach, might overlook power relations, justice, and sufficiency, thus limiting its effectiveness in solving sustainability issues.

This touches on whether circular economy is pursued as part of an "eco-modernist" agenda that seeks to retain conventional economic growth patterns with technical fixes, or as a genuinely transformative agenda that might require reducing overall material consumption and rethinking socio-economic goals.

Why GDP Falls Short in the Context of Sustainability

The preceding sections have highlighted general criticisms of GDP and introduced the circular economy as a sustainability paradigm. The focus now turns to the intersection of these issues: why is GDP an especially poor guide for policy in a world facing sustainability imperatives? And conversely, why does the sustainability context epitomized by circular economy thinking demand new metrics and approaches beyond GDP?

1. **Environmental Externalities and Resource Depletion:** The most immediate issue is that GDP not only ignores environmental externalities but can perversely cast environmental degradation as economic gain. Many environmental harms do not come with market prices attached, for example, CO_2 emissions, deforestation, loss of biodiversity, or pollution of a river are typically not subtracted from any national accounts. In fact, activities that cause these harms add to GDP by the value of the extracted commodities or products. The costs such as climate change, species extinction, health effects are borne outside the market and thus outside GDP calculations. As a result, an economy could be in ecological overshoot but still report positive GDP growth and appear "successful" by that metric. This is not a hypothetical scenario but it has been the reality for decades. Global GDP grew exponentially in the second half of the 20th century but humanity's ecological footprint has also grown so much that the Earth's regenerative capacity has now been exceeded in many areas (Rockström et al., 2009). A WEF analysis succinctly noted that "as global annual GDP peaked, people's ecological footprint did so too, leading to an ecological deficit", forests were felled for farms and industry, oceans overfished, fossil fuels burnt, yielding short-term growth but long-term damage to health, wealth, and well-being (Vanham, 2025). GDP offered no warning of this trade-off on the contrary, it celebrated the throughput as progress. By not accounting for the depreciation

of natural capital, GDP gives an illusion of sustainable prosperity even as the foundations for future prosperity such as clean air, stable climate, fertile soil are eroded. This is fundamentally at odds with the ethos of a circular economy, which strives to protect and regenerate natural capital rather than run it down. In the context of sustainability, indicators that monitor environmental health such as carbon emissions, material footprints or nature indices are needed alongside or integrated with economic performance however, GDP alone cannot achieve this.

2. **Climate Change and Unpriced Carbon:** Climate change is a prime example of GDP's blind spot. For decades, industrial growth pumped greenhouse gases into the atmosphere with essentially no reflection of this accumulating risk in economic statistics. Nations with high GDP growth often also had high emissions growth. GDP only counts the positive output from fossil-fuel driven industries and it does not deduct the negative externality of climate damages. As a result, policies purely targeting GDP growth may encourage continued fossil fuel use until catastrophic climate impacts start hurting economic output, a lagging recognition that comes too late. A sustainable standard of living, in contrast, would require proactively limiting emissions to prevent dangerous climate change, even if that means certain GDP-sacrificing actions like leaving coal and oil reserves untapped or investing in costlier renewable infrastructure now for long-term benefit. GDP is simply not equipped to guide such decisions. Alternative approaches, like incorporating a carbon price or using measures like "Green GDP" which adjusts GDP by estimating environmental costs, have been proposed and trialed China, for instance, experimented with Green GDP accounting in the 2000s. These attempts often showed significantly lower growth once environmental degradation was netted out, reinforcing the point that conventional GDP was overstating true sustainable income. In short, an economy can appear to grow steadily in GDP terms while it is on an unsustainable emissions path only when climate change impacts tangibly lower output might GDP signal a problem, and by then severe damage is done. This lag makes GDP a dangerous compass for sustainable development.
3. **Overemphasis on Quantitative Growth vs. Qualitative Improvement:** In sustainability discourse, there is a critical distinction between growth quantitative increase in size of the economy and development qualitative improvement in well-being. The circular economy emphasizes development without growth in material and energy use. However, GDP conflates the two, any increase in monetary economic activity is "growth" and is assumed beneficial. This leads to what some call the tyranny of GDP growth policymakers feel pressured to maximize GDP in the short term, sometimes at the expense of qualitative improvements or long-term considerations. For example, cutting down a forest for

timber export will boost GDP, whereas protecting it yields no immediate GDP gain even if it provides ecosystem services and future tourism revenue. Under political focus on GDP, the former is rewarded despite being less sustainable. A beyond GDP approach would value the qualitative aspects, e.g., forest conservation might register as a positive in a "Genuine Progress Indicator" or a well-being index, whereas in GDP it's practically invisible.

In a circular economy, value is created by maintaining quality and utility through repair, remanufacture, etc., not by sheer volume of new production. Yet GDP, by counting only new production, can undercount the benefits of circular activities. For instance, if consumers buy fewer new goods because they are reusing durable products longer or sharing products thus saving resources and reducing waste, GDP might show a slowdown, even though from a welfare perspective nothing is lost, people may enjoy the same services with less spending. This is often perceived as a "GDP paradox" in sustainability what is good for sustainability such as reduced consumption of materials, longer product lifetimes may show up as bad for GDP. Thus, clinging to GDP as the yardstick can discourage or undervalue precisely the changes needed for a circular, sustainable economy. By failing to capture qualitative distinctions, GDP biases decisions toward throughput-intensive strategies rather than efficiency and preservation.

4. **The Disconnect Between GDP and Well-being in Affluent Societies:** Another sustainability-related shortcoming of GDP is evident in wealthy countries where basic material needs are largely met. In such contexts, relentless pursuit of GDP growth may yield only marginal gains in wellbeing, while often exacerbating environmental harm. As noted earlier, the Easterlin Paradox and subsequent research have shown that in developed economies, increases in GDP per capita over time have little correlation with increases in average happiness or life satisfaction (Easterlin, 1974). Instead, social cohesion, mental health, work-life balance, and environmental quality become critical for well-being. However, these factors can be compromised by an excessive growth focus for instance, longer working hours and higher stress might raise output but reduce quality of life heavy industrial activity might raise GDP but worsen air quality and health. The WEF report highlighted that "in the West, GDP does not grow like it used to, and well-being stopped increasing a long time ago", suggesting a decoupling of GDP and genuine progress in advanced economies (Vanham, 2025). This realization is at the heart of movements like degrowth or post-growth economics, which argue that high-income countries should shift away from GDP growth as a goal and focus on distributing resources fairly and improving conditions in nonmaterial terms. The circular economy could be an avenue to operationalize

this. By shifting value creation to regenerative and service-oriented activities, focusing on meeting human needs in innovative ways, and reducing excess consumption, societies might maintain or improve well-being with lower resource throughput. But if policymakers remain tethered to GDP growth targets, they might resist or underprioritize such measures.

For example, repairing goods locally creates skilled jobs and saves resources, but it might contribute less to GDP than producing new goods overseas due to how value-added is measured. Yet from a sustainability and local well-being perspective, the repair economy is highly beneficial. This indicates that as societies progress, metrics of success must evolve, a point made clearly by New Zealand's Treasury when it declared, "life is about more than just money," in justifying the country's shift to a well-being budget framework (Martin, 2018).

5. **GDP and the Policy Trap:** Finally, it is worth noting the feedback loop between metrics and policy. Because GDP has been the de facto scorecard, policies are often crafted to maximize GDP, sometimes inadvertently aggravating unsustainability. Subsidies for fossil fuels, urban sprawl development, consumer credit expansion, these can all boost short-term GDP, but at long-term costs. The singular focus on GDP can crowd out or subordinate environmental and social policy objectives ("how will it affect growth?" is often the first question). This policy trap is dangerous in the context of urgent issues like climate change, which require bold action that may not always align with short-term GDP maximization. For instance, phasing out coal power might slightly reduce GDP in the short run closing plants, transitioning industries but is crucial for sustainability. A GDP-focused lens might delay this. In contrast, if success is measured in terms of carbon reduction, renewable energy adoption, or well-being improvements, policy choices might tilt differently. In other words, using the wrong metric can lead to the wrong policies. This has led to calls for "beyond GDP" policy frameworks at the highest levels. The United Nations, for example, has launched initiatives to develop inclusive wealth accounts and better capture human and natural capital. The EU and OECD have programs on well-being and sustainable development indicators and emphasize that what is measured drives what is strived for. A recent UN initiative referenced in a Chatham House report advocates aligning the post-2030 development agenda with a Beyond GDP approach so that global progress is measured by ecological and social contributions to well-being, not just output. The logic is straightforward. To achieve an inclusive, circular future, indicators are needed that promote and track inclusive circular outcomes such as circular jobs, resource efficiency and ecosystem health (Schröder & Barrie, 2024).

Rethinking Standards of Living in a Circular Economy

If it is accepted that GDP is an inadequate measure of well-being and that a sustainable future requires new models, the question arises: how should "standards of living" be redefined and measured under the circular economy paradigm?

Success in a circular economy is not about extracting maximum resources for maximum production, but about meeting needs and creating well-being with minimum new inputs and minimum waste. This means that what is considered a good life or a high standard of living is changing. Key aspects of this rethinking include an emphasis on well-being and quality of life, the concept of sufficiency, and the incorporation of environmental balance into the very notion of living standards.

1. **Focusing on Well-being and Quality of Life (Beyond Material Consumption):** In a circular economy context, well-being becomes the centerpiece of evaluating living standards. This means prioritizing health, happiness, fulfillment, and ecological harmony over sheer material throughput. A high standard of living could be understood as one where people's essential needs are met to a high standard, nutritious food, decent housing, healthcare, education, meaningful work, and leisure, within the planet's ecological limits. The vision aligns with what Kate Raworth's Doughnut Economics framework encapsulates: ensuring no one falls short on life's essentials while not overshooting planetary boundaries. The "social foundation" of the doughnut represents the minimum living standards that every human being should enjoy in line with the Sustainable Development Goals while the "ecological ceiling" represents the biophysical limits that must be respected. Between these lies the safe and just space for humanity to thrive. Rethinking living standards in these terms means that a country or community's success is measured by how well it brings its population above the social foundation such as eliminating deprivations like hunger, illiteracy, avoidable illness without breaching the ecological ceiling e.g., keeping carbon emissions, nutrient cycles, biodiversity loss within safe levels.

In practical terms, this could translate into composite indices or dashboards replacing GDP. For instance, a Circular Well-being Index might track indicators such as employment rates in circular sectors, access to repaired/refurbished goods, air and water quality, community reuse initiatives, average material footprint per capita, and subjective life satisfaction. There are already signs of this approach. The Happy Planet Index by the New Economics Foundation combines well-being life satisfaction, life expectancy, inequality of outcomes, and ecological footprint into a single index of sustainable wellbeing. Similarly, Gross National Happiness (GNH) in Bhutan includes environmental conservation and equitable socio-economic development as core pillars of living standards, explicitly balancing material with non-material facets (Martin, 2018).

The circular economy naturally dovetails with these approaches because it seeks prosperity that does not come at the cost of environmental degradation. In a circular economy society, one might expect quality to be valued over quantity: longer-lasting high-quality products, more localized and relationship-based services, and greater emphasis on health and community, all of which improve life quality without necessarily increasing consumption. For example, if people shift from owning many low-quality garments to owning fewer, durable garments and participating in clothing rental or secondhand exchanges, their material standard of living is maintained or even enhanced, while resource use plummets. Traditional GDP accounting might register a drop in new clothing sales, but from a living standard perspective nothing is lost and potentially much is gained.

2. **Embracing Sufficiency and Post-Consumerist Values:** A circular economy rethinking of living standards also involves the idea of sufficiency, the notion of "enough." In contrast to the ever-expanding consumerism that characterized late 20th-century growth, sufficiency is about provisioning everyone with what they need for a good life and not excessively beyond that. It recognizes diminishing returns of consumption: once comfortable, healthy and nourished, more consumption yields little additional well-being and can even undermine it through stress, waste management burdens, ecological damage. Therefore, a high standard of living in a circular economy might mean having enough and no more "living better with less" in terms of material accumulation. This does not imply hardship or austere sacrifice rather, it means decoupling the idea of prosperity from the volume of stuff owned. For individuals, it could translate into preferences for products that last, multi-functional goods, sharing or renting when possible, and taking pride in minimal waste lifestyles. At a societal level, it could manifest as shorter workweeks and more time affluence since ultra-high production is not the goal, people could work less and enjoy life more. Empirical evidence shows that beyond a moderate income, additional leisure time contributes more to well-being than additional income (Easterlin, 1995). Thus, a circular economy standard of living might prioritize time prosperity, time to spend with family, community, in nature, as a key component of living well, in lieu of ever-higher income. Policies like incentivizing repair over replacement also reinforce sufficiency if products are repaired and reused, consumers save money and resources, potentially spending their saved money on services or experiences that enrich their lives without heavy material impact.

The challenge is that sufficiency stands in contrast to decades of messaging equating "more is better." However, cultural shifts toward valuing sustainability, simplicity, and wellness are already underway in many places e.g., the minimalism movement, zero-waste lifestyles, slow food movement. A circular economy narrative can bolster these by showing that living standards can improve in qualitative terms even as material consumption levels stabilize or decline. For example, widespread cycling infrastructure like in the Netherlands can replace some car use. This might lower fuel consumption and GDP from fuel sales, but it raises living standards via better health, less pollution, and often quicker urban travel. Similarly, a diet shift from high quantities of meat to a plant-rich diet might reduce agricultural GDP slightly but improve public health and reduce environmental pressure. In these cases, less consumption is more well-being and sustainability, a mantra of sufficiency.

3. **Integrating Environmental Health into Living Standards:** Traditionally, standard of living metrics considered only human-centric outcomes. A rethinking under circular economy would integrate environmental health and ecosystem services as intrinsic to living standards. Clean air, clean water, green space, and a stable climate are not just external factors they directly affect quality of life and are part of what makes life good. Therefore, maintaining them is part of maintaining a high standard of living. In circular economy terms, the environment is a beneficiary of closed loops and the human standard of living rises because people enjoy a healthier environment. For instance, if a city adopts circular waste management and circular design, the city's environment becomes cleaner. Residents benefit through better health and aesthetics. These improvements should be recognized as enhancements to living standards. Indices of living standards in a circular economy might thus include metrics like air quality index, water quality scores, per capita urban green space, or biodiversity measures in living areas. New Zealand's Wellbeing Budget approach, for example, explicitly requires that policy proposals be evaluated for their impacts on natural capital and environmental sustainability, treating those as equally important to citizens' welfare as economic impacts (Martin, 2018). This signals a governance mindset where environmental quality is considered part of the "standard of living" delivered to the populace. In a sense, it aligns policy with what many people intuitively value. Surveys often show that beyond a certain income, people prioritize things like health, environment, and community over further material gain. A circular economy strives to deliver on those priorities by design.
4. **Community and Resilience as Components of Prosperity:** Rethinking living standards also involves social and community dimensions. A circular economy often emphasizes localism which can strengthen community ties and resilience.

For example, repair cafes and sharing libraries not only reduce resource use but also foster social interaction and mutual help, which improve social capital. In many well-being studies, social support networks and trust are significant determinants of life satisfaction. A high standard of living could thus be measured by social cohesion indicators as much as by consumption volumes. One could argue that a society in which neighbors share items and co-operate might have lower per-capita consumption but higher overall welfare than a society of isolated consumers each owning redundant sets of infrequently used items. The COVID-19 pandemic provided some insight at this point. Communities with stronger local networks and diversified local production were more resilient and maintained better well-being in the face of global disruptions, whereas those reliant on long supply chains for essentials saw vulnerabilities. A circular economy inherently builds more local loops, contributing to resilience. Measures of resilience, such as supply diversity, self-sufficiency ratios, and levels of emergency preparedness, can serve as important indicators of societal well-being. They reflect a society's capacity to absorb and adapt to shocks while preserving overall quality of life, thereby offering a broader and more robust understanding of living standards.

5. **Education and Mindset Shifts:** To support this reimagined standard of living, education and cultural mindset are key. People need to value longevity, stewardship, and shared prosperity. The measure of "standard of living" may shift from "How much do I own and consume?" to "How healthy and secure am I? How strong are my relationships? Do I have meaningful activities? Is my environment clean and beautiful?". These are harder to quantify but far more aligned with human well-being. The circular economy does not automatically guarantee such a shift, it provides the conditions through design and system change for more sustainable living, but individuals and societies must also embrace different aspirations. The literature on sustainable consumption suggests that beyond moderate income levels, further well-being comes from improvements in quality of goods, services, environment, and time use rather than quantity of goods (Nielsen & Hakala, 2022). For instance, one study noted that many products and services that improve life such as cars, appliances, convenience goods also "have been perceived as reducing QoL by polluting the environment, being wasteful, and encouraging materialism and over-consumption" (Nielsen & Hakala, 2022).

The circular economy aims to break that pattern, offering ways to get the benefits such as mobility, comfort, convenience without those downsides, e.g. electric shared vehicles instead of individual gas guzzlers. Therefore, when assessing the standard of living in a circular economy, the following question should be asked: Are the sought-after functional benefits and satisfactions achieved with minimal harm? If yes, then living standards are sustainably high.

In practical policy terms, rethinking standards of living might involve developing new national accounts or dashboards that complement GDP. These could include measures like Adjusted Net Savings which include changes in natural and human capital, Inclusive Wealth such as monetary valuation of produced, human, and natural capital, and subjective well-being indices. Governments like New Zealand and Iceland are already incorporating well-being and environmental indicators into budgeting, effectively treating them as goals on par with or above GDP (Martin, 2018). Cities like Amsterdam have adopted the Doughnut model to assess city progress, for example, checking what percentage of residents have access to basic needs and what the city's carbon footprint is, and striving to improve the former while shrinking the latter (Raworth, 2017). These are concrete steps toward a new understanding of prosperity consistent with circular economy principles.

Innovative Policy Making for a Post-GDP Circular Transition

Translating the above ideas into reality requires retooling governance and policy. A transition to a post-GDP, circular economy model calls for innovative policies on multiple fronts such as new indicators and budgeting practices, regulations and incentives for circular business, education and labor reforms, and international cooperation. This section will discuss key policy approaches that emerge from the literature and current experiments, illustrating how governments can foster a circular economy while moving beyond GDP as the lodestar of progress.

1. **Adopting Well-being and Sustainability Indicators in Governance:** One of the most fundamental shifts is for governments to officially adopt alternative indicators to guide policy and measure success. This means developing statistical frameworks that go beyond GDP to track things like population health, education outcomes, inequality, environmental quality, and subjective well-being and using these in policy planning and evaluation. An example is New Zealand's Wellbeing Budget initiative, launched in 2019. Under this approach, the NZ Treasury is mandated to assess budget proposals against a range of well-being dimensions aligned with the OECD's Well-Being Framework rather than just their impact on economic growth.

In practice, this meant that ministries had to justify spending based on how it would improve outcomes in areas such as mental health, child welfare, indigenous rights, and environmental sustainability. The Treasury was instructed that it "can no longer only consider the impact of policies on GDP growth", but must also weigh social, human, and natural capital impacts (Martin, 2018). This represents a direct operationalization of beyond-GDP thinking at the highest budgetary level. As Prime Minister Jacinda Ardern put it, New Zealand aimed to be “the first place in the world where our budget… demonstrates the overall well-being of our country and its people”. The early outcomes included significant investments in areas like mental health services, poverty reduction, and environmental programs that might have been hard to justify under a pure GDP-growth lens (Meredith, 2023). By changing what is measured, governments create space for circular economy policies that might not maximize short-term GDP but improve long-term welfare. For example, preserving a forest might not boost GDP, but if your metrics include biodiversity or air quality, it becomes a “gain” in those terms, supporting conservation policy. Furthermore, statistical agencies are innovating with satellite accounts for natural capital and ecosystem services. The UN’s System of Environmental-Economic Accounting (SEEA) is one initiative to integrate environmental data with national accounts. With SEEA, a country can track depletion of minerals, forests, fish stocks, etc., alongside GDP, giving a fuller picture of how sustainable its growth is. These measures do not replace GDP but complement it, allowing policymakers to target a balance which is moderate GDP growth with improvements in natural capital and social metrics, rather than growth at all costs. Over time, some propose that a single synthetic measure like “Genuine Progress Indicator (GPI)” could substitute GDP as the headline figure. The GPI adjusts personal consumption which is the largest GDP component by factors such as income distribution, adds positive components like value of household work, and subtracts negatives like cost of pollution and climate damage (Alberich et al., 2023). Studies in various countries have shown GPI per capita often plateauing or declining after a certain point even while GDP kept rising, reflecting unsustainable or inequitable growth. Including such an index in official reporting would signal a paradigm shift. In policy terms, a region could set targets to increase GPI or HDI and decrease carbon emissions per capita, rather than focusing on GDP. In sum, measurement innovation is a critical policy tool: “Measuring what matters” aligns government priorities with circular and welfare outcomes (Martin, 2018).

2. **Embedding Circular Economy Principles through Regulation and Incentives:** To drive the economy itself in a circular direction, policymakers are employing a mix of regulations, standards, and economic instruments. A few notable examples and proposals can be found below:
    - **Extended Producer Responsibility (EPR):** EPR schemes make producers financially (and sometimes physically) responsible for the end-of-life management of their products. This creates incentives to design products for easier recycling or longer life. The EU has EPR policies

for electronics (WEEE Directive), batteries, vehicles, and packaging, requiring producers to fund collection and recycling programs. Such policies encourage circular design and closed-loop supply chains. They effectively internalize what used to be externalized costs (waste disposal) into producer decision-making. EPR can be seen as a regulatory nudge aligning market signals with circular economy goals.

- **Right to Repair and Durability Standards:** Several jurisdictions are implementing "right to repair" laws that require manufacturers to make repair manuals, tools, and spare parts available to consumers and independent technicians. The EU, for instance, introduced eco-design requirements that mandate certain appliances (like washing machines, TVs) be built so that key components can be replaced rather than the whole unit discarded. France has even instituted a Repairability Index for electronics, scoring products on how easy they are to fix. These measures fight planned obsolescence and promote a culture of maintenance, directly contributing to longer product lifetimes and waste reduction. As a result, new service businesses (repair cafes, refurbishment centers) are bolstered, boosting jobs in those sectors which could improve social well-being while reducing the need for new manufacturing which might slow raw GDP growth but is beneficial in sustainability terms. Over time, as repair and reuse become mainstream, the metrics of success may shift from number of new units sold to things like product longevity and customer satisfaction.
- **Resource and Pollution Taxation:** Shifting the tax base from labor to resource use or pollution is a frequently suggested policy for a circular economy. For example, a higher landfill tax and virgin resource extraction fees encourage recycling and use of secondary materials. Carbon pricing (carbon tax or cap-and-trade) internalizes climate externalities, making circular, low carbon processes more competitive. Some economists propose a broad "materials levy" on non-renewable resource inputs which would drive materials efficiency and substitution.

Such Pigouvian taxes correct the market signal that GDP growth alone fails to, by ensuring that environmental costs are reflected in prices. If implemented revenue-neutrally (e.g., returning revenues via lower income taxes or dividends), they can change behavior without harming overall welfare, in fact, by reducing pollution, they often improve welfare. A practical example: Sweden and several other countries tax landfill and incineration, which has led to very high recycling rates and even waste import for energy because domestic waste is so minimized. In a beyond-GDP framework, success might be measured by low per-capita waste generation or high recycling percentages, rather than just production output.

- **Circular Public Procurement:** Governments are large consumers, so incorporating circular criteria in public procurement can create significant market pull for circular products and services. For instance, requiring that a certain percentage of materials in construction projects be recycled content, or that furniture procured for offices is remanufactured, helps develop those industries. The city of Amsterdam, as part of its circular strategy, committed to pursue 100% circular procurement by 2030, meaning every euro spent by the city will go into products that meet circular standards (recyclable, non-toxic, service-based, etc.). This not only reduces the city's footprint but signals demand that private suppliers respond to, accelerating the transition. It also sets an example for private consumers regarding the viability and quality of circular products.
- **Legislation for Specific Sectors:** Some sectors have bespoke circular economy policies. For example, the EU's Circular Economy Action Plan targets plastics (with a single-use plastics ban directive), textiles (strategy for sustainable textiles to address fast fashion waste), and electronics (the aforementioned right-to-repair rules). China's approach included mandated waste exchange platforms in industrial parks and targets for resource productivity improvement. These targeted policies are often accompanied by quantitative goals (e.g., recycling 75% of packaging by 2030, reducing food waste by X%). These goals themselves reflect a move beyond GDP, as they set performance metrics in physical terms (material flow targets, waste reduction) rather than just monetary terms.

All these measures help align economic activity with circular principles. But it's important to note that some may appear to constrain traditional growth. For instance, durability and repairability mean consumers buy replacements less often, potentially slowing manufacturing output. Yet from a post-GDP perspective, that's acceptable if well-being is maintained or improved (consumers save money, less pollution, new repair jobs). One study on circular business strategies noted both environmental and social gains can result, but also cautioned about "unintended consequences, especially at the societal level" (Nielsen & Hakala, 2022). For example, if industries shrink due to efficiency, workers might need re-skilling to transition to new jobs in repair, recycling, or services. This implies supportive policies are needed for labor.

3. **Labor and Social Policies for a Circular Economy:** A truly innovative approach ties in social policies such as labor regulations, education, and social security,

to facilitate a circular transition. For instance, if a society decides to prioritize well-being over pure output, it might encourage work-time reduction (like a four-day workweek or 6-hour workday) to share work and reduce unemployment as productivity rises. This could help balance any GDP slowdown and ensure people still have jobs and income while enjoying more leisure (a direct well-being improvement). Some European countries have experimented with such models, motivated partly by quality-of-life and environmental considerations (people with more time might engage in lower consumption lifestyles, like cooking at home, which can be less resource-intensive than fast food, etc.).

Additionally, education and training systems need to reorient toward circular skills. As identified in research, integrating circular economy concepts into curricula and vocational training is vital (Schröder & Barrie, 2024). For example, training programs for repair technicians, recycling engineers, product designers specialized in cradle-to-cradle design, and circular business model innovation can build the human capital required. The EU's Skills Agenda now highlights green and circular skills, and some countries (like Finland) have started introducing the circular economy in school education. By valuing these skills, the standard of living in terms of meaningful employment can be preserved or enhanced in the new economic model.

Social security policies might also adapt. Proposals like universal basic income (UBI) often enter the conversation in post-growth discourse. UBI could decouple livelihood security from the need for ever-increasing production, thereby making it politically feasible to prioritize well-being and environment. If people's basic needs are guaranteed, an economy could pursue slower or different kinds of growth without mass hardship. While UBI is still experimental, a few pilot programs (in Finland, Canada, etc.) showed positive effects on well-being and did not significantly reduce willingness to work, indicating it could support a transition where perhaps less total labor is needed due to efficiency gains.

4. **Rethinking Financial and Corporate Incentives:** Innovative policy also involves the financial sector and corporate governance. If GDP is no longer the sole goal, companies might also be encouraged to broaden their objectives beyond profit to include social and environmental value (sometimes termed the triple bottom line). Governments can incentivize this through mechanisms like integrated reporting requirements (firms reporting on ESG, Environmental, Social, Governance performance) or even revising corporate fiduciary duty to consider stakeholders other than shareholders. This is happening through moves such as benefit corporation statutes, which allow companies to formally pursue public benefits. On the finance side, central banks and finance ministries could start aligning monetary and fiscal policy with climate and

circular economy targets (e.g. "green quantitative easing" or requiring banks to account for climate risk). New Zealand's Treasury, for example, developed a Living Standards Framework to guide its advice, which includes natural and social capital considerations alongside financial metrics (Martin, 2018). The emergence of green bonds, sustainability-linked loans, and circular economy investment funds are market innovations that policy can accelerate by providing guarantees or interest subsidies. One interesting idea is conditional economic stabilizers tied to environmental metrics: for instance, stimulus spending that automatically increases when carbon emissions drop too steeply (to prevent recession) or that is directed into green sectors. This is speculative but reflects creative thinking on how to manage an economy not for maximizing output but for achieving a safe and just operating space.

5. **International and City-level Collaboration:** Many circular economy and beyond-GDP policies require coordination beyond national borders. Internationally, sharing best practices and setting collective goals is key. The UN's 2030 Agenda (SDGs) already implies beyond-GDP thinking by including goals on inequality, climate action, biodiversity, etc., not just economic growth (SDG 8 is about "decent work and economic growth" but even it emphasizes per capita economic growth "in accordance with national circumstances" and job quality).

The OECD, through its Well-Being Framework and the High-Level Expert Group on Measuring Economic Performance (Stiglitz-Fitoussi-Durand report 2018), provides guidelines to countries on implementing these measures. The EU's Circular Economy packages (2015, 2020) compel member states to adopt certain laws and set a vision of a "competitive, climate-neutral, circular economy" by 2050, effectively acknowledging that the old growth model must change. On the beyond-GDP front, the EU has a "Beyond GDP" initiative since 2007 and is exploring measures like adjusted GDP or complementary indicators for inclusion in official processes. The fact that major institutions are involved lends legitimacy and technical support for national innovative policies.

Cities are also hotbeds of experimentation. Many cities such as Amsterdam, Copenhagen, Ljubljana, etc. have declared goals to become 100% circular or zero-waste by specific dates. They innovate with policies like circular building codes requiring use of secondary materials in construction), urban mining (recovering materials from demolition sites, and community repair and sharing programs. Cities network and others facilitate peer-learning among cities on these strategies. For example, Amsterdam's circular strategy is explicitly tied to social goals, like creating jobs for marginalized communities in refurbishing activities, thus marrying circularity with inclusive development. City-level implementation is crucial because cities control waste management, local transport, and can influence citizen behavior directly. A city might measure success by neighborhood well-being indices and waste reduction stats rather than just business activity. This local approach can feed upwards into national and global progress.

6. **Ensuring a Just Transition:** Innovative policy must include measures to ensure the transition is fair the concept of a "just circular transition." This means protecting those who might lose out for example, workers in extractive industries or manufacturing of disposable goods and enabling them to find roles in the new economy. Policies like strong social safety nets, retraining programs, regional redevelopment funds, and stakeholder engagement in planning are critical. The circular economy should ideally create more and better jobs than it disrupts, and studies often suggest net job gains due to increased recycling, remanufacturing, and local services. But those jobs may be in different places and require different skills than the ones lost. So active labor market policies and investments in education are needed to avoid inequality worsening. The literature points out that many existing macro indicators and policies are "agents of the status quo" but some can disrupt GDP's dominance and create conditions for a more ambitious circular economy (Alberich et al., 2023).

Those "disruptive" indicators and policies often involve challenging power structures and vested interests (e.g., fossil fuel lobbies, planned obsolescence profit models). Hence, transparency, public participation, and a strong evidence base are important to drive change.

CONCLUSION AND RECOMMENDATIONS

This study has demonstrated that GDP, while historically central to measuring economic performance, fails to capture the multidimensional nature of well-being in the 21st century. In the face of planetary boundaries, social inequalities, and a changing climate, the need for rethinking how people define and measure standards of living has become both urgent and foundational. The circular economy offers a transformative framework that decouples prosperity from material consumption and ecological degradation. It reorients the goals of economic systems toward sustainability, resilience, and human flourishing by embedding principles such as resource efficiency, durability, shared value creation, and regenerative design. In a circular paradigm, prosperity is no longer defined by the accumulation of goods but by the quality of life achieved within ecological limits. Furthermore, the integration of circular economy thinking into policy frameworks supported by alternative indicators such as well-being indices, inclusive wealth measures, and ecosystem health metrics which represents a shift toward post-GDP governance. As illustrated through examples like New Zealand's Wellbeing Budget and the European Union's CE initiatives, this transition is not only conceptually sound but increasingly politically feasible. Ultimately, rethinking standards of living through a circular lens enables societies to pursue long-term well-being over short-term output, aligning economic structures with the imperatives of environmental sustainability and social justice. Following recommendations can be made based on the findings:

1. **Develop Integrated Well-being Dashboards**: Governments should implement multi-criteria indicators that combine social, environmental, and economic dimensions such as the Genuine Progress Indicator (GPI), Human Development Index (HDI), or circular well-being indices to assess national performance beyond GDP.
2. **Mainstream Circular Economy Principles in Public Policy**: Regulatory frameworks should mandate eco-design, extended producer responsibility, right-to-repair standards, and circular procurement policies, thereby embedding circularity into economic systems.
3. **Support Cultural and Behavioral Transitions**: Policies and educational initiatives must encourage a shift from consumerist values to sufficiency-based lifestyles, promoting the idea of "living better with less" and valuing time, community, and environmental quality.
4. **Redesign Fiscal Incentives**: Governments should introduce tax reforms that penalize resource extraction and pollution while rewarding circular practices, such as repair services, secondary markets, and renewable energy use.
5. **Ensure a Just Circular Transition**: To avoid social disruption, policymakers must implement inclusive labor policies that invest in circular skills training, protect vulnerable workers, and create meaningful employment opportunities in low-carbon, resource-efficient sectors.
6. **Align Finance with Sustainability**: Financial systems should be restructured to favor circular investments through green bonds and integrated reporting. Companies should be incentivized to account for environmental and social value alongside profits.
7. **Localize Circular Innovation**: Municipal governments and cities should be empowered to experiment with circular solutions tailored to community needs, enabling decentralized action and fostering social capital through repair networks, urban sharing systems, and local production loops.

Overall it can be said that building a post-GDP society requires more than new metrics it demands a cultural, institutional, and structural reimagining of what it means to live well. The circular economy provides the conceptual and operational tools to enable this shift, placing human well-being and planetary boundaries at the center of policy innovation.

REFERENCES

Aghion, P., & Howitt, P. (1992). A model of growth through creative destruction. *Econometrica*, *60*(2), 323–351. DOI: 10.2307/2951599

Alberich, J. P., Llorente-González, L. J., Ramezankhani, M. J., Bimpizas-Pinis, M., & Lowe, B. (2023). Using macroeconomic indicators to enact an ambitious circular economy. *Circular Economy and Sustainability*, *3*(3), 1515–1544. DOI: 10.1007/s43615-022-00232-3

Anderton, A. (2006). *Economics* (4th ed.). Pearson Education.

Barro, R. J., & Sala-i-Martin, X. (2004). *Economic growth* (2nd ed.). MIT Press.

Blomsma, F., & Brennan, G. (2017). The emergence of circular economy: A new framing around prolonging resource productivity. *Journal of Industrial Ecology*, *21*(3), 603–614. DOI: 10.1111/jiec.12603

Boulding, K. E. (1966). The economics of the coming spaceship Earth. In Jarrett, H. (Ed.), *Environmental quality in a growing economy* (pp. 3–14). Resources for the Future/Johns Hopkins University Press.

Dasgupta, P., & Weale, M. (1992). On measuring the quality of life. *World Development*, *20*(1), 119–131. DOI: 10.1016/0305-750X(92)90141-H

Desrochers, P. (2004). Industrial symbiosis: The case for market coordination. *Journal of Cleaner Production*, *12*(8–10), 1099–1110. DOI: 10.1016/j.jclepro.2004.02.008

Easterlin, R. A. (1974). Does economic growth improve the human lot? Some empirical evidence. In David, P. A., & Reder, M. W. (Eds.), *Nations and households in economic growth* (pp. 89–125). Academic Press. DOI: 10.1016/B978-0-12-205050-3.50008-7

Easterlin, R. A. (1995). Will raising the incomes of all increase the happiness of all? *Journal of Economic Behavior & Organization*, *27*(1), 35–47. DOI: 10.1016/0167-2681(95)00003-B

Easterlin, R. A. (2000). The worldwide standard of living since 1800. *The Journal of Economic Perspectives*, *14*(1), 7–26. DOI: 10.1257/jep.14.1.7

Finlayson, J. A. (2002). Living standards: How does British Columbia compare? *Polish Perspectives*, *9*(4), 1–4.

Ison, S., & Wall, S. (2007). *Economics* (4th ed.). Prentice Hall.

Kakwani, N. (1993). Performance in living standards: An international comparison. *Journal of Development Economics, 41*(2), 307–336. DOI: 10.1016/0304-3878(93)90061-Q

Kirchherr, J., Reike, D., & Hekkert, M. (2017). Conceptualizing the circular economy: An analysis of 114 definitions. *Resources, Conservation and Recycling, 127*, 221–232. DOI: 10.1016/j.resconrec.2017.09.005

Korhonen, J., Honkasalo, A., & Seppälä, J. (2018). Circular economy: The concept and its limitations. *Ecological Economics, 143*, 37–46. DOI: 10.1016/j.ecolecon.2017.06.041

Martin, B. (2018). New Zealand goes beyond GDP. *Green Economy Coalition.* https://www.greeneconomycoalition.org/news-and-resources/new-zealand-goes-beyond-gdp

Meredith, S. (2023). The world's in a 'polycrisis'—and these countries want to quash it by looking beyond GDP. *CNBC.* https://www.cnbc.com/2022/12/26/well-being-these-countries-are-looking-beyond-gdp-and-economic-growth.html

Nielsen, I. B., & Hakala, H. (2022). Circular business strategies and quality of life. *Sustainability (Basel), 14*(3), 1782. DOI: 10.3390/su14031782

Parkin, M. (2003). *Economics* (6th ed.). Addison-Wesley.

Preston, S. H. (2007). The changing relation between mortality and level of economic development. *International Journal of Epidemiology, 36*(3), 484–490. DOI: 10.1093/ije/dym075

Raworth, K. (2017). *Doughnut economics: Seven ways to think like a 21st-century economist.* Chelsea Green Publishing.

Reike, D. (2024). *Understanding the circular economy: From synthesized conceptual foundations to system-oriented progress measurement* [Doctoral thesis, Utrecht University].

Rockström, J., Steffen, W., Noone, K., Persson, Å., Chapin, F. S.III, Lambin, E. F., Lenton, T. M., Scheffer, M., Folke, C., Schellnhuber, H. J., Nykvist, B., de Wit, C. A., Hughes, T., van der Leeuw, S., Rodhe, H., Sörlin, S., Snyder, P. K., Costanza, R., Svedin, U., & Foley, J. A. (2009). A safe operating space for humanity. *Nature, 461*(7263), 472–475. DOI: 10.1038/461472a

Schröder, P., & Barrie, J. (2024). How the circular economy can revive the Sustainable Development Goals. *Chatham House.* https://www.chathamhouse.org/2024/09/how-circular-economy-can-revive-sustainable-development-goals

Sen, A. (1987). *The standard of living – The Tanner lecture 1985.* Cambridge University Press.

Stahel, W. R., & Reday-Mulvey, G. (1981). *Jobs for tomorrow: The potential for substituting manpower for energy.* Vantage Press.

Stiglitz, J. E., Sen, A., & Fitoussi, J. P. (2009). *Report by the Commission on the Measurement of Economic Performance and Social Progress.* https://ec.europa.eu/eurostat/documents/8131721/8131772/Stiglitz-Sen-Fitoussi-Commission-report.pdf

Vanham, P. (2025). A brief history of GDP – and what could come next. *World Economic Forum.* https://www.weforum.org/stories/2021/12/stakeholder-capitalism-episode-1-a-brief-history-of-gdp/

Chapter 2
Green Capital for Circular Economies:
The Evolving Role of Financial Institutions

Ahmad Ashaal
https://orcid.org/0000-0001-6021-966X
Lebanese International University, Lebanon

Mohamad Saad
Lebanese International University, Lebanon

Fadi Ghosn
https://orcid.org/0000-0002-2450-0478
Lebanese International University, Lebanon

Mohamad Hijazi
https://orcid.org/0009-0005-9054-0557
Lebanese International University, Lebanon

ABSTRACT

This chapter examines how the financial sector is changing to promote economic circularity. It shows how green capital—sustainable financing and investments—can enable the transformation from linear "take-make-waste" to circular business models. Finance may assist in achieving circular economy goals, managing risk, and providing competitive investor returns. Recent studies show that circular economy solutions reduce investment payback default risk and improve risk-adjusted performance, indicating comprehensive risk management and future market growth. It will discuss green bonds, ESG-focused mutual funds, and sustainability-linked loans that support circular innovations as part of the circular economy transformation.

DOI: 10.4018/979-8-3373-3852-1.ch002

It will provide global case examples of how banks, investors, and policymakers are using green capital to support circular solutions and offer recommendations and policy frameworks for finance, policy, and sustainability professionals to integrate circular economy aspects into their financial systems.

INTRODUCTION

The circular economy (CE) offers a different lens on economic growth. It recasts the former linear solutions tied to "take, make, dispose" in terms of reuse, repair, recycle, and regenerate natural systems, thereby unlinking economic growth from resource consumption (Kandpal, Jaswal, Santibanez Gonzalez, & Agarwal, 2024). The baseline idea for this move is green capital - those cash flows to environmentally just activities that implement CE processes designed to reduce waste, implement closed-cycle production, and sustainable resource exploitation (Gennari, 2024; Lawrence, 2025; Vangeri et al., 2024).

The rise in global environmental issues, including biodiversity loss and greenhouse gas emissions, has generated international interest in circularity. UNEP (2021) asserts that over 50% of global emissions come from resource extraction and processing. The studies cited by the World Economic Forum (2020) estimate that CE could unlock $4.5 trillion in global economic value by 2030; however, this will require more than environmental intent; it will require a shift in the financial systems we use.

Financial entities have a profound role in unleashing these transformational pressures. Banks, asset management firms, venture capitalists, and development banks are responsible for directing capital flows. When they embed circularity criteria into lending or investment assessments, they drive behavioral and infrastructural change in the corporate sphere (Relano, Paulet, & Mavoori, 2024). Daumas (2024) notes that failing to incorporate circularity into financial models can result in stranded assets, regulatory risk, and vulnerable resource security.

Evidence shows companies adopting circularity are frequently realizing operational savings, increased resilience, and investor confidence (Pan et al., 2024; Alghababsheh, 2024). Specifically, Bocconi University, Ellen MacArthur Foundation, and Intesa Sanpaolo (2021) provide evidence that circular businesses will realize lower default rates and better risk-adjusted returns. The financial upside has created the emergence of CE-themed products: circular economy-based ETFs, green bonds and sustainability-linked loan facilities are explicitly designed to achieve CE outcomes (da Silva & Sehnem, 2025; Xavier, Ottoni, & Lepawsky, 2021).

Policy developments now reinforce the momentum. The European Union Sustainable Finance Taxonomy interprets the circular economy into its list of specific environmental objectives and creates indicators for access to capital through green eligibility (UNEP, 2024). Multilateral development banks, such as the World Bank and the IDB, are utilizing forms of blended finance to de-risk circular economy projects in the Global South (Van Opstal et al., 2024). In the meantime, national governments are incorporating CE targets into their national policies, such as industrial policies and green recovery plans, and making them part of their ESG disclosure obligations (Kumar et al., 2024).

This chapter has important implications for policymakers, potential responsibilities for financial professionals, and practical ideas for sustainability leaders and researchers. Policymakers should prioritize the establishment of a circular economy in planning and public finance. Financial professionals will see the emergence of new tools and techniques to support circular economy investments and de-risking investments. Sustainability leaders and researchers will consider the practical ways to align the environmental goals with financial innovation. The presence of green capital could emerge as the source of economic resources that drive systematic change when stakeholders are jointly motivated to work together.

THE CIRCULAR ECONOMY AND ITS FINANCIAL DIMENSIONS

I. Understanding the Circular Economy

The circular economy is a drastically different economic model from the traditional linear "take-make-waste" approach. In a circular economy, design helps to renew value. It replaces the linear paradigm with methods that limit waste and pollution, extend the lifetime of materials, and restore natural systems (Kandpal, Jaswal, Santibanez Gonzalez, & Agarwal, 2024; UNEP, 2024). This means designing recyclable, durable, and repairable products; reusing, remanufacturing, and recycling materials to keep them in use; and carefully reintroducing biological materials into the ecosystem. These basic concepts aim to distinguish between the use of limited resources for economic development and environmental degradation. By carefully organizing waste and routinely cycling commodities and resources, a circular economy may preserve natural capital while boosting innovation and competitiveness (Morelli et al., 2024). Prominent corporations, such as the Ellen MacArthur Foundation, claim that a circular economy is "restoring and regenerative by intention," meaning it seeks to ultimately benefit businesses, society, and the environment equally (Bocconi University, Ellen MacArthur Foundation, and Intesa Sanpaolo, 2021).

In response to mounting environmental problems, the circular economy has gained increasing prominence on the agendas of world governments over the past decade. With the linear consumption model exacerbating pollution, biodiversity loss, and climate catastrophe, it is becoming increasingly important as a method of addressing all of these issues (Andersen, 2021). For instance, over half of the world's greenhouse gas emissions originate from resource extraction and processing; adopting circular approaches could significantly reduce this proportion (World Economic Forum, 2020). Likewise, with just one use per year in today's linear system, 95% of the value of plastic packaging is lost to the economy; therefore, failed circular business models may not be able to address this issue within the linear system. These realities have encouraged politicians, businesses, and financial actors to see the circular economy as an essential component of projects aiming at sustainable development. Approaching the "decade to deliver," circular economy solutions are imperative to fulfill the UN Sustainable Development Goals and climate objectives by 2030, as business as usual is no longer an option (World Economic Forum, 2020). The circular economy offers a framework for reevaluating value creation, potentially leading to financial growth and environmental and social benefits.

II. The Financial Effects of Circular Economy Transition: Risk, Resilience and Returns.

The financial ramifications of implementing circular economy concepts are substantial for banks, investors, individual businesses, and national economies. Reorienting financial flows and upfront investments with careful risk and reward analysis is necessary for adopting circularity.

Financial potential and cost savings: Adopting circular models can have a significant, worldwide, beneficial economic impact. According to the World Economic Forum (2020), waste reduction and the creation of new business value might result in an economic potential of $4.5 trillion by 2030. This value is derived from several sources, including increased manufacturing efficiency, new income streams from creative services (such as product leasing or sharing platforms), and material cost reductions through recycling and reuse. Circular approaches, for instance, could have a substantial positive impact on plastics and food systems (Urugo et al., 2024). Improving the reuse of plastic materials could preserve billions of dollars of material value that is currently lost annually, and implementing circularity in the production and management of food could cut associated greenhouse gas emissions by almost half (UNEP, 2021). Companies that use circular strategies at the corporate level frequently discover that they may increase operational efficiency, create more value products because of their sustainability, and lower input costs by using recycled materials or creating more lasting products (Alghababsheh, 2024; Pan, Wong, Wong, Boon-itt, & Li, 2024). Collectively, these advantages contribute to an increase in profit margins over time.

Additionally, adopting circular supply chains protects businesses from unstable raw material prices. By relying more on recovered materials or product-as-a-service models, businesses can reduce their vulnerability to fluctuations in commodity prices and supply disruptions (UNEP, 2024). This improved resource security can thus improve long-term financial performance and corporate resilience.

Resilience and risk reduction: A circular transition is a response to the substantial financial risks associated with the status quo, presenting an opportunity for growth. Businesses and investors who rely on the linear model are more vulnerable to shifting customer tastes, regulatory fines, and resource limitations (Kanwal, Yadav, & Dewasiri, 2025). On the other hand, investment portfolios and activities may be made less risky by using circular business models. Banks and investors can mitigate their exposure to supply chain shocks and resource price volatility by funding circular operations, such as recycling initiatives, remanufacturing, and product-service systems (Raj & Choudhary, 2025). Capital may gradually shift from linear to circular assets to successfully hedge against the risks associated with the resource-intensive, high-waste economy (UNEP, 2024). According to an examination of over 200 businesses across 14 industries, a company's probability of debt default over one to five years decreases with its level of circularity. Stated differently, circular businesses are generally more financially stable (UNEP, 2024), most likely due to their flexible business structures and safer inputs.

Furthermore, businesses with greater circularity have demonstrated greater resilience to economic shocks. The COVID-19 pandemic demonstrated that businesses with circular business models performed better during the crisis and outperformed those with linear business models in the post-shock period (UNEP, 2024). Lenders and investors in those businesses profit financially from their resiliency.

On the other hand, increasing hazards are associated with funding the linear economy. As resource limits tighten and environmental regulations become more stringent, traditional "take-make-waste" industries may become less feasible (Haar, 2024). Financial institutions may face a surge of stranded assets that lose value prematurely due to market, legal, or environmental changes if they continue to make significant investments in linear business models (UNEP, 2024). As virgin resources become more expensive or scarce, industries that rely on inexpensive virgin materials may significantly decline the value of their assets. Ignoring these patterns puts banks and investors at risk of suffering losses. Therefore, balancing portfolios favoring circular, future-fit companies is crucial from a fiduciary standpoint. The shift to a circular economy can be seen as a risk management strategy for the financial industry since it positions financial institutions to prosper in a low-carbon, resource-efficient economy while lowering exposure to the legal, reputational, and market risks associated with unsustainable practices (Gennari, 2024; Kandpal, Jaswal, Santibanez Gonzalez, & Agarwal, 2024; Kumar et al., 2024; Todaro & Torelli, 2024).

Capital reallocation and investment requirements: A substantial amount of capital will be required to implement a circular economy on a large scale (Heikkinen, Kujala, & Blomberg, 2023). New technologies, such as material recovery innovations, circular product design, and infrastructure like sophisticated recycling and composting facilities, as well as reverse logistics networks for product take-back and remanufacturing factories, must be financed (Vangeri et al., 2024). Businesses will also require funding to develop goods and retool processes for circularity. Although estimates of the required investment differ, it is obvious that hundreds of billions of dollars will need to be raised. Indeed, more than USD 300 billion in funding has been allocated to circular economy projects worldwide since 2019, indicating a sharp increase in capital inflow into this field (Ellen MacArthur Foundation, 2020). This covers corporate expenditure on circular supply chains, venture capital investments in circular businesses, and project funding for extensive circular initiatives. However, substantially more financial support from the public and commercial sectors will be needed to close the gap to a truly circular economy. Particularly in emerging nations where upfront costs may be a hurdle, governments and international lenders can help de-risk early-stage circular initiatives or offer concessional financing when the business case is still in its infancy. Thankfully, the financial benefits of these expenditures outweigh the effort. According to the UNEP (2021), the shift to circularity is expected to increase economic output by USD 4.5 trillion by 2030, highlighting the significant returns on investment in jobs and growth.

Returns on investments made in a circular economy: Crucially, preliminary data indicate that, with proper management, investments in the circular economy might yield competitive, if not greater, financial returns. Recent estimates from the OECD and the Ellen MacArthur Foundation suggest that countries transitioning to circular economic systems could experience 0.5-1.0% annual GDP growth by 2035, particularly when combined with digital innovation and industrial retooling. According to a 2021 research conducted in collaboration with Bocconi University, the Ellen MacArthur Foundation, and Intesa Sanpaolo, a significant European bank, incorporating the concepts of the circular economy has a "de-risking effect" and can result in higher risk-adjusted returns for businesses and their investors (UNEP, 2024). Improved waste management and resource efficiency immediately reduce costs, while the introduction of new circular goods and services creates new sources of income (Karim, Waaje, Roshid, & Yeamin, 2025; Sarkhoshkalat, Afkham, Bonyadi Manesh, & Sarkhosh, 2024). These benefits can raise a company's shareholder value and return on investment. Companies that exhibit circular practices are expected to be rewarded more by markets over time, as they are perceived to be more aligned with sustainable growth patterns and less vulnerable to future shocks. As part of broader ESG (environmental, social, and governance) concerns, investors are beginning to incorporate the performance of the circular economy into their value models (Lawrence, 2025). As lenders and investors perceive less risk, a company with higher degrees of circularity may have a cheaper cost of capital. Switching to circular models can improve long-term financial performance by reducing risk, expanding markets, and reducing expenses simultaneously. However, it necessitates a mindset change upfront and often significant capital investments shortly; financial institutions will be crucial in tackling this problem (Relano, Paulet, & Mavoori, 2024).

Nonetheless, there are risks associated with circular investments. The initial support to set them up can be high cost, and we also look at untested business models, and mixed policy environments, especially in the emerging markets, can reduce investors' willingness to take a chance on some investments. Without policy support and blended finance tools to de-risk projects for all parties in circular initiatives, there are some instances where a circular initiative can under- or overperform. The implications of risk and the need for financial innovation revolve around both reward systems and risk sharing.

THE EVOLVING ROLE OF FINANCIAL INSTITUTIONS IN A CIRCULAR ECONOMY

The transition to a circular economy is significantly facilitated by financial institutions, such as banks, asset managers, institutional investors, and development banks. Their choices regarding capital allocation, risk assessment, and product development significantly impact how rapidly circular business models can expand, as they are the guardians of "green capital." How these organizations view and interact with the circular economy has changed in recent years.

Supplying financial items and capital: Commercial banks and investors increasingly offer customized financial products and services to promote circular initiatives. Financial institutions, especially banks, are essential because they provide capital that helps companies implement circular business models, save resources, and cut waste. This covers tools such as circular economy finance facilities, sustainability-linked loans, and green loans (Zahid, Hayat, Rahman, & Ali, 2024). For instance, some banks offer favorable lending terms or credit lines to businesses implementing circular economy ideas, such as establishing a remanufacturing plant or implementing a product take-back program. New debt products are appearing on the capital markets side. Sustainability and green bonds were issued especially to finance initiatives related to the circular economy. Intesa Sanpaolo's €750 million "circular economy" green bond, issued in 2019 and linked to a larger €6 billion loan portfolio designated for circular economy initiatives, is a noteworthy example (UNEP, 2024). This bond drew investors by emphasizing circular outcomes and showing how capital markets can promote circularity. Financial institutions acting as investors have also begun introducing theme funds focusing on breakthroughs in the circular economy. These days, specialized venture capital and private equity firms look for entrepreneurs in product-as-a-service platforms, circular packaging, and advanced recycling (World Economic Forum, 2020). A recent development that reflects investor interest in the prospects in this field is the growth of specific investment funds devoted to circular enterprises (da Silva & Sehnem, 2025; Kanda, Klofsten, Bienkowska, Henry, & Hjelm, 2024). By 2020, we anticipate that large asset managers will collaborate with specialists in the circular economy to develop investment vehicles. One example is an index fund created in collaboration with the Ellen MacArthur Foundation to invest in leaders in the circular economy. This type of financial innovation is essential because it directs funds to the appropriate areas and conveys assurance that circular enterprises are the future (Agrawal et al., 2024).

Rethinking risk assessment: Financial institutions have been compelled to enhance their risk and value assessments in response to the growing movement towards a circular economy. The danger of new circular initiatives may be overestimated (UNEP, 2024). In contrast, the long-term hazards of linear ones may be underestimated by traditional credit risk models and investment assessments, which frequently depend on past data and linear economic assumptions (Daumas, 2024). Progressive banks, particularly in Europe, are developing new tools to assess circular business proposals on their own merits more effectively (UNEP, 2024). One such instrument was created by a group of Dutch banks and called the Circular Risk Scorecard. These tools evaluate a company's capacity for circular innovation—that is, using recycled inputs, managing product lifetimes, and optimizing resources. Lenders can more precisely estimate the credit risk of circular projects by considering these factors, often determining that they are more creditworthy than traditional models would suggest. Banks also consider the risk associated with linear business models when making decisions. Forward-thinking banks could, for example, impose a higher risk premium or urge a client firm to migrate if its value chain relies heavily on virgin resources and an impending shortage or regulatory problems are anticipated. Both market factors and regulatory expectations, such as stress-testing for environmental and climatic risks, contribute to this change. To prevent being caught off guard by the hidden risks of linearity, financial institutions are broadening their due diligence to include circular economy metrics. It is still a work in progress to overcome the apprehension surrounding circular models; many banks agree that the circular economy is a relatively new concept and that further data and approaches are needed before it can be widely adopted. Nonetheless, pilot projects and knowledge-sharing programs are fostering the development of expertise in the financial industry (Scorrano, Borin, Thrassou, Cavallo, & Mastroleo, 2025).

New services and business models: Often connected to the circular economy, new business models—such as sharing models, product-as-a-service, and reverse logistics operations—require new financing solutions. A Product-as-a-Service (PaaS) model, for example, alters the cash flow profile by allowing a company to retain ownership of a good and present it as a service. This model yields regular payments rather than one-time sales income, and the asset remains on the provider's balance sheet (Hidalgo-Crespo et al., 2024). Instead of using traditional inventory or receivables finance, banks have had to adjust by funding these businesses using methods that consider the residual asset value and the dependability of service contracts. Due to leasing and pay-per-use structures, lenders must have a comprehensive understanding of depreciation and the secondary market. Insurance and warranty services are also becoming increasingly critical to ensure optimal performance. In response, several banks have established internal teams or "innovation labs" dedicated to financing solutions for the circular economy, gaining knowledge on how to collateralize assets intended for recycling or reuse (Intesa Sanpaolo, 2025). Banks such as BBVA have offered reverse factoring to circular suppliers, allowing businesses to acquire recycled materials or remanufactured parts with improved financing (BBVA, 2023). At the same time, we observe an increase in reverse factoring and supply chain finance solutions targeted at circular supply chains. Financial institutions are successfully co-designing new business models with companies by introducing innovative financing arrangements (such as blue bonds, green bonds, etc.), which make circular strategies possible that would not have been feasible under traditional financing terms.

Participation and collaboration: To promote circularity, financial institutions are assuming a more active engagement with stakeholders and customers, extending beyond just offering goods (Tabas, Rehman, Khitous, & Urbinati, 2025). Nowadays, many top banks offer their corporate customers strategic advice on sustainability and the circular economy, helping them discover circular opportunities within their supply chains and business models. For instance, the Circular Economy Desk at Intesa Sanpaolo's Innovation Center oversees the bank's circular bond issue and provides clients with circular innovation advice. To increase capacity, banks are collaborating with specialized groups. One example is Bancolombia, one of the biggest banks in Latin America, which established the circular economy as a strategic goal in 2021. To strengthen its knowledge of the circular economy, Bancolombia became the first corporation in Latin America to collaborate with the Ellen MacArthur Foundation and formed a specialized internal team focused on the circular economy. Through initiatives like "Hub Círculos" and Circular Economy Diagnostics, Bancolombia is funding projects that support circular business models in different sectors, thereby matching their activities with the sustainability goals of the nation. Banks in South Africa, Australia, and Canada have participated in information exchanges on circular finance, demonstrating how this collaboration model is being duplicated overseas. Financial institutions are also working together on global platforms. Banks, businesses, and governments collaborate to identify investment opportunities and challenges in the circular transition through the Platform for Accelerating the Circular Economy (PACE), a global public-private partnership initiated with support from the World Economic Forum (GreenBiz, 2021). These partnerships enable the sharing of technical and financial resources, conveying a unified message of dedication to the growth of the circular economy.

Finance for development and inclusivity: Recognizing the importance of the circular economy in achieving climate and sustainable development goals, multilateral development banks and development finance organizations are integrating it into their missions (Van Opstal et al., 2024; Zahid, Hayat, Rahman, & Ali, 2024). These organizations often operate in developing nations where there is a need to strengthen the business case for circular initiatives. Using a combination of public, private, and charitable funding, they increasingly utilize blended financing tools to launch circular businesses that yield significant social and environmental benefits. For example, the Inter-American Development Bank (IDB) has funded projects meant to establish inclusive recycling systems all throughout the Caribbean and Latin America in planning and execution. By integrating informal garbage pickers into official systems and strengthening the infrastructure for waste collecting and recycling, such initiatives create social and environmental advantages that help workers live better. Private investors who perceive risks or lower immediate returns may be put off, but they are drawn to these projects thanks to the IDB's assistance, which is frequently provided through concessional loans or guarantees. Similarly, the World Bank and the African Development Bank have initiated programs to fund elements of the circular economy, including plastic reduction, municipal waste management, and industrial symbiosis—the process by which waste from one industry is converted into an input for another. In addition to making portfolios greener, these initiatives ensure that the shift to a circular economy is inclusive, benefiting disadvantaged populations and emerging countries. Development organizations are demonstrating that, with the proper support, circular initiatives can be financially viable, opening the door to future expansion of commercial finance.

Yet still, while the circular economy can create employment, it can also create job loss in traditional linear employment sectors. It is crucial to have a just transition; policies must enable retraining, ensure social protection, and direct financial flows towards inclusive development goals to prevent or alleviate inequality.

GLOBAL CASE EXAMPLES AND TRENDS

To see how these processes play out in practice, consider a few case studies from around the world and instances of circular economy financing. These stories highlight the numerous methods in which financial institutions engage across different geographies and the concrete effects of such efforts:

Intesa Sanpaolo, Italy, issued a €750 million green bond in 2019 to promote the circular economy (Iannuzzi, Labini, & D'Apolito, 2023). The bond proceeds were awarded to enterprises that met circular criteria, including efficient resource use, recycling, and the development of innovative circular goods, resulting in a pipeline of financed circular business loans. This was coupled with a multibillion-euro loan line that the bank set up to support the circular economy. Intesa increased its green financing options by introducing this approach and proved that circular projects are appealing to mainstream finance as well as being sensible. The bond received good responses from investors, suggesting the need for such targeted impact investments. Intesa's example has prompted other European banks to adopt similar "use-of-proceeds" tools for the circular economy, consistent with the EU's overall thrust.

Latin America - Strategic Bank Initiatives (Bancolombia, Colombia): The bank's strategy integrates the circular economy into its basic business model. Bancolombia would have assembled an internal team to promote the circular economy and aggressively created financial structures and alliances to help circularity in its markets by 2021 (UNEP, 2023). The bank created a "Circular Economy Taxonomy," for instance, to classify and monitor loans and investments in circular businesses. It also initiated initiatives such as "Circular Credits," which provide preferential financing to businesses that adopt circular practices. It held innovation competitions, such as "Circulatón," to find and encourage circular entrepreneurs. The bank's collaboration with the Ellen MacArthur Foundation provided access to worldwide knowledge and confirmation of its strategy. By matching its portfolio with Colombia's environmental goals, Bancolombia is funding projects ranging from creative reuse business models to renewable material research. This event emphasizes the importance of creating market banks outside of the EU in order to support the circular economy as part of their sustainable development objective.

North America: Investment Funds and Corporate Engagement: While government circular economy policy has been decentralized in the United States and Canada, the financial sector and corporate investors have begun to mobilize (Xavier, Ottoni, & Lepawsky, 2021). Major global investors have launched circular economy equity funds; for example, in 2019, a large asset management firm collaborated with the Ellen MacArthur Foundation to launch a Circular Economy exchange-traded fund (ETF), which directs capital into publicly traded companies that excel in circular practices. Furthermore, venture capital in Silicon Valley has increased financing for circular technologies, such as chemical recycling businesses and circular supply chain software (Espuny et al., 2025; Schumacher & Green, 2023). Large firms, under pressure from shareholders and activist investors, are now making direct investments in circular innovation or acquisitions. Financial institutions support this trend through instruments such as sustainability-linked loans. In one case, a Canadian bank loaned a packaging company at a lower interest rate if the company met specific circular economy targets, such as achieving a certain percentage of recycled product content. These market-driven examples illustrate how North American investor pressure and customer demand drive enterprises toward circularity, with financial incentives in place to encourage the transition (Gagnon, Tanguay, Amor, & Imbrogno, 2022).

Policy-driven finance throughout Asia, including China and beyond. In Asia, China stands out for incorporating the circular economy into its national objectives and leveraging governmental funding. With circular economy development goals included in China's 14th Five-Year Plan (2021–2025), state-owned banks and local governments are funding projects, including large-scale recycling facilities (Raza & Quaye-Kumah, 2024), and industrial symbiosis parks, where several businesses share waste and byproducts as inputs. The China Development Bank and other policy banks have issued green bonds to support circular economy initiatives, such as waste-to-resource conversion projects (Lin & Hong, 2022). Furthermore, in Southeast Asia, public-private partnerships are being formed to combat ocean plastic pollution by investing in waste management infrastructure and circular economy financing backed by foreign philanthropies, development banks, and local banks. For example, in Indonesia and India, blended financing vehicles supported by institutions such as the World Bank's International Finance Corporation (IFC) and donor governments are funding efforts to increase recycling and garbage collection, both of which are essential for a circular plastics economy (Ramli & Kasih, 2024). These projects show how top-down legislative requirements and international cooperation often provide financial momentum throughout Asia, therefore assuring that money is available to achieve governments' ambitious circular economy aspirations.

Furthermore, Kenya has introduced mobile-based microfinance for waste collection cooperatives in Sub-Saharan Africa, giving informal workers access to funding for recycling interventions. In the Philippines, the Green Turismo initiative is providing circular tourism financing through a combination of private capital and government-supported guarantees. These examples support the importance of considering the local institutional environment when developing circular finance mechanisms.

Every example reveals a more general trend: global financial institutions are beginning to take notice of the circular economy and respond accordingly. They are forming partnerships, developing new financial products, and reevaluating risk and return models to enable money to flow into circular solutions. However, problems still exist. Many companies and banks are still developing their systems to enable them to explore circular projects. To assess how well circularity is working, we need standard metrics, such as carbon footprints. Through more standardized standards and reporting approaches for the circular economy, individuals will be able to make more informed financial decisions. Initiated by the WBCSD, projects such as the Circularity Indicators Project and the EU reporting guidelines provide a clear path forward. Similarly, ensuring a fair transition is crucial: financiers must consider social outcomes to ensure that the shift to a circular economy enhances people's lives and promotes fairness (for example, by funding circular projects that create jobs in recycling or retraining programs for workers transitioning from linear industries).

In essence, the circular economy is rethinking concepts of value and risk in the financial industry. The proactive participation of financial institutions as innovators, risk managers, and capital suppliers will help to determine their broad adoption. The financial aspects of circularity involve mitigating the negative consequences of the current linear paradigm and capitalizing on the opportunities presented by a new sustainable strategy. Banks, investors, and other financial actors have a clear path to incorporating circular economy concepts into their operations as supporting regulations progress, and successful case studies demonstrate the viability of these concepts. The deployment of "green capital" depends critically on integrating finance with the circular economy, ensuring that capital generates financial returns while advancing a regenerative, circular economic model for the future.

THE IMPORTANCE OF INTEGRATING ALL FINANCIAL SYSTEM IN CE

The circular economy is a comprehensive economic system that has defined outputs and objectives. To finance such a comprehensive system, we need a tailored financial system that supports and meets the financing needs of the circular economic system. Given that, no single financial institution, such as an ESG fund or a sustainable bank, can play such a significant role alone. At the same time, one financial market, such as a green bond market, cannot play such an important financing role alone. Moreover, the investors in a given financial system cannot alone effectively contribute to such a comprehensive system unless they are directed, regulated, and motivated to adapt their investment literacy and philosophy accordingly. What is needed is a comprehensive financial system that incorporates all the components of a conventional financial system, updated and upgraded to financially support other economic segments, thereby meeting the objectives of the desired circular economy.

I. Literature review about integration (PPP, ESG, SRI, and Impact investing)

Larivière and Smit (2022) designed a framework that integrates the people, planet, and profit, known as the Triple-P, which is found to contribute to a better, sustainable world. Regardless of the origin and initial objective of this model or framework, the integration part of this model is the most crucial element required in any suggested model aimed at promoting and supporting the circular economy. In other words, when the impacts on people, planet, and profit are studied simultaneously, we can contribute to a better, more sustainable world, where one of the three dimensions alone cannot contribute.

Nogueira, Gomes, and Lopes (2023) revealed that the Triple-P was developed due to the need for sustainable economic development.

The evolving view on corporate and economic sustainability stresses the importance of balancing and integrating the economic, environmental, and social dimensions of the Triple Bottom Line equally, without prioritizing one dimension over the others (Hahn, Pinkse, Preuss, & Figge, 2015).

According to Aldowaish et al. (2022), the market pressure exerted by regulators and investors on firms to report ESG results and performance, has significantly affected the view of these firms toward impact investing, ESG, and sustainability. In response to this pressure, firms began to apply ESG practices rather than thoughtfully integrating sustainability and ESG values into their core business models and operations. In addition, this market pressure has contributed to critical issues such as ESG performance manipulation practices, such as blue washing, green washing, and in extreme cases, value washing. Aldowaish et al. (2022) suggested reforming the internal business models of firms to integrate ESG and sustainability practices into their core business operations. Based on this, although ESG has emerged from the need to integrate the benefits of the three different dimensions —mainly environment, social, and governance —the integration process should start within the firm before proceeding to the external social, economic, and financial environment surrounding it.

We have an urgent need to clarify and discover how integrated actions and measures taken by different financial institutions, such as banks, funds, and other investment companies, can have meaningful effect on the real economy (Heeb, Kellers, & Kölbel, 2022).

Moreover, integrating ESG principles with the concepts of SRI (socially responsible investing), ethics, and impact investing is an effective way to ensure that financial markets are efficient enough to promote sustainability.

II. Conceptual links between existing financial instruments and the circular economy

To ensure we have a comprehensive and integrated financial system that can support and contribute to the circular economy, we don't need to create new financial institutions as the current financial system already includes all types of institutions, such as banks, brokerage companies, credit unions, investment companies, insurance companies, funds, etc. that can perform all functions and fulfill all primary needs. Given this diversity, creating entirely new financial institutions is not necessary. Instead, promoting and ensuring integration among such financial institutions is a needed approach to ensure we have an integrated financial system. Similarly, the market does not need to attract new investors, as the current financial system already serves a wide range of investors with diverse budgets, sizes, risk-return profiles, and investment horizons. Instead, we need to pay special attention to the behaviors and the mentality of these investors to ensure that we can integrate them into the comprehensive financial system designed to support the circular economy.

Although the current financial system offers a wide range of financial instruments, there is an urgent need to design and create new financial instruments to be integrated into a comprehensive financial system that supports the circular economic system. This need is behind the creation of sustainability-oriented instruments, such as green bonds, blue bonds, and ESG funds, which aim to promote sustainability and contribute to the circular economy. Before proposing new financial instruments or designing a conceptual framework for an integrated financial system that supports a circular economy, we should first describe how existing financial instruments align with the objectives of a circular economy.

Green bond instruments are designed to support the transition from a traditional economy to a circular economy. If we assess the objectives of a circular economy, we can clearly see that green bonds can directly support the achievement of these objectives. For example, by issuing green bonds to finance recycling projects or to support plants implementing waste-to-energy initiatives, this green instrument will play a key role in promoting the resource efficiency and waste reduction objectives of a circular economic system. While traditional bonds attract traditional investors, green bonds attract only investors who are ESG-oriented.

After comparing the yields of green municipal bonds with the yield of traditional municipal bonds, Li et al. (2023) concluded that green bonds offer lower yields relative to traditional bonds. This lower yield is reflected in a premium charged on green bonds, known as the greenium. Li et al. (2023) argued that the size of greenium indicates the extent to which investors are interested in and engaged with investing in and demanding Environmental, Social, and Governance (ESG) securities. Li et al. (2023) concluded that the level of greenium is positively correlated with investors' green preferences in the municipal bond markets.

Similarly, Blue bonds are a sustainable debt instrument tailored to finance and promote sustainable ocean and water projects. A blue bond is a key financial instrument that supports the circular economy by financing projects with the primary objective of reducing marine pollution and plastic waste. Additionally, blue bonds can be utilized to finance projects that promote circular water management, a crucial prerequisite for a circular economic system. Moreover, such blue bonds can be issued to finance ocean projects that require sustainable fisheries, thereby promoting sustainable fishing practices.

In addition, ESG funds, which serve as funds with integrated dimensions of sustainability, can play a strategic role in channeling capital from different investors toward different segments in the circular economy. Circular exchange-traded fund (Circular ETF), previously described in this chapter, is a good example of ESG funds. Specifically, the ESG funds are using the capital in hand to invest in recycling technology startups and sustainable material developers. ESG funds will have enough power to exert pressure on corporations to adopt strategies that ensure sustainability objectives are targeted and to ensure zero-waste tactics are followed. This way, ESG funds help investors to align their portfolios with planetary boundaries, attracting a new generation of investors to start a strategic change toward a waste-free circular economy.

Moreover, Sustainability-Linked Loans (SLLs) is an innovative debt financial instrument that is tailored to support and motivate corporations to adopt circular economy principles and to meet sustainability performance targets (SPTs). Unlike conventional loans, Sustainability-Linked Loans (SLLs) require borrowers to achieve sustainability-linked metrics, such as waste reduction, resource efficiency, and product lifecycle extension, thereby strategically aligning with the circular economy. This alignment will be the first step in transitioning from "take-make-waste" systems to circular systems. Sustainability-linked loans (SLLs) are a modern type of debt instrument designed to motivate firms to adopt circular practices. However, for a bank to offer SLLs, it also needs to attract funding that aligns with similar sustainability goals. One way to achieve this is by issuing Sustainability-Linked Certificates of Deposit (CDs), a type of deposit product directly linked to circular economy objectives.

III. Conceptual framework

After identifying the conceptual link each financial instrument has with the circular economy, we should integrate all of the components of a financial system to make it a comprehensive system that has the potential to finance other economic segments in order to meet the principles of the targeted circular economy. The integrated financial system presented in Figure 1 brings together the dynamic interplay between investors, instruments, institutions, and the CE ecosystem. It demonstrates how investor types (i.e., conservative versus aggressive) match with corresponding financial instruments (e.g., green bonds, ESG funds) through institutions (i.e., banks, funds) to fund a range of CE-aligned projects. This alignment is key to bridging capital supply with developing CE requirements.

Figure 1. Integrated Financial System Tailored to Finance Circular Economy

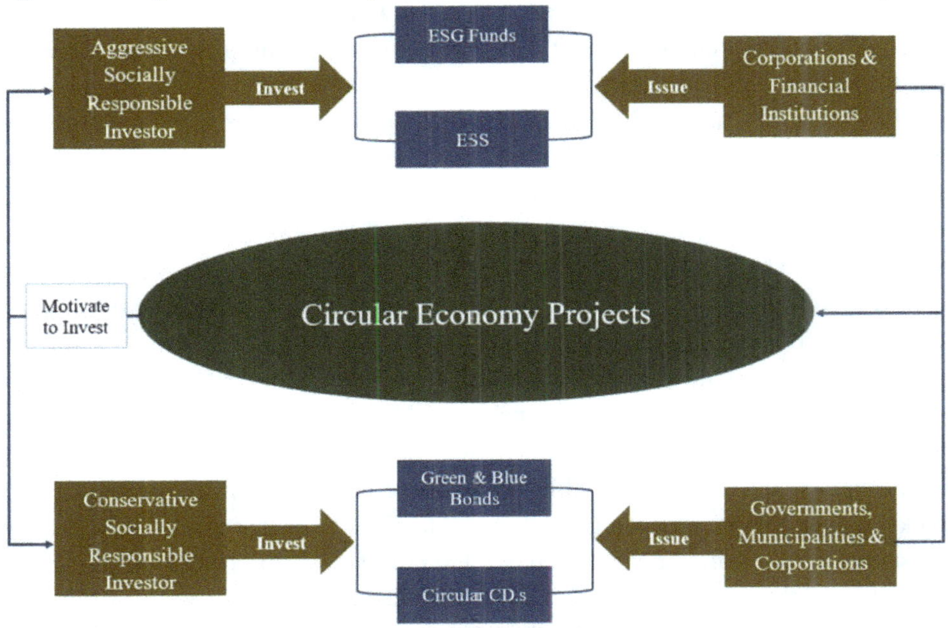

Source: Author

As the circular economy is expected to require a wide variety of circular projects, a corresponding diversity in investor styles and profiles is also necessary. This is illustrated in Figure 1, where two investment styles—conservative and aggressive—are both needed. Being a socially responsible investor does not contradict being an aggressive or risk-taking investor; therefore, both risk-averse and risk-taking investors are essential for a healthy and circular financial system. Additionally, a broad range of financial instruments is required to attract diverse investors on the one hand, and to meet the needs and preferences of various projects on the other. Different financial institutions and entities must play managerial, financial, and intermediary roles by linking investors who demand financial instruments with circular projects that need capital.

EFFICIENT AND SUSTAINABLE STOCKS (ESS): CHALLENGES AND OPPORTUNITIES

After reviewing the literature on green and sustainable financial instruments and their conceptual links with the objectives of the targeted circular economy, we have identified a critical gap in researching and designing equity instruments that can be linked to environmental performance metrics or circular economy principles. Stocks related to the circular economy often show less market efficiency. Because this concept is still relatively new, it introduces more uncertainty for global investors than traditional sustainable investment strategies do.

This gap exists across three important dimensions that are suggested to have growing literature in the future. First, there is no existing universal standard that can be used to classify stocks as sustainable stocks. Stocks represent ownership in public companies, and therefore, the value of such ownership is directly linked to the company's profitability and the stock price movements in the market. Unlike the case with bonds, such stock ownership will make it harder to isolate the sustainable value or green value, known as greenium, from the overall stock value.

Second, there is no general literature review about the relationship between market efficiency and market sustainability. As previously mentioned, isolating the sustainable value component from the overall stock value is considered a key requirement to qualify a sustainable stock. Therefore, we require a strong form of stock market efficiency to determine a fair value of the stock that reflects all available information, including information related to the sustainability component of such value. Given that stock market inefficiency delays the discovery of stock prices, such market inefficiency would also delay the development of a sustainability-linked stock market as a result. Moreover, the presence of an inefficient stock market may be considered a sign of a socially irresponsible market. In other words, persistent stock market inefficiencies, which can ultimately lead to market bubbles and crashes, may contribute to socially irresponsible outcomes. Finally, despite their focus on sustainability, would socially responsible investors be motivated to invest in an inefficient stock market? Since socially responsible investors play a key role in financing a sustainable and circular economy, the inability to attract them in an inefficient stock market will also delay the development of sustainability-linked stock markets. Therefore, we can assume that stock market efficiency is a key condition for ensuring stock market sustainability.

Third, short-termism refers to the short-term horizon investors have in the stock market. Similarly, Short-termism refers to the short-term outlook and vision a firm might have when planning its business future. In other words, short-termism prevails when the overall stock market focuses on immediate and short-term financial outcomes, even if such immediate results come at the expense of long-term stock value creation or sustainability investments that offer environmental and social benefits.

Dow et al. (2024) show that short-termism prevails when investors become traders who prefer to make gains sooner in the short term than later in the long term. According to Dow et al. (2024), firms would benefit if their stocks were traded by informed, rational, and emotion-free investors, since the resulting informative stock values would eventually enhance long-term firm value. Dow et al. (2024) argued that such short-termism can potentially reduce the benefits from the stock market by up to 100%.

Behavioral finance is also crucial. The persistence of heuristics such as herding and status quo bias may limit ESG take-up in equity markets. Incorporating some 'nudges' into sustainable investment frameworks—including sustainability scoring and ESG auto-enrollment—may increase investor alignment with longer-term circular outcomes.

Based on this, short-termism undermines the stock market's ability to finance the circular economy. Therefore, we can add another assumption, which implies that short-termism behaviors must be strictly regulated before designing a sustainable stock market. Regulators and policymakers are advised to take action against this dangerous behavior that is prevalent in the most important capital market in the economy. Addressing the key drivers of short-termism behaviors is the most crucial step to take before designing and implementing structural reforms in the capital markets, thereby transitioning to greater efficiency and sustainability. The quarterly earnings pressure exerted on firms listed in stock markets is a key driver of short-termism. Speculative behaviors, by converting shareholders into share traders, represent another key driver of short-termism in the market, where traders seek immediate rewards in order to maintain a high level of Dopamine in the brain. Thus, High-Frequency Trading (HFT) and Algorithmic Trading can be likened to High-Dopamine Trading (HDT), which can mitigate the negative impact of short-termism on a circular economy.

There is another key driver that is driving not only the short-termism but also the first two drivers previously described. The existing stock pricing mechanism, which is primarily based on free market forces, where supply and demand determine the stock price without any restrictions, is the most significant driver of short-termism in the stock market. This free market, although it sounds attractive, opens the door for speculative behaviors, high-frequency trading, and scalping, thus leveraging the short-termism of the stock market, where emotions, instead of rationality, set the market stock prices which might increase or decrease far away from the fundamental and intrinsic value of respective stocks. Such behaviors will eventually lead to bubbles and crashes that deter socially responsible and long-term investors from investing in such volatile and inefficient markets. Therefore, regulating and reforming the stock market pricing mechanism is the most crucial step to take in order to enhance stock market efficiency and, consequently, address the issues of short-termism. After that, the market will be ready to accept a new financial instrument such as a sustainable stock.

The existing regulatory measures taken to improve efficiency are not integrated, resulting in more market inefficiency. For example, stock price limits aim to protect and enhance market efficiency. However, they are not effective as the fair stock value is often traded outside the limits. Before designing such regulations, the existing stock pricing mechanism should be reformed and regulated.

Stocks represent ownership in a firm and cannot be treated like consumable goods and products. Therefore, the traditional laws of supply and demand should not apply to stocks. While free supply and demand forces determine the price of goods in the consumer market, the equity market operates differently. In other words, a high number of sellers in the stock market indicates that investors, also known as shareholders, are choosing to no longer participate in the business, which is not considered a healthy position for profitable companies. Therefore, is using the law of supply and demand for determining the value of stocks considered appropriate for a financial asset purchased for ownership or speculation purposes? Applying the economic law of supply and demand to price a financial asset, such as a stock, implies that irrational behaviors and psychological factors, driven by emotional traders, influence market stock prices. Saad et al. (2025), given the strong evidence of the stock market's inefficiency, suggested that such inefficiency problem has arisen after delegating the stock pricing task to emotional traders. Therefore, regulators should assign this important task to the firms that have issued these stocks, through a regulated stock valuation process that should be performed outside the stock market, far away from the emotional forces exerted by the speculative market.

Saad et al. (2025) proposed that shareholders in each company agree on a common and efficient stock valuation model that will be adopted by the firm and supervised and regulated by the stock market regulator in order to generate fundamental stock values. After that, shareholders buy and sell at the fair value generated from such an efficient model, which would vary based on the fundamentals reflected in the stock valuation model agreed upon by shareholders. According to Saad et al. (2025), such structural reform in the stock market, which eliminates the impact of emotional traders and short-termism on the stock pricing mechanism, aims to redirect the market's focus to fundamental factors and thereby improve stock market efficiency.

Any regulatory measure imposed by the regulator, such as financial taxes, trading halts, price limits, etc., if imposed in isolation, will be ineffective. According to Saad et al. (2025), the proposal aims to introduce an integrated and updated regulatory framework that encompasses all relevant measures collectively. For instance, the updated stock pricing mechanism, previously discussed, when complemented with stock price limits set by the regulator around the fair stock value derived from the agreed-upon stock valuation model, would ensure that stock values always reflect all available information, and thus would improve stock market efficiency. Similarly, Saad et al. (2025) concluded that a maturity tax, tied to investor holding periods, is expected to encourage and promote long-term investment while curbing short-termism behaviors. One of the main conditions required to develop an efficient stock pricing mechanism is the identification of a list of efficient stock valuation models that have the potential to reflect all available information pertaining to the issuing firms. Then, shareholders in each firm can select an efficient valuation model from this regulated list based on the risk-return profile of the issuing firm (Saad et al., 2025).

Saad (2023) has developed the Net Asset Present Value (NAPV) model, which is considered a potential efficient model for use in this regulated stock pricing mechanism. The NAPV valuation model, after being tested for information efficiency, has shown a significantly higher level of information efficiency than other traditional valuation models. The NAPV model reflects four main value components per share, including basic net asset value (Basic NAV), revaluation per share (RPS), present value of running projects (PVRP), and net present value (NPV). These value components capture the basic book value, inflation value, current economic profit value, and expected growth value, respectively. After identifying the fair value of a stock using an efficient valuation method, regulators can set price limits, not to restrict the market, but to help protect that value. These limits will prevent over- and undervaluation in the market. Within this price range, investors still have the freedom to share their views, whether that means paying a premium because they are optimistic or asking for a discount if they are more cautious.

Finally, our contribution can be stated clearly now. Stocks that are priced under the regulated stock market mechanism, which was previously discussed, will be considered information efficient and are expected to retain this efficiency for the long run. At the same time, the stock value that is generated using an efficient model, such as the NAPV model, can be decomposed into different value components. This value decomposition allows us to create and design new sustainable equity instruments that have the potential to be linked with environmental performance metrics or circular economy principles. This can be done by adding a value component to the stock value generated using NAPV, which reflects the green and sustainability preferences of investors in the stock markets. In other words, within the price range set by regulators around the fair stock value generated by the efficient valuation model, investors can pay a premium because they are optimistic or because they prefer instruments that finance circular economy principles. Given that, such new designed instruments, which can be called Efficient and Sustainable Stocks (ESS), have the potential to reflect the greenium value component in addition to other financial and economic value components, mainly the fundamental book value, the inflation value, the current economic profit value, and the expected growth value. Thus, ESS investors will be compensated in both cases, when companies generate profit, and when sustainable and circular objectives are achieved.

CONCLUSION AND POLICY RECOMMENDATION

The changes made in the financial sector's contributions towards circular economy discussed within this chapter point in a direction that sustainability and finance are heading toward a more common space. A central idea throughout our discussion is that applying the circular economy principles can help manage risks while achieving decent financial returns. Companies and the financiers that work with them face many risks by being bound to traditional linear models of creating value. These risks include increasing commodity prices, supply chain disruptions, regulatory issues, and reputational risks associated with waste and pollution. Firms can manage all of these risks through adopting a circular approach, such as, recycled inputs, reusing materials, and providing a service that involves a product. Evidence supports this point; for example, companies demonstrating greater circularity tend to have lower credit risk (such as a reduced probability of defaults) and better risk-adjusted stock performance compared to their less circular peers. Circular economy strategies can also act as a form of de-risking; that is, because you are relying less on resource consumption and waste generation for growth as a result of implementing circular economy strategies. Likewise, circular economy strategies can improve the resilience of supply chains. By reusing, recycling, and using secondary materials, businesses are less reliant on supply chains made up of raw materials subject to shortage and volatility. Additionally, circular models can create new revenues and cost savings (e.g., savings in energy costs or material reuse), which lead to better profit and long-term returns on capital. These benefits are reflected in the growing shift of investor interest in the circular economy, as evidenced in the emergence of new circular economy investment indices and funds that have outperformed many of the traditional benchmarks.

A variety of financial instruments and mechanisms have been mobilized to capitalize on circular economy opportunities. This chapter presents several examples of these instruments, illustrating their operation and highlighting their successful applications. The most prominent instrument is the green bond, which has been issued since 2007 and is a type of bond designed explicitly for expenditures on projects that have positive environmental impacts. Green bonds are developing to meet demand for financing circular projects (e.g., recycling facilities, new renewable materials, waste-to-resource infrastructure) as eligible uses of the proceeds. Many leading banks and corporations have issued circular economy bonds, a sub-category of green or sustainable bonds, which serve to finance circular economy projects and reflect a clear commitment to achieving circular outcomes. In fact, over the past couple of years, we have seen at least ten corporate bonds issued for specifically circular economy projects by major institutional players. Another innovative instrument are sustainability-linked loans (SLLs) where the interest rate on corporate borrowing is connected to the borrower's sustainability performance (which can measure rates of recycled inputs or reclaimed product returns – i.e., circular metrics for business models). This prompts companies to improve their circular performance for a better interest rate. On the equity phase, ESG investment funds and dedicated circular economy funds are directing investor capital toward companies with circularity-focused practices. With the emergence of circular economy equity indexes and exchange-traded funds by market players (ECPI's Circular Economy Leaders index, MSCI's materials circularity index, etc.), investors have vehicles for investing in baskets of circular-focused companies. Prominent asset managers have created actively managed funds that target circular innovators, driven by increased demand from investors seeking exposure to these types of investments. Together, these technologies—green bonds, sustainability-linked financing, equity funds, venture capital for circular start-ups, and others— form an expanding toolbox for circular finance. They allow capital to be deployed toward circular solution on many different scales and vehicles, including large infrastructure projects and novel new business models.

The chapter also presented global cases of how financial institutions and policies are, importantly, demonstrating change on the ground across both sectors and regions. These examples emphasize, more than anything, that the circular economy is not uniform, but rather shows up in many different ways. For example, multilateral development banks have financed initiatives about waste management and recycling, sustainable textiles and fashion, remanufacturing electronic goods, and recovering critical materials from used goods. Each case study in this chapter highlights the implications for policy and practice: European circular business incubators funded through public-private investment, Asian countries investing in large-scale recycling infrastructure with proceeds from green bonds, and remarkable reuse or remanufacturing startups in Africa that receive support from microfinance. A consistent pattern is that blended finance models (using public or development finance institutions in the investment with private investors) can reduce risk and entice private capital for new circular economy opportunities. The case studies also highlighted that many circular economy projects offered co-benefits. For example, many circular economy projects yielded social and economic outcomes in addition to environmental benefits (such as reduced waste or emissions) that included new jobs in remanufacturing, lower costs for consumers, or enhanced supply chain security. For example, companies investing in circular supply chains observed better control and predictability in their sourcing, lower costs, and less risk in operationalizing. These field examples show it is possible to combine financial thinking with approaches consistent with circular economy principles. They also show the role of local context (as in the policy support, market demand, and partnership opportunities often critical for success).

This means that while the strategies may be localized, the fundamental principles of finance can be deployed in different contexts.

While momentum is accelerating, the chapter also noted some challenges and gaps that need to be addressed and filled before the financial system can be fully aligned with circular economy goals. A significant problem is that the current financial paradigm does not fully price in the environmental and resource risks associated with disruption under a linear model. Most financial models do not yet fully internalize the numerous risks associated with operating in a linear economy, including potential future regulations on single-use plastics or limits on extraction capacity. Therefore, linear risks are typically not adequately reflected in company valuations or assessed when calculating lending risk. On the other hand, today's markets do not allow for identification or reward of positive impacts with financial returns, including long-term savings, of circular business models. A financing gap can occur because circular projects, especially innovative ones and those at an early stage, are often perceived as riskier or less bankable than they genuinely are. In addition, a challenge that is intertwined is the lack of comparable and standardized data and metrics for circular economy performance. Financial institutions are data-dependent; they must utilize data and data evaluation mechanisms to inform their investment decisions. Many circular economy initiatives (e.g., new product-as-a-service initiatives, advanced recycling technologies) nevertheless do not have as much historical data. Because there are no established category-wide methods for metrics comparable to carbon emissions for climate finance, data in these areas is limited and challenging to understand, which presents price risk to risk officers and investors who need to be able to evaluate commitments into circular ventures with relative ease. As noted, the practice of risk assessment and credit risk models often requires adjustments. It may not offer the same opportunities for financiers who lack a deep understanding of circular models as traditional models do. As familiarization and capacity building are still ongoing in these new areas, many financial institutions are only now figuring out how to create the internal know-how, frameworks, tools, and products to support both circular economy and circular economy innovation opportunities actively. These analyses, conducted in light of survey findings, revealed a vice-captively related need for awareness-raising movements and capacity building within financial institutions, specifically in identifying circular economy projects and structuring deals that support a circular economy. These bottlenecks will be critical if practitioners in the circular economy wish to grow circular economy finance from a niche activity to being a more integrated part of the total global finance.

To address these gaps and develop a cohesive and integrated financial system that advances circular economy objectives, this chapter presents a definitive set of recommendations for policy and strategic actions. These recommendations are aimed at both government policy activities and actions from the financial sector, acknowledging the systemic nature of circular economy finance and thus the need to work together to shift incentives and infrastructure for circular finance. The key recommendations are:

1. Integrate circularity in financial taxonomies and ESG standards: National and regional regulators should adapt their green finance frameworks to include an explicit requirement for CE criteria (UNEP, 2024). Metrics such as material reuse, product longevity, and recyclability should all be standardized.
2. Use public and blended finance: Multilateral banks and government agencies should co-finance CE projects through guarantees, concessional loans, and early-stage funding to stimulate private investment (Van Opstal et al., 2024).
3. Enhance risk assessment frameworks: Credit rating agencies and commercial banks should develop and incorporate CE risk indicators, such as exposure to virgin material prices or waste regulatory risk, into their due diligence frameworks (Gennari, 2024).
4. Incentivize financial innovation: Policymakers should facilitate the establishment of new circular finance instruments, which could include, for example, blue bonds for water-related projects or CE insurance products for take-back schemes (Espuny et al., 2025).
5. Build institutional capacity: Financial actors require capacity building on CE concepts. Likewise, regulators can foster cross-sectoral platforms to encourage the sharing of data, the piloting of tools, and the assessment of impact (Scorrano et al., 2025).

Fundamentally, the circular economy is more than a technological and environmental transition; it is also a financial transition. Green capital is the glue that ties political ambition to innovation for business. With good regulation, innovative instruments, and cooperative leadership among stakeholders, financial institutions can become facilitators of a regenerative economy for the future.

At the same time, the overall economic transformation to circularity has significant macroeconomic implications. In addition to firm-level returns, economies will see reallocation of labor between sectors. Linear industries will transition to contracted workers while circular industries transition to more steady and increased levels of employment. The inclusion of re-skilling and inclusive labor market policies in circular finance will enhance economic resilience. Overall, instilling circular models at the system level can mitigate long-term inequality and create sustainable productivity growth.

REFERENCES

Agrawal, R., Agrawal, S., Samadhiya, A., Kumar, A., Luthra, S., & Jain, V. (2024). Adoption of green finance and green innovation for achieving circularity: An exploratory review and future directions. *Geoscience Frontiers*, *15*(4), 101669. DOI: 10.1016/j.gsf.2023.101669

Aldowaish, A., Kokuryo, J., Almazyad, O., & Goi, H. C. (2022). Environmental, social, and governance integration into the business model: Literature review and research agenda. *Sustainability (Basel)*, *14*(5), 2959. DOI: 10.3390/su14052959

Alghababsheh, M. (2024). Understanding whether, how and when circular supply chain management influences firm performance. *Business Strategy and the Environment*, *33*(7), 7139–7161. DOI: 10.1002/bse.3865

Andersen, I. (2021, Feb 24). *United Nations Environment Programme*. Retrieved April 2025, from https://www.unep.org/news-and-stories/speech/circularity-transition-leaving-no-one-behind

BBVA. (2023). *BBVA and Tiendas Ara now offer reverse factoring in Colombia with a social impact.* Retrieved May 2025, from https://www.bbva.com/en/sustainability/bbva-and-tiendas-ara-now-offer-reverse-factoring-in-colombia-with-a-social-impact/

Bocconi University. Ellen MacArthur Foundation; Intesa Sanpaolo. (2021). *The circular economy as a de-risking strategy and driver of superior risk-adjusted returns.* White paper. Retrieved from https://content.ellenmacarthurfoundation.org/m/244d98bd9b1a3cc5/original/The-circular-economy-as-a-de-risking-strategy-and-driver-of-superior-risk-adjusted-returns.pdf?_gl=1*1qidc3p*_ga*MjI1NjY2MTMwLjE3NDcwNTExMzE.*_ga_V32N675KJX*czE3NDcwNTExMjgkbzEkZzAkd

da Silva, T. H., & Sehnem, S. (2025). The utilization of Industry 4.0 technologies to enhance the circular economy through the engagement of stakeholders in Brazilian food technology companies. *Business Strategy and the Environment*, *34*(1), 129–161. DOI: 10.1002/bse.3954

Daumas, L. (2024). Financial stability, stranded assets and the low-carbon transition–A critical review of the theoretical and applied literatures. *Journal of Economic Surveys*, *38*(3), 601–716. DOI: 10.1111/joes.12551

Dow, J., Han, J., & Sangiorgi, F. (2024). The short-termism trap: Catering to informed investors with limited horizons. *Journal of Financial Economics*, *159*, 103884. DOI: 10.1016/j.jfineco.2024.103884

Ellen MacArthur Foundation. (2020). *Financing the circular economy: Capturing the opportunity.* Ellen MacArthur Foundation. Retrieved from https://www.ellenmacarthurfoundation.org/financing-the-circular-economy-capturing-the-opportunity

Espuny, M., Reis, J. S., Giupponi, E. C., Rocha, A. B., Costa, A. C., Poltronieri, C. F., & Oliveira, O. J. (2025). The role of the triple helix model in promoting the circular economy: Government-led integration strategies and practical application. *Recycling*, *10*(2), 50. DOI: 10.3390/recycling10020050

Gagnon, B., Tanguay, X., Amor, B., & Imbrogno, A. F. (2022). Forest products and circular economy strategies: A Canadian perspective. *Energies*, *15*(3), 673. DOI: 10.3390/en15030673

Gennari, F. (2024). Strategic risk-based approach for the circular economy. *European Journal of Business and Management Research*, *9*(3), 24–32. https://hdl.handle.net/11379/599545. DOI: 10.24018/ejbmr.2024.9.3.2294

GreenBiz. (2021, May). Retrieved from The Potential Impact of a Circular Economy: https://givingcompass.org/article/the-potential-impact-of-a-circular-economy

Haar, G. (2024). Transition to a Circular Economy. In *The Great Transition to a Green and Circular Economy* (pp. 89–126). Springer, Cham., DOI: 10.1007/978-3-031-49658-5_9

Hahn, T., Pinkse, J., Preuss, L., & Figge, F. (2015). Tensions in corporate sustainability: Towards an integrative framework. *Journal of Business Ethics*, *127*(2), 297–316. DOI: 10.1007/s10551-014-2047-5

Heeb, F., Kellers, A., & Kölbel, J. (2022). *Does ESG integration impact the real economy. A theory of change and review of current evidence.* Bern: Federal Office for the Environment (FOEN). Retrieved from https://www.csp.uzh.ch/dam/jcr:ac4406e3-ae17-43c0-8fa1-f967cd5abacb/BAFU%20Report_DIGITAL_pages.pdf

Hidalgo-Crespo, J., Riel, A., Golinska-Dawson, P., Peeters, J. R., Werner-Lewandowska, K., & Duflou, J. R. (2024). Facilitating circularity: Challenges and design guidelines of Product-as-a-Service (PaaS) business model offers for electrical and electronic equipment. *Procedia CIRP*, *128*, 567–572. DOI: 10.1016/j.procir.2024.03.037

Iannuzzi, A. P., Labini, S. S., & D'Apolito, E. (2023). Sustainability and the circular economy: the role of the financial sector and the response of Intesa Sanpaolo. In P. M. Falcone, E. Sica, & 1st (Ed.), *Sustainable Finance and the Global Health Crisis* (pp. 193-213). Routledge. DOI: 10.4324/9781003284703

Intesa Sanpaolo. (2025). *Support to the Circular Economy.* Retrieved May 2025, from https://group.intesasanpaolo.com/en/sustainability/support-to-esg-transition/support-to-circular-economy

Kanda, W., Klofsten, M., Bienkowska, D., Henry, M., & Hjelm, O. (2024). Challenges of circular new ventures: An empirical analysis of 70 cases. *Journal of Cleaner Production, 442*, 141103. DOI: 10.1016/j.jclepro.2024.141103

Kandpal, V., Jaswal, A., Santibanez Gonzalez, E. D., & Agarwal, N. (2024). Circular economy principles: shifting towards sustainable prosperity. In *Sustainable energy transition: Circular economy and sustainable financing for environmental, social and governance (ESG) practices* (pp. 125–165). Springer, Cham., DOI: 10.1007/978-3-031-52943-6_4

Kandpal, V., Jaswal, A., Santibanez Gonzalez, E. D., & Agarwal, N. (2024). Sustainable energy transition, circular economy, and ESG practices. In *Sustainable Energy Transition: Circular Economy and Sustainable Financing for Environmental, Social and Governance (ESG) Practices* (pp. 1–51). Springer, Cham., DOI: 10.1007/978-3-031-52943-6_1

Kanwal, P., Yadav, A. K., & Dewasiri, N. J. (2025). Entrepreneurial orientation and green supply chain management (GSCM). In *Impacts of Entrepreneurial Orientation on Supply Chain Management* (pp. 197-236). IGI Global. DOI: 10.4018/979-8-3693-3386-0.ch008

Karim, R., Waaje, A., Roshid, M. M., & Yeamin, M. B. (2025). Turning the waste into wealth: Progressing toward global sustainability through the circular economy in waste management. In *Sustainable Waste Management in the Tourism and Hospitality Sectors* (pp. 507–552). IGI Global Scientific Publishing., DOI: 10.4018/979-8-3693-6110-8.ch019

Kumar, B., Kumar, L., Kumar, A., Kumari, R., Tagar, U., & Sassanelli, C. (2024). Green finance in circular economy: A literature review. *Environment, Development and Sustainability, 26*(7), 16419–16459. DOI: 10.1007/s10668-023-03361-3

Larivière, B., & Smit, E. G. (2022). People–planet–profits for a sustainable world: Integrating the triple-P idea in the marketing strategy, implementation and evaluation of service firms. *Journal of Service Management, 33*(4/5), 507–519. DOI: 10.1108/JOSM-01-2022-0033

Lawrence, J. M. (2025). Impact of Environmental, Social, and Governance (ESG) and the Circular Economy (CE) on Financial Decision-Making. In *Fintech for ESG and the Circular Economy* (pp. 119-148). DOI: 10.1002/9781394234035.ch7

Li, B., Wang, B., & Yu, J. (2023). *The Emerging Greenium*. The Brookings Institution., Retrieved from https://www.brookings.edu/wp-content/uploads/2023/05/GreenBonds_20230711.pdf

Lin, L., & Hong, Y. (2022). Developing a green bonds market: Lessons from China. *European Business Organization Law Review*, *23*(1), 143–185. DOI: 10.1007/s40804-021-00231-1

Morelli, G., Pozzi, C., Gurrieri, A. R., Mele, M., Costantiello, A., & Magazzino, C. (2024). The role of circular economy in EU entrepreneurship: A deep learning experiment. *Journal of Economic Asymmetries*, *30*, e00372. DOI: 10.1016/j.jeca.2024.e00372

Nogueira, E., Gomes, S., & Lopes, J. M. (2023). Triple bottom line, sustainability, and economic development: What binds them together? A bibliometric approach. *Sustainability (Basel)*, *15*(8), 6706. DOI: 10.3390/su15086706

Pan, X., Wong, C. W., Wong, C. Y., Boon-itt, S., & Li, C. (2024). The influences of Circular Economy practices on manufacturing firm's performance: A meta-analytic structural equation modeling study. *International Journal of Production Economics*, *273*, 109267. DOI: 10.1016/j.ijpe.2024.109267

Raj, A., & Choudhary, B. (2025). Amalgamation of Corporate Social Responsibility With the Principles of the Circular Economy for Sustainable Growth. In *Driving Business Success Through Eco-Friendly Strategies* (pp. 21–46). IGI Global Scientific Publishing., DOI: 10.4018/979-8-3693-9750-3.ch002

Ramli, I. M., & Kasih, M. C. (2024). *Integrative Report on Implementation of the Circular Economy in ASEAN*. Economic Research Institute for ASEAN and East Asia (ERIA). Retrieved from www.eria.org/uploads/Integrative-Report-on-Implementation-of-the-Circular-Economy-in-ASEAN.pdf

Raza, R., & Quaye-Kumah, N. (2024). *People's Republic of China Country strategic opportunities programme 2025–2030*. IFAD.

Relano, F., Paulet, E., & Mavoori, H. (2024). Addressing the climate–finance interaction in a new light: From green to brown assets disclosure in the banking industry. *Strategic Change*, *33*(5), 399–416. DOI: 10.1002/jsc.2593

Saad, M. (2023). How a Novel Stock Valuation Model Outperforms Traditional Models in Information Efficiency: Implications for Shareholders and Regulators. *Journal of Financial Economics*, *11*(2), 113–130. DOI: 10.12691/jfe-11-2-5

Saad, M., Bajalan, S., & Tehrani, R. (2025). Integrating and updating the stock market regulation: A significant approach to enhance the information efficiency of the stock market. *Interdisciplinary Journal of Management Studies, 18*(4), 669-684. DOI: 10.22059/ijms.2025.379692.676885

Sarkhoshkalat, M. M., Afkham, A., Bonyadi Manesh, M., & Sarkhosh, M. (2024). Circular Economy and the Recycling of E-Waste. In *New Technologies for Energy Transition Based on Sustainable Development Goals: Factors Contributing to Global Warming* (pp. 319-354). Singapore: Springer Nature. DOI: 10.1007/978-981-97-2527-4_16

Schumacher, K. A., & Green, M. L. (2023). Circular economy in a high-tech world. *Circular Economy and Sustainability, 3*(2), 619–642. DOI: 10.1007/s43615-022-00220-7

Scorrano, P., Borin, E., Thrassou, A., Cavallo, F., & Mastroleo, G. (2025). Knowledge sharing between businesses and stakeholders for systemic and sustainable regional development. Insights in the agri-food sector. *Journal of Knowledge Management, 29*(4), 1278–1300. DOI: 10.1108/JKM-05-2024-0517

Tabas, A. M., Rehman, M. A., Khitous, F., & Urbinati, A. (2025). Stakeholder and customer engagement in circular economy ecosystems: A systematic literature review and research agenda. *Business Strategy and the Environment, 34*(1), 402–416. DOI: 10.1002/bse.3989

Todaro, D. L., & Torelli, R. (2024). From greenwashing to ESG-washing: A focus on the circular economy field. *Corporate Social Responsibility and Environmental Management, 31*(5), 4034–4046. DOI: 10.1002/csr.2786

UNEP. (2021). *The circularity transition: leaving no one behind.* Retrieved April 2025, from https://www.unep.org/news-and-stories/speech/circularity-transition-leaving-no-one-behind

UNEP. (2023). *Unlocking Circular Economy Finance in Latin America and the Caribbean: The Catalyst for a Positive Change.* Retrieved from https://www.unepfi.org/publications/unlocking-circular-economy-finance-in-latin-america-and-the-caribbean-the-catalyst-for-a-positive-change/

UNEP. (2024). *Circular Economy as an Enabler for Responsible Banking.* Retrieved April 2025, from https://www.unepfi.org/wordpress/wp-content/uploads/2024/07/PRB_CE-Climate-Nexus_Guidance-Doc.pdf

UNEP. (2024). *Circular Economy as an Enabler for Responsible Banking:Leveraging the Nexus between Circularity and Sustainability Impact.* UNEP. Retrieved April 2025, from https://www.unepfi.org/wordpress/wp-content/uploads/2024/07/PRB_CE-Nexus_Guidance-Doc.pdf

Urugo, M. M., Teka, T. A., Gemede, H. F., Mersha, S., Tessema, A., Woldemariam, H. W., & Admassu, H. (2024). A comprehensive review of current approaches on food waste reduction strategies. *Comprehensive Reviews in Food Science and Food Safety*, *23*(5), e70011. DOI: 10.1111/1541-4337.70011

Van Opstal, W., Borms, L., Brusselaers, J., Bocken, N., Pals, E., & Dams, Y. (2024). Towards sustainable growth paths for work integration social enterprises in the circular economy. *Journal of Cleaner Production*, *470*, 143296. DOI: 10.1016/j.jclepro.2024.143296

Vangeri, A., Bathrinath, S., Anand, M., Shanmugathai, M., Meenatchi, N., & Boopathi, S. (2024). Green Supply Chain Management in Eco-Friendly Sustainable Manufacturing Industries. In *Environmental Applications of Carbon-Based Materials* (pp. 253–287). IGI Global., DOI: 10.4018/979-8-3693-3625-0.ch010

World Economic Forum. (2020, Jan 22). https://www.weforum.org/stories/2020/01/the-world-needs-a-circular-economy-lets-make-it-happen. (F. v. Houten, & N. Ishii, Eds.) Retrieved April 2025, from https://www.weforum.org/: https://www.weforum.org/stories/2020/01/the-world-needs-a-circular-economy-lets-make-it-happen

Xavier, L. H., Ottoni, M., & Lepawsky, J. (2021). Circular economy and e-waste management in the Americas: Brazilian and Canadian frameworks. *Journal of Cleaner Production*, *297*, 126570. DOI: 10.1016/j.jclepro.2021.126570

Zahid, M., Hayat, M., Rahman, H. U., & Ali, W. (2024). Is the financial industry ready for circular economy and sustainable development goals? A case of a developing country. *Qualitative Research in Financial Markets*, *16*(5), 962–992. DOI: 10.1108/QRFM-06-2023-0135

Chapter 3
Green Investors in the Circular Economy:
Catalyzing Sustainable Finance for a Regenerative Future

Fadi Ghosn
https://orcid.org/0000-0002-2450-0478
Lebanese International University, Lebanon

Mohamad N. Hijazi
https://orcid.org/0009-0005-9054-0557
Lebanese International University, Lebanon

Mohamad Saad
Lebanese International University, Lebanon

Ahmad Ashaal
https://orcid.org/0000-0001-6021-966X
Lebanese International University, Lebanon

ABSTRACT

The chapter explores the critical role of green investors in promoting and scaling the circular economy, a regenerative economic model designed to eliminate waste, maximize resource efficiency, and create long-term sustainability. It examines how investment strategies aligned with environmental, social, and governance (ESG) principles can support circular business models, and how financial markets are evolving to meet the demands of sustainability-focused stakeholders. Through a blend of theoretical perspectives, case studies, and policy analysis, the chapter identifies key investment trends, actors, challenges, and enabling mechanisms that link

DOI: 10.4018/979-8-3373-3852-1.ch003

capital markets with circular economy transitions. It also discusses how financial innovation, impact measurement tools, and regulatory frameworks are shaping the behavior of green investors.

1. INTRODUCTION

Imagine a world where every dollar invested doesn't just grow wealth, it heals the planet. That's the promise of green investors in the circular economy, a financial revolution turning waste into wealth and pollution into prosperity. These forward-thinking financiers aren't just avoiding harm; they're actively rebuilding broken systems, funding innovations that make trash obsolete and designing business models where everything is reused, repurposed, or regenerated. From venture capitalists backing startups that transform plastic waste into premium materials, to pension funds demanding circular design in every company they invest in, this movement is proving sustainability and profitability can go hand-in-hand. The numbers speak volumes: circular economy strategies could generate $4.5 trillion in global economic benefits by 2030 (Ellen MacArthur Foundation, 2023), with green investors serving as the critical bridge between bold ideas and real-world impact.

In an era where climate change, resource scarcity, and environmental degradation pose existential threats, the need for regenerative economic models is more urgent than ever. The circular economy offers a transformative blueprint that challenges the linear 'take-make-waste' paradigm, emphasizing continuous material loops and systemic efficiency. However, scaling circular innovations demands not just policy shifts but also financial ecosystems that prioritize long-term ecological and social returns over short-term profits. This chapter explores how green investors—ranging from individual ethical savers to institutional giants—mobilize capital to accelerate this transition.

Despite growing interest, the literature remains fragmented in addressing how behavioral theories of green investors explicitly shape circular finance mechanisms. While significant studies explore sustainable finance and circular economy independently, there is a gap in integrating investor behavior models (such as Priority Theory, System Disruption Theory) into the analysis of circular investment strategies, especially within emerging economies where financial ecosystems are less mature. A comparative analysis of existing literature reveals a concentration of research efforts in Europe and North America, where policy support, mature financial markets, and extensive institutional backing have accelerated the development of circular finance frameworks. Conversely, emerging economies in MENA, Southeast Asia, and Latin America exhibit significant circular economy initiatives but remain underrepresented in academic discourse. This geographic imbalance underscores the need to incorporate diverse regional perspectives to enrich global understanding of circular finance dynamics.

We have added new real-world examples to fill this gap, including the UAE's Masdar City, a $22 billion eco-city financed by green bonds and sovereign wealth funds; Chile's Green Hydrogen Fund, a public-private initiative that positions the nation as a leader in renewable energy; and Southeast Asia's Grab Holdings, which has integrated circularity into its ride-hailing model by investing in EV fleets. These examples demonstrate how emerging economies are using green finance for circular innovation, while also broadening the chapter's geographic focus.

This chapter examines the vital role green investors play in advancing and expanding the circular economy, a regenerative economic model aimed at eliminating waste, improving resource efficiency, and promoting long-term sustainability. It explores how investment strategies aligned with Environmental, Social, and Governance (ESG) principles can support circular business models, and how financial markets are adapting to meet the growing expectations of sustainability-oriented stakeholders. By combining theoretical insights, real-world case studies, and policy analysis, the chapter highlights key investment trends, major actors, challenges, and enabling factors that connect capital markets with circular economy transitions. It also explores the influence of financial innovation, impact measurement tools, and regulatory frameworks on shaping the actions and decisions of green investors.

This chapter's conceptual framework connects five key elements: (1) Circular Economy Principles; (2) Green Investor Types; (3) Green Investment Instruments; (4) Obstacles to the Transition to the Circular Economy; and (5) Green Finance Enablers. The foundation is provided by the principles of the circular economy, which place an emphasis on waste reduction, resource efficiency, and system regeneration. Using tools like green bonds, ESG ETFs, carbon credits, and sustainability-linked loans, green investors—who can be divided into retail, institutional, impact, venture capitalists, green bond buyers, and philanthropists—raise money. Barriers like market failures, capital intensity, and policy fragmentation moderate the interaction between these actors and tools, while facilitators like advanced data metrics, public-private partnerships, and regulatory incentives promote the shift to a regenerative economic model.

This chapter uses a qualitative approach that combines synthesis of case studies, secondary data analysis, and a thorough literature review. The theoretical framework was developed through a systematic review of industry publications, academic journals, and institutional reports (OECD, WEF, Ellen MacArthur Foundation). In order to ensure that both developed and emerging market perspectives were represented, empirical examples were chosen based on their applicability to circular economy investments across a range of geographic locations. The chapter attempts to provide a comprehensive analysis of green investment dynamics in the circular economy by fusing conceptual theories with real-world examples.

This chapter is structured as follows: Section 2 explores the theoretical foundations of circular economy principles and green finance theories. Section 3 analyzes the investor landscape, categorizing investor types and financial instruments. Section 4 highlights current investment trends in circular economy sectors, while Section 5 addresses barriers hindering the transition. Section 6 discusses key enablers that facilitate circular economy investments. Section 7 reviews regulatory and policy frameworks, followed by Section 8, which delves into the importance of data, metrics, and transparency. Finally, Section 9 presents real-world case studies demonstrating successful green investments in circular enterprises.

2. THEORETICAL FOUNDATIONS

2.1. Circular Economy Principles

In recent years, the idea of a circular economy has gained a lot of attention and is becoming more popular. Terms like "circular economy" and "circular principles" often appear in academic studies and reports from different organizations. The meaning of circular economy can vary depending on the issue being addressed, who the audience is, or the author's point of view. For some, it's about using materials more efficiently and closing resource loops. For others, it's about creating new business models, planning, or designing innovative products.

Without a solid understanding of the circular economy, we risk missing valuable chances to connect it with current frameworks. For instance, it becomes hard to answer important questions like: How does the circular economy support the Sustainable Development Goals? What actions can help reduce emissions and meet the targets set by the Paris Agreement of COP21? Which strategies work best in different industries for promoting sustainability? And what kinds of political efforts are needed in various countries?

Over the past 60 years, the concepts of sustainable development and environmental protection have gradually advanced from almost nothing to the more sophisticated idea of the circular economy that we see today. The concept of a circular economy is not unique to any one individual or period of time; rather, it has a long history. Nonetheless, two primary strategies for the circular economy can be identified based on worldwide research:

The first is a resource-focused approach, which aims to create a closed loop for materials, energy, and waste. This can be done by reusing products through repair or refurbishment, reusing parts in manufacturing, or recycling materials. The second approach is economy-focused, where the circular economy is seen as an economic system that emphasizes reusing materials and conserving natural resources, while creating value for both people and the economy throughout the entire system.

When the Ellen MacArthur Foundation was established in 2010, the idea of the Circular Economy became well-known. Combining the two previous methods, the Foundation's experts' definition is the one that is most frequently cited. A circular economy, according to their definition, is one that is intended to be restorative and regenerative, with an emphasis on maintaining goods, parts, and materials at their maximum worth and usefulness at all times. This method makes a distinction between biological and technical cycles.

In 2014, the World Economic Forum, together with the Ellen MacArthur Foundation and McKinsey & Company, released a report titled "Towards the Circular Economy: Accelerating the Scale-Up Across Global Supply Chains". In this report, they identified five key principles of the circular economy:

2.1.1. Design Out Waste

By reducing waste in the design phase, both environmental and operational gains can be realized. The intention is to reduce waste through developing products that are easily disassembled and arranged to refurbish, therefore allowing them to mirror the cycles of biological and technical materials.

2.1.2. Build Resilience Through Diversity

A system that is diverse, with characteristics like modularity, flexibility, and adaptability, becomes less vulnerable to external disruptions.

2.1.3. Relying on Energy From Renewables

As great amounts of energy are typically used during production processes, using renewable resources should be the aim for manufacturing systems.

2.1.4. Think in Systems

The circular economy is informed by natural systems, where the emphasis is on systems as a whole, rather than components. The key is understanding how the systems interact with each other.

2.1.5. Waste is Food

Products and materials, whether technological or biological, should move through the economy to different uses before their nutrients are returned to the natural environment.

The five principles originate from an earlier and significant articulation of circular economy thinking based on biomimicry and cradle-to-cradle thinking. Well known leaders and advocates such as Michael Braungart and William McDonough (see Cradle to Cradle) and supported by the Ellen MacArthur Foundation in its early systems thinking work.

Although these five principles describe a systems-based approach to circular economy, addressing waste reduction, resilience, and optimization of the system, the framework continues to evolve to be, and be perceived as, more succinct and usable. However, as the vision became more widely adopted, then it became apparent a simplified and more strategic model was needed to make action at a constitutive scale and to incorporate major sustainability frameworks. This led to the development of the three core principles:

2.1.6. Design Out Waste and Pollution

The first rule focuses on creating products and systems that reduce waste and pollution from the start. Instead of thinking waste is just a normal part of making and using things, this approach aims to prevent waste before it happens. In a circular economy, waste isn't seen as unavoidable but something that can be avoided by planning better and coming up with new, smarter products, with the following key elements:

Product Design: Products should be created in a way that makes it easy to reuse, fix, or recycle when they're no longer needed. This means designing them with separate parts that can be taken apart easily and using materials that can be used again and again.

Preventing Pollution: Whenever processes are poorly managed, pollution tends to occur. Companies can mitigate detrimental emissions and avoid harming the environment, from the initial extraction of raw materials from nature through to disposal, by enhancing product and system design procedures.

Design for Longevity: Creating durable products that require less frequent replacement can significantly reduce waste. Designing durability, repairability, and upgradeability extends the lifecycle of products and reduces the need for new resources.

Real-World Example: Fair phone designs smartphones with easily changeable parts-like the screen or battery-so when things break, consumers only need to swap out or repair the part instead of the entire phone. Patagonia is another example from the clothing industry, focused on creating durable, long-lasting clothes that can be repaired and don't contribute to waste from fast fashion.

2.1.7. Keep Products and Materials in Use

The second principle is keeping products and materials useful for as long as possible. This means finding ways to reuse, repair, or upgrade them instead of throwing them away. The idea is to keep things in use and avoid waste by making the most out of what we already have.

Reuse: Products and materials should be used more than once whenever possible, this can include small objects, everyday items, or even parts of machines and equipment for new production.

Repair and refurbishment: Products should be designed to be able to be repaired or upgraded. This not only makes them last longer, but it decreases the likelihood of needing to buy something new. Companies can assist with this by providing repair services or designing their products to be repaired easily.

Remanufacturing: When a product or part wears out, it can be rebuilt or upgraded to work like new again giving it another life instead of being thrown away.

Sharing Models: Some businesses use sharing systems, like bike- or car-sharing, where many people use the same product. This reduces the number of items that need to be made, saving resources.

Real-World Example: IKEA is designing more of its products so they can be taken apart, repaired, or upgraded to help reduce waste and facilitate reuse. Zipcar offers a service that allows people to share cars rather than owning one, thereby reducing the number of cars on the road, and the resources required to make them.

2.1.8. Regenerating Natural Systems

The third principle of the circular economy goes beyond just reducing harm to helping nature heal. Instead of only trying to do less damage, businesses should aim to restore ecosystems and bring natural resources back to life.

Restoring Ecosystems: The circular economy supports ways of working that help nature recover and thrive. This can mean putting nutrients back into the soil, protecting wildlife, and using farming or forestry methods that improve natural habitats.

Using Renewable Resources: Instead of relying on limited resources, this approach promotes using energy from renewable resources such as the sun and wind. This approach to design also encourages the making of products from materials that naturally decompose or can regenerate quickly.

Cradle to Cradle: This idea means designing products so that when they're no longer useful, they can safely return to nature or be reused in new products, without creating waste or pollution.

Real-World Example: The Body Shop encourages regeneration using responsibly sourced ingredients in ways that help nature regenerate rather than harming it. Patagonia's "Worn Wear" program extends clothing life, and is also involved with projects like regenerative farming, which helps improve the health of their soil and supports biodiversity.

Implementing circular economy strategies like designing for reuse, promoting repairability, or investing in renewable resources, requires more than just innovation in design or production. These changes often involve higher upfront costs, long-term planning, and supportive financial systems. As a result, the transition to a circular economy is closely linked to the growing field of green investment and sustainable finance. These financial approaches aim to direct capital toward environmentally responsible projects, including those that support circular practices. Understanding how sustainable finance operates is essential to scaling up circular solutions and achieving broader environmental and economic goals. Beyond the resource-focused and economy-centric perspectives, additional approaches enrich the circular economy discourse. These include:

2.1.9. Design-Centric Approach

Emphasizes product innovation and lifecycle thinking, where materials and products are designed from inception for durability, reparability, and eventual reintegration into production cycles.

2.1.10. Regenerative Approach

Focuses on enhancing and restoring natural systems, going beyond sustainability to actively improve ecosystems, often linked with practices such as regenerative agriculture and eco-restorative industrial processes.

2.1.11. Social and Equity-Focused Approach

Recognizes that circularity must also address social justice, ensuring that circular transitions create inclusive economic opportunities, reduce inequalities, and involve community participation.

These approaches often overlap with resource and economic models, but they provide a systemic overview as well. A conceptual framework (Figure X) showing the intersection of these approaches has been created, outlining the connection between design approaches, regenerative intentions and equity considerations alongside materials cycles and economic value creation, where green investors become the enablers to actualize this whole approach.

2.2. Green Investment and Sustainable Finance Theories

Sustainable development is now a major global priority. It means meeting the needs of people today without harming the ability of future generations to meet theirs. The idea first emerged in the 1980s as a way to balance economic growth, social well-being, and environmental protection (IUCN, 1980). Achieving this balance is not possible without effective use of financial resources. Green finance refers to using money in ways that support the environment and help achieve sustainable development. Wang and Zhi (2016) describe it as the connection between financial activities and eco-friendly practices. In simple terms, green finance is essential for sustainability, because if money isn't used responsibly and with care for the environment, long-term development goals cannot be reached.

There isn't one single definition of "green finance." In general, it refers to providing financial services and carrying out financial activities in ways that positively impact the environment. The European Banking Federation defines green finance as it covers a wide range of areas. It includes environmental issues like pollution, biodiversity loss, and air or water quality. It also involves efforts to tackle climate change, such as investing in renewable energy, improving energy efficiency, and reducing the risks of extreme weather events. On the other hand, the Organization for Economic Co-operation and Development (OECD) defines green finance as a finance that supports economic growth in a way that cuts down pollution and greenhouse gas emissions, reduces waste, and uses natural resources more efficiently. The government of Germany defines green finance as a way to involve the financial sector in helping economies shift toward using fewer carbon emissions and resources, while also supporting efforts to adapt to climate change.

The term "sustainable development" is now commonly used by companies, politicians, universities, and many other organizations. It has become a key concept that shapes how modern society thinks and plans for the future. At its core, sustainable development is about creating progress that brings benefits to many sectors, crosses national boundaries, and considers the needs of both current and future generations. The International Institute for Sustainable Development (IISD) defines sustainable development as a way of meeting today's needs without harming the ability of future generations to meet theirs. The main goal of sustainable development is to keep both the economy and the environment strong over the long term. To achieve this, economic, environmental, and social issues must all be considered and balanced in every decision-making process.

Green finance and sustainable development are closely connected for several key reasons. First, sustainability cannot be achieved without green finance. Second, the goal of meeting the needs of the present without compromising the ability of future generations to meet their own needs cannot be realized without green finance in the economy. Lastly, green finance is specifically designed to promote sustainability, making it incomplete without the broader objective of sustainable development. On the other hand, sustainable finance has become a big focus as people around the world try to make financial systems support long-term environmental, social, and economic goals. To really get why businesses and investors care about sustainability, it helps to know the key ideas behind it. The following section breaks down some important theories that explain why sustainable finance matters, how it works, and what results we can expect from it.

2.2.1. Priority Theory of Sustainable Finance

The priority theory of sustainable finance posits that the effort economic agents put into achieving sustainable finance goals reflects how important these goals are within a specific country or region (Wilson, 2010; Kuhn, 2020; Krauss et al., 2016). This prioritization can be observed through three main aspects: the level of coordinated, independent, and collaborative actions taken by economic actors, the speed at which consensus is reached on sustainable finance initiatives, and the promptness of implementation toward these goals. Economic agents often manage multiple priorities, ranking them based on their perceived importance. The position of sustainable finance goals within this hierarchy indicates how seriously these agents take them. Over time, shifts in economic, political, or environmental conditions can alter these rankings (Kuhn, 2020). When sustainable finance is prioritized, it typically receives more dedicated resources and strategic focus. Conversely, if it is deemed less important, it may attract minimal attention or investment (Krauss, Krüger, & Meyer, 2016). For instance, financial institutions that prioritize sustainability often integrate their principles into their core business strategies, making sustainability a fundamental aspect of their operations (Setyowati, 2020; Cunha, Meira, & Orsato, 2021). However, prioritizing sustainable finance comes with trade-offs. Elevating these goals may necessitate the de-prioritization or postponement of other significant objectives. In developing economies, where immediate needs like poverty alleviation or GDP growth take precedence, sustainable finance may be viewed as a secondary concern. This perspective can lead to resistance against reshuffling priorities, especially when the short-term costs of such changes appear high.

The theory provides two important benefits: It acknowledges that economic agents function in a field of conflicting interests, and sustainable finance is a priority among them. It allows for public communication of the priority that economic agents give to sustainability goals in the form of strategic plans, policies or pronouncements (Pinchot & Christianson, 2020). However, there are drawbacks to the theory. First, priority does not ensure success, and planning for sustainable goals does not necessarily lead to success. Second, sustainable finance goals remain attainable even without priority settings - this occurs when the private sector independently makes sustainable finance decisions even in the absence of national strategies.

2.2.2. The Peer Emulation Theory of Sustainable Finance

This theory suggests that people and organizations often follow the lead of others they admire when working toward sustainability goals (Setyowati, 2020; Cunha et al., 2021). When there aren't clear, universal rules for how to finance sustainable projects, it's common for countries or institutions to copy what their peers are doing. This usually happens when those peers share similar views about sustainability, politics, or economics. For example, countries that take the same approach to climate change are likely to adopt similar green finance strategies. There are many benefits to this process. First, it helps groups to measure their goals and values against peers with similar interests. Second, you are able to replicate existing work, which means you will usually spend less time, as you will have a few adjustments to make. Third, it is often less expensive than writing an entirely new original plan. Fourth, you take what someone else has done and build off of it; there may be room for improvement to existing policies. Lastly, this theory of cooperation as opposed to competition helps to engage others in the process. However, there are disadvantages too, and the foremost comes from the lack of creativity and learning a group won't gain if they are only following someone else's original ideas and solutions. Secondly, a policy that worked exceptionally well in one country may not be as useful as being copied in another country. Differences in laws, financial systems, and the support of government can make considerable differences in the implementation and success of a policy that you merely copy.

2.2.3. The Life Span Theory of Sustainable Finance

This theory builds on Vernon's product cycle hypothesis. It suggests that people's interest in sustainable finance depends on how long they think sustainable finance products, like green bonds, eco-friendly policies, or funding schemes, will last. According to this theory, experienced economic players understand that these products go through stages: they're introduced, they grow, they mature, and eventually, they may decline (Vernon, 1966; Brest & Born, 2021). Based on this understanding, these agents make decisions about whether to support a sustainable finance initiative in the short term, long term, or not at all. Their level of support depends on how long they believe a specific sustainable finance tool will stay relevant. For example, if investors think a sustainable finance product is just a trend that won't last, they may only make short-term commitments or none. But if they believe the product will stick around or even become the new normal, they're more likely to invest for the long haul. This theory has a few advantages. First, it helps explain why demand for items like green bonds may increase or decrease. If one has a positive view of the demand for green bonds into the future, they are likely to invest. Second, this theory helps identify how important people's expectations are in determining whether or not to support sustainable finance products. However, this theory also has a couple of disadvantages. One disadvantage is that it is common to be biased or subjective in making predictions about how long a sustainable finance product will be around. A second disadvantage is that a prediction can be incorrect; therefore, the person can forego an opportunity that is positive or support an opportunity based on incorrect assumptions.

2.2.4. System Disruption Theory of Sustainable Finance

This theory suggests that shifting to sustainable finance could shake up the existing traditional financial system and negatively affect businesses that depend on it (Pinchot & Christianson, 2020; Stavins, 2023). This kind of change might lead to some economic actors, like banks, companies, or investors, to resist or hesitate in supporting sustainable finance, especially if they fear their business models or incomes will suffer. The theory proposes that economic agents make decisions based on two factors: if they think the benefits outweigh the risks and the degree to which they think the change is going to impact their work or livelihoods. If the process seems disruptive with little or no clear upside, these economic agents are likely to retract their support. To help curb this resistance, the theory recognizes that an element of transparency and clarity will help. Economic agents need to know the specifics of how the shift towards supporting sustainable finance is evolving: Which existing systems are going to be phased out? Are any new systems going to be put in place? Are there any kind of support or compensatory measures available to those affected? Through these staged or transitional elements in the process, trust in nevertheless difficult process will be harnessed and introduced. This theory has two notable strengths. First, it accurately recognizes that moving toward sustainable finance will not be without difficulty and disruptions. Second, it nice emphasizes information sharing as an important aspect of this shift so that people are able to understand the rationale for the change and less likely to reject it. The theory has one critical weakness: the theory assumes that in order to adopt sustainable finance, there needs to be a complete shift in the current system. Sustainable finance could potentially be simply an additional avenue for traditional finance to blend existing and new models and give businesses the option to include environmental, social, and governance (ESG) factors in their financial decision making.

2.2.5. Positive Signaling Theory

The positive signaling theory suggests that businesses and governments have a strong reason to share good news about their commitment to sustainable finance (Rodin & Brandenburg, 2021; Financial Times, 2022). By doing this, they send a positive signal to outsiders, like investors or international partners, who might support their efforts. These signals often come in the form of public announcements or extra financial and non-financial details in reports. For example, a company might talk about its new green bonds or sustainable finance tools to attract investors who are specifically looking to support environmentally responsible firms. Similarly, a government might announce plans to launch a national sustainable finance policy. This not only boosts its reputation as a sustainability-minded country but can also attract foreign investment and technical help for green projects. One big advantage of this theory is that it helps reduce information gaps between companies and investors. When firms share more information, investors feel more confident about where their money is going. However, the theory has some downsides. Just because an organization shares positive information doesn't mean it will take meaningful action. Also, some companies might use these positive announcements to distract from bad news—like financial losses from fossil fuel investments—by talking up their sustainable finance intentions instead.

2.2.6. Resource Theory of Sustainable Finance

This theory explains that some countries can achieve their sustainable finance goals faster than others because they have more and better human-made resources. These resources include things like strong financial systems, large foreign reserves, advanced financial technology, low national debt, effective climate monitoring systems, and well-informed citizens who care about sustainability (McKinsey & Company, 2022; GCEC, 2023). Countries that also have many institutional investors willing to fund green projects are in an even better position. Because of these advantages, such countries can transition from traditional finance to sustainable finance more smoothly and quickly than countries that lack these resources. On the other hand, countries with weaker financial systems, high debt, limited access to technology, and fewer investors face greater challenges and may take longer or struggle altogether to reach their sustainable finance goals.

This theory suggests that we cannot expect all countries to move at the same pace but rather allow every country to process at a pace that reflects the resources it has.

A country with fewer resources may lose ground and there may be countries that do not reach their goals—not because they did not try, but because their limitations are real. Resource theory does have two major strengths. First, it accepts that differences in resources available are a significant reason as to why some countries succeed faster than others. Second, it accepts that differences in levels of development impact a country's ability to pursue sustainable finance. Development is fundamentally about building up these human-made resources. There are some limitations to resource theory. The first was mentioned earlier in that it may be used to unfairly judge or discriminate against countries that are lagging. Another drawback is that it does not quite understand how long it takes to build these resources up that all countries do need to build. As a result, some countries may use the excuse of lacking resources to delay or not take action toward sustainable finance. Table 1, below, summarizes the sustainable finance theories compared based on core focus, strengths, weaknesses and perspectives of sustainability.

Table 1. Comparative Analysis of Sustainable Finance Theories

Theory	Core Focus	Strengths	Limitations	Sustainability Perspective
Priority Theory	Goal prioritization by economic agents	Highlights goal-setting dynamics	Prioritization does not guarantee execution	Aligns sustainability importance with action
Peer Emulation Theory	Mimicry among similar agents	Facilitate policy diffusion, lowers transaction costs	Can discourage innovation due to over-reliance on peers	Encourages alignment of practices in ecosystems
Life Span Theory	Perceived longevity of sustainable tools	Explains temporal variations in support	Heavily influenced by subjective biases	Long-term viability shapes investor decisions
System Disruption Theory	Fear of disrupting existing systems	Realistically accounts for resistance factors	May overstate systemic resistance	Highlights need for transparent transition plans
Positive Signaling Theory	Reputation enhancement through disclosure	Reduces information asymmetry	Risks superficial compliance or 'greenwashing'	Encourages transparency and external validation
Resource Theory	Availability of enabling resources	Contextualizes disparities in green finance progress	May justify inertia in resource-poor regions	Emphasize capacity building for circularity

Source: Done by the author.

3. INVESTOR LANDSCAPE

3.1. Types of Green Investors

According to the Global Sustainable Investment Alliance (2022), green investors are individuals or institutions that align their investment decisions with environmental values by directing capital toward businesses and initiatives focused on ecological protection. They're part of the socially responsible investing world, but with a special focus on eco-friendly solutions. These investors look for opportunities that make both financial sense and a positive environmental impact, like renewable energy companies, energy-efficient technologies, sustainable transportation options, and other initiatives that work to combat climate change. What sets them apart is their commitment to supporting ventures that don't just turn a profit, but also contribute to a cleaner, healthier planet for future generations. Whether it's funding solar farms or backing green startups, their investments reflect a belief that good business and environmental responsibility can go hand in hand. Many green investors want their money to do good while growing. They put their cash into businesses that share their concern for the planet - companies that work clean, waste less, and take real steps to protect the environment. Before investing, they'll often check how much pollution a company creates, how it handles its trash, and other green factors that show whether a business walks its eco-friendly talk.

3.1.1. Retail Investors

Retail green investors are individual, non-professional investors who use their personal savings to support environmentally conscious companies through stocks, green ETFs (exchange-traded funds), or sustainable mutual funds (GSIA, 2021). These everyday investors are typically motivated by personal ethics rather than pure financial returns, often expressing sentiments like "I want my retirement savings to contribute to clean energy solutions" (Riedl & Smeets, 2017). The choices they made for investing illustrate an increasing trend toward values-based decision making in personal finance. People are aligning their investments with their values, especially where environmental issues are concerned. One common example is being able to use a mobile brokerage app to buy shares of solar energy companies like First Solar or SunPower, where even small investors can participate in the renewable energy transition (Morningstar, 2022). Although retail investors usually invest less than institutional investors, their investment choices collectively represent meaningful demand for sustainable investment products.

3.1.2. Institutional Investors

Institutional green investors—including pension funds, insurance companies, and university endowments—manage trillions in assets and wield significant influence over sustainable finance markets (UNPRI, 2023). These large-scale investors are increasingly motivated by both financial and non-financial factors, particularly the need to mitigate long-term climate-related risks to their portfolios and comply with growing ESG (Environmental, Social, and Governance) regulations (Krueger et al., 2020). A prominent example is Norway's $1.4 trillion Government Pension Fund Global, which has systematically divested from fossil fuel companies since 2015, citing both ethical concerns and financial risk management (NBIM, 2022). Similar to Harvard University's $53 billion endowment targeting net-zero greenhouse gas emissions by 2050—illustrating how institutional investors react to stakeholder pressures while working through systemic climate challenges (Harvard Management Company, 2021). The investment decisions of institutional investors often have wide market implications, as when California Public Employees' Retirement System (CalPERS) and several other large pension funds undertook substantial capital allocations to new renewable energy infrastructure assets indicating that institutional capital can help facilitate transitioning capital toward low-carbon economies (Clark et al., 2022).

3.1.3. Impact Investors

Some people and groups put their money into projects not just to make a profit, but also to do good for society or the environment. Impact investors are a unique type of investor who focuses more on making a real positive impact on the environment than on earning the highest possible profits. These change-makers put their dollars behind ventures that can prove they're making a real difference, whether that's cutting carbon emissions, cleaning up waterways, or developing green technologies (Brest & Born, 2021). You'll often hear them say things like, "I need to see exactly how my investment will shrink a company's carbon footprint," because for them, success is measured in metric tons reduced, not just percentage returns (GIIN, 2022. For instance, the rise of investor-backed startups like SES or QuantumScape are two examples of companies developing next-generation EV batteries that could potentially reduce costs and ease access to electric vehicles (PitchBook, 2023). Notably, the unique aspect for these investors involves their 'active' or 'hands on' support, they keep on providing mentorship and industry connections along with their capital - forming an entire support system for green startups to endure the early years (Rodin & Brandenburg, 2021).

3.1.4. Venture Capitalist

Green tech venture capitalists are the people who are willing to take risks in sustainable finance. They put a lot of money into early-stage startups that could change the way we deal with climate change. These VCs don't play it safe like regular investors do. Instead, they look for disruptive innovations in sustainability, like Upside Foods, which makes lab-grown meat, or LanzaTech, which makes hydrogen fuel (CleanTech Group, 2023). They are driven by the huge growth potential in areas like clean energy, circular economy solutions, and decarbonization technology (IEA, 2022). Bill Gates-backed Breakthrough Energy Ventures has invested millions in everything from next-gen nuclear reactors to carbon capture startups. This shows that high-risk capital can help make breakthroughs that save the planet (BEV, 2023). Many green VCs also look at environmental impact metrics, like tons of waste, to see how successful they are.

3.1.5. Green Bonds Buyers

Investors in green bonds are a diverse group of individuals who are concerned with both environmental preservation and prudent financial decision-making. Governments, corporations, and private citizens are among the investors who purchase bonds designed to finance green initiatives, such as constructing wind farms, putting in solar panels, or enhancing building energy efficiency (Climate Bonds Initiative, 2023). They want the consistent, predictable returns that bonds usually provide, but they also insist on knowing exactly how their money is benefiting the environment, which sets them apart from ordinary bond investors. "I need to see the solar panels my investment paid for," stated one portfolio manager (Financial Times, 2022). Apple's 2022 $2.2 billion green bond issuance is a notable example.

3.1.6. Philanthropic Investors

Instead of using a spreadsheet, these investors make decisions based on their emotions. Environmental nonprofits typically receive grants and donations from affluent individuals, family foundations, or corporate philanthropies with no expectation of financial return (Brest, 2020). Their only incentive? generating observable ecological advantages, such as preventing climate change, preserving threatened ecosystems, or creating clean water solutions (McKinsey & Company, 2022). A prime example of this strategy is the Gates Foundation's ambitious $1.4 billion commitment to water sanitation projects throughout Africa, which funds everything from innovative filtration systems to hygiene education initiatives (Gates Foundation Annual Letter, 2023). These donors only consider success in terms of better lives or less carbon emissions, in contrast to impact investors who look for both social good and financial returns (Stanford Social Innovation Review, 2021). Their adaptable funding frequently bridges vital gaps, assisting with risky conservation initiatives.

Table 2. Investor Types and Motivations

Investor Type	Primary Motivation
Retail Investors	Ethical alignment, long-term environmental impact
Institutional Investors	Portfolio risk mitigation, regulatory compliance
Impact Investors	Measurable environmental and social returns
Venture Capitalists	High-growth potential in green technologies
Green Bond Buyers	Stable returns with environmental accountability
Philanthropic Investors	Pure ecological benefits, no financial returns

Source: Done by the author.

The motivations, risk appetites, and impact expectations of green investors are not all the same; they are not a homogenous group. Mapping how various investor profiles use particular financial instruments to promote circular economy outcomes requires an understanding of this diversity. These tools are broken down in Section 3.2 to show how each fits with the strategic goals of different kinds of investors.

3.2. Green Investment Instruments:

To translate their environmental ideals into tangible effects, green investors require useful tools. Green investment tools can help with that. These financial innovations function as specialized pipelines, carefully allocating funds to conservation and climate change initiatives (Harvard Business Review, 2023). For example, green bonds legally mandate that issuers use the funds for certain environmental projects, such as constructing flood-resistant infrastructure in Jakarta or putting up wind turbines in Texas (Climate Bonds Initiative, 2023). With more than $2 trillion issued globally since 2007, their combination of environmental responsibility and financial restraint has caused them to soar from the niche to the mainstream (BloombergNEF, 2023). Bonds are only one tool in the toolbox, though.The sustainable finance revolution has spawned everything from ESG ETFs, exchange-traded funds that invest in a diversified portfolio of stocks and bonds based on Environmental, Social, and Governance (ESG) criteria, letting people invest everyday with their values (think of them like climate-friendly mutual funds) to carbon credit systems that put a price tag on pollution. Below are the key vehicles shaping sustainable finance today:

3.2.1. Green Bonds

A novel class of debt instruments created especially to fund environmentally friendly projects are known as "green bonds." These securities require that all funds raised be used for verifiable sustainability projects, such as pollution control systems or renewable energy installations, in contrast to traditional bonds (Climate Bonds Initiative, 2023). Their importance goes beyond their competitive returns, which are comparable to those of traditional fixed-income products and typically range between 4 and 6%, as well as their innovative transparency standards. Issuers are required to set a new benchmark for accountability in sustainable finance by providing comprehensive public reporting on the particular projects they fund, including infrastructure for electric vehicles and wind energy facilities (Financial Times Sustainable Investing Review, 2023). The transformative potential of this instrument is best demonstrated by the €250 billion green bond program of the European Union. Instead of being incorporated into overall budgets, these funds are directly funding.

Green bonds, which provide investors with a structured way to finance environmentally beneficial projects, have become a key tool in sustainable finance. Their risk-return profile, however, raises special questions. Like conventional bonds, green bonds are subject to market volatility, which is exacerbated by regulatory risks whereby changing green taxonomies could change a project's eligibility. Concerns about transparency and "greenwashing" also remain if issuers don't meet their promised environmental results. Notwithstanding these difficulties, investors are drawn to green bonds because of their competitive returns, which frequently match those of conventional fixed-income instruments—while also offering advantages related to impact and reputation. As an illustration of how environmental responsibility and financial success can coexist, Apple's $2.2 billion green bond not only provided steady yields but also funded 17 renewable energy projects. Additionally, investors frequently consider green bonds to be

3.2.2. ESG ETFs and Mutual Funds

Environmentally conscious exchange-traded funds (ETFs) represent a transformative innovation in retail investing, packaging diversified portfolios of companies that meet strict sustainability criteria into single tradable securities (Riedl & Smeets, 2021). These instruments track specialized indices focused on clean energy, low-carbon technologies, or other ESG (environmental, social, and governance) themes, allowing individual investors to align their portfolios with their values without requiring extensive financial expertise (Baker et al., 2022). Their significance lies in solving two critical challenges simultaneously: providing instant diversification across hundreds of holdings while systematically excluding fossil fuel producers, tobacco companies, and other controversial industries (Berg et al., 2023). The operational mechanics reveal their appeal. When investors purchase shares of funds like BlackRock's iShares Global Clean Energy ETF (ICLN), they gain exposure to 100+ renewable energy companies worldwide, from solar panel manufacturers to hydrogen fuel innovators, with the same ease as buying individual stocks (BlackRock, 2023). With $6 billion in assets under management, ICLN exemplifies how these instruments scale impact: according to MSCI's impact calculations, every $1,000 invested theoretically displaces approximately 0.8 metric tons of carbon emissions annually through capital reallocation. This "passive activism" allows teachers, nurses, and other non-professional investors to collectively shift market capital toward sustainable sectors, a phenomenon that is now influencing corporate behavior worldwide (Dimson et al., 2022). Investing in funds such as BlackRock's iShares Global Clean Energy ETF (ICLN) enables investors to gain exposure to more than 100 renewable energy companies worldwide, from solar panel manufacturers to hydrogen fuel innovators (BlackRock, 2023).

3.2.3. Carbon Credits

Each tradable unit of carbon credits certifies that one metric ton of carbon dioxide has either been removed from the atmosphere or prevented from entering it, serving as a financial representation of environmental action (World Bank, 2022). These tools function at the nexus of economics and ecology, producing a measurable currency for emission reductions that governments, businesses, and even individuals can purchase, sell, or retire (Stavins, 2023). When a business must decide between buying cleaner technology or offsets, the carbon market turns environmental responsibility into a line item in the budget, transforming intangible climate goals into tangible financial decisions (Koch et al., 2021). Both promise and complexity are revealed by the actual implementation. According to Microsoft's 2023 sustainability report, the company purchased 1.3 million tons of CO2 equivalent in reforestation-derived credits, mostly from third-party verified afforestation projects in Latin America (Microsoft, 2023). This transaction is a prime example of the twofold benefit: creating economic value for forest communities and having an immediate climate impact (through funded tree growth that sequesters carbon) (Chhatre et al., 2022). However, the system's efficacy is dependent on strict criteria; registries such as Verra and Gold Standard enforce that projects show "additionality" (demonstrating that the carbon reduction would not have happened without credit revenue) and permanence (ensuring stored carbon isn't later released) (Greenhouse Gas Protocol, 2023).

3.2.4. Sustainability-Linked Loans

Imagine a loan that gets cheaper when a company meets its environmental targets—that's the innovative premise behind sustainability-linked loans (SLLs). These loans represent financial instruments where the interest rate adjusts based on verified progress toward predefined ESG goals, whether that's cutting water usage by 20% or diverting 95% of waste from landfills (Loan Syndications & Trading Association, 2023). The brilliance of this model lies in its accountability: companies can't just issue glossy sustainability reports; they must hit concrete, third party-audited benchmarks to secure better terms (International Capital Market Association, 2022). For instance, Unilever's groundbreaking €1 billion SLL. The consumer goods giant tied its borrowing costs to ambitious plastic reduction targets, lower rates kick in only if they achieve 100% reusable, recyclable, or compostable packaging by 2025 (Bloomberg, 2022). This creates what bankers call "skin in the game": Unilever saves millions in interest payments by delivering actual circular economy results, not just pledges (Financial Times, 2023). Analysis by BNP Paribas shows such loans now represent over $300 billion globally, with a particularly strong uptake in food/beverage and manufacturing sectors where resource efficiency directly impacts profitability (BNP Paribas Sustainable Finance Report, 2023).

3.2.5. Green Venture Capital

Imagine a financial system in which investors seek out planetary impact rather than just profits. This daring frontier, where patient capital meets scientific audacity, is exemplified by climate tech venture capital. These are equity stakes in startups addressing civilization-scale issues, such as transforming food production and decarbonizing steel production, rather than the usual Silicon Valley bets on the next app (Gates, 2021). Their penchant for "high-risk, high reward" science is what distinguishes these investments (IEA, 2023). For instance, consider Breakthrough Energy Ventures' $2 billion war chest which specifically targets technologies that sound like science fiction today but might save the climate tomorrow (BEV, 2023). Their portfolio is like a climate superhero roster: companies developing hydrogen-powered aviation, ultra-deep geothermal drilling, and even nuclear fusion reactors (BEV Portfolio Report, 2023). MIT researchers estimate that every $1 of venture funding in this space leverages $4 of follow-on investment once technologies prove viable (MIT Energy Initiative, 2022), creating a multiplier effect that turns lab breakthroughs into market realities. These investors combine knowledge of climate science with sound financial principles. To determine if a carbon capture startup is ready for pilot plants or is still in the petri-dish stage, they use "technology readiness assessments" (TRLs) (DOE, 2023). Furthermore, many of them mandate that startups pair climate scientists with business experts on their founding teams, demonstrating that they are more than just passive check writers (Harvard Business Review, 2023). Although there are risks (roughly 60% of cleantech startups fail, according to McKinsey, 2022), there are also benefits that go beyond financial gain. These venture capitalists are the architects of the new economy, as the Global Commission on the Economy and Climate estimates that every $1 trillion invested in climate technology each year could result in $26 trillion in economic benefits by 2030 (GCEC, 2023).

3.2.6. Green Real Estate Investment Trusts (REITs)

Imagine owning a piece of a solar-powered apartment complex or a wind farm, without ever having to fix a leaky roof or repair a turbine. That's exactly what green Real Estate Investment Trusts (REITs) offer. These aren't typical property funds; they're specialized investment vehicles that pool money to buy and manage eco-friendly buildings and infrastructure (U.S. EPA, 2023). Think of them like mutual funds for sustainable real estate, where you can invest in anything from LEED-certified office towers to community solar projects (FIRST, 2023). For example, Hannon Armstrong (ticker: HASI) is a cutting-edge REIT that specializes only in climate-positive properties, making it a favorite among sustainable investors. Their portfolio resembles a wish list for sustainability: geothermal heating systems on college campuses, energy-efficient military housing that reduces power consumption by 40%, and even carbon-sink-doubling forest conservation projects (Hannon Armstrong, 2023). According to their most recent impact report, they measure success not only in rental income but also in metric tons of carbon avoided, with over 5 million tons avoided annually (HASI Impact Report, 2023).

3.2.7. Transition Bonds

Not every business can go green right away, particularly in sectors where oil rigs and smokestacks have long been commonplace. Transition bonds can help with that. Whether it's converting cargo ships to run on ammonia fuel or retrofitting a steel mill to run on hydrogen, these specialized financial instruments help finance the messy but necessary process of turning "brown" industries green (Climate Bonds Initiative, 2023). They are contentious because they specifically provide funding to fossil fuel companies, but only under stringent guidelines that demand quantifiable advancements toward sustainability goals (Financial Times, 2023). Cadent Gas's 2023 £500 million transition bond is a good illustration. The UK utility is using these funds to replace outdated methane pipelines with hydrogen-ready systems rather than abandoning its gas infrastructure (Bloomberg, 2023). Ironclad clauses in the bond's fine print state that 100% of proceeds must go toward pre-approved transition projects, that annual emissions reductions must be verified by third-party auditors, and that interest rates will rise if decarbonization goals are not met (Cadent Gas Prospectus, 3023).

3.2.8. Green Securitization

The power of green asset-backed securities (ABS) can be visualized as a single investment product that combines thousands of rooftop solar installations or electric vehicle leases. When hundreds or thousands of small-scale green loans or leases are combined into tradable securities that institutional investors can purchase, these financial products function similarly to a sustainability snowball (Climate Bonds Initiative, 2023). It is a financial innovation that addresses a significant issue: although individual EV leases or solar panel loans may be too small for large investors to contemplate, combining them creates the scale required to draw significant capital (International Finance Corporation, 2023). This idea is exemplified by Tesla's $520 million green ABS deal in 2023. By bundling together thousands of customer solar roof leases, Tesla created a security large enough for pension funds and insurers to invest in (BloombergNEF, 2023). The mechanics are clever: Homeowners' monthly lease payments become the security's income stream, then risk is spread across thousands of geographically diverse installations and third-party verifiers confirm the environmental benefits (Solar Energy Industries Association, 2023). This approach is revolutionizing clean energy financing. According to the Rocky Mountain Institute, green ABS can reduce solar financing costs by up to 20% by connecting Main Street sustainability projects with Wall Street's deep pockets (RMI, 2023). To facilitate understanding of the distinct features of each instrument, Table 3 summarizes key attributes.

Table 3. Key Features of Green Investment Instruments

Instrument	Risk Level	Return Profile	Impact Focus	Key Strength
Green Bonds	Low-Medium	Stable, predictable	Infrastructure, large-scale projects	High transparency, earmarked capital
ESG ETFs & Mutual Funds	Medium	Diversified, market-linked	Broad ESG sectors	Easy access for retail investors
Carbon Credits	Variable	Volatile, market-dependent	Emission reductions, ecosystem restoration	Creates a market incentive for sustainability

continued on following page

Table 3. Continued

Instrument	Risk Level	Return Profile	Impact Focus	Key Strength
Sustainability-Linked Loans	Medium	Incentivized through rate adjustments	Corporate ESG performance improvement	Directly ties financing cost to sustainability metrics
Green Venture Capital	High	High-risk, high reward	Disruptive green technologies	Catalyzes innovation, early-stage support
Green REITs	Medium	Real estate-driven returns	Sustainable buildings & infrastructure	Income-generating with tangible asset base

Source: Done by the author.

4. INVESTMENT TRENDS IN CIRCULAR ECONOMY SECTORS

The way that things are made, used, and reused around the world is undergoing a quiet revolution. Forget the outdated "take-make-waste" paradigm; the circular economy of today is repurposing waste, changing the way products are made from the ground up, and utilizing digital intelligence to extend the life of materials (Ellen MacArthur Foundation, 2023). The World Economic Forum refers to this change as "the biggest economic opportunity since the Industrial Revolution," with $4.5 trillion at stake by 2030 (WEF, 2023). It's not just tree-hugging idealism. The three revolutionary circular economy strategies that forward-thinking investors are funding include "waste wizardry," in which innovators recover value from previously discarded materials using biological and chemical processes, such as enzyme-driven breakdowns and plasma gasification (Journal of Cleaner Production, 2023); "design do-overs," with businesses. Together, these approaches prove that sustainability and profitability can go hand in hand. Necessity is fueling this gold rush, with raw material prices skyrocketing (copper up 300% since 2000) and landfills overflowing (2 billion tons of waste annually), and partly because it's just better business (World Bank, 2023). As IKEA's CEO recently put it: "We're not just saving the planet; we're saving our bottom line" (Financial Times, 2023). Investors are capitalizing on three interconnected opportunity areas:

4.1. Waste & Resource Recovery

The days of recycling bins and scrap metal drives are long gone. The most creative waste management techniques of today are turning items that were once thought to be completely useless—such as cigarette butts, dirty diapers, and even hazardous e-waste—into useful resources (National Geographic, 2023). Two groundbreaking approaches are leading this charge: First, nature-inspired alchemy, where startups deploy hungry bacteria to do what machines cannot. Companies like Mint Innovation use microbial "bioleaching" to extract gold from old smartphones with 80% efficiency, which nearly triple the recovery rate of traditional smelting (Journal of Cleaner Production, 2023). It's like having microscopic miners working around the clock. Second, molecular rebirth, where chemical processes break materials down to their building blocks. Seattle-based Evrnu made headlines by converting discarded Levi's jeans into virgin-quality nylon fibers, securing $45 million from investors who see textile waste as tomorrow's raw material (GreenBiz, 2023). With landfills overflowing and new bans on waste exports (like China's 2018 "National Sword" policy), the waste management market is projected to hit $530 billion by 2025 (Grand View Research, 2023). As one waste CEO quipped: "We're not just cleaning up the planet, we're building the next Fortune 500 companies from what others throw away" (Waste Dive, 2023).

4.2. Circular Manufacturing and Design

A quiet rebellion against throwaway culture is being witnessed. Forward-thinking companies are rejecting the planned obsolescence model and instead creating products that are built to last, designed to be taken apart, and engineered for endless rebirth. This isn't just better for the planet, it's proving to be better for business too (Ellen MacArthur Foundation, 2023). For example, modular electronics, such as smartphones made by Fairphone, which just raised $90 million. These gadgets are easy to upgrade the camera and replace the battery because they snap together like Legos. As a result, phones now have a lifespan of five or more years rather than the usual two (TechCrunch, 2023). To turn old bumpers into new door panels without sacrificing quality, companies such as Recycle Track are collaborating with major automakers to 3D print car parts using recycled materials (McKinsey, 2023). The numbers speak for themselves: by lowering material requirements and waste, circular design principles can cut manufacturing costs by 18–25% (Ellen MacArthur Foundation, 2023). According to Yvon Chouinard, the founder of Patagonia, "The most sustainable product is the one that never needs to be replaced" (Patagonia, 2022).

4.3. Sharing Platforms and Digital Enablers

Ownership is becoming optional in the new era. Similar to how Uber turned idle cars into sources of income, a flurry of digital innovations is currently assisting companies in extracting as much value as possible from their tangible assets, such as raw materials, office furniture, and factory equipment (Harvard Business Review, 2023). Cutting costs is only one aspect of this; another is a fundamental rethinking of the way resources move through our economy. By enabling factories to "rent out" their costly equipment during downtime, EQUOTA's equipment-sharing platform has assisted manufacturers in reducing machinery idle time by 60% (BCG, 2023). Alternatively, Circularis's blockchain-driven "material passports," which serve as industrial components' birth certificates and track them throughout their whole lifecycle to make sure nothing is wasted (Forbes, 2023). Even consumer products are becoming more intelligent, with. As the World Economic Forum notes, these digital enablers could unlock $4.5 trillion in economic value by 2030 simply by making better use of what we already have (WEF, 2023). The message is clear: in the circular economy, the most valuable asset isn't what you own, it's what you can share.

Masdar City in the United Arab Emirates, a $22 billion eco-city project that combines financing from the government's sovereign wealth funds with green bonds, is a great illustration of the concepts of the circular economy in action. The Green Hydrogen Fund in Chile, which is supported by both public and private investors, aims to establish Chile as a global leader in renewable energy, demonstrating how emerging economies are leveraging green finance to promote circular innovation. With the help of green venture capital, Grab Holdings has integrated circular principles into its ride-hailing business in Southeast Asia by making investments in fleets of electric vehicles.

5. BARRIERS TO CIRCULAR ECONOMY TRANSITION

5.1. Infrastructural and Policy Deficiencies

Before engaging in a circular economy (CE), systemic change is required. Unfortunately, key barriers exist. There is still a lack of infrastructure for waste collection and treatment, little scientific research at the national and regional levels, and weakness in applying environmental policies (Melece, 2016). For example, Latvia has a lot of biodegradable waste going to landfill, with very few municipalities introducing separate bio-waste collection; this shows weaknesses in terms of infrastructure and governance. A further issue is the absence of respectively reliable statistics, making it impossible to implement good policies and measure progress (Melece, 2016).

5.2. Structural and Regional Disparities

The Transition to a circular economy, governed by the European Green Deal (EGD), comes with significant opportunities but even greater challenges. The structural challenges include existing technologies, significant costs of innovation, regional differences in green transition capability, and socio-economic inequities across EU member states (Kuci & Fogarassy, 2021; Pianta & Lucchese, 2020). While there are sizable policy impulses, many Central and Eastern European countries are still reluctant to move forward due to how carbon intensive their economies are and the risk of de-industrialization (Siddi, 2020).

5.3. Capital Intensity and Upfront Costs

Moving towards a circular economy often comes with a significant expense to cover initial costs, such as capital costs, research and development, building infrastructure and stranded asset management. For example, the British Government estimates a successful recycling and recovery system would come with GBP 13 billion in costs and scaling that up to the European level would be GBP 110 billion (Tian, 2018). The significant costs represent a challenge and barrier to public and private investments, which creates an urgent need for financial systems for the circular economy.

5.4. Institutional Limitations and Global Inequities

Green investment through the circular economy is a complex and multifaceted area subject to institutional readiness, consumer behavior, market maturity and engagement from the financial sector. Although environmental awareness and regulation has, in both Europe and the United States, opened the door to increased green investments, systemic and institutional factors still hinder wider green investment globally. These are fragmented policy contexts, underdeveloped financial guarantees, and investor capability (Tian, 2018). In China, for example, although strategic directions and national plans mention green economy and circular economy promotion, there is a gap between the policies and the capabilities of the financial system. Most banks in China do not employ any environmental and social (E&S) risk assessors, nor do they have financial systems that adhere to even basic sustainable investment principles. In addition, without financial guarantees and insurance, the private sector is not engaging (PwC HK, 2013).

5.5. Risk Perception and Market Failures

The primary hurdle for greater green investment for circular economy projects is the perception of higher financial risk as well as uncertainty in the market. Even though these projects have considerable positive environmental and economic outcomes with time, they are frequently considered financially uncertain, especially when operating in developing markets like bio-based materials or resource recovery systems (Kandpal, Jaswal, Santibanez Gonzalez, & Agarwal, 2024). The perception of high-risk in green investments is exacerbated by high capital cost requirements, long investment time horizons, and the lack of common performance compliance, and these factors represent a caution to a conservative investor. Market failures compound this scenario, particularly the systemic underpricing of environmental externalities. Without proper carbon pricing or adjustments for sustainability-dependent endeavors, traditional economic investments still appear relatively profitable, and therefore the opportunity cost of deploying capital to the betterment of sustainability available in a green investment is not as attractive (Kandpal et al, 2024).

5.6. Regulatory Gaps and Policy Inconsistencies

The impact of regulation has a dual outcome for green investment. On one hand, disjointed and inconsistent policy environments hamper investment by creating uncertain frameworks for sustainability (Chen et al., 2020). International conventions, such as the Basel, Stockholm, and Rotterdam Conventions, set the minimum expectations to manage toxic waste and enhance chemical safety; however international instruments are often ineffective beyond setting minimum expectations (Chen et al., 2020). National level implementation and monitoring gaps often undermine international efforts. The arguments presented above outline national level policy implementation and monitoring challenges as a ratio which should be focused on strengthening regulatory processes that link global frameworks to local enactment for effective systemic transformations.

5.7. Data Gaps and Transparency Issues

Investors are increasingly requesting reliable data and standardized metrics to assess their portfolios' sustainability performance, but the absence of transparent, comparable ESG data continues to impose prohibitive barriers for green investing at a large scale (Kandpal et al., 2024). When it comes to investment-ready data, particularly to emerging sectors, it is non-existent. Additionally, the absence of standardized data disclosure does not streamline due diligence and risk assessment that would otherwise occur in the valuation phase of the investment process.

6. ENABLERS OF CIRCULAR ECONOMY TRANSITION

6.1. Financial Instruments and Public-Private Synergies

A key enabler of investments in circular economy initiatives is the increasing availability and diversity of green financial instruments. Green financial instruments are financing vehicles, including green bonds, sustainability-linked loans, environmental, social, and governance (ESG) themed exchange-traded funds (ETFs), and blended finance structures that seek to mobilize finance in connection with projects or initiatives that have an environmentally responsible focus. For example, green bonds have become a well-recognized financing mode for financing infrastructure such as renewable energy systems, waste recovery facilities, and energy-efficient buildings because of their transparency, standard documentation, and relatively low risk to the investor (European Commission, 2020).

At the same time, public-private partnerships (PPPs) are emerging as a prominent force in supporting the circular economy transition. Partnerships allow public actors to share risk and provide longer time horizons, together with private sector actors who can bring technical insights, know-how, and capital. PPPs have been particularly applicable in more infrastructure-heavy projects where public subsidies or guarantees can be aligned with private sources of capital. By lowering barriers to entry for high-impact capital-intensive circular economy opportunities for the public, these partnerships offer the opportunity to be more innovative and efficient in sectors such as waste to energy, bioeconomy, and resource-efficient production.

In addition, the growth of impact-oriented capital is altering the behavior of investors. Both institutional and retail investors are increasingly putting funds into vehicles that provide financial returns and allow them to have a positive impact in relation to environmental and social outcomes. The growth of ESG globally has contributed notably to this shift. Investors are factoring sustainability into risk assessment, asset valuation, and decision making. This has become part of their fiduciary responsibility when allocating capital into financial markets.

Governments have also contributed to stimulating private investment via subsidies, tax incentives, and regulatory frameworks supportive of circular business model innovation. Examples include tax credits for companies who invest in eco-design, grants for startups in closed-loop technology, and public procurement criteria with an emphasis on circular solutions.

Yet despite these positive developments, the one of the longest standing obstacles remains the absence of scalable, replicable investable models. Many circular projects are either extremely localized, or oriented towards small niche markets, so institutional investors cannot deploy capital on scale. Also, the long gestation period, along with technological uncertainty and difficulty quantifying long term returns associated with many circular innovations also deter traditional financiers. More credible financial engineering, standardization of impact metrics, and platforms that combine smaller scale CE projects into investable portfolios are needed to address these constraints.

6.2. Policy Support and Political Momentum

Effective and coherent policy frameworks at the national and supranational levels are essential for enabling circular economy transitions. In the European context, coordinated EU policies, such as the European Green Deal, the Circular Economy Action Plan, and the EU Taxonomy regulation, have borne substantial responsibility in advancing circularity within the sustainability agenda, generating more predictable regulatory atmospheres and sending strong signals in the marketplace for investors and businesses (European Commission, 2020). These initiatives have promoted harmonization of definitions, established mandatory disclosure practices, and have provided phased roadmaps for circular transition across sectors such as construction, textiles, plastics, and electronics.

Political will is being built globally, evidenced by increasing commitments by national governments and local authorities to climate action, decarbonization, and zero waste targets. This political alignment is important because it can shape long-range planning, mobilize resources, integrate circular strategies with wider development agendas, and provide public funding and other incentives where possible. The circular economy is increasingly being recognized for unlocking economic and social co-benefits, like creating jobs, increased competitiveness for local industry, and energy security, in an era where the costs of inaction are considerable.

Another enabling element includes rising public awareness and consumer demand for sustainable products and responsible corporate behaviors. Citizens tend to put increased pressure on policymakers and businesses to move more rapidly away from linear consumption based models of sustainability. On a similar front, investor awareness has also grown considerably, with stakeholders increasingly looking for alignment on international climate targets, particularly the Paris Agreement and United Nations Sustainable Development Goals (SDGs), resulting in financial institutions demanding increased sustainability practices from portfolio companies.

Public-private partnerships and eco-innovation funding approaches including innovation hubs, living labs, and green technology accelerators are further enabling ways of converting political intention to operational change. These mechanisms facilitate experimentation, scaling, and commercialization of circular technologies while fostering collaboration among industry, academia, and government. Similarly, fiscal mechanisms such as environmental taxes, extended producer responsibility (EPR) regimes, and differential VAT on circular products have been adopted by some jurisdictions in ways to encourage circular behaviours by both producers and consumers.

Nevertheless, one of the key constraints that persist is the fragmentation of policy frameworks across multiple regions, sectors, and levels of governance. This poor coordination often leads to inconsistent implementation, unnecessary duplication of effort and confusion for businesses and investors trading across borders (Altenburg & Rodrik, 2017). Overcoming these gaps will depend on better intergovernmental collaboration, policy coherence, and multi-level structures of governance that can make sure that local, national, and international CE agendas, remain aligned and co-oriented.

6.3. Green Finance Mechanisms

Green finance presents itself as a strategic enabler to work around financial barriers to transitioning companies to circularity. It can help redirect capital flow into sustainable projects. As Tian (2018) states, the financial system must evolve to change the industrial structure and subject to sustainability, for instance, through lowering interest rates, lengthening credits and making concessions for circular vehicles. Therefore, financing mechanisms are shifting to become a core enabling mechanism to direct the transition to a circularity.

6.4. Strong Regulatory Frameworks

Strong regulatory frameworks can also serve as an enabler by encouraging innovation and minimizing investment risk. To illustrate, policies on extended producer responsibility, green subsidies, and eco-design rules help create stability in the market and reward long-term environmental performance.

6.5. Standardization and ESG Metrics

The Globally Harmonized System (GHS) for chemical classification and other measures developed by the World Business Council for Sustainable Development (WBCSD) mark important first steps toward comparability (Chen et al., 2020), but much wider uptake of ESG metrics that are based on sector and material specific qualities, still need to happen.

6.6. Market Failures and Financial Risk Perception

Market failures, from the inability to internalize environmental externalities and the presence of information asymmetries, were significant barriers to financing the circular economy. Market failures distort the pricing of environmental goods, leading to persistent under-investment in green industries (Melece, 2016; Siddi, 2020). Traditional finance considers circular business activities high-risk endeavors because the technology is unproven, investment horizons are long, and historical performance data are lacking. This view is reinforced by the lack of comparable entrepreneurial models that incorporate environmental and social returns, which leads to a bias towards short-term profitability (Tian, 2018).

Information asymmetry further fuels financial institutions' risk aversion, particularly when SMEs emerge to disrupt the status quo. For eco-innovative SMEs, there will generally be a lack of visibility and credit history which would force lenders and investors to guess the possible returns. Therefore, it is necessary to have public risk-sharing mechanisms and blended finance with equity based capital to erase the capital failure and drive down the perception of risk. The EU Resource Efficiency Scoreboard shows evidence of improvements of resource efficiency across Eastern European countries, despite large financing gaps for circular SMEs remaining due to little support for venture capital and demonstrative funding (EC, 2016; Melece, 2016).

The ramifications of stranded asset risks also bear on investment decisions. As environmental regulation becomes more stringent and technologies advance, the value of assets related to pollution could diminish in price relatively quickly. Investors do not want to risk funding an asset tied to such risks, especially in sectors like fossil fuels, waste-intensive activities, and unsustainable manufacturing (Siddi, 2020). Ultimately, when environmental externalities are not accurately priced or harmful acts do not incur penalties for polluters, traditional investments seem to fare better in terms of return, which could further diminish the pooling of capital toward sustainable resources (Kandpal, Jaswal, Santibanez Gonzalez, & Agarwal, 2024).

Legal liability often leads to trepidation in capital deployment. In the US, the Comprehensive Environmental Response, Compensation, and Liability Act (1980) enhances the financial exposure of lenders that have environmental remediation associated with them. China's structural risks remain due to its reliance on bank lending more than equity or bond markets by 2.7 times, restricting long-term financing for green firms (Tian, 2018). Additionally, banks within China do not have standardized environmental, social, or human rights risk assessment standards, which further stymies the availability of capital to circulate projects.

To fill the circular investment gap of more than € 1 trillion to meet European Union's budget goals for 2030, there needs to be strong policy signals, de-risking instruments, and strong economic incentives within a market-based framework. Policy signals and mechanisms will need to tackle both real and perceived financial risks to access capital measures for a circular business. (Pianta et al., 2020)

7. REGULATORY AND POLICY ENVIRONMENT

7.1. EU Circular Economy Directives and Waste Legislation

The European Commission (EC) has adopted a complete suite of policies and financial measures to enable the circular economy across member states. There are directives for municipal waste recycling goals of 70% and for packaging recycling goals of 80% by 2030, and a ban on landfilling materials that can be recycled by 2025 (EC, 2016). EU cohesion policy adds to these initiatives through the structural funds provided for the development of sustainable waste management infrastructure within the EU, especially in member states, like Latvia, that are lacking institutional capacities (Melece, 2016).

But, although there is clarity in the regulatory direction, at the implementation stage there is a less clear path across the EU. Many member states cannot align their national policies with an EU-focused approach. For member countries, like Latvia, infrastructure deficiencies and inertia combined with other factors impede overall compliance; thus, there is a gap between EU directives and the national approaches used to enact those directives. Closing that gap is vital for achieving transformative goals with respect to a circular economy.

7.2. The European Green Deal and Investment Mobilization

The European Green Deal (EGD) pushes the EU's environmental framework even further and incorporates circular economy aspects into wider climate neutrality objectives. It offers a roadmap for emissions reductions, energy efficiency, and renewable energy implementation by 2050 (European Commission, 2019; Siddi, 2020). The EGD outlines two main instruments; the Sustainable Europe Investment Plan and the Just Transition Mechanism, both used to mobilize capital flows towards sustainable projects. Global staff reforms to the European Investment Bank support this realignment, as the EU is moving toward green lending (Kuci & Fogarassy, 2021).

Nevertheless, limitations to enforcement and the presence of environmentally harmful subsidies diminish the transformative potential of the policy (Pianta et al., 2020). Furthermore, a wide array of capacity among regions in the EU, both in terms of economic structure and infrastructure, necessitates contextually variable approaches that build from local contexts into broader policy frameworks.

7.3. National Green Finance Instruments and Institutional Support

National governments play an important role in providing an enabling environment for circular economy investments. One example is the Green Investment Bank launched by the UK in 2012 with US$5 billion in public capital. It focused on offshore wind, energy efficiency, and recycling infrastructure. This focus attracted significant additional private sector co-financing (Tian, 2018). Institutions like the Green Investment Bank address market failures by absorbing the early-stage risk of a project, encouraging private sector involvement.

Globally, international agreements, such as the Paris Agreement and the Sustainable Development Goals (SDGs), establish frameworks for climate finance and green investment. These agreements provide direction and legitimacy but fail to provide traction in most emerging markets. For example, a lack of environmental safeguards in the financial systems of ASEAN countries leads to poor mobilization of sustainable capital (Tian, 2018).

7.4. Comparative Perspectives: China and the EU

China has made considerable advancements in embedding circular economy principles in practice. The Circular Economy Promotion Law (2009) and a succession of Five-Year Plans, have provided a vision that spans pollution control, the environment, and efficiency (Tian, 2018). The document from the State Council in 2012 conceptualized energy saving and emissions reductions through a greater understanding of energy inputs as an integrated top-down process. Likewise, European countries have proposed changes to regulation through instruments such as Germany's feed-in tariffs, the EU Emissions Trading Scheme, and the Dutch Green Funds that can reduce financial uncertainty for and promote sustainable investment (UNEP FI, 2007).

Despite these developments, hurdles remain. Regulatory fragmentation, uneven enforcement and inconsistent definitions of green finance have all contributed to challenges for engagement from the finance sector (CPC Central Committee, 2012). This speaks to the importance of having organized frameworks and improved institutional capacity, such as across jurisdictions, to fully leverage circular economy investment potential.

8. ROLE OF DATA, METRICS, AND TRANSPARENCY

8.1. Importance of Data Infrastructure and Standardized Metrics

A well-developed data infrastructure and standardized environmental criteria are critical steps to embedding a circular economy and mobilizing sustainable financing. Transparency and consistency in reporting provide the supply chain with the confidence urgently needed by investors, while also facilitating the important role of monitoring green investments and evidence-based policy-making - yet even among EU Member States there remain challenges, especially emerging economies - insufficient infrastructures to produce statistics are severely limiting the ability develop the facts and figures around waste volumes, rates of recycling, and material recovery (Melece, 2016) - the lack of harmonized data means that we cannot accurately assess progress towards a circular economy - and therefore inform responsive policy-making.

8.2. Harmonization and Technology

To further assist with these limitations, the European Commission has recommended integrating common metrics for circularity and strong Environmental Social Governance (ESG) reporting frameworks for measuring material usage, emissions, and sustainability outcomes accurately (Kuci & Fogarassy, 2021). Many tools such as Equator Principles and Green Bond Principles exist to enhance comparability and transparency (Equator Principles Association, 2013). Digital tools e.g. IoT and blockchain will also assist with supply chain traceability and real-time reporting, allowing developments in environmental impact, and supporting data-driven decision making (Tian, 2018).

8.3. Regional Disparities and Verification Challenges

Nonetheless, data fragmentation and verification are still significant barriers. For instance, in China, circular economy statistics are often confused with environmental expenditures, undermining the impact of targeted markets as investments go toward unverified practices (Tian, 2018). Second, most financial institutions reporting the impact of investments depend on self-reported EIA data from borrowers with virtually no verification, collectively undermining the working integrity of investment reporting. As is the case with global programs like the UN Principles for Responsible Investing, their calls for disclosure ultimately rely on voluntary disclosure, thereby undermining transparency and accountability in the green finance system. As Smol et al. (2017) contend, without common metrics and sustainability indicators in real-time, the ability to effectively establish policy and mobilize capital is limited.

9. REAL-WORLD EXAMPLES OF GREEN INVESTMENT IN CIRCULAR ENTERPRISES

Green investment in circular economy (CE) activities has taken many forms, across regions and sectors, including institutional lending and public–private partnerships, venture capital, and technological innovation.

9.1. Regional Pilot Projects and Public–Private Partnerships

Green investment in the Baltic region, particularly Latvia, has supported pilot projects in bio-waste composting and resource efficiency in construction. These projects showed that with targeted funding and institutional collaboration, circular investments could deliver impactful change (Melece, 2016). Public–private partnerships have been instrumental in demonstrating effective composting facilities, establishing eco-industrial parks, and using circular approaches in packaging. Current limitations to scaling are a consequence of poor data systems at the local level and a failure to harmonize policy to support local implementation, which indicates a wider need for an enabling investment ecosystem with financial flows directed to suits the local capacity for implementation (Melece, 2016).

9.2. Enterprise-Led Circular Innovations

Numerous enterprises across Europe have started testing circular business models, with funding and support given by private investors and innovation funds. For instance, Renewcell in Sweden focuses on textile recycling via chemical processing and Fairphone in the Netherlands makes modular, repairable smartphones with recycled and ethically sourced materials. These firms received EU innovation funding along with assorted private funds, placing themselves at the forefront of sustainable production (Kandpal et al. 2024).

9.3 Historical and Institutional Foundations

There are historical examples of integrating green finance and CE development. GLS Bank in Germany has been granting preferential loans for social and ecological projects since being founded in 1974. Around 23,000 projects have been financed to date (Tian 2018). In the USA, a regulatory basis was provided by the Comprehensive Environmental Response, Compensation, and Liability Act (Superfund) of 1980 to provide cleanup and sustainable financing. Both efforts speak to the role of regulation in shaping behaviors which, if exhibited consistently enough, result in more predictable green pathways.

9.4. Growth of the Green Bond Market

The green bond market has appeared as an important mechanism for scaling circular investment. Globally, green bond issuance increased from US$0.4 billion in 2008 to almost US$42 billion in 2015, with supporting frameworks like the Green Bond Principles and institutional programs such as the Green Finance Initiative in London (Tian, 2018). The voluntary principles have increased transparency, market confidence and enabled investors to allocate capital to projects that have transparent and measurable environmental impact.

9.5. National Policy Instruments and Financial Innovation

In addition, national policy instruments have promoted investment in circular practices. The feed-in tariff enables Germany to rely on distributed solar energy, and the Green Funds Scheme provides financial benefits for ecology-related investments in the Netherlands (UNEP FI, 2007). The additional transparency and confidence provided by these instruments have increased capital to sustain energy and sustainable packaging projects. The Industrial Bank in China was the first to publicly disclose the adoption of the Equator Principles, as the company was used as an example of responsible banking. The Shanghai Pudong Development Bank, then, incorporated environmental and social (E&S) risk metrics into performance-based assessments of branch offices (Tian, 2018).

9.6. Emerging Models in Green Chemistry and Biotechnology

Innovative projects in green chemistry and biotechnology demonstrate the expanding scope of circular investments. For example, a textile waste valorization initiative in Hong Kong utilizes biological processes to extract sugars from biodegradable fibers, showcasing both material recovery and commercial scalability (To et al., 2019). Moreover, the development of bio-based polymers and green chemical substitutes aligns with CE goals by reducing reliance on fossil-based inputs and minimizing industrial waste (Kaur, Uisan, Ong, & Kansedo, 2018). These models reflect the potential for integrating scientific innovation with sustainable finance.

9.7. Investment Returns and Environmental Outcomes

Circular investments, especially those based on green chemistry and lifecycle innovation, are providing ESG (Environmental, Social, and Governance) and financial returns. Kandpal et al. (2024) demonstrate that diversified portfolios of green assets - and rigorously assessed impact - often create and preserve more value in the long run compared to traditional portfolios. Concrete outcomes such as reducing carbon emissions, improving resource efficiency, and achieving a better form of circularity are increasingly being recognized as critical success indicators. These outcomes mitigate regulatory and reputational risk and improve the profit potential and strength of the circular business model.

9.8. Analysis of Outcomes, Returns, and Impact

a. **Economic Performance and Material Efficiency**: Circular investments provide various benefits that go beyond the usual financial return. Studies done by the European Commission showed that countries that have greater performance on waste recycling and energy efficiency also have a greater gross domestic product (GDP) per unit of material input. This finding implies that sustainable-practice countries have a stronger economic productivity that justifies the best practitioner's rationale for generating and progressing with circular economy (CE) investment (Melece, 2016).

However, the fundamental characteristics of CE investments, longer time horizons and the challenge of monetizing environmental externalities, creates difficulty with traditional investors. In this case, comprehensive life-cycle analysis (LCA) and an ecosystem of standardized value measurement frameworks can provide the transparency of environmental and economic performance necessary to provide solid data for the creation of bankable risk profiles for circular investments (Smol et al., 2020).

b. **Financial Viability and Investment Horizon:** Empirical studies demonstrate that circular companies can outperform traditional companies over time, in large part by reducing input costs, mitigating regulations and enhancing brand value. But in most cases, these returns are delayed, requiring investors to be willing to accept returns that flow late and patient capital (Kandpal et al., 2024).

From an acceptable investment strategy, this requires patient capital and adaptable capital instruments that match the temporal nature of sustainability outcomes. If circular projects are not financed in a way that aligns with their value proposition, they risk being under financed

c. **Social and Environmental Co-benefits:** Beyond economic returns, circular investments also generated environmental and social returns, such as job creation, reductions in greenhouse gases, and increase resource-efficiency (Smol et al., 2020). In addition, projects which comply with frameworks such as the Equator Principles may include social safeguards and stakeholder engagement plans to promote inclusive development and promote social cohesion (Equator Principles Association, 2013).

However, there is a likelihood that the returns generated will not be equally distributed across geographic regions. The limitation of institutional capacity or the lack of policy support may hinder CE outcomes to be realized in some locations. In this way, inclusive policy design is even more important to create equitable access to environmental and economic returns.

d. **National and Sectoral Case Studies:** It is instructive to consider the UK Green Investment Bank, which represents a model showcasing how dedicated green financial resources can effectively mobilize private capital and generate real environmental impacts. Through the bank's investments, it helped improve the energy efficiency of millions of UK homes and helped mobilize private sector investments in low-carbon infrastructure (Tian, 2018). This model shows the possibility of how well-designed public capital is focused, de-risking investments and attracting market-enabled solutions.

In contrast, the Chinese experience highlights some fundamental limitations. While the Industrial Bank and Shanghai Pudong Development Bank are pursuing green lending activities, many projects, especially pollution prevention projects and projects for ecological restoration, lack liquidity or experienced delays in their economics (Tian, 2018). Further, there is no seriousness about post-loan environmental and social (E&S) monitoring, which complicates performance assessment as well as downgrading investor confidence. All these conditions can deepen the reliance on blended finance models and further erode regulatory oversight.

e. **Systemic Impacts and Risk Mitigation:** Investing in circular economy initiatives offers systemic positives that positively contribute to company reputations, market competitiveness, and regulatory uncertainty. For example, in Europe, organizations with sustainability missions have cited reputational improvements that yield indirect positive contributions to market performance by increasing stakeholder trust. Regulatory instruments like price guarantees or tax inducements create greater certainty for investors in a landscape of uncertainty (UNEP FI, 2007).

Unless governments support or provide policies to deliberately influence the uptake of circular investment opportunities, there may always be a limited uptake in some sectors without financial returns. For this reason, adopting systemic risk mitigation instruments backed by supporting governments or concessional capital is necessary in order to scale green investment for the circular economy.

10. POLICY AND STRATEGIC RECOMMENDATIONS FOR INVESTORS, REGULATORS, AND ENTREPRENEURS

10.1. Policy Recommendations for Governments and Regulators

Governments and regulators play a foundational function in building an enabling ecosystem for green investments in the circular economy (CE). They can enact laws, develop policy instruments, and use fiscal measures that reshape markets, de-risk innovation and enable new pathways to a sustainable circular system. Many creative policy interventions are essential to fast-track the scaling-up of circular models:

a. Fiscal and Regulatory Incentives

Developing fiscal instruments that promote sustainable behaviors is critical. The government can develop progressive measures, such as introducing landfill taxes, eco-tariffs and tax-reliefs for businesses adopting circular technologies. They create disincentives that penalize environmentally harmful behaviors and create incentives for those trying to operate in a circular manner and shift market behaviors in favor of sustainable approaches (Melece, 2016). For example, landfill taxes discourage the waste disposal of an item in favor of recycling, or getting materials recovered.

b. Risk Reduction and Financial Support

Perceptions of investment risk remain significant barriers to private capital mobilization to circular projects. Governments should work to establish green investment banks that can help mitigate project-specific financial risk and encourage institutional investors. Blended finance mechanisms, where public funds are effectively used to absorb some of the risk to catalyze private investment, have already been particularly effective in assisting early-stage circular economy (CE) innovations that may not have a market pull but can generate significant social or environmental value (European Commission, 2020). Public co-investment acts as a catalyst to improve the risk-return profile of such ventures to realize large-scale participation of private sector capital.

c. Standardization and data infrastructure

Differences in sustainability metrics and limited data access are barriers to transparency and comparability of circular investments. Governments should assist with the establishment and enhancement of standards for frameworks for environmental, social, and governance (ESG) reporting, while at the same time improving data infrastructure, e.g., environmental impact databases and registries of circular business models and so on, which can help enhance investor and regulatory decision making (Smol et al., 2020). In addition to the need for robust environmental and social liability frameworks to hold firms accountable for pollution and resource misuse and internalize negative externalities.

d. Inclusive Transition Mechanisms

Policymakers must keep in mind that moving towards a circular economy must be socially inclusive and equitable. Funding such as the EU's Just Transition Mechanism is an important tool for directing money to specific areas and training people from workers, and investment for community in regions, and labor markets that are significantly dependent on fossil-fuel-intensive industries (European Commission, 2020). Ensuring that no region or demographic group is disproportionately disadvantaged during the transition, that will strengthen public support, reduce opposition and support long-term socio-economic resilience.

10.2. Strategic Guidelines for Investors

Institutional and private financing will play an important role in implementing the transition to a circular economy. Investors can shift flows of capital to sustainable sectors as they can have economic returns and systemic environmental benefits. The following strategic recommendations should be considered:

a. Incorporate Circularity in ESG Strategies

Investors should broadly incorporate the circular economy in their ESG assessments and investment filters. This would mean assessing long-term sources of risk, resource dependency, regulatory risk, and climate-related liabilities (Kandpal et al., 2024). This will allow investors to foresee disruptions to linear operating models and be strategic in their investments and portfolios for resilience against resource scarcity. Incorporation of circularity in ESG can also offer investors pathways to align with global sustainability initiatives, including the EU Green Taxonomy and the UN SDGs.

b. Use of Blended Finance and Green Products

Investors are also recommended to engage in innovative financing, including green financing, green-bonds, impact investing platforms and blended finance products to accelerate capital mobilization. Investors can achieve market rates of return whilst generating environmental and social outcomes (Tian, 2018). These financing mechanisms use public-private risk sharing and targeted subsidies to improve the bankability of great circular economy project ideas and increase the pipeline of investable opportunities.

c. Capacity Building and Transparency

Investors need to build a commitment to internal capacity to assess the environmental and social risks facing future CE sectors. They need to actively engage with the sustainability performance of companies and to support better disclosures and reporting practices, in the interest of accountability (Smol et al., 2020). Additionally, investors can support their role in the ecosystem as facilitators by being supportive of data platforms that enhance project visibility, readiness for investment, and the standardization of circular metrics.

10.3. Entrepreneurial Strategies for Circular Innovation

Entrepreneurs can rethink product designs, supply chains, and value creation to put them at the forefront of CE principles. They can further broaden and accelerate their impact by aligning with policies, markets, and investors, using one of the following strategies.

a. Business Model Innovation and Policy Alignment

Circularity can minimize environmental footprints through durable, repairable, and recyclable products help with the challenges of circularity. It also can facilitate their alignment with emerging and changing policy frameworks and sustainability funding practices (Melece, 2016). Improving alignment of companies with globally accepted goals, such as the SDGs, can also improve access to public capital and as well as impact investors purposefully looking for mission aligned enterprises.

b. Collaborate on Research and Development

Partnerships with universities and technical institutions can strengthen innovation capacity and provide technological readiness. Europe has introduced a range of instruments that offer funding and knowledge transfer for CE research and demonstration projects that can include partnerships (European Commission, 2020). Collaborations can also facilitate cross disciplinary collaboration that captures the skills learned from integration of science, engineering, economics, and policy insights to have better outcomes for solving for CE.

c. Transparent Impact Measurement and Capacity Development

Entrepreneurs need to adopt standardized metrics to measure the environmental and social impacts of a circular business model. Providing transparency in the various reporting standards will provide credibility to a range of stakeholders. Targeted investments in workforce training, operating systems and institutional capacity are also required to develop circular business models and adapt to new regulatory frameworks (Kaur et al., 2018).

10.4. Multi-stakeholder engagement and aligning systems

The success of the transition to the circular economy is dependent upon the collective action of a variety of stakeholders. Cross-sectoral collaboration is needed to align incentives, jointly develop policies, reduce transaction costs, and develop innovative ecosystems that support the scaling of circular solutions. Multi-stakeholder engagement platforms can be public-private dialogues, innovation hubs or sectoral roundtables to identify systemic barriers, build consensus and ensure coherence across policy, finance and market systems (UNEP FI, 2007). Only when systemic alignments are in place can circular business models and profitability co-exist for the long-term business development and environmental regeneration value proposition.

11. CONCLUSION

The circular economy principles offer a rounded toolset for rethinking resource use, product design, and value creation in economic systems. By prioritizing waste prevention, resource efficiency, and natural systems regeneration, these principles advance beyond traditional linear models, and align with wider sustainability outcomes, such as the SDGs or the Paris Agreement. As circular economy continues to evolve, the practical integration of its major strategies and supporting financial mediums and policy requirements will be essential for it to reach adoption and be an effective long-term solution.

Research into green investment and sustainable finance needs to become a fundamental pillar to achieving global sustainable development. Based on the goal of economic growth, environmental protection and social equity, green finance is the finance and investment arm of this process. Various theories, priority theory, peer emulation theory, life span theory, system disruption theory, positive signalling theory and resource theory, offer varied, but complementary perspectives on green finance; they have similarities but offer varied perspectives on the reasons for financing, the available challenges and outcomes. Ultimately, they highlight that while it is important to have global agreement of sustainability outcomes, what matters more in terms of successful outcomes are location based objectives, availability of the necessary material resources, and the communicative strategies employed. Understanding these theoretical underpinnings equips policymakers, investors, and institutions with the insight needed to navigate the complexities of transitioning toward a more sustainable financial system.

Green investors come in all forms, from ethically driven retail investors and strategically oriented institutions to mission-driven impact and philanthropic investors, each playing a distinct yet complementary role in financing the transition to a sustainable future. Through direct equity, venture capital, green bonds, or philanthropic grants, these investors are aligning capital with the environment, scaling up clean technologies, financing low-carbon infrastructure, and advancing ecological conservation. Their varied motivations, from risk management and long-term value creation to moral imperative and environmental stewardship, demonstrate that sustainable investing is no longer a niche but a multi-faceted movement reshaping global finance.

Green investment products are revolutionizing the intersection of finance and environmental sustainability by converting sustainability into actionable, measurable outcomes from a checklist of principles. Be it through green bonds and ESG ETFs, sustainability-linked loans, or green venture capital, the products enable investors, both institutional and retail, to align financial returns with climate action. They foster accountability, transparency, and innovation across sectors, and accelerate global transition to a low-carbon economy. Collectively, they not only allocate trillions of capital to green objectives but also reshape financial markets to reward long-term environmental performance, making sustainable investing a hallmark of modern finance.

Investment in circular economy sectors is rapidly reshaping how sectors approach sustainability and the use of resources. Through innovation in waste recovery technologies, promotion of durable and modular design of products, and application of digital platforms for sharing resources, investors are unleashing significant economic and environmental value. These trends validate that circular business models are not only crucial to addressing raw material shortages and waste challenges but also yield vast financial opportunities. With the circular economy on the rise, it has the potential to change conventional ways of production and consumption into a more robust and profitable future.

Transitions to a low-carbon, resource-productive, and regenerative circular economy (CE) need a fundamental reorganization of market behavior, regulation, and finance. A raft of discrete environmental modifications, rather than much more than that, the circular economy is a transformative economic system, characterized by high operation efficiency, low resource consumption, and low emissions, that makes environmental protection a source of long-term economic resilience.

Green finance is at the forefront of this shift towards mobilizing capital, de-risking circular investments, and ramping up the deployment of green technologies. There is emerging evidence from Asia, China, the United States, and ASEAN countries that point both to potential and complexities of green financial tools. Europe, for instance, highlights the strengths of holistic policy mechanisms, data harmonization, and multi-stakeholder coordination under agendas such as the European Green Deal. On the contrary, the Chinese record serves to highlight the structural challenge of balancing rapid economic growth with ecologically focused goals, particularly in high-capital and lower-margin endeavors such as pollution abatement and resource efficiency.

Despite growing momentum, persistent barriers such as scattered regulation, deficient financial tools, asymmetry of information, and institutional capacity remain to hinder the large-scale uptake of circular solutions. These issues especially impact small and medium-sized enterprises (SMEs), which are likely to face stringent financing constraints and regulatory ambiguity.

To address these challenges, there needs to be the development of an integrated green finance system. Policy coherence, as a first point, must be ensured through coordination among fiscal instruments, regulatory incentives, and sustainability standards. This includes the development of progressive tax regimes, phasing out environmentally harmful subsidies, and mandatory disclosure of sustainability.

Second, governments and institutions should come forward with creative financial instruments, including green bonds, credit guarantees, environmental investment funds, and special green banks. These products diversify funding sources, reduce investment risk, and mobilize institutional capital for high- gestation, high-impact investments.

Third, mobilizing private capital on a scale must include active involvement of institutional investors, and such must be supported by policies such as tax benefits for green investments, expedited clearance processes, and robust ESG integration into risk models. Combinations of finance structure blends and public-private partnerships are also capable of bridging investment gaps and securing bankability for projects.

Fourth, global cooperation and knowledge exchange are essential to harmonize standards, build financial resilience, and facilitate cross-border investment. Global cooperation among development banks, regulators, and industry bodies will enhance market clarity and provide an international consistent framework for green finance.

Ultimately, green investors, supported by a robust ecosystem of regulators, entrepreneurs, and civil society, are at the core of driving the shift towards a regenerative circular economy. While challenges exist, real case studies demonstrate that when flows of capital are directed toward ESG objectives and sustainability performance metrics, circular investments can yield competitive financial returns alongside substantial environmental and social value.

Systemic realignment, with roots in strategic policy formulation, institutional creativity, market motives, and collective governance, is the recipe for a successful shift. Overcoming structural constraints and scaling up sustainable finance will allow the full potential of the circular economy to be unleashed and an inclusive, fair, and regenerative future to be brought about.

REFERENCES

Altenburg, T., & Rodrik, D. (2017). Green industrial policy: Accelerating structural change towards wealthy green economies. *Green Industrial Policy*, *1*, 2–20.

Apple Inc. (2023). Environmental Progress Report. https://www.apple.com/environment/

As You Sow. (2023). Decarbonize your portfolio [Investment report series]. https://www.asyousow.org

Baker, M., Berg, F., & Kölbel, J. F. (2022). *The sustainable corporate governance debate: Evidence from ESG ETFs*. European Corporate Governance Institute.

BCG. (2023). Industrial sharing platforms: The $900 billion opportunity. https://www.bcg.com

Berg, F., Kölbel, J. F., & Rigobon, R. (2023). Aggregate confusion: The divergence of ESG ratings. MIT Sloan Research Paper No. 5822-21.

BlackRock. (2023). Global Sustainable Investing Survey. https://www.blackrock.com/sustainability

BlackRock. (2023). iShares Global Clean Energy ETF (ICLN): Annual fund report. https://www.ishares.com

BlackRock. (2023). iShares Global Clean Energy ETF (ICLN): Prospectus. https://www.ishares.com

Bloomberg. (2023, June 15). UK gas networks bet big on hydrogen with £500m bond. https://www.bloomberg.com

Bloomberg. (2023, June 8). *ThreadUp's AI-powered resale engine drives valuation to $1.2B*. https://www.bloomberg.com

Bloomberg, N. E. F. (2023). *Global green bond market retrospective 2023*. Bloomberg Finance L.P.

Bloomberg, N. E. F. (2023). Green securitization market outlook. https://about.bnef.com

Breakthrough Energy Ventures (BEV). (2023). Investment Portfolio. https://www.breakthroughenergy.org

Brest, P. (2020). *The Strategic Value of Philanthropy*. Stanford University Press.

Brest, P., & Born, K. (2021). When Can Impact Investing Create Real Impact? *Stanford Social Innovation Review*.

Cadent Gas. (2023). Hydrogen transition bond framework. https://www.cadentgas.com

Carbon Brief. (2023). The state of voluntary carbon markets 2023. https://www.carbonbrief.org

Chen, T. L., Kim, H., Pan, S. Y., Tseng, P. C., Lin, Y. P., & Chiang, P. C. (2020). Implementation of green chemistry principles in circular economy system towards sustainable development goals: Challenges and perspectives. *The Science of the Total Environment*, *716*, 136998. DOI: 10.1016/j.scitotenv.2020.136998 PMID: 32044483

Chhatre, A., Lakhanpal, S., & Nelson, A. (2022). Community benefits from forest carbon credits: Evidence from Mozambique. World Development, *158*, 1-14. https://doi.org/DOI: 10.1016/j.worlddev.2022.105963

Clark, G. L., Feiner, A., & Viehs, M. (2022). *From the stockholder to the stakeholder: How sustainability can drive financial outperformance*. University of Oxford.

CleanTech Group. (2023). 2023 Global Cleantech 100 Report. https://www.cleantech.com

Climate Bonds Initiative. (2023). Green bond market summary: Annual report 2023. https://www.climatebonds.net

Climate Bonds Initiative. (2023). Green securitization state of the market.

Climate Bonds Initiative. (2023). Transition finance state of the market. https://www.climatebonds.net

CPC Central Committee. (2012). Decisions of the CPC Central Committee on Several Major Issues Concerning the Comprehensive Deepening of Reform adopted at the Third Plenum of the 18th CPC Congress.

Cunha, F. A. F. S., Meira, E., & Orsato, R. J. (2021). Sustainable finance and investment: A review of trends and challenges in the Global South. *Journal of Cleaner Production*, *312*, 127789. DOI: 10.1016/j.jclepro.2021.127789

Dimson, E., Marsh, P., & Staunton, M. (2022). Responsible investing: The ESG-efficient frontier. Journal of Financial Economics, *145*(2), 1-24.

Ellen MacArthur Foundation. (2023). Circular economy investment opportunities. https://ellenmacarthurfoundation.org

Ellen MacArthur Foundation. (2023). The circular design advantage: Economic benefits of durable products. https://ellenmacarthurfoundation.org

European Commission. (2016). Resource Efficiency Scoreboard 2015. Brussels. *European Union, 2016*, 72.

European Commission. (2019) The European Green Deal, COM 640 final, 11 December. https://ec.europa.eu/info/sites/info/files/european-green-deal-communication_en.pdf

European Commission (2020). Sustainable Europe Investment Plan/European Green Deal investment plan. Communication from the commission to the European Parliament, the European Council, the Council, the European Economic and Social Committee and the Committee of the Regions 21.

European Commission. (2023). European green bond standard: Implementation report. https://ec.europa.eu

Financial Times. (2022, March 15). "How Green Bonds Went Mainstream." https://www.ft.com

Financial Times. (2023, March 15). How Unilever's plastic pledge is reshaping packaging finance. https://www.ft.com

Financial Times. (2023, March 15). IKEA's circular business model pivot. https://www.ft.com

Financial Times. (2023, March 8). The contentious rise of transition bonds. https://www.ft.com

Financial Times. (2023). Sustainable investing review 2023. https://www.ft.com/reports/sustainable-investing

FIRST. (2023). Guide to sustainable REIT investing. https://www.first.org

Forbes. (2023, April 15). Circularise's blockchain solution tracks materials through supply chains. https://www.forbes.com

Gates, B. (2021). *How to avoid a climate disaster*. Knopf.

Gates Foundation. (2023). Annual Goalkeepers Report. https://www.gatesfoundation.org

Global Commission on the Economy and Climate. (2023). Unlocking the inclusive growth story of the 21st century. https://newclimateeconomy.report

Global Impact Investing Network (GIIN). (2022). Annual Impact Investor Survey.

Global Sustainable Investment Alliance. (2022). Global sustainable investment review 2022. https://www.gsi-alliance.org

Global Sustainable Investment Alliance (GSIA). (2021). Global Sustainable Investment Review 2020. https://www.gsi-alliance.org

Grand View Research. (2023). Waste management market analysis. https://www.grandviewresearch.com

Green Finance Institute. (2023). Innovations in asset-level sustainability data. https://www.greenfinanceinstitute.co.uk

GreenBiz. (2023, April 12). Evrnu's $45M bet on fashion's circular future. https://www.greenbiz.com

Greenhouse Gas Protocol. (2023). *Carbon credit accounting guidelines*. World Resources Institute.

Hannon Armstrong. (2023). Annual sustainability report. https://www.hannonarmstrong.com

Harvard Business Review. (2023, June 15). The new rules of impact investing. Harvard Business Review, 101(4), 56-67.

Harvard Business Review. (2023). The asset-light revolution. https://hbr.org

Harvard Business Review. (2023). The modular design revolution. https://hbr.org

Harvard Management Company. (2021). *Harvard endowment sets 2050 net-zero goal*. https://www.hmc.harvard.edu_https://www.climatebonds.net

International Capital Market Association. (2022). Sustainability-linked bond principles. https://www.icmagroup.org

International Energy Agency. (2023). Cleantech innovation and venture capital trends. https://www.iea.org

International Energy Agency. (2023). Financing clean energy transitions in industry. https://www.iea.org

International Energy Agency (IEA). (2022). Special Report on Startups and Innovation. https://www.iea.org

International Finance Corporation. (2023). Scaling small-scale renewables through securitization. https://www.ifc.org

IUCN. (1980). *World Conservation Strategy: Living Resource Conservation for Sustainable Development*. International Union for Conservation of Nature and Natural Resources. https://portals.iucn.org/library/efiles/documents/WCS-004.pdf

Journal of Cleaner Production. (2023). Advanced waste recovery technologies. https://www.sciencedirect.com

Journal of Cleaner Production. (2023). Bioleaching efficiency in e-waste recovery, 412(1), 1-12. https://doi.org/DOI: 10.1016/j.jclepro.2023.135000

Kandpal, V., Jaswal, A., Santibanez Gonzalez, E. D., & Agarwal, N. (2024). Sustainable investment strategies for renewable energy and circular economy projects. In *Sustainable Energy Transition: Circular Economy and Sustainable Financing for Environmental, Social and Governance (ESG) Practices* (pp. 201–216). Springer Nature Switzerland. DOI: 10.1007/978-3-031-52943-6_6

Kaur, G., Uisan, K., Ong, K. L., & Lin, C. S. K. (2018). Recent trends in green and sustainable chemistry & waste valorisation: Rethinking plastics in a circular economy. *Current Opinion in Green and Sustainable Chemistry*, *9*, 30–39. DOI: 10.1016/j.cogsc.2017.11.003

Kirchherr, J., Reike, D., & Hekkert, M. (2017). Conceptualizing the circular economy: An analysis of 114 definitions. *Resources, Conservation and Recycling*, *127*, 221–232. DOI: 10.1016/j.resconrec.2017.09.005

Koch, N., Fuss, S., & Grosjean, G. (2021). Pricing carbon when costs are hidden. *Nature Climate Change*, *11*(3), 218–224. DOI: 10.1038/s41558-021-00988-w

Krauss, J. E., Krüger, P., & Meyer, J. (2016). Sustainable finance prioritization: A global perspective on economic agents' strategies. *Environmental Economics and Policy Studies*, *18*(3), 405–423. DOI: 10.1007/s10018-016-0156-2

Krueger, P., Sautner, Z., & Starks, L. T. (2020). The importance of climate risks for institutional investors. *Review of Financial Studies*, *33*(3), 1067–1111. DOI: 10.1093/rfs/hhz137

Kuci, A., & Fogarassy, C. (2021). European Green Deal Policy for the Circular Economy: Opportunities and Challenges. *Hungarian Agricultural Engineering*, *39*(39), 65–73. DOI: 10.17676/HAE.2021.39.65

Loan Market Association. (2023). Sustainability-linked loan principles. https://www.lma.eu.com

Loan Syndications & Trading Association. (2023). U.S. sustainability-linked loan market report. https://www.lsta.org

Lomax, G., Workman, M., & Lenton, T. (2023). Reframing carbon removals for net-zero policy. *Climate Policy*, *23*(2), 1–18.

McKinsey & Company. (2022). Philanthropy's Role in Energy Transition.

McKinsey & Company. (2022). The dawn of the climate tech boom. https://www.mckinsey.com

McKinsey & Company. (2023). Additive manufacturing in automotive: The circular opportunity. https://www.mckinsey.com

McKinsey & Company. (2023). Digital platforms for industrial symbiosis. https://www.mckinsey.com

Melece, L. (2016). Challenges and opportunities of circular economy and green economy. *Engineering for Rural Development*, *25*, 1162–1169.

Microsoft. (2023). Sustainability report: Carbon removal portfolio. https://www.microsoft.com/sustainability

MIT Energy Initiative. (2022). Venture capital's role in energy transition. https://energy.mit.edu

Morgan Stanley. (2023). Sustainable REITs: Performance and growth trends. https://www.morganstanley.com

Morningstar. (2022). Sustainable Funds U.S. Landscape Report. https://www.morningstar.com

MSCI. (2023). MSCI ESG Impact Metrics Methodology. https://www.msci.com

NAREIT. (2023). ESG reporting guidelines for REITs. https://www.reit.com

National Geographic. (2023, January). The waste revolution.

Norges Bank Investment Management (NBIM). (2022). Government Pension Fund Global annual report. https://www.nbim.no

Paribas, B. N. P. (2023). Sustainable finance market trends Q2 2023. https://cib.bnpparibas.com

Patagonia. (2022). Built to last: Our design philosophy. https://www.patagonia.com

Pianta, M., & Lucchese, M. (2020). Rethinking the European Green Deal: An Industrial Policy for a Just Transition in Europe. *The Review of Radical Political Economics*, *52*(4), 633–641. DOI: 10.1177/0486613420938207

Pinchot, A., & Christianson, G. (2020). *System disruption and sustainable finance: Navigating economic transitions*. Stanford Social Innovation Review. https://ssir.org/articles/entry/system_disruption_and_sustainable_finance

PitchBook. (2023). Emerging Technologies in Sustainable Transportation Report.

Pricewaterhouse Coopers Consultants (PWC). (2013). Exploring green finance incentives in China. China: PwC.

Reclaim Finance. (2023). Transition bonds: Greenwashing or genuine progress? https://www.reclaimfinance.org

Riedl, A., & Smeets, P. (2017). Why do investors hold socially responsible mutual funds? *The Journal of Finance*, *72*(6), 2505–2550. DOI: 10.1111/jofi.12547

Riedl, A., & Smeets, P. (2021). Social preferences and portfolio choice: Evidence from ESG ETFs. *The Journal of Finance*, *76*(6), 1–42.

Rocky Mountain Institute. (2023). Lowering clean energy financing costs. https://rmi.org

Rodin, J., & Brandenburg, M. (2021). *The Power of Impact Investing*. Wharton School Press.

Securities and Exchange Commission. (2023). ABS disclosure and reporting requirements. https://www.sec.gov

Setyowati, A. B. (2020). Governing sustainable finance: Insights from Indonesia's peer emulation strategies. *Climate Policy*, *20*(8), 1015–1030. DOI: 10.1080/14693062.2020.1795321

Siddi, M. (2020). The European Green Deal: Asseasing its current state and future implementation. Upi Report, 114.

Smol, M., Kulczycka, J., & Avdiushchenko, A. (2017). Circular economy indicators in relation to eco-innovation in European regions. *Clean Technologies and Environmental Policy*, *19*(3), 669–678. DOI: 10.1007/s10098-016-1323-8

Solar Energy Industries Association. (2023). Solar loan performance metrics. https://www.seia.org

Stanford Social Innovation Review. (2021). "When Grants Outperform Investments."

Stavins, R. N. (2023). *The future of carbon pricing*. Harvard Environmental Economics Program.

TechCrunch. (2023, May 15). Fairphone's $90M funding round signals shift toward repairable tech. https://techcrunch.com

Tian, H. (2018). Establishing green finance system to support the circular economy. In *Industry 4.0* (pp. 203–210). Empowering ASEAN for the Circular Economy.

To, M. H., Uisan, K., Ok, Y. S., Pleissner, D., & Lin, C. S. K. (2019). Recent trends in green and sustainable chemistry: Rethinking textile waste in a circular economy. *Current Opinion in Green and Sustainable Chemistry*, *20*, 1–10. DOI: 10.1016/j.cogsc.2019.06.002

United Nations Environment Programme Finance Initiative (UNEP FI). (2007). *'Green Financial Products & Services: Current State of Play and Future Opportunities', A Report of the North American Task Force (NATF) of the UNEP*. UNEP FI.

United Nations Principles for Responsible Investment (UNPRI). (2023). Global trends in sustainable investing. https://www.unpri.org

Urban Green Council. (2023). New York City building emissions law impact study. https://www.urbangreencouncil.org

U.S. Department of Energy. (2023). Technology readiness levels handbook. https://www.energy.gov

U.S. Environmental Protection Agency. (2023). Green buildings and investment opportunities. https://www.epa.gov

Vernon, R. (1966). International investment and international trade in the product cycle. *The Quarterly Journal of Economics*, *80*(2), 190–207. DOI: 10.2307/1880689

Wang, Y., & Zhi, Q. (2016). The role of green finance in environmental protection: A global perspective. *Energy Economics*, *58*, 123–134. DOI: 10.1016/j.eneco.2016.07.012

Waste Dive. (2023). CEO interviews: The new economics of trash

Wilson, C. (2010). Prioritizing sustainability: Economic agents and the pursuit of green finance. *Journal of Sustainable Finance & Investment*, *1*(2), 95–110. DOI: 10.1080/20430791003780485

World Bank. (2022). State and trends of carbon pricing 2022. https://www.worldbank.org/carbonpricing

World Bank. (2023). Global waste management outlook. https://www.worldbank.org

World Economic Forum. (2022). The Green Venture Capital Playbook. https://www.weforum.org

World Economic Forum. (2023). Circular economy economic potential. https://www.weforum.org

World Economic Forum. (2023). Digital platforms for resource efficiency. https://www.weforum.org

Chapter 4
Innovative Policy Making for Circular Economy: A Strategic Perspective on CSR Communication

Gizem Ölçekciler
Independent Researcher, Turkey

Caner Yazıcıoğlu
https://orcid.org/0000-0001-8067-4563
Independent Researcher, Turkey

ABSTRACT

This study has underscored the strategic convergence between Corporate Social Responsibility (CSR) and the circular economy (CE), emphasizing that CSR communication serves as a powerful enabler for innovative policy development. Through a thorough theoretical investigation, it has been demonstrated that CSR communication does more than inform stakeholders, it strategically frames sustainability narratives, fosters trust, and mobilizes diverse stakeholder groups to support and co-develop circular initiatives. CSR and CE together constitute a synergistic pathway where ethical responsibility and operational sustainability reinforce one another. Crucially, the study shows that transparent and credible CSR communication can build the legitimacy required to introduce systemic shifts and that stakeholder engagement facilitated through communication is not only a governance tool but a catalyst for transformative change.

DOI: 10.4018/979-8-3373-3852-1.ch004

1. INTRODUCTION

Contemporary global challenges such as climate change, resource scarcity, and waste accumulation have catalysed a paradigm shift towards sustainable development models. One prominent model is the circular economy (CE), which seeks to transcend the traditional linear "take-make-dispose" economic framework. A circular economy aims to decouple growth from resource use by designing out waste and keeping products and materials in continuous use (Eickhoff, 2024). In practical terms, this involves principles of reducing, reusing, and recycling resources to create closed-loop systems that regenerate natural capital and minimize environmental impact. For example, the European Union's Circular Economy Action Plan (CEAP) of 2020 which is considered as a key pillar of the European Green Deal, emphasizes a regenerative growth model whereby the value of products and materials is maintained as long as possible through reuse, repair, remanufacture, and recycling (Resourcify, 2023). The CEAP not only targets technical solutions (such as improved recycling rates and material efficiency) but also underscores the need for collaboration among stakeholders and supportive policy innovations to achieve a sustainable economic system (Safdie, 2024). In tandem with the rise of the circular economy, Corporate Social Responsibility (CSR) has evolved from a voluntary corporate ethos to a strategic imperative. CSR broadly refers to the responsibility of enterprises for their impacts on society and the environment, going beyond profit-making to include social and environmental considerations. It covers diverse issues such as fair labour practices, human rights, community development, and environmental stewardship. A distinguishing feature of CSR is its voluntary nature companies adopt CSR initiatives that often exceed legal requirements, driven by ethical values or stakeholder expectations (Boatright, 1997). In essence, CSR embodies the notion of good corporate citizenship, where businesses commit to moral obligations and societal expectations to contribute to sustainable development. Notably, sustainable environmental practices (like pollution prevention, resource efficiency, and now circular economy initiatives) form a core pillar of CSR commitments.

A critical link between CSR and the circular economy lies in policy making and communication. As firms integrate circular principles into their operations (for instance, through eco-design, waste reduction, or product life-cycle extension), these initiatives often emerge under the umbrella of CSR strategies (Hong et al., 2023). In fact, the circular economy has recently been described as an "innovative business model for firms to transform CSR into actions" (Hong et al., 2023). This suggests a convergence where CSR provides the ethical and strategic rationale for pursuing circular innovations, while circular economy practices give concrete, operational form to CSR commitments in environmental sustainability. For such a convergence to drive innovative policy making, effective communication is indispensable. CSR communication which is defined as a company's disclosure and dialogue with stakeholders regarding its social and environmental initiatives, plays a strategic role in shaping stakeholder perceptions, legitimising corporate policies, and influencing broader policy agendas. Through transparent and proactive CSR communication, companies can build credibility and stakeholder trust, thereby creating a supportive context for bold changes such as the adoption of circular economy models. Moreover, CSR communication can frame sustainability issues (e.g. waste reduction, recycling, circular product design) in ways that resonate with stakeholders' values, mobilizing their support and even prompting collaborative policy innovation between businesses, governments, and civil society.

This study provides a comprehensive theoretical exploration of how innovative policy making for a circular economy can be enabled through a strategic perspective on CSR communication. The discussion is entirely literature-based, drawing primarily on conceptual foundations from contemporary CSR and sustainability scholarship. The aim is to integrate these theoretical perspectives into a cohesive understanding of innovative policy making for circular economy through the lens of CSR communication.

2. THEORETICAL BACKGROUND

2.1. Circular Economy Concepts

The circular economy (CE) has emerged as a transformative concept for sustainable development, proposing a systemic alternative to the linear economic model of extraction, production, consumption, and disposal. In a seminal attempt to synthesize numerous definitions, Kirchherr et al. (2017) define the circular economy as "an economic system that is based on business models which replace the 'end-of-life' concept with reducing, alternatively reusing, recycling and recovering materials in production, distribution and consumption processes, operating at the micro (product, company, consumer), meso (eco-industrial parks), and macro (city, region, nation) levels, with the aim of accomplishing sustainable development, thereby creating environmental quality, economic prosperity, and social equity for the benefit of current and future generations" (Resourcify, 2023). This comprehensive definition highlights several key principles of CE:

Resource Looping: Instead of treating products and materials as waste at the end of their life, CE emphasizes keeping them in the loop through strategies like recycling, remanufacturing, refurbishing, and reusing. The classic "3Rs" (Reduce, Reuse, Recycle) are often expanded with additional strategies such as redesign, repair, recover, and regenerate, all aimed at minimizing virgin resource use and waste generation (Kirchherr et al., 2017).

Systems Approach: CE operates across multiple levels. At the micro level, individual companies and consumers engage in circular practices (e.g., a business using recycled inputs or a consumer choosing products-as-a-service). At the meso level, industrial symbiosis can occur, one firm's waste becomes another's input, forming a network of material exchange (an example of industrial ecology) (Safdie, 2024). At the macro level, cities or nations implement policies like recycling infrastructure, material circularity indicators, and circular procurement to enable a supportive environment (Resourcify, 2023). This multi-level nature means that CE requires coordination among various stakeholders and alignment of incentives.

Decoupling and Sustainable Development: The ultimate goal of a circular economy is to decouple economic growth from environmental degradation and resource depletion (de Hallgren et al., 2024; Eickhoff, 2024). By maintaining the value of resources for as long as possible and designing waste out of the system, a CE aims to achieve triple bottom line benefits: environmental quality (e.g., lower pollution and greenhouse gas emissions, reduced resource extraction), economic prosperity (new business opportunities, cost savings, job creation), and social equity (resource availability for future generations, inclusive growth) (Resourcify, 2023). In fact, the EU explicitly frames the circular economy as integral to achieving climate neutrality and the Sustainable Development Goals (SDGs) (Safdie, 2024).

It is important to recognize that the CE concept is rooted in earlier ideas of sustainability and industrial ecology. Kenneth Boulding's 1966 vision of a "spaceship earth" economy (a closed-loop system with limited inputs and outputs) and the laws of thermodynamics highlight that endless linear growth is biophysically unsustainable (Eickhoff, 2024). The CE draws on these insights, proposing a restorative system that functions within planetary boundaries. It also builds on the notion of cradle-to-cradle design (McDonough & Braungart, 2002) and performance economy (Stahel, 2016), where products are designed for disassembly and reuse, and consumers obtain services rather than owning products.

Policy making has played a crucial role in advancing circular economy principles. Governments and international bodies have begun to implement policies that incentivize or mandate circular practices. For example, the European Commission's CEAP (2020) sets targets for recycling (such as a 65% municipal waste recycling rate by 2035) and introduces measures like extended producer responsibility and eco-design requirements (Safdie, 2024). China incorporated CE into law as early as 2008, focusing on resource efficiency and recycling industries. These policies illustrate innovative policy making, in that they often move beyond command-and-control regulation to include market-based instruments, public private partnerships, and information-based policies encouraging voluntary action. However, policy innovation for circular economy is not only top-down. It often requires bottom-up initiatives and corporate leadership. This is where the synergy with CSR emerges. Businesses, through their CSR programs, have significant freedom to pilot circular solutions ahead of or beyond regulatory requirements. For instance, a company might voluntarily eliminate single-use plastics from its supply chain or invest in product take-back schemes as part of its CSR environmental commitments. Such corporate initiatives can, in turn, inform and inspire public policy (e.g., an industry-wide voluntary standard might later become regulation, or successful pilots may shape national circular economy roadmaps). The relationship between CSR-driven innovation and formal policy development is thus interactive. In summary, the circular economy provides a strategic framework for sustainability that redefines how value is created and preserved. It aligns with CSR in its emphasis on environmental stewardship and long-term societal benefit, but CE specifically offers concrete operational models (like closed-loop supply chains, circular product design, and resource recovery systems).

2.2. Corporate Social Responsibility and Communication

Corporate Social Responsibility (CSR) has evolved over decades of scholarship and practice, encompassing a broad array of concepts about business responsibilities to society. One widely cited framework is Carroll's Pyramid of CSR, which delineates four layers of responsibility: economic (profitable operation), legal (obeying laws and regulations), ethical (doing what is right, just, and fair beyond mere compliance), and philanthropic (voluntarily contributing to community well-being). Carroll (1991) emphasized that fulfilling these responsibilities makes a corporation a "good citizen" in society. In practical terms, CSR activities can range from ensuring workplace safety and fair labour practices, to reducing environmental impacts, engaging in charity or community development, and ensuring transparent governance. Notably, sustainable environmental management is an integral part of CSR often classified under the ethical or philanthropic domain but increasingly seen as a fundamental corporate duty given global sustainability challenge. A critical aspect of CSR, beyond the activities themselves, is how companies communicate their CSR policies, initiatives, and performance to stakeholders (Luo et al., 2023). CSR communication refers to an organization's disclosure of information and messaging about its social and environmental contributions (or impacts) to both internal stakeholders (employees, managers, shareholders) and external stakeholders (customers, communities, regulators, NGOs, etc.). The goals of CSR communication include informing stakeholders, building the company's reputation and legitimacy, and persuading stakeholders to support or participate in the company's CSR-related endeavours (Bartikowski & Berens, 2021).

Podnar (2008) suggests that CSR communication is the process by which social and environmental issues are integrated into corporate communication strategy, thereby creating points of mutual interest between the company and its stakeholders. In essence, effective CSR communication turns CSR from a set of internal policies into a platform for stakeholder engagement and dialogue (Bartikowski & Berens, 2021). Several theoretical perspectives shed light on the nature and challenges of CSR communication:

Stakeholder Information vs. Response vs. Involvement Strategies: Morsing and Schultz (2006) propose that companies can adopt different communication strategies vis-à-vis stakeholders. In an information strategy, communication is one-way in which the company simply disseminates information about its CSR (e.g., through reports or websites) to project a positive image. A response strategy involves two-way but asymmetrical communication in which the company seeks feedback but mainly to adjust its messaging or actions to stakeholder expectations. An involvement strategy is two-way and symmetrical in which stakeholders are actively engaged in dialogue and partnership, co-creating CSR initiatives or policies. This latter approach often leads to higher stakeholder trust and legitimacy because stakeholders feel heard and involved in corporate responsibility efforts. In practice, firms might use a combination of these: e.g., publishing a CSR report annually (informing), responding to public concerns or media exposés on issues (responsive), and hosting stakeholder forums or multi-stakeholder initiatives to shape CSR programs (involving).

Persuasive vs. Informative Communication: McWilliams et al. (2006) distinguish between CSR communication designed to persuade and that designed to inform. Persuasive CSR communication tends to resemble marketing in which CSR is used to enhance brand image and consumer purchase intention. For instance, a company might highlight a cause-related marketing campaign (donating a portion of sales to a cause) to persuade ethically minded consumers to buy their product. Such communication is often overt, emotive, and seeks to differentiate the product or company via its social responsibility credentials. Kotler and Lee (2005) provide examples like companies aligning with credible animal rights movements to attract supporters of that cause. In contrast, informative CSR communication focuses on factual, transparent disclosure of what the company is actually doing in terms of CSR, without direct advertising or sales appeals. Examples include detailed sustainability reports, sections on a corporate website dedicated to CSR practices, or integrated reporting (financial + non-financial information). Morsing and Schultz (2006) note that when CSR information is communicated in a subtle way (e.g., embedded in annual reports or dedicated sustainability webpages) rather than as flashy advertisements, stakeholders tend to respond more favourably. The reason is that informative communication is perceived as more sincere and less self-congratulatory, thereby enhancing credibility.

Channels and Tools of CSR Communication: Traditional and new media channels are used to convey CSR messages. Traditional channels include annual reports, press releases, brochures, and press conferences. Academic studies highlight that annual reports (and standalone CSR or sustainability reports) have been a primary vehicle for CSR disclosure (Luo et al., 2023). Even as companies have adopted digital media, annual reports (often available online in PDF or interactive form) remain crucial because they are official, comprehensive, and targeted at investors and regulators (stakeholders with a "vested interest"). Press releases are another tool, often used to broadcast specific CSR initiatives or achievements via mass media. While press releases may not always gain broad coverage, they serve to inform journalists and the public in a factual tone. Whysall (2005) argues that press releases can be effective in addressing multiple stakeholder expectations by covering key messages such as new environmental initiatives, community programs, or improvements in social performance. Beyond these, companies now extensively use websites and social media to communicate CSR. Corporate websites typically have a CSR or sustainability section providing policy statements, case studies, and data (often updated more frequently than annual reports). Social media platforms (Twitter, LinkedIn, Facebook, etc.) allow more interactive and real-time CSR communication. For instance, sharing stories of community engagement, responding to customer questions about ethical sourcing, or promoting events like Earth Day campaigns. These interactive platforms can foster stakeholder dialogue but also expose companies to immediate public scrutiny and feedback.

One of the fundamental challenges in CSR communication is credibility. Stakeholders today are often sceptical of corporate claims, given widespread concerns about "greenwashing" which is the practice of portraying products or policies as more environmentally friendly or socially responsible than they truly are. Thus, a recurring theme in the literature is that CSR communication must be balanced, honest, and backed by performance, otherwise it can backfire and erode trust (Morsing et al., 2008; Dawkins, 2004). Consistency between what a company says (through CSR communication) and what it does (actual CSR performance) is critical to maintaining legitimacy.

In conclusion, CSR communication is not merely an ancillary public relations activity, it is a strategic process that can reinforce or undermine the impact of CSR initiatives. Effective CSR communication builds transparency and invites stakeholder engagement and thereby enhances the perceived legitimacy of the company's policies and actions. This has direct implications for how companies can lead or influence policy innovations in arenas like the circular economy, where stakeholder buy-in and multi-actor cooperation are vital.

2.3. CSR and Stakeholder Theory

Any discussion of CSR is inextricably linked with stakeholder theory, as the latter provides the underlying logic for why firms should be socially responsible and to whom. R. Edward Freeman's classic definition encapsulates the essence: a stakeholder is "any group or individual who can affect or is affected by the achievement of a corporation's purpose" (Freeman, 1984). Stakeholder theory posits that corporations have obligations not just to shareholders (owners) but to a wide array of stakeholders including employees, customers, suppliers, communities, creditors, regulators and even the environment (some scholars consider the natural environment or future generations as stakeholders in a broader sense). Freeman's work challenged the dominant managerial model focused solely on shareholder interests, expanding the corporate strategic horizon to account for external influences and expectations. In an increasingly complex business environment, this approach provided "legitimate solutions to challenges of modern world" by encouraging managers to balance and integrate multiple stakeholder concerns in decision-making.

From a CSR perspective, stakeholder theory provides the normative justification and strategic impetus for corporate social responsibility. If a firm's survival and success depend on its ability to manage relationships with key stakeholders, then attending to those stakeholders' legitimate needs and demands becomes a matter of enlightened self-interest (Donaldson & Preston, 1995; Freeman et al., 2010). For instance, treating employees well (beyond what the law requires) can improve morale and productivity, addressing customer concerns about product sustainability can preserve brand loyalty and supporting community development can maintain a company's social license to operate. As Carroll (1991) noted, ethical and philanthropic responsibilities in his CSR pyramid are often fulfilled in service of stakeholders, ensuring no stakeholder group is harmed and that some are benefited by corporate operations.

Stakeholder legitimacy is a key concept here. It refers to the perceived validity or appropriateness of a stakeholder's claim on the company. Not all stakeholders are equal in influence they vary in power, legitimacy, and urgency (Mitchell et al., 1997). However, the concept of legitimacy implies that beyond power dynamics, companies ought to respond to stakeholders whose claims are socially legitimate (e.g., environmental NGOs highlighting pollution have a legitimate issue even if they lack coercive power). This ties to legitimacy theory, which suggests that corporations seek to operate within the bounds and norms of their respective societies to ensure continual approval of their objectives and activities. According to legitimacy theory, society grants legitimacy to a firm as long as the firm's value system aligns with that of the society. If a disparity arises (for example, the public perceives the firm's operations as violating social or environmental norms), the firm's legitimacy is threatened, which can manifest in protests, boycotts, or regulatory backlash. When legitimacy is at risk, companies often resort to communication strategies to restore alignment. Lindblom (1994) identified four such strategies for organizations to employ in the face of legitimacy gaps:

- Informing stakeholders about changes in the organization's performance or policies (e.g., publicly announcing a new sustainability initiative to address a known concern).
- Changing perceptions of stakeholders without necessarily changing actual behaviour (e.g., re framing an issue by highlighting positive aspects or comparisons, sometimes bordering on greenwash if substantive action is lacking).
- Deflecting attention from the issue by associating the company with positive actions in another area (a diversion tactic, such as donating to charity to overshadow an environmental mishap).
- Changing external expectations of performance (e.g., lobbying to shape industry standards or public opinion so that what the firm is doing appears acceptable under new norms).

While not all of these strategies are laudable, they underline how critical stakeholder perceptions and communications are to maintaining legitimacy. In fact, Farache and Perks (2010) argue that companies often use CSR disclosures explicitly to bolster their legitimacy by showcasing alignment with societal values. Empirical evidence supports that firms in industries with greater environmental and social impacts (like oil and gas, mining, chemicals) tend to engage more in CSR reporting to justify their operations to the public. As Branco and Rodrigues (2006) note, society expects such firms to communicate how they are mitigating negative impacts as part of maintaining their license to operate.

Stakeholder engagement is another crucial element. Beyond just identifying stakeholders and acknowledging their stakes, engagement implies a process of active dialogue and partnership. Engagement can take forms such as stakeholder meetings, advisory panels, participatory decision making in community projects, and collaborative initiatives (for example, industry-NGO alliances for sustainable supply chain standards). The literature suggests that effective stakeholder engagement can lead to more robust CSR strategies and innovations, as it brings diverse perspectives and knowledge to the table (Andriof & Waddock, 2002). Moreover, engagement enhances stakeholder buy-in and reduces scepticism, because stakeholders who are involved in shaping CSR initiatives are more likely to view them as credible and worthwhile. For instance, Maignan and Ferrell (2004) and Podnar (2008) both stress that encouraging interaction with stakeholders' positions CSR managers in a pivotal role of building corporate image in line with stakeholder expectations.

Rather than a top-down approach, CSR becomes a collaborative effort, improving both outcomes and perceptions.

In summary, stakeholder theory reinforces that CSR is fundamentally about managing a business in a way that balances the interests and values of all those affected by the business. Companies that excel in CSR often demonstrate a stakeholder-oriented mindset, assessing their success not just by financial metrics but by the well-being of their employees, satisfaction of their customers, strength of their supplier relationships, health of the communities in which they operate, and minimal environmental footprint. CSR communication, in turn, is the conduit through which these stakeholder relationships are nurtured, informing, responding, involving, and through which companies maintain legitimacy.

Considering the link CSR with the circular economy, stakeholder theory reminds that the transition to circular models requires considering who the winners and losers are, how stakeholders are engaged or compensated, and how the narrative is framed so that the change is seen as positive and necessary by those it impacts.

2.4. CSR and Circular Economy Convergence

The concepts of CSR and circular economy (CE) are complementary facets of the broader pursuit of sustainable business, and their convergence represents a holistic approach to corporate sustainability strategy. At the heart of both lies the principle of sustainability, meeting present needs without compromising the ability of future generations to meet theirs. CSR provides the strategic and ethical orientation, urging companies to be accountable to society and the environment, while the circular economy provides a practical blueprint for sustainable operations, particularly in the environmental and economic domains. Several points of convergence can be identified:

Environmental Responsibility: Environmental stewardship is a cornerstone of CSR (often seen in commitments to reduce pollution, manage carbon footprints, and protect biodiversity), and it is also the primary focus of the circular economy (emphasizing waste elimination, resource efficiency, and ecosystem regeneration). Implementing circular economy practices is one tangible way companies fulfil their CSR environmental commitments. For example, a firm that pledges under CSR to mitigate its environmental impact can operationalize that pledge by redesigning products for durability and recyclability, establishing take-back programs, or switching to recycled raw materials, all hallmark actions in a circular model. In this way, the CE acts as an implementation arm of CSR goals. Indeed, some scholars argue that the circular economy transforms CSR from abstract principles into concrete actions and outcomes (Hong et al., 2023). By moving towards circular production and consumption patterns, companies demonstrate accountability for the full life-cycle impacts of their products, which is a key expectation in modern CSR.

Stakeholder and Institutional Pressure: The drive towards both CSR and CE often comes from similar stakeholder pressures and institutional incentives. Regulators, consumers, investors, and NGOs are increasingly vocal about sustainability. As Frynas (2005) observed in the context of oil and gas industries with significant environmental impacts are under high pressure to adopt responsible practices. Today, such pressure frequently includes expectations to embrace circular economy principles. For instance, governments and international bodies promote circularity to address waste crises and resource security, while consumers might Favour products with recycled content or minimal packaging. From a CSR standpoint, responding to these pressures is part of being attuned to stakeholder concerns and maintaining legitimacy. When governments encourage circularity (through legislation or incentives), forward-thinking companies integrate these expectations into their CSR strategies pre-emptively, turning potential compliance requirements into voluntary initiatives. Conversely, companies with strong CSR track records can influence or pre-empt policy for example, an industry CSR coalition might develop circular economy guidelines for its sector, which could later inform public regulations. Thus, CSR and CE converge in the sense that stakeholder and policy landscapes are aligning to favour businesses that contribute to a circular, sustainable economy (Boas & Machado, 2024).

Triple Bottom Line and Value Creation: Both CSR and CE are founded on the idea of creating value not just economically but also socially and environmentally (the "triple bottom line"). A circular economy operationalizes this by finding economic value in what was once waste (environmental and economic gain) and potentially creating new employment sectors in recycling, remanufacturing, or maintenance services (social and economic gain). CSR's long-term orientation similarly advocates for businesses to create shared value, value for shareholders as well as for society (Resourcify, 2023). When companies adopt circular business models (like product-service systems, sharing models, or resource recovery enterprises), they often unlock innovations and efficiencies that align profitability with sustainability, which is the ideal scenario CSR theorists envision (where doing good and doing well financially reinforce each other). For instance, using recycled materials can reduce costs and supply chain risks (an economic benefit) while also reducing landfill and energy use (an environmental benefit), thus satisfying both CSR objectives and economic objectives.

Reporting and Metrics: As CSR practices have matured, so have standards for reporting them (e.g., GRI – Global Reporting Initiative, and integrated reporting frameworks). Now, there is a push to incorporate circular economy metrics into corporate reporting. Some companies publish "circularity reports" or include metrics like percentage of recycled input, product recyclability, waste reduction percentages, etc., in their CSR reports. This melding of reporting shows convergence: a company's sustainability report might simultaneously serve as a CSR report and a circular economy progress report. It demonstrates to stakeholders how the company's CSR commitments to the environment are being met through circular strategies. Furthermore, investors focused on ESG (Environmental, Social, Governance criteria) increasingly evaluate how companies manage resource circularity as part of environmental performance. Thus, integrating CE into CSR reporting aligns with the broader trend of quantifying and communicating sustainable performance.

Ethical and Social Dimensions of Circularity: While the environmental and economic aspects of CE are well-known, its social dimension is sometimes less explicit but still significant. CSR, with its strong social focus (labour rights, community impacts, etc.), ensures that the move to a circular economy also considers social equity. For example, CSR would urge companies to ensure that as they implement circular practices (e.g. shifting to recyclable materials or refurbishing operations), they consider the impact on workers (re-skilling workers in linear processes to work in circular processes), on communities (like waste-picker communities in developing countries who might be affected by changes in waste flows), and on customers (ensuring products remain affordable and accessible). A just circular transition, one that is fair and inclusive, is fundamentally a CSR concern. This is reflected in concepts like the inclusive circular economy, which advocates that circular strategies should benefit a broad range of stakeholders and not create new inequalities. In essence, CSR values inject considerations of equity, human rights, and community well-being into the technical agenda of circular economy, ensuring that CE initiatives are not just eco-efficient but also socially responsible.

Overall, CSR and circular economy converge as strategic approaches for sustainable business that reinforce each other. CSR provides the broad commitment to accountability and stakeholder wellbeing, which sets the stage for adopting circular economy innovations. Meanwhile, those innovations make CSR tangible and results-driven, allowing companies to showcase real contributions to sustainability (e.g., quantifiable reductions in waste and emissions). The convergence is increasingly visible in corporate strategies, many leading companies now articulate "circular economy" as a part of their CSR or sustainability vision. For example, a retail company's CSR policy on environment might explicitly state goals to move toward circular packaging or 100% recyclable products, blending the language of CSR (commitment, responsibility) with CE (specific circular goals). This convergence also means that policy making for a circular economy can leverage CSR communication and engagement frameworks.

3. CSR COMMUNICATION

CSR communication serves as a platform for establishing common ground with stakeholders by integrating social and environmental issues into the corporate communication agenda (Podnar, 2008).

Figure 1. CSR Communication

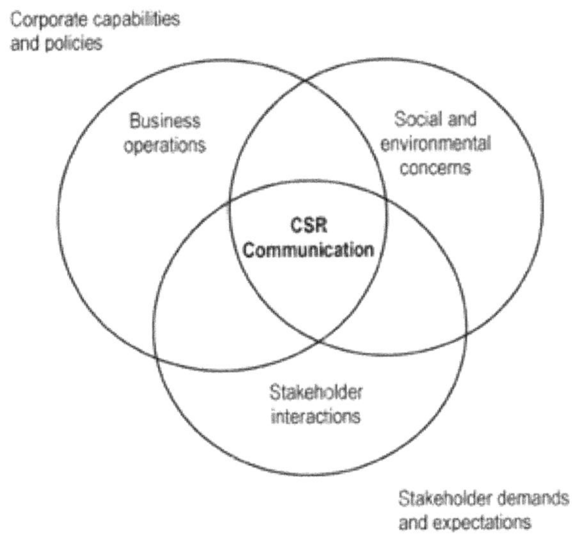

Source: Podnar (2008)

The practical implementation of CSR highlights its growing importance for both public and private sectors, as stakeholders increasingly demand corporate involvement in socially responsible initiatives, particularly emphasizing transparent communication of such activities (Beckmann et al., 2006). Corporations, in turn, focus strongly on consumers, acknowledging their expectations regarding responsible business conduct. Consumers anticipate that companies will act ethically, adopt fair employment practices, and support community initiatives such as local schools (Harrison et al., 2006). To recognize a company as socially responsible, stakeholders, especially consumers, require clear communication about CSR initiatives (Podnar, 2008). When companies neglect certain responsibilities or engage in irresponsible actions, external pressures from consumers and media outlets intensify, compelling them to reconsider and align with societal expectations (Podnar, 2008).

To ensure effective knowledge and information exchange with internal and external stakeholders, corporate communication managers must approach CSR communication from two perspectives. First, CSR communication should be strategically evaluated in terms of its influence on corporate performance and profitability. Second, companies should adopt communication strategies and tools tailored to meet the diverse expectations of stakeholders, particularly consumers, regarding CSR practices.

Strengthened and transparent CSR communication not only enhances corporate reputation but also builds stakeholder trust and contributes to perceived product quality (McWilliams et al., 2006). Moreover, CSR communication professionals act as mediators between corporate behavior and stakeholder expectations, shaping the company's CSR image and encouraging stakeholder engagement (Podnar, 2008). According to McWilliams et al. (2006), CSR communication can be either persuasive or informative. Persuasive communication relies on influencing consumer attitudes and purchase intentions by showcasing a company's responsible image. For example, CSR-oriented promotions such as highlighting support for animal rights can persuade socially conscious consumers to buy related products. Informative communication, by contrast, provides straightforward details about a company's practices without overtly promoting a cause or advertising its CSR image. While persuasive strategies aim directly at driving purchases, informative communication fosters a broader belief in the company's commitment to social responsibility.

4. CSR Communication as an Enabler of CE Policy Innovation

Having established the theoretical linkages, it can now be delved into how CSR communication functions as a catalyst for innovative policy making in the realm of circular economy (CE). Policy innovation here refers not only to formal public policies (like laws or regulations) but also to the adoption of new norms, standards, and practices that guide the transition to a circular economy. CSR communication can enable these innovations in several ways: by disseminating knowledge and shaping narratives (making circular principles widely understood and accepted), by building trust and legitimacy (so that stakeholders support the changes), and by influencing stakeholder behaviour and expectations (which can drive both corporate self-regulation and governmental action). This section explores specific dimensions of this enabling role: the tools and channels through which CSR and CE messages are communicated, the framing of circular economy policies within CSR narratives, and the critical factors of transparency, credibility, and stakeholder influence that determine success.

4.1. Communication Tools in CSR for CE

Communication tools are the vehicles carrying CSR messages. To effectively promote circular economy ideas and practices through CSR, organizations rely on a mix of traditional and modern communication tools.

Sustainability and CSR Reports: These comprehensive reports (often annual or biennial) are a cornerstone of CSR communication. Traditionally, CSR or sustainability reports cover performance on various issues (environmental metrics, social impact, governance). To serve the cause of circular economy, companies have started including specific sections or indicators related to circularity. For example, a sustainability report might highlight a company's material circularity index, the percentage of products designed for reuse, or case studies of closed-loop initiatives (like a take-back program for recycling products). The rigor and detail of such reports help in institutionalizing circular economy goals within the corporate agenda and communicating progress transparently. According to Day and Woodward (2009), annual reports (and by extension integrated CSR reports) are considered highly credible channels for stakeholders because they present audited data and comprehensive information. When a company reports, for instance, that it achieved a 30% reduction in waste this year by recycling and this is in a verified report, stakeholders are more likely to believe and appreciate that progress. Reports also allow for comparability over time and between companies, which can spur a healthy competition towards circular economy leadership. Morsing and Schultz (2006) contended that CSR communication gains wider societal approval when conducted through subtle means, such as issuing annual reports on CSR practices or creating dedicated websites for CSR causes, rather than relying on overtly persuasive campaigns. They emphasized the responsibility of managers to both inform and respond to stakeholder expectations in order to build consensus and incorporate diverse inputs into the development of effective CSR communication. Yet, the theoretical and practical progress of CSR communication directed at customers, as the primary stakeholder group, remains underdeveloped and requires further consolidation (Beckmann et al., 2006). Currently, annual reports serve as the most common medium through which companies communicate CSR activities (Podnar, 2008). However, corporations face the challenge of embedding CSR practices more deeply into their structural frameworks. Annual reports, which typically provide audited financial statements and information on company operations, also offer an avenue for disseminating CSR-related messages. Communicating CSR through annual reports holds distinct advantages compared to other media channels. Despite considerable academic attention to CSR communication, there is still debate among scholars about which reporting methods are most effective, given the diversity of approaches available. Nevertheless, comparative studies highlight similarities across annual and CSR reports from various companies, enabling the establishment of coherent cross-firm assessments (Podnar, 2008).

Since annual reports outline financial performance and strategic plans, the credibility of these documents becomes essential, particularly regarding the inclusion of CSR information (Beckmann et al., 2006). Critics, however, argue that using annual reports for CSR communication may create tension between genuine social responsibility efforts and the declarative nature of corporate statements. In this view, reporting CSR through annual reports risks reducing meaningful social engagement to a matter of corporate positioning rather than substantive action.

Corporate Websites and Online Platforms: The digital presence of a company is a dynamic tool for CSR communication. Many companies have dedicated sustainability or CSR microsites. These are increasingly interactive, featuring infographics on circular economy initiatives, videos explaining how consumers can participate (e.g., returning used items for recycling), and progress dashboards. One advantage of web-based communication is that it can be updated continuously, unlike annual reports. So, if a company launches a new CE pilot project or forms a partnership for circular innovation, it can publish a news update or blog post immediately. For example, a fashion retailer might use its website to promote a new line of clothing made from recycled fibres and include customer stories or Q&A about product care and eventual recycling effectively using content marketing to reinforce circular economy principles as part of its CSR story. Moreover, social media amplifies this reach. Through platforms like Twitter or LinkedIn, companies share bite-sized updates (e.g., "We've achieved 90% recyclable packaging - moving closer to our #CircularEconomy goal! #Sustainability"). Social media also invites engagement. Stakeholders can comment, share, or ask questions, making CSR communication a two-way street. However, with this immediacy comes scrutiny any claims made online are open to public challenge, which incentivizes companies to ensure their communications are accurate and substantiated.

Press Releases and Media Engagement: When companies have significant achievements or policy changes aligned with CSR and CE (such as committing to phase out single-use plastics by a certain date, or investing in a new recycling facility), they often issue press releases. Press releases serve to frame the narrative in a favourable way for the media and public. For instance, a press release might highlight that a company's circular initiative will "reduce waste to landfill by X tons and create Y new green jobs", thus appealing to both environmental and social dimensions. As Kotler et al. (1999) note, such proactive communications through mass media aim to extend reach and create awareness in an "impartial" manner (since a news article is seen as more neutral than an advertisement). Whysall (2005) observed that well-crafted press releases can simultaneously address the interests of multiple stakeholders by covering various angles employment opportunities, environmental benefits, community impacts, etc. In the context of CE, this holistic communication is useful. It helps people see circular economy efforts not as isolated environmental projects, but as integrated business strategies with broad societal benefits.

Workshops, Webinars, and Stakeholder Meetings: These tools are more focused but powerful for engagement. A company might organize workshops or webinars about its circular economy efforts, targeting specific stakeholder groups, for example, a webinar for suppliers explaining how they can contribute to the company's circular supply chain goals, or a townhall with employees about integrating circular thinking into product design. Such forums allow detailed communication and dialogue. They double as capacity-building exercises, effective CSR communication in these settings empowers stakeholders with knowledge (e.g., educating suppliers on new materials or customers on product return processes). Many companies also host multi-stakeholder roundtables as part of their CSR engagement when the topic is circular economy, they might invite NGOs, academics, and policymakers to discuss challenges and collaborative solutions. The communication tool here is the structured conversation itself, often summarized later in reports or press releases to inform a wider audience of the key outcomes.

Storytelling and Case Studies: While not a tool per se, storytelling is a technique applied across the above tools to humanize and contextualize CSR and CE progress. For example, in a CSR report or on a website, a company might include a case study about a particular product's journey in a circular system, maybe an electronics manufacturer describing how a returned device gets refurbished and given a second life, including quotes from the engineers involved or the customers benefiting. This narrative approach makes the concept of circular economy relatable and demonstrates the company's commitment in real terms. It also underscores transparency by showing how things are done, not just touting results. As Harrison et al. (2006) argue in the CSR context, stakeholders (especially ethically conscious consumers) want to know the story behind products that companies are conducting themselves in an acceptable and responsible manner throughout their operations. By communicating such stories, firms not only inform but also build emotional connection and credibility.

In utilizing these tools, a few best practices have emerged to ensure they effectively enable policy innovation for CE:

Consistency and Alignment: The messaging across different tools and channels should be consistent. If a company's sustainability report extols circular economy, then its advertising, social media, and stakeholder communications should not simultaneously suggest a conflicting message (for example, promoting disposable products without context). Consistency builds trust. Moreover, aligning the CSR communication with actual business strategy is key, if communications set bold circular economy goals, the company must ensure internally that plans and resources are in place to work towards them, otherwise communications can be dismissed as empty rhetoric.

Fact-based and Data-driven Communication: Particularly for an area like CE which involves technical aspects (recycling rates, material science, lifecycle analysis), providing data lends credibility. McWilliams et al. (2006) highlight that effective disclosure of information strengthens corporate image and trust. So, rather than just saying "we are becoming more circular," leading companies provide metrics (e.g., "this year 40% of our raw materials were from recycled sources, up from 25% last year"). Such data, when verified, can influence external policy by demonstrating feasibility and progress, and perhaps encouraging regulators to set industry wide benchmarks based on what frontrunners achieve.

Tailoring to Audience: Different stakeholders may prefer different tools. Investors might focus on official reports and data, consumers might be more reached by social media and product labelling (e.g., a product label indicating recyclability or recycled content is a form of CSR communication right at the point of sale). Meanwhile, policymakers often pay attention to broader industry reports or media coverage. Thus, enabling CE policy innovation requires communicating through multiple tools so that each stakeholder group gets the message in a form that resonates with them. For instance, to influence policy, a company might contribute to a white paper or an industry coalition report on circular economy progress, a tool that carries more weight in policy circles, while simultaneously using more accessible tools to bring consumers on board with circular behaviours. In conclusion, the arsenal of communication tools in CSR can be effectively employed to advance circular economy objectives. Each tool from the detailed annual report to the quick tweet plays a role in educating, persuading, and mobilizing stakeholders. Through strategic use of these tools, companies become not just implementers of circular practices, but also advocates and thought leaders, shaping the discourse and policies around circular economy in their industry and society at large.

4.2. CSR Communication and Policy Framing

Framing refers to the way information and issues are presented and interpreted. In the context of CSR communication, how a company frames its messages about sustainability and circular economy can significantly influence stakeholder support and the broader policy discourse. Essentially, companies engaged in CSR communication are not just reporting facts, they are also shaping narratives, about the importance of certain issues, the responsibilities of various actors, and the solutions that should be pursued.

One important aspect is framing the circular economy as an opportunity rather than a burden. Traditionally, environmental regulations and sustainability measures might be framed negatively by businesses (as costs or constraints). However, CSR communication allows companies to reframe these as positive, future-oriented changes. For example, a company might frame its transition to circular practices as "innovation for competitive advantage and community benefit", highlighting that circular economy policies (internal or external) will lead to jobs in recycling, reduced pollution in local communities, and a more resilient business. This aligns with findings that many consumers and stakeholders respond well to optimistic, solution-focused messaging in CSR (Bartikowski & Berens, 2020). By framing CE initiatives as win-win (for both business and society), companies can build a coalition of support that includes customers willing to perhaps pay a bit more for sustainable products, suppliers willing to collaborate on new materials, and local governments seeing the company as a partner in achieving environmental goals.

Policy framing through CSR communication also involves legitimizing certain policy measures. If a firm publicly supports the idea of extended producer responsibility (EPR) laws or higher recycling mandates, it uses its CSR platform to normalize and advocate those policies. For instance, in its CSR report or blog, the company might discuss the need for industry-wide standards on recyclable packaging, effectively framing regulation not as an external threat but as a logical step aligned with the company's own values and practices. This can influence policymakers by demonstrating industry buy-in. It can also sway public opinion, stakeholders hear from a trusted company that such policies are desirable, which might contrast with other voices that portray regulation as harmful. Thus, the voice of CSR communication can add to the policy debate, often tilting it towards more progressive environmental policy because credible businesses speaking positively about regulation can undermine the narrative that all businesses are against stricter environmental rules.

Another dimension of framing is linking circular economy to broader societal goals and values. CSR communication often connects company actions to things people care about, like health, quality of life, intergenerational equity, or national pride. For example, a company in the food and beverage sector might frame its reduction of plastic and increase of biodegradable packaging in terms of protecting oceans and marine life (thus resonating with public concern about ocean plastic) and in terms of ensuring safe, clean communities for children. By doing so, the company situates circular economy initiatives within widely accepted moral frameworks (protecting nature, caring for future generations), which can build a moral case for certain policies. This echoes the notion of a "social contract" from legitimacy theory: society allows business to operate as long as business contributes positively to societal values. Through framing, companies underscore that contribution, for instance, implying "our business supports a circular economy because it's the right thing to do for society and our shared future". Such framing can pre-empt resistance, stakeholders may come to view a circular economy transition not as an abstract, technocratic initiative, but as an ethically necessary evolution of our economic system.

Effective framing in CSR communication also involves addressing stakeholder concerns and expectations, essentially speaking to what matters for each audience. If research shows that consumers worry about product quality in remanufactured goods, a company's communications might frame its policy of refurbishing products as delivering "like-new quality with added environmental benefits," thus reassuring consumers that circular products are not inferior. Similarly, if policymakers are concerned about economic growth, companies might frame CE actions as boosting efficiency and opening new markets (for example, "the market for recycled materials is growing and we are positioning ourselves at the forefront, which will bring investment to our region"). This approach resonates with Morsing and Schultz's (2006) concept of stakeholder responsiveness, shaping messages in response to stakeholder attitudes to gain acceptance.

A case in point of framing can be seen in industry coalitions and collective CSR communication. When an entire industry sector voluntarily comes together to announce circular economy commitments (a form of collective CSR), they often frame it as shaping the future of the industry. For example, if a group of electronics manufacturers jointly communicate that they are setting a standard for electronics take-back and recycling, they frame it as "the electronics industry stepping up for sustainability, ensuring products do not become toxic e-waste." This not only sends a strong signal to policymakers that regulation in this area would be welcome (or even that it might be unnecessary if self-regulation works), but it also frames the narrative such that companies not part of the coalition may feel pressure to join so as not to be seen as laggards. In essence, framing via CSR communication can help create peer pressure and normative shifts in industries, a soft form of policymaking where the policy is a voluntary code or standard, influenced by communication.

Transparency and disclosure also relate to framing. By being transparent about challenges and setbacks, a company frames itself as honest and committed rather than deceitful. For example, if a company's CSR report openly states "We aimed to achieve 50% recycled content in our packaging but reached only 30%; here is why and here is how we will improve," it frames the narrative around continuous improvement and learning. Stakeholders are more likely to remain supportive and engaged because the issue is framed as a journey that everyone is on together, rather than a binary success/failure which might invite criticism. This honest framing can ironically make external policy support stronger, regulators might see that companies are trying but facing certain barriers (like lack of recycling infrastructure), which could prompt them to address those barriers through policy interventions.

Lastly, framing through CSR often uses metaphors and terms that resonate. The term "circular economy" itself is a framing device and it conveys completeness and renewal, as opposed to a "linear economy" which might evoke wastefulness. Companies might amplify this by using phrases like "closing the loop" (implying no leakage of waste, everything has value) in their communications or referring to "waste as resource" (a classic reframing that helped spawn industrial symbiosis projects). By consistently framing waste as lost value or pollution as a design flaw that can be corrected, CSR communications change mindsets, which is a precursor to changing policies and behaviours. In fact, Blomsma and Brennan (2017) describe the circular economy as an evolving "umbrella concept" in which part of its success has been due to effective framing that unites various sustainability practices under an appealing narrative. Businesses have played a role in popularizing that narrative through their CSR messaging.

In summary, CSR communication contributes to policy innovation not just by sharing information but by framing the circular economy in ways that build understanding, alignment, and momentum among stakeholders. By highlighting opportunities, aligning with societal values, and addressing concerns through careful framing, companies help create a more favourable environment for the implementation of circular economy policies whether those are internal corporate policies, industry standards, or public regulations. The framing ensures that these policies are seen as positive, necessary, and viable, which significantly smooths the path for innovative changes.

4.3. Transparency, Credibility, and Stakeholder Influence

The effectiveness of CSR communication in driving circular economy initiatives hinges on transparency and credibility. These qualities determine whether stakeholders trust the messages and are willing to support or participate in the proposed changes. Additionally, stakeholder influence, the capacity of stakeholders to shape corporate behaviour and policy, is both something to be managed by communication and a force that can be harnessed for positive change.

Transparency in CSR communication means openly disclosing information, including both successes and shortcomings. Transparent communication is crucial for circular economy endeavours because these often involve complex processes and trade-offs that stakeholders need to understand. For instance, a company might introduce a new biodegradable packaging but be transparent that it only breaks down under industrial composting conditions (thus urging municipalities to provide appropriate waste processing). If the company were not transparent about this, consumers might dispose of it improperly, undermining the intended environmental benefit. A culture of transparency is also linked to accountability, by disclosing targets and performance data related to circularity, a company holds itself accountable to stakeholders for making progress. Sweeney and Coughlan (2008) emphasize that for reports to be perceived as credible, they must provide correct and complete information about CSR efforts. In CE perspective, that implies sharing, for example, the percentage of materials recycled, the carbon footprint reductions achieved, or the challenges faced in sourcing sustainable materials. When stakeholders see that a company is forthcoming with data and even admits where it has not yet reached its goals, it fosters trust.

Credibility is built not just by transparency, but by consistency and evidence of follow-through. One of the biggest pitfalls in CSR communication is when companies are seen as saying one thing and doing another. This credibility gap can severely backfire, as illustrated by incidents where companies have been accused of greenwashing. To maintain credibility, companies must ensure their CSR communication aligns with actual performance. Beckmann et al. (2006) point out that stakeholders often pressure organizations to implement and disclose socially responsible initiatives. If a company talks extensively about supporting a circular economy but fails to implement basic measures (like recycling in its own operations), stakeholders will quickly call out the discrepancy, particularly in the age of social media where inconsistencies can go viral. Therefore, credible CSR communication often includes third-party validations. For example, mentioning that an independent auditor verified the recycling rate, or that the company's circular initiatives won an award or certification. This external endorsement can strengthen stakeholder belief that the company's claims are real. One concrete example of building credibility is through pilot projects and transparent results sharing. If a firm is unsure about a new circular approach, it might run a pilot (e.g., a single store operating on circular principles or one product line using 100% recycled input) and then share honest results. Were there cost increases? How did customers react? What was the environmental outcome? By reporting these in a balanced way, the company signals that it cares about outcomes, not just optics. Such credibility can garner patience and goodwill from stakeholders and they may be more forgiving of incremental progress if they believe the company is earnestly learning and improving.

Stakeholders can be both an audience of CSR communication and protagonists that drive CSR and circular policies forward. As discussed under stakeholder theory, groups like consumers, investors, and NGOs have varying degrees of power, legitimacy, and urgency. Effective CSR communication recognizes these dynamics. It not only tries to influence stakeholders (e.g., persuade consumers to recycle products by communicating how to do so and why), but also to be influenced by them, that is, to listen and respond, giving stakeholders a voice in shaping strategies. A vivid illustration of stakeholder influence is the role of consumer pressure. In retail, for example, if consumers begin to favour sustainable products, their purchasing power influences companies to adopt circular practices (like using recycled materials or offering product take-back). CSR communication can amplify this influence by raising awareness. Consider a campaign where a company informs customers that a certain percentage of them returning used packaging could enable the company to recycle and reuse that packaging. This both informs (transparency about what is possible) and invites action (stakeholder influence on outcomes). Should customers respond positively (influence through behaviour change), the company can then justify scaling up such circular programs and possibly advocate for supportive public policies (like recycling infrastructure) by demonstrating consumer buy-in.

Investor influence is also critical. Many investors now scrutinize companies' sustainability performance. Transparent CSR communication regarding circular economy initiatives can attract responsible investors and satisfy rating agencies. On the flip side, if a company's communications reveal they are lagging in managing waste or resources, investors might pressure them to improve. In one sense, every target and figure published in a CSR report becomes a potential hook for stakeholder influence. If targets are missed, activist investors or NGOs can challenge the company at shareholder meetings or in the press, urging accountability. This might sound like a risk, but it is precisely this mechanism of influence that keeps companies progressing. A company anticipating such scrutiny may proactively strengthen its initiatives or collaborate with stakeholders to ensure targets are met, thereby improving actual performance. The power of mass media and public opinion (stakeholders at large) can be observed when companies face crises or criticism. Podnar (2008) notes that when stakeholders and mass media place significant pressure on an organization over perceived irresponsibility, the organization is often forced to review its practices and policies and respond acceptably. This highlights that stakeholder influence, when communicated (for example, media coverage of an issue raises public awareness, which in turn forces a corporate response), can drive policy changes within the firm. In some cases, companies have changed course on environmental practices after public campaigns. CSR communication can serve as an early warning system by engaging with stakeholders and hearing concerns through dialogue, a company can address issues before they escalate into full-blown legitimacy crises. Conversely, if a crisis does hit (say a company is found dumping waste illegally), the credibility and goodwill built by years of honest CSR communication can be crucial for recovery stakeholders might give the company a chance to make amends if historically it has been responsible and transparent. Finally, transparency and stakeholder engagement are linked to the concept of co-creation of policy. A highly credible CSR communication approach can evolve into a platform where stakeholders actually participate in defining solutions. For instance, a company could publish a draft of its circular economy roadmap and invite feedback from employees, customers, and experts. This level of radical transparency, sharing plans and seeking input, can yield innovative ideas (stakeholders might suggest practical improvements or point out blind spots) and also makes stakeholders co-owners of the policy. When people feel they had a hand in shaping an initiative, they are more likely to support and champion it. This collaboration can extend outward. Companies might partner with NGOs or government agencies, effectively blurring the line between internal policy and public policy. A credible CSR record often makes such partnerships easier to form, because external actors trust the company to be a genuine and competent collaborator.

In summary, transparency and credibility in CSR communication are foundational for engaging stakeholders and leveraging their influence positively. Transparent, trustworthy communications build a reservoir of goodwill and a culture of accountability, which not only helps avoid backlash and cynicism but actively engages stakeholders as allies. Stakeholder influence, when channelled through participatory and responsive communication processes, becomes a driving force to refine and amplify CSR and circular economy policies. Companies that master this dynamic, being open about their journey and responsive to stakeholder voices, are typically more successful in implementing ambitious sustainability initiatives and often take on leadership roles in shaping industry norms and public policies. As evidence, one need only look at how certain industries have progressed. Sectors like retail and consumer goods have seen rapid adoption of circular practices (recycled packaging, sustainable sourcing) largely because consumer-facing companies communicated these issues, gained consumer support, and collectively influenced suppliers and regulators to follow suit.

5. CONCLUSION AND RECOMMENDATIONS

This study has underscored the strategic convergence between Corporate Social Responsibility (CSR) and the circular economy (CE), emphasizing that CSR communication serves as a powerful enabler for innovative policy development. Through a thorough theoretical investigation, it has been demonstrated that CSR communication does more than inform stakeholders, it strategically frames sustainability narratives, fosters trust, and mobilizes diverse stakeholder groups to support and co-develop circular initiatives. CSR and CE together constitute a synergistic pathway where ethical responsibility and operational sustainability reinforce one another. Crucially, the study shows that transparent and credible CSR communication can build the legitimacy required to introduce systemic shifts and that stakeholder engagement facilitated through communication is not only a governance tool but a catalyst for transformative change. Based on findings, following recommendations can be given:

1. **Integrate Circular Economy Metrics into CSR Communication**: Companies should move beyond generic sustainability claims and adopt clear, measurable

indicators of circularity within their CSR reports and digital platforms. This includes metrics like material circularity index, waste reduction rates, and product recyclability.

2. **Adopt a Multi-Channel Communication Strategy**: Businesses should leverage a variety of communication tools from formal reports to social media to effectively reach and influence a broad spectrum of stakeholders, including consumers, investors, regulators, and NGOs.
3. **Focus on Stakeholder-Centred Framing**: CSR communication should be aligned with the concerns and values of targeted stakeholder groups. Framing circular economy actions as opportunities for innovation, employment, and social equity can help build broad-based legitimacy and support.
4. **Promote Transparency and Credibility**: To counteract scepticism and avoid perceptions of greenwashing, companies must maintain transparency in their progress and setbacks. Independent verification of circular economy claims and open disclosure of implementation challenges will enhance stakeholder trust.
5. **Encourage Co-Creation through Communication**: Companies should use CSR communication as a participatory platform by involving stakeholders in designing and refining circular initiatives. Mechanisms like feedback loops, public consultation on sustainability roadmaps, and collaborative workshops can facilitate shared ownership and policy alignment.

In conclusion, CSR communication, when applied strategically, has the potential not only to amplify a company's circular economy agenda but also to contribute meaningfully to wider societal and policy-level transformations toward sustainability.

REFERENCES

Andriof, J., & Waddock, S. (2002). Unfolding stakeholder engagement. In Andriof, J., Waddock, S., Husted, B., & Rahman, S. S. (Eds.), *Unfolding Stakeholder Thinking: Theory, Responsibility and Engagement* (pp. 19–42). Greenleaf. DOI: 10.9774/GLEAF.978-1-909493-28-5_3

Bartikowski, B., & Berens, G. (2020). Message Framing in CSR Communication: An Abstract. In Pantoja, F., Wu, S., & Krey, N. (Eds.), *Enlightened Marketing in Challenging Times* (pp. 175–176). Springer., DOI: 10.1007/978-3-030-42545-6_46

Bartikowski, B., & Berens, G. (2021). Attribute framing in CSR communication: Doing good and spreading the word – But how? *Journal of Business Research, 131*, 700–708. DOI: 10.1016/j.jbusres.2020.12.059

Beckmann, C. S., Morsing, M., & Reisch, L. (2006). Strategic CSR Communication: An Emerging Field. In Morsing, M., & Beckmann, S. C. (Eds.), *Strategic CSR Communication*. DJOF Publishing.

Blomsma, F., & Brennan, G. (2017). The Emergence of Circular Economy - A New Framing Around Prolonging Resource Productivity. *Journal of Industrial Ecology, 21*(3), 603–614. DOI: 10.1111/jiec.12603

Boas, F. R. V., & Machado, C. F. (2024). Chapter 9 - Social responsibility as a lever for the circular economy. *Circular Economy and Manufacturing*, 217-238. DOI: 10.1016/B978-0-443-14028-0.00011-6

Boatright, J. R. (1997). *Ethics and the Conduct of Business* (2nd ed.). Prentice-Hall.

Branco, M. C., & Rodrigues, L. L. (2006). Corporate social responsibility and resource-based perspectives. *Journal of Business Ethics, 69*(2), 111–132. DOI: 10.1007/s10551-006-9071-z

Carroll, A. B. (1991). The Pyramid of Corporate Social Responsibility: Toward the Moral Management of Organizational Stakeholders. *Business Horizons, 34*(July-August), 39–48. DOI: 10.1016/0007-6813(91)90005-G

Dawkins, C. J. (2004). *The public's views of Corporate Responsibility 2003.* MORI White Papers.

Day, R., & Woodward, T. (2009). CSR reporting and the UK financial services sector. *Journal of Applied Accounting Research, 10*(3), 159–175. DOI: 10.1108/09675420911006398 de Hallgren, S. C., Julca, A., Lucio, J. P., Ferrufino, R., & Costa, H. S. P. (2024). New Economics for Sustainable Development: Circular Economy. https://www.un.org/sites/un2.un.org/files/circular_economy_14_march.pdf

Donaldson, T., & Preston, L. E. (1995). The stakeholder theory of the corporation: Concepts, evidence, and implications. *Academy of Management Review*, *20*(1), 65–91. DOI: 10.2307/258887

Eickhoff, H. (2024). The appeal of the circular economy revisited: On track for transformative change or enabler of moral licensing? *Humanities & Social Sciences Communications*, *11*(301), 301. Advance online publication. DOI: 10.1057/s41599-024-02815-x

Farache, F., & Perks, K. J. (2010). CSR advertisements: A legitimacy tool? *Corporate Communications*, *15*(3), 235–248. DOI: 10.1108/13563281011068104

Freeman, R. E. (1984). *Strategic Management: A Stakeholder Approach*. Pitman.

Freeman, R. E., Harrison, J. S., Wicks, A. C., Parmar, B. L., & De Colle, S. (2010). *Stakeholder Theory. The State of the Art*. Cambridge University Press. DOI: 10.1017/CBO9780511815768

Frynas, J. (2005). The False Development Promise of Corporate Social Responsibility: Evidence from Multinational Oil Companies. *International Affairs*, *81*(3), 581–598. DOI: 10.1111/j.1468-2346.2005.00470.x

Harrison, R., Newholm, T., & Shaw, D. (2006). *The Ethical Consumer*. Sage Publications.

Hong, T., Ou, J., Jia, F., Chen, L., & Yang, Y. (2023). Circular economy practices and corporate social responsibility performance: The role of sense-giving. *International Journal of Logistics*, *27*(11), 2208–2237. DOI: 10.1080/13675567.2023.2237914

Kirchherr, J., Reike, D., & Hekkert, M. (2017). Conceptualizing the circular economy: An analysis of 114 definitions. *Resources, Conservation and Recycling*, *127*, 221–232. DOI: 10.1016/j.resconrec.2017.09.005

Kotler, P., Armstrong, G., Saunders, J., & Wong, V. (1999). *Principles of Marketing* (2nd European edition). Prentice-Hall.

Kotler, P., & Lee, N. (2005). *Corporate Social Responsibility: Doing the Good for Your Company and Your Cause*. John Wiley & Sons.

Lindblom, C. K. (1994). The implications of organizational legitimacy for corporate social performance and disclosure. *In* Critical Perspectives on Accounting Conference, New York.

Luo, Y., Jiang, H., & Zeng, L. (2023). Linking Informative and Factual CSR Communication to Reputation: Understanding CSR Motives and Organizational Identification. *Sustainability (Basel), 15*(6), 5136. DOI: 10.3390/su15065136

Maignan, I., & Ferrell, O. C. (2004). Corporate Social Responsibility and Marketing: An Integrative Framework. *Journal of the Academy of Marketing Science, 32*(1), 3–19. DOI: 10.1177/0092070303258971

McDonough, W., & Braungart, M. (2002). *Cradle to Cradle: Remaking The Way We Make Things*. Vintage.

McWilliams, A., Siegel, S. D., & Wright, P. M. (2006). Corporate Social Responsibility: Strategic Implications. *Journal of Management Studies, 43*(1), 1–18. DOI: 10.1111/j.1467-6486.2006.00580.x

Mitchell, R. K., Agle, B. R., & Wood, D. J. (1997). Toward a Theory of Stakeholder Identification and Salience: Defining the Principle of Who and What Really Counts. *Academy of Management Review, 22*(4), 853–886. DOI: 10.2307/259247

Morsing, M., & Schultz, M. (2006). Corporate Social Responsibility Communication: Stakeholder Information, Response and Involvement Strategies. *Business Ethics (Oxford, England), 15*(4), 323–338. DOI: 10.1111/j.1467-8608.2006.00460.x

Morsing, M., Schultz, M., & Nielsen, K. U. (2008). The 'Catch 22' of communicating CSR: Findings from a Danish study. *Journal of Marketing Communications, 14*(2), 97–111. DOI: 10.1080/13527260701856608

Podnar, K. (2008). Communicating Corporate Social Responsibility. *Journal of Marketing Communications, 14*(2), 75–81. DOI: 10.1080/13527260701856350

Resourcify, (2023, February 16). Find value in your waste: Circularity Benefits in Business. https://www.resourcify.com/blog/circular-economy-benefits-business#:~:text=The%20circular%20economy%20action%20plan,for%20as%20long%20as%20possible

Safdie, S. (2024, March 28). Circular Economy: Definition and Principles. https://greenly.earth/en-us/blog/company-guide/circular-economy-definition-and-principles

Stahel, W. R. (2016). The circular economy. *Nature, 531*(7595), 435–438. DOI: 10.1038/531435a PMID: 27008952

Sweeney, L., & Coughlan, J. (2008). Do Different Industries Report Corporate Social Responsibility Differently? An Investigation Through the Lens of Stakeholder Theory. *Journal of Marketing Communications*, *14*(2), 113–124. DOI: 10.1080/13527260701856657

Whysall, P. (2005). Retailers' Press Release Activity: Market Signals for Stakeholder Engagement? *European Journal of Marketing*, *39*(9/10), 1118–1131. DOI: 10.1108/03090560510610752

Chapter 5
Innovative Policy Making for Circular Economy: A Political Economy Perspective

Ali Eren Balıkel
https://orcid.org/0009-0007-4743-0867
İstanbul Kent Üniversitesi, Turkey

ABSTRACT

This theoretical study examines the transition to a circular economy (CE) through the lens of political economy, emphasizing that circularity is not merely a technical or managerial challenge, but a fundamentally political and institutional transformation. Drawing on classical and contemporary political economy frameworks including Sector Governance Analysis, Power Analysis, Drivers of Change, and the CAR and CEL models, the study explores how power asymmetries, vested interests, institutional path dependencies, and ideological narratives shape the design and implementation of CE policies. By analysing how governance quality, stakeholder dynamics, and socio-political contexts influence reform feasibility, the research highlights the limitations of conventional economic models that ignore the politics of change. Instead, it argues for an integrated and anticipatory approach to CE policy-making, one that addresses not only the "what" but also the "how" of transition.

INTRODUCTION

The transition to a circular economy (CE), an economic system aimed at eliminating waste and continually reusing resources, is increasingly recognized as a necessary paradigm shift for sustainable development. Governments, businesses, and communities worldwide have embraced CE principles in pursuit of "closing

DOI: 10.4018/979-8-3373-3852-1.ch005

the loop" on resource flows, yet meaningful progress remains slow and uneven. A growing body of research suggests that conventional economic and policy models are ill-equipped to enable a full CE transition (Keblowski et al., 2020; Kirchherr et al., 2017). These traditional approaches often assume that technological innovation and market adjustments alone will drive circularity, neglecting the complex social, political, and institutional dynamics that fundamentally shape economic outcomes. In other words, the CE challenge is not purely technical or managerial, it is deeply political.

This study argues that a political economy perspective is essential for innovative CE policy making. "Political economy" refers to an analytical lens that examines how political forces, power relations, and institutional contexts affect economic processes and policy outcomes (Serrat, 2017). In the context of CE, a political economy approach asks critical questions: Who stands to gain or lose from circular transitions? Which interest groups support or resist CE policies, and why? How do existing institutions, governance structures, and path dependencies facilitate or hinder the shift from a linear "take-make-waste" model to a circular one? Such questions go beyond the scope of conventional environmental economics and management frameworks, illuminating the power asymmetries, stakeholder interests, and institutional constraints that must be addressed for CE initiatives to succeed.

Notably, insights from political economy complement those from management and organization studies. Scholars in management and organizational science have examined how firms innovate with circular business models and how organizational change toward sustainability can be led from within. However, these analyses often abstract away from the broader political and institutional environment, treating policy and market conditions as exogenous. By integrating the political economy lens, the micro-level focus of management studies is combined with the macro-level forces that determine what organizations can achieve. This intersection highlights that even the most well-intentioned corporate circular initiatives will falter if the "rules of the game", shaped by policies, regulations, and power relations, remain aligned with the linear economy. Thus, a key premise of this study is that effective CE policy innovation requires an understanding of why existing systems are locked into unsustainable patterns and how to redesign governance to overcome those lock-ins, drawing on political economy frameworks developed by thinkers such as Karl Polanyi and contemporary development scholars (e.g. Serrat, Unsworth, etc.).

In the following pages, this study first outlines the limitations of conventional economic and policy models in catalyzing CE transitions. It then introduces key concepts from political economy, highlighting work on sector governance, drivers of change, power analysis and related frameworks, and provides a conceptual foundation for analyzing CE policy. The core of the study provides a thorough conceptual analysis of how political economy methods can be adapted to CE governance.

A range of analytical frameworks (e.g., Sector Governance Analysis, Drivers of Change, Power Analysis, etc.) is discussed, illustrating how each framework can illuminate different facets of the circular transition, including power dynamics, stakeholder incentives, institutional path dependency, and knowledge flows. Throughout the discussion, the emphasis remains theoretical and conceptual rather than empirical, although occasional examples or hypothetical scenarios are used for illustrative purposes. In conclusion, study summarized the conceptual contributions of a political economy perspective to CE policy innovation and reflected on how integrating political economy with insights from management and organization studies can yield more effective and enduring sustainability strategies. The overarching aim is to demonstrate that innovative policy making for the CE must explicitly account for politics, power, and institutions, not as obstacles to be bypassed, but as structural realities to be understood and strategically leveraged for transformational change.

THE CIRCULAR ECONOMY TRANSITION AND ITS CHALLENGES

The CE has emerged as a visionary framework to address the failures of the traditional linear economic model, which is characterized by resource extraction, one-time use, and disposal. In a CE, in contrast, materials and products are kept in use for as long as possible through strategies like reuse, repair, remanufacturing, and recycling, thereby reducing both resource input and waste output. The promise of CE lies in its potential to achieve a triple dividend: environmental sustainability (through lower resource depletion and pollution), economic benefits (through new business opportunities and efficiency gains), and social gains (through job creation in repair, recycling, and remanufacturing sectors) (Becque et al., 2016).

Over the past decade, this promise has spurred numerous policy initiatives, from the European Union's Circular Economy Action Plans to China's Circular Economy Promotion Law, aimed at accelerating the transition. At the same time, major companies and cities have announced CE strategies, and the concept has been "hyped" in sustainability discourse as a win-win solution for growth and the environment (Kirchherr et al., 2017).

However, moving from concept to reality has proven daunting. Early experiences reveal that technical solutions and piecemeal policies alone are insufficient to overcome ingrained linear practices. Many CE pilot projects remain small-scale or short-lived, and overall global resource use and waste generation continue to rise.

A fundamental challenge is that transitioning to circularity entails systemic change, reconfiguring production and consumption systems, supply chains, business models, and consumer behaviors, which disrupt established interests and routines.

This systemic nature means that straightforward policy fixes (such as recycling targets or landfill bans) often encounter structural barriers and pushback that are not immediately apparent in engineering or economic analyses. As one study of CE barriers in the EU found, the most significant obstacles were not technological but cultural and institutional: for example, low consumer awareness, entrenched business habits favoring linear models, and misaligned incentives like cheap virgin materials and subsidies for resource extraction (Kirchherr et al., 2017). These findings underscore that the transition is as much about changing mindsets, power structures, and rules of the game as it is about new technologies or business models.

A key limitation of conventional policy approaches is their tendency to treat the CE transition as a primarily technical or economic optimization problem. Traditional environmental policy, grounded in neoclassical economics, often focuses on correcting market failures (e.g. through pricing carbon or taxing waste) and assumes that once the "right" price signals or regulations are in place, markets will efficiently innovate toward circular solutions. While market-based instruments and regulations are indeed important, this technocratic approach overlooks the deep political nature of market transformations. Policies that impose costs on certain industries (for instance, mandating the phasing out of single-use plastics or requiring producers to take back products at end-of-life) will inevitably create winners and losers, provoking political contestation (Becque et al., 2016). Incumbent firms that profit from the linear status quo, such as fossil fuel companies (for plastics production), mining interests, or manufacturers built on planned obsolescence, may perceive CE measures as threats to their market share and will mobilize to resist change. For example, the transition to a CE in plastics "creates winners and losers" and thus "is politically contested", as noted by Becque et al. (2016). Conventional models, which assume frictionless policy implementation, fail to account for how such opposition can dilute, delay, or derail CE initiatives. Indeed, stakeholder resistance and power struggles have already manifested in real-world CE policy debates, from the EU's circular economy package encountering industry lobbying, to local recycling reforms facing public skepticism.

Another shortcoming of traditional approaches is the neglect of institutional and path-dependent constraints (Poole, 2011). Economists often model policy interventions as if they operate on a blank slate, but in reality policies must contend with existing institutions and infrastructures that were designed for the linear economy (Strange, 1970). Decades of investments in landfills, waste incinerators, fossil-fuel based energy systems, and global supply chains optimized for disposable products have created a strong path dependency, a form of systemic inertia that perpetuates linear practices (Sustainability Directory, 2025).Once a city has sunk costs into a large incinerator, for instance, there is a financial incentive to keep it operating at high capacity (and thus keep feeding it waste) for decades, undermining recycling efforts. Likewise, if tax revenues or jobs in a region depend heavily on virgin resource extraction (oil, minerals, timber), there will be political and social resistance to policies that might curtail those activities. These policies and infrastructural lock-ins are often invisible to standard cost-benefit analyses yet pose significant obstacles to circular transitions. Overcoming them may require transformative public investments and governance innovations, for example, redirecting subsidies from virgin to recycled materials, re-training workers for circular jobs, or redesigning waste management contracts, actions that are fundamentally political in nature (Haider & Rao, 2010).

Finally, conventional models typically assume a unitary policymaker acting in the public interest, whereas in practice policy design and implementation are influenced by power asymmetries and governance quality (Fritz, Kaiser, & Levy, 2009). In some cases, regulatory agencies may be "captured" or unduly influenced by powerful industry lobbies, resulting in weak enforcement of CE-related rules or loopholes that favor incumbents. In other cases, government officials might genuinely champion CE reforms but face constraints from bureaucratic silos, limited state capacity, or competing policy priorities. For instance, an environment ministry promoting circular policies might clash with an industry ministry focused on short-term economic growth, reflecting an internal power tussle. Additionally, differing levels of government (local, national, supranational) might have misaligned agendas. A city trying to ban certain disposables might be stymied by national legislation, or vice versa. Conventional analyses that ignore these multi-level governance dynamics may overestimate the efficacy of isolated policy tools. In sum, a purely economic or technocratic lens offers an incomplete picture of the CE transition, often leading to optimistic assumptions that "good policies" will naturally prevail. The sobering reality is that CE policies operate within a contested political arena, shaped by vested interests, institutional inertia, and public sentiment.

THE NEED FOR A POLITICAL ECONOMY LENS

Given the above challenges, there is a clear need to reimagine CE policy making through a political economy lens (Edelmann, 2009). Political economy, in its classical sense, is the study of the interplay between economic and political forces in society. It recognizes that economic outcomes, such as who benefits from a policy or how resources are allocated, are not determined solely by market efficiency or technological feasibility, but also by power relations, institutional contexts, and ideological narratives. As Serrat (2017) succinctly defines, political economy analysis investigates "the interaction of political and economic processes in a society" by understanding three key dimensions: (1) the distribution of power and authority among groups and the interests and incentives that drive their actions, (2) the role of formal and informal institutions (laws, norms, organizations) in governing resource allocation, and (3) the influence of values and ideas (culture, ideologies, belief systems) on shaping human behavior and policy choices (Serrat, 2017). Adopting this lens in the context of CE means examining how these factors (power, institutions, and ideas) condition the prospects for circular transition. It moves the analysis from asking "What technical solution would maximize recycling?" to also asking "Why are existing systems linear to begin with? Who might oppose or support a shift to circularity, and how can their incentives be realigned? What institutional reforms are necessary to embed circular principles into the economy?".

The value of a political economy perspective becomes evident when one considers the historical relationship between markets and governments. The work of economic historian Karl Polanyi is particularly illuminating. Polanyi (2001) argued that the attempt to disembed the economy from society (treating the market as an autonomous, self-regulating sphere separate from political and social control) was both a utopian vision and a source of deep social dislocation. Polanyi (2001) observed that markets are always, to some degree, creations of the state and society, and that markets and governments are not adversaries but part of a combined whole. He noted that the notion of a pure free market, separate from politics, was an idealized construct that ultimately proved flawed, culminating in severe crises such as the Great Depression. According to Polanyi (2001), legislative and policy-making institutions play a foundational role in shaping market dynamics through instruments such as legal frameworks, property rights, and monetary policy. Conversely, economic actors, including firms and investors, actively seek to influence political decision-making through lobbying and strategic engagement. This reciprocal relationship underscores the inseparability of economic transformation from political processes. When this perspective is applied to the transition toward a CE, it becomes evident that the shift cannot be expected to occur solely on the basis of economic rationality or environmental necessity. Rather, it demands intentional political intervention aimed at re-embedding economic activity within institutional structures and normative frameworks that foreground sustainability as a core principle (DFID, 2009). Just as laissez-faire markets did not spontaneously curb their own excesses without social "counter-movements", a fully CE likely requires a powerful societal push (and new institutional arrangements) to constrain the linear throwaway culture and institutionalize circular practices. In Polanyian terms, one might view today's sustainability initiatives (like CE) as part of a "double movement", a societal response aimed at protecting humans and nature from the ravages of an unrestrained linear industrial system (Keblowski et al., 2020).

Another way political economy enriches one's understanding is by highlighting the importance of historical legacies and path dependence. As Polanyi (2001) notes, land (nature) and labor were treated as "fictitious commodities" in the rise of industrial capitalism, meaning they were subjected to market mechanisms despite being fundamentally social and natural entities not produced for sale (Polanyi, 2001). The environmental degradation currently observed, such as overflowing landfills, ocean plastic pollution, and resource scarcity, can be understood, in part, as a consequence of the historically dominant market ideology, which systematically externalized ecological costs. A political economy perspective prompts a critical examination of the institutional transformations necessary to shift prevailing paradigms, moving away from the treatment of nature as an inexhaustible commodity toward its recognition as a finite and vulnerable system requiring active stewardship (Collinson, 2003). From this standpoint, incremental policy measures, such as modest taxation schemes or voluntary corporate commitments, are unlikely to generate the scale of change required. Instead, more profound structural reforms may be needed, including the redefinition of property rights (e.g., through extended producer responsibility mechanisms), the restructuring of environmentally harmful subsidies, or the establishment of legal frameworks that formally acknowledge ecological boundaries. Such systemic interventions inherently involve navigating complex political trade-offs and entrenched power relations, thereby reinforcing the limitations of purely technocratic approaches in addressing environmental challenges of this magnitude.

Crucially, a political economy perspective provides tools to analyze and manage the power asymmetries and conflicts inherent in CE transitions (Bjuremalm, 2006). Rather than assuming harmonious implementation, it starts by mapping out the stakeholders of a given policy, identifying which groups have a stake in maintaining the linear status quo and which could champion change. For instance, if a government aims to implement a circular policy like banning certain single-use plastics, a PEA (political economy analysis) would investigate the positions and power of the plastics industry, alternative material producers, consumer organizations, environmental NGOs, and end-users. It would ask how the policy's costs and benefits are distributed and how those distributions translate into political support or opposition. By doing so, it provides foresight into potential resistance and alliances. As one practical guide suggests, advocates should "assess what the real or perceived impacts on key stakeholder groups could be and their power to rally in favor of or resist the change" (Becque et al., 2016). This kind of analysis enables policymakers to craft strategies to preempt or mitigate resistance, for example, by compensating losers, building coalitions of winners, sequencing reforms, or reframing the narrative to appeal to broader values (The World Bank, 2012).

In summary, embracing a political economy lens means recognizing that CE transitions are not automatic or apolitical, but rather negotiated processes that unfold within existing power structures and institutional frameworks. It means shifting from asking "What is the optimal policy?" to also asking "What is politically feasible, and how can feasibility be expanded by altering incentive structures and power relations?". The next section introduces specific frameworks and tools from the political economy field that can be applied to analyze and guide CE policy-making.

POLITICAL ECONOMY FRAMEWORKS FOR CIRCULAR ECONOMY POLICY DESIGN

A range of political economy analytical frameworks has been developed within the fields of development studies and governance to explain the conditions under which reforms succeed or fail (Underhill, 2000). This section examines several of these frameworks and explores how each can be adapted to the specific context of CE policy-making.

The frameworks considered include Poverty and Social Impact Analysis (PSIA), the World Bank's Political Economy of Policy Reform approach, the Sector Governance Analysis Framework, Drivers of Change analysis (originally developed by the UK's Department for International Development), Power Analysis (as employed by the Swedish International Development Agency, Sida), the Capability, Accountability, Responsiveness (CAR) framework, and the Context, Evidence, Links (CEL) framework from the Overseas Development Institute.

Each framework offers a distinct analytical entry point, ranging from distributional impacts and institutional dynamics to stakeholder incentives, but together, they constitute a comprehensive toolbox for interpreting and navigating the political economy dimensions of CE transitions (Serrat, 2011). Although these tools were not originally designed with CE objectives in mind, their conceptual application demonstrates clear relevance. By utilizing such frameworks, policymakers can better identify points of resistance and leverage within the system, thereby enabling the formulation of more innovative, adaptive, and resilient CE policies.

Poverty and Social Impact Analysis (PSIA)

Poverty and Social Impact Analysis (PSIA) is an approach developed and frequently used by the World Bank (and other development agencies) to evaluate the distributional effects of policy reforms on different social groups. In essence, PSIA asks: who are the winners and losers of a given policy change, especially among the poor and vulnerable? According to World Bank guidance (World Bank, 2012), PSIA provides a "systematic and rigorous analysis of the impact of policy reforms on the welfare of different stakeholder groups, particularly the poor and marginalized". It typically combines economic analysis (such as modeling how a subsidy removal affects household expenditures) with stakeholder analysis (identifying which groups benefit or are harmed). The goal is twofold: to inform the design of policies so that adverse impacts can be mitigated (or positive impacts enhanced), and to anticipate political economy issues by understanding who might oppose or support the reform based on its distributional outcomes. In the context of a CE transition, PSIA is highly pertinent because many CE policies have uneven impacts across society.

For example, consider a policy initiative to impose landfill taxes and encourage recycling. A PSIA of this reform would examine effects such as: Will low-income households face higher waste collection fees, and can they afford them? Will certain worker groups (e.g. employees in the landfill or incineration industry) face job losses, and are there alternative employment opportunities or retraining programs for them? Conversely, which industries stand to gain (e.g. recycling companies, manufacturers of recycling equipment) and are they hiring locally? By answering these questions, a PSIA can guide policymakers to incorporate just transition measures, ensuring that the shift to circularity does not exacerbate social inequalities or provoke backlash from communities who feel unfairly burdened. For instance, if analysis shows that a landfill tax would hit poorer households hardest, the policy could be paired with offsetting measures (like targeted rebates or improved recycling services in low-income neighborhoods) to maintain equity and public support. Additionally, PSIA highlights potential points of resistance, if a policy significantly harms a particular interest group's income, that group is likely to mobilize against it. Knowing this in advance, authorities can engage in dialogue with the group, adjust the policy design, or prepare compensation schemes. In summary, PSIA brings a social equity and political feasibility lens to CE policies by rigorously mapping out their welfare impacts and the likely responses of affected stakeholders. This aligns with the political economy emphasis on understanding incentives: those "benefited from and damaged by the change" can be identified and their concerns addressed to reduce conflict.

Political Economy of Policy Reform

The World Bank's Political Economy of Policy Reform approach is another analytical framework that can be instructive for CE transitions. This approach, detailed in various World Bank publications (e.g. World Bank, 2012), provides an "analytical and operational framework to assess and address the context, content, and process of sector policy reforms". In practice, it means looking at a proposed reform through multiple lenses: the structural context (economic and institutional conditions in that sector), the interests and stakeholder positions, the reform process (how the policy is formulated and implemented), and the actual outcomes and feedback. What sets this framework apart is its emphasis on being both analytical (diagnosing problems) and actionable, it aims to generate insights that directly inform how to manage the reform process.

For example, an analysis might reveal that a water sector reform failed in the past due to opposition from a certain lobby and lack of public communication. With that knowledge, the new reform design can include a robust outreach campaign and negotiation with that lobby (Harris, Kooy, & Jones, 2011).

Applying this to circular economy, imagine a government is attempting a major reform like a "circular economy package" that introduces multiple policy measures across waste, product design, and consumer behavior (similar to the EU's CE packages). A Political Economy of Reform analysis would start by examining the sectoral context: How is the waste management sector currently structured? Who are the dominant players (public or private)? Are there entrenched contracts or corruption issues? It would also assess the broader macro-economic context: Is the country in an economic downturn or boom (which affects willingness to adopt environmental regulations)? Next, it identifies stakeholders and drivers: the businesses affected (manufacturers, retailers, waste handlers), government agencies (environment ministry, industrial ministry, local governments), civil society (environmental groups, consumer associations), and maps their interests, who stands to gain or lose from the CE reform. Importantly, it would analyze the power resources of each stakeholder: for instance, do waste management firms have strong political connections? Do consumer groups have broad public support?

The framework also examines the process of reform formulation: Is it being done transparently, with stakeholder consultation, or behind closed doors? Experience shows that inclusive processes can sometimes disarm opposition by giving stakeholders a voice, whereas top-down approaches might trigger greater resistance. The World Bank approach encourages thinking about "winners and losers" of reform in dynamic terms: not just identifying them, but devising strategies to bolster the winners' influence and mitigate the losers' opposition (Becque et al., 2016). For example, if analysis finds that small and medium enterprises (SMEs) worry about compliance costs for new circular standards, the reform could include subsidies or technical assistance for SMEs, turning a potential opponent into at least a neutral party, if not an ally. Additionally, this approach values lesson-learning from case studies and empirical evidence. In CE terms, that could mean studying similar reforms in other jurisdictions (e.g. how did another country successfully implement an extended producer responsibility scheme for electronics, and what political challenges did they overcome?). By grounding the reform in both local context and cross-case evidence, the policy design becomes more robust.

In essence, the Political Economy of Policy Reform framework helps policymakers to "think politically" about CE reforms: plan not only the content (the what of the policy) but also the politics of how to get it adopted and implemented (Castles et al., 2011). It stresses that good technical policy is not enough. One must also navigate the "terrain" of interests and institutions. For example, one output of such an analysis might be an explicit stakeholder engagement strategy: identify champions (like progressive businesses or local leaders who support circular practices) and empower them to advocate for the reform, while concurrently devising responses to anticipated opposition (like phasing the policy to give industries time to adjust, or offering side-payments such as transition aid). By doing so, the reform's chances of success increase. In summary, this framework is about moving from a naive "announce and hope" strategy to a strategic, politically savvy implementation plan for CE policies, which is a hallmark of innovative policy making (Castles et al., 2011).

Sector Governance Analysis Framework

The Sector Governance Analysis Framework, as used for example by the European Commission (Unsworth & Williams, 2011), is a tool specifically geared towards understanding the governance and power dynamics within a given sector of the economy. It "systematically investigates the main power and political factors at the sector level, especially how power and politics affect the functioning and outcomes of the sector". Essentially, it's about doing a deep dive into a particular sector (like energy, waste management, agriculture, etc.) to see how decisions are made, who holds influence, and why certain policies might be working or failing in that sector. The framework typically combines political science and institutional analysis: it looks at formal institutions (like the sector's regulatory agencies, laws, and policies), informal norms (like networks, patronage relationships, or industry culture), key actors (public agencies, private companies, interest groups, users), and accountability relationships (who is accountable to whom, and where are the gaps). Unsworth and Williams (2011) note that a strength of this framework is having a solid theoretical basis coupled with practical "operational propositions," meaning it offers concrete hypotheses or entry points for reform based on the analysis. For CE, this framework is invaluable because many CE initiatives are inherently sector-specific. For example, making the construction industry circular (through material reuse and modular design) is a very different challenge from making the food system circular (through composting, waste reduction, etc.) or the fashion/textile industry circular (through recycling fabrics, extended producer responsibility for clothing).

Each sector has its own structure of interests and governance. By conducting a Sector Governance Analysis for a priority sector, policymakers can identify what specific political economy factors are enabling or obstructing circular practices in that domain. This can be illustrated with the waste management sector, which is central to CE. A sector governance analysis of waste might reveal, for instance, that in a given country, waste services are handled by a few large private contractors who have long-term contracts and cozy relationships with municipal authorities (a power concentration that might resist disruptive change like zero-waste goals) or perhaps the analysis finds that the informal sector (waste pickers, recyclers) actually handles a significant portion of recycling but lacks legal recognition, leading to a governance gap. Or that there is a fragmentation of authority (with responsibilities split between city councils, environment ministries, and public health departments), causing incoherent policies. These findings point to very different policy interventions. In one case, perhaps tightening procurement and transparency in contracting to break undue corporate influence. In another, integrating informal recyclers into the formal system (as partners or employees) to improve outcomes and equity. In the third, creating a coordinating body or clarifying mandates to align the governance framework.

Moreover, sector analysis will consider how political incentives align with sector outcomes. For example, if a local government's revenue is partly tied to landfill fees or if it politically gains from providing jobs in waste collection, it may have an incentive to favor linear waste disposal over circular recycling. It is an insight that would not surface without looking at the governance of the sector. By mapping out such incentives and relationships, a Sector Governance Analysis highlights where leverage points for change are. It may uncover reform "champions" too: e.g., a progressive city mayor who has made zero-waste a political platform, indicating an opportunity to support and replicate that leadership elsewhere.

In summary, the Sector Governance Analysis Framework brings to light the sector-specific institutional constraints and power relations affecting CE policies. It reminds that "one size fits all" policy solutions often fail because each sector might require a tailored approach. A CE policy that succeeds in the energy sector (like feed-in tariffs for renewable energy and material circularity) might flop in the agriculture sector if it does not account for rural power structures or land tenure issues.

Therefore, using this framework, policymakers can design sector-tailored circular economy interventions that address the unique governance challenges, whether that's adjusting power imbalances, improving accountability, or introducing new institutional mechanisms, in that sector. This targeted approach increases the likelihood that circular policies will actually take root in each domain of the economy.

Drivers of Change Analysis

The Drivers of Change (DoC) approach, originally developed by the UK's Department for International Development (DFID) in the early 2000s, is a broad political economy tool used to analyze country-level political and institutional dynamics. It seeks to understand the fundamental "drivers" that shape a country's development trajectory, including its governance environment and capacity for reform. According to DFID's usage (Poulton, 2012), a Drivers of Change analysis looks at the interrelationships between structural features (such as the country's historical legacies, social and economic structure, class, ethnicity, natural resource endowments), institutions (formal rules like constitutions and laws, and informal norms and power structures), and agents (key actors or groups such as political leaders, private sector, civil society, donors). The goal is to identify deep-seated factors that enable or constrain change. In DFID's context, DoC was often used to inform development assistance strategies by revealing, for instance, why certain reforms might be blocked by elite interests or how social trends (like urbanization or education expansion) could open a window for change. It's essentially a diagnostic of the political-economic system at large, highlighting points of entry for reformers (Serrat, 2017).

Translating Drivers of Change analysis to the CE agenda means stepping back to look at a country or region's overarching political economy and asking what are the underlying factors that could drive or impede a transition to circularity? This is important because while individual policies and sector efforts matter, the success of a CE transition also depends on macro-level conditions, such as political will, governance capacity, societal values, and economic structure. For example, a Drivers of Change (DoC) analysis might examine whether a country's economic structure is heavily reliant on linear activities such as mining or oil extraction. In such cases, this structural dependence on resource rents may pose a significant barrier to the adoption of circular economy models, as both powerful economic interests and substantial government revenues are closely linked to extractive industries (Becque et al., 2016).

It would also examine historical legacies: perhaps past attempts at environmental reform failed due to corruption, leading to public distrust, which must be addressed if new CE policies are to gain legitimacy. Or it might note that a country has a legacy of strong state planning (as in some East Asian or European contexts), which could be a driver enabling ambitious coordinated CE strategies, as opposed to more laissez-faire contexts where the state is reluctant to intervene in markets (Harris, Kooy, & Jones, 2011).

Institutional factors in DoC would include the overall quality of governance, for instance, rule of law and regulatory effectiveness. If environmental regulations are generally not enforced due to weak rule of law, that signals that simply enacting CE policies on paper will not suffice, and attention must be paid to enforcement mechanisms and capacity building. Informal institutions are equally critical. Is there a culture of consumerism and disposability that's deeply ingrained (a cultural norm that might resist circular values of reuse and repair)? Or conversely, perhaps cultural traditions of thrift and repair exist in the society (as is the case in some communities) which could be positive drivers for circular practices if tapped into (Kirchherr et al., 2017).

The "agents" dimension of a Drivers of Change (DoC) analysis entails a broad mapping of key stakeholders relevant to environmental sustainability within the national context. This includes identifying principal advocates for sustainability in the political sphere, such as the presence and influence of green parties, environmental non-governmental organizations (NGOs), and youth-led climate movements. It also involves examining the position of the business sector, whether prominent business leaders are actively promoting circular innovations or whether industry actors predominantly exhibit resistance, adhering to entrenched linear economic models. Furthermore, the analysis considers public attitudes, assessing the extent to which there is societal awareness of and demand for circular economy solutions, or conversely, a prevailing sense of indifference. By delineating the coalitions that support or oppose transformative change and assessing their relative power and influence, a DoC analysis provides a structured understanding of the political and institutional landscape within which circular economy policy initiatives are likely to unfold. For instance, a Drivers of Change analysis in a country might reveal that "economic diversification away from oil" is a stated government priority due to declining oil revenues (a structural driver), which could align well with promoting a circular economy as a new economic paradigm, thus creating a political opening.

At the same time, it might reveal that the "patronage networks in politics" rely on revenues from state-owned extractive industries (an institutional/agent factor), meaning those networks could obstruct policies that threaten the extractive sector. Recognizing this, CE advocates might strategically frame circular economy initiatives as complementing, not substituting, certain industries (at least in the short term) or ensure that influential political patrons are brought on board by demonstrating how they can benefit from CE investments (Keblowski et al., 2020).

Overall, Drivers of Change provides a big-picture view. When applied to CE, it encourages reformers to align their strategies with the grain of positive drivers (like demographic change, public opinion shifts, international commitments) and to devise ways to work around or gradually transform the negative ones (like elite resistance or institutional voids). It answers the "why" question ("Why is the economy stuck in a linear mode? What fundamental changes might shift it?") which is crucial for devising long-term strategies for systemic transition. By understanding the deep drivers, policy makers can be more realistic and strategic about the pace and sequencing of CE reforms: for example, focusing first on areas where there is latent support or less resistance, building momentum, and then tackling the tougher structural barriers as conditions become more favorable (Poole, 2011).

Power Analysis

Power Analysis (as developed in particular by Sida, the Swedish aid agency) is a methodology explicitly focused on mapping out power relations in a society, understanding who holds power, in what forms, and how that power is exercised to influence outcomes. Sida's Power Analysis, as described by Mcloughlin (2012), looks at both visible power (formal decision-making authority, like government positions, laws, official budgets) and behind-the-scenes power (informal influence, vested interests, clientelism, control of information or narratives). It often pays attention to how power dynamics affect poverty reduction and marginalized groups, given Sida's mandate, examining issues of voice, accountability, and responsiveness. The key premise is that unequal power distribution often lies at the heart of governance failures and to promote change (like pro-poor or sustainable policies), one must confront or alter these power dynamics.

A power analysis will identify the actors or groups with the greatest power (e.g. political elites, oligarchs, corporations, military, etc. depending on context) and evaluate how their interests align or conflict with the reform in question. It also considers the "space" for less powerful voices, for instance, are civil society and communities able to organize and influence policy, or are they excluded?

In applying Power Analysis to the circular economy transition, the focus would be on unveiling the power asymmetries that shape environmental and economic policy. CE often challenges established industries and practices, so it is crucial to know which actors have the power to either block or propel such changes. For example, an analysis of the global plastics economy through the lens of power analysis may reveal that a small number of dominant petrochemical firms and multinational consumer goods corporations exert disproportionate influence over plastics-related policy processes (Kirchherr et al., 2017). This influence is often exercised through mechanisms such as lobbying activities, political campaign financing, and the strategic shaping of public discourse, particularly by promoting narratives that emphasize individual responsibility and recycling, thereby deflecting attention from systemic regulatory reform. These incumbents might strategically promote certain solutions (like recycling or anti-litter campaigns) while resisting others (like plastic production caps or bans) to preserve their business model (Auty, 2024). In light of such dynamics, proponents of CE policies may need to recalibrate their strategies by fostering broader coalitions capable of counterbalancing the influence of entrenched corporate interests. Alternatively, they might pursue policy designs that align incentives in a way that encourages cooperation from powerful actors, for example, through public-private partnerships aimed at developing recycling infrastructure, thereby transforming potential opponents into active stakeholders in the transition (Keblowski et al., 2020).

Power Analysis also sheds light on why certain unsustainable policies persist, often, it is because they benefit powerful groups. For instance, consider fossil fuel subsidies or mining concessions that lead to wasteful resource use: these may persist not because they are economically rational (they are often not), but because politically influential actors (a fuel lobby or mining tycoons) profit from them. Similarly, a city might hesitate to implement waste reduction policies because the private concessionaire managing the local landfill, a politically connected firm, profits from more waste, not less.

By identifying such power-driven conflicts of interest, one can better target policy interventions. In some cases, it might mean confronting that power (e.g. through anti-corruption efforts, transparency, mobilizing public opinion against a harmful practice), while in others it might mean co-opting or negotiating with power (e.g. offering incumbent firms new business opportunities in the circular model so they feel invested in change rather than threatened) (Keblowski et al., 2020).

An important aspect of power analysis is also to highlight the voices that are not being heard in the current system. For the circular economy, this might include future generations (who obviously have no voice, but whose interests in sustainability are at stake), informal workers (like waste pickers who might lack formal representation in policy dialogues), or local communities affected by linear economy externalities (such as communities near landfills, incinerators, or mines). These groups often have limited power to influence decisions that nonetheless deeply affect them (Becque et al., 2016). Power Analysis would encourage policy designers to incorporate mechanisms for these less powerful stakeholders to be heard, for instance, community consultations, participatory decision-making forums, or protections to ensure vulnerable groups benefit from CE policies (e.g. including informal recyclers in formal recycling programs rather than displacing them). This aligns with the principle that a transition will be more politically and socially sustainable if it is inclusive and perceived as fair.

Applying Power Analysis to CE means explicitly asking: "Where are the power imbalances in our economic system that keep it linear, and how can a shift to circularity redistribute power or overcome power blocks?". It might reveal that certain powerful narratives need changing too, for example, the pervasive message that continuous consumption equals prosperity is a form of ideological power benefiting linear economy advocates. Changing that narrative (to value sufficiency, longevity of products, etc.) can be part of shifting power towards more sustainable norms. Indeed, Mcloughlin (2012) notes that power analysis has a strong grounding in scholarly literature on authority, voice, and accountability, meaning it is not only about raw power but also about legitimacy and narratives. For CE, promoting new narratives (like the economic opportunities of circular jobs, or the health benefits of less pollution) can help undercut the influence of those clinging to old paradigms.

By revealing both the hard power (money, political clout) and soft power (ideas, public support) at play, power analysis arms CE policymakers with knowledge to craft strategies that are politically astute.

Capability, Accountability, Responsiveness (CAR) Framework

The Capability, Accountability, Responsiveness (CAR) framework is an approach used notably by DFID to assess governance in terms of three critical dimensions of state performance. A well-functioning system, according to this framework, is one where the state has the capability to carry out its responsibilities (i.e., the resources, expertise, and organizational competence to implement policies and deliver services), is accountable to its citizens (through mechanisms like elections, audits, transparency, and democratic oversight that ensure the state answers for its actions), and is responsive to the needs of the public (listening and reacting to citizens' concerns and requirements). In DFID's use, the CAR framework was often linked to the idea that poverty reduction and good development outcomes occur when political leaders and institutions are capable, accountable, and responsive to their people's needs. It is a diagnostic that can highlight, for example, that a government might be capable but not accountable (leading to technocratic but potentially unjust policies), or accountable in form but not truly responsive (due to elite capture of the political process, so the state responds only to certain interests). Applying the CAR lens to circular economy governance provides a structured way to evaluate whether the institutional environment is conducive to designing and implementing CE policies effectively. Each component in the CE context are:

- **Capability:** Do the relevant institutions (ministries, environmental agencies, local governments, etc.) have the technical know-how, financial resources, and organizational capacity to implement circular economy initiatives? For instance, shifting to a CE might require new skills in life-cycle analysis, new infrastructure for waste collection and sorting, or better data systems to track materials. If a government lacks these capabilities, even well-intended policies may flounder in execution. Identifying capability gaps can lead to recommendations like investing in capacity building, training programs for civil servants on CE concepts, or establishing dedicated units (e.g., a Circular Economy task force or innovation lab) with the expertise to pilot and coordinate circular projects.
- **Accountability:** Are policymakers held accountable for environmental and sustainability outcomes, or only for short-term economic metrics? Often, political accountability (through elections or public scrutiny) skews toward

things like jobs, prices, and immediate visible issues, whereas long-term environmental stewardship can be under-prioritized.

However, if there is robust accountability (e.g. active media and civil society monitoring of government's environmental promises, legal requirements to report progress on waste reduction, or even constitutional environmental rights that citizens can use in court) then officials have stronger incentives to follow through on CE commitments. A CAR analysis might find, for example, that while a country has published a shiny circular economy strategy, there are no clear accountability mechanisms (no regular progress reports, no independent body evaluating results, no budget transparency on green spending). The recommendation could then be to strengthen accountability by, e.g. setting up a parliamentary committee on circular economy oversight, involving independent watchdog NGOs in monitoring progress, or integrating CE targets into the performance evaluation of public agencies. Accountability also ties to fighting corruption. If vested interests can bribe their way out of regulations (like illegal dumping or circumventing recycling mandates), that undermines CE. So anti-corruption measures and transparency in sectors like waste management become relevant, these ensure that policies enacted on paper actually translate into action (Serrat, 2017).

- **Responsiveness:** This pertains to whether the policy process actively responds to citizen needs and feedback. In the context of CE, responsiveness could mean engaging the public and businesses in consultations about new CE regulations (so that policies address real obstacles people face and get buy-in), or it could mean flexibility, adjusting policies if they are not working on the ground. For example, if a city imposes a strict recycling separation regime but residents struggle to comply because of practical issues (like lack of space in small apartments for multiple bins), a responsive approach would detect this issue through citizen feedback and adapt the policy (maybe by investing in better public sorting facilities or adjusting collection frequency). A non-responsive system might just lament poor compliance and penalize citizens, breeding resentment. Responsiveness also means proactively identifying what citizens might need to embrace circular practices, such as educating and raising awareness or ensuring that circular options (like repair services or refill stations) are accessible and convenient. A CAR assessment might reveal that a government's environmental agency possesses considerable technical expertise and operates in an insulated, expert-driven manner, indicating a high level of capability. However, limited public engagement may result in policies that fail to gain societal traction, highlighting the need for more participatory mechanisms, strategic communication efforts, and institutionalized feedback loops (Keblowski et al., 2020).

The CAR framework applied to CE governance ensures that examine the institutional quality and public-sector dynamics behind the lofty goals. A country could have ambitious CE targets on paper, but if the civil service is under-resourced (low capability), if powerful polluters can evade rules with impunity (weak accountability), or if policies are designed without consulting those affected (poor responsiveness), the transition will stall. Conversely, improving these dimensions can create an enabling environment where innovative circular policies can flourish. For instance, Serrat (2017) noted in context of CAR that poverty reduction is most effective when political authorities are capable, accountable, and responsive to society. Analogously, circular economy initiatives will be most effective under those same conditions, capable institutions to implement and regulate, accountability to keep them on track and honest, and responsiveness to refine policies in line with societal input. So, CAR provides a checklist for governance reform alongside CE policy reform. It reminds that policies do not implement themselves. The implementation depends on governance capacities and relationships, which themselves might need strengthening as part of the CE transition. Innovative CE policy-making, then, might involve not just new environmental regulations, but also meta-reforms like training judges on environmental law (capability), creating public dashboards of waste and recycling statistics (accountability/transparency), or establishing citizen advisory panels on local circular economy plans (responsiveness and participation).

Context, Evidence, Links (CEL) Framework

The Context, Evidence, Links (CEL) framework, popularized by researchers at the Overseas Development Institute (ODI) (Serrat, 2017), is a tool for understanding how research and evidence inform (or fail to inform) policy-making. It posits that the degree to which evidence (data, studies, analysis) influences policy depends on three broad factors. Context (the political and institutional environment into which the evidence is introduced), Evidence (the credibility, communication, and relevance of the research itself), and Links (the networks and relationships between researchers and policymakers that facilitate knowledge transfer). In simpler terms, even the best evidence-based policy ideas need a conducive context and effective channels of communication to actually impact decisions. This framework is especially useful in areas like environmental policy, where scientific evidence of an issue (e.g. climate change or resource depletion) might be strong, but translating that evidence into policy action is non-trivial.

Applying the CEL framework to the circular economy highlights the importance of knowledge and ideas in driving the transition and why good ideas sometimes do not get adopted due to political economy reasons.

Evidence: Over the past years, numerous studies and pilot projects have demonstrated that circular economy approaches can bring economic benefits, create jobs, and reduce environmental harm. For example, reports by organizations like the Ellen MacArthur Foundation have quantified potential GDP and employment gains from circular strategies. From an evidence standpoint, one might think this makes an irrefutable case for CE policies. However, the CEL perspective asks how this evidence is packaged and perceived. Is the evidence seen as credible and policy-relevant? Are there concrete case studies in the specific national context, or is it all general and theoretical? Often, policy makers are more convinced by localized evidence or by seeing a successful example in a peer country. Also, how evidence is communicated matters. If evidence shows, for instance, that "a CE strategy could create X thousand jobs and save Y amount of resources by 2030", those findings need to be translated into messages that resonate with current political priorities (e.g. "this can help our manufacturing sector become more competitive and create jobs in your constituency"). So, enhancing the salience and communication of CE evidence is part of the task.

Context: The uptake of evidence depends on the political context. Is the government even looking for solutions? Perhaps circular economy is not on their radar because they are preoccupied with other issues, or maybe there's skepticism or ideological opposition to the source of the evidence (for example, a government might distrust studies by international NGOs or see the CE as a foreign agenda). The political context includes factors like timing (evidence presented at a moment of crisis or change can have more impact), ideology (a neoliberal-oriented administration might be less receptive to policies seen as interventionist, whereas an administration focused on green growth might be eager for evidence in support), and existing policy processes (if a national development plan or industrial strategy is being written, that's a window to insert CE evidence). Also, context involves the presence of policy champions, individuals or units in government who are inclined to push for CE and can act as internal translators of evidence to policy proposals. If the context is lacking such champions, evidence might languish in reports.

ODI's framework emphasizes understanding what kind of evidence is persuasive in a given context; e.g., in some contexts anecdotal evidence or pilot demonstrations might convince better than abstract numbers; in others, a cost-benefit analysis is essential to get finance ministries on board (Kirchherr et al., 2017).

Links: This aspect deals with the networks and relationships through which information flows. For evidence to influence CE policy, there often needs to be a bridge between researchers (who generate knowledge about i.e. material flows or lifecycle impacts) and policymakers (who control regulations and investments). These links can be formal (like advisory councils, or including researchers in government task forces) or informal (personal connections, regular dialogues between academia, industry, and government). If these linkages are weak, for instance, if the circular economy community (academics, environmental experts) operates in silo, publishing papers but not engaging with decision-makers, then a lot of valuable evidence might not penetrate the policy arena. Strengthening the links could involve creating multi-stakeholder platforms on circular economy that convene scientists, entrepreneurs, and policymakers, or leveraging existing networks (like business councils or environmental forums) to disseminate research findings to key people. Serrat (2017) notes that the CEL framework provides insight into the "politics of the research-policy nexus," essentially who needs to talk to whom to get evidence heard.

In the CE context, a good example is how evidence on plastic pollution built up for years, but only started shifting policy markedly when it was coupled with strong advocacy networks (links) and a political moment (context) around public outrage over ocean plastic (vivid images of marine wildlife harmed). That combination forced policymakers to listen, leading to bans on single-use plastics in many jurisdictions. On the other hand, even in cases where substantial evidence exists, such as the documented benefits of industrial symbiosis, wherein firms utilize each other's waste streams, such insights may remain underrepresented in policy frameworks. This disconnect may stem from weak institutional linkages between researchers and industrial policymakers, or from a contextual environment in which the absence of an immediate crisis diminishes the urgency to prioritize such approaches within the policy agenda (Poole, 2011).

The CEL framework underscores that knowledge, in isolation, is insufficient to drive policy change. It must be embedded within effective communication strategies, supported by robust networks, and attuned to the prevailing political and institutional context. In the realm of innovative CE policy-making, this insight highlights the importance of strengthening the interface between analysis and action. It necessitates deliberate efforts to ensure that empirical data (such as material flow analyses, evidence from pilot initiatives, and economic assessments of circular models) are communicated in accessible and policy-relevant formats to those involved in drafting legislation and strategic plans. Moreover, it may require building institutional capacity within government to both understand and demand such evidence. This could involve training a cohort of policymakers in systems thinking and CE principles, thereby enabling them to actively seek out and integrate research findings into the policy development process. In short, CEL is about bridging the gap between the experts and the executors. By using this framework, one can plan how to effectively "market" the circular economy idea within government and industry circles (who to inform, how, and when) to maximize the chance that solid evidence translates into solid policies. This is an often underappreciated but crucial element of political economy ideas and knowledge are a form of power too, but only if they are mobilized in the right way (Haider & Rao, 2010).

COMMON POLITICAL ECONOMY CHALLENGES IN CIRCULAR ECONOMY TRANSITIONS

Having reviewed a range of analytical frameworks and conceptual lenses, it is now possible to distill several recurrent political economy challenges that commonly arise in the context of CE policy-making. These challenges represent overarching patterns that emerge when the aforementioned tools are applied to empirical or hypothetical scenarios. Identifying such obstacles constitutes a crucial first step in formulating strategies to effectively address them. Among the most prominent challenges are power asymmetries and vested interests, as well as institutional path dependency and policy lock-in. Additional barriers include stakeholder resistance and issues of social acceptability, alongside ideological or cognitive lock-ins, namely, entrenched mental models and dominant paradigms that inhibit the uptake of innovative approaches. Each of these challenges is examined in the sections that follow, with attention to how they manifest within CE transitions and drawing on earlier insights regarding potential strategies for their mitigation (Auty, 2024).

1. **Power asymmetries and vested interests.** The most evident political economy challenge is that circular economy transitions inevitably create winners and losers, and those who perceive themselves as potential losers often have the incentive and means to resist change. As previously noted, incumbent industries that depend on linear economic models, such as fossil fuel companies, mining corporations, manufacturers reliant on high volumes of virgin resource extraction, and large retail chains driven by rapid consumer turnover, often exert disproportionate influence over policy processes. In contrast, emerging circular economy actors, including repair services, recycling startups, and firms based on product-service systems, tend to have less political leverage due to their smaller scale, relative novelty, or limited access to decision-making channels. These incumbents may use their power to lobby against stringent CE regulations, to shape policies in their favor (for example, supporting superficial recycling measures over more transformative waste reduction mandates), or to stall implementation. A classic example can be seen in the plastics sector even as evidence mounted about plas-

tic pollution, major plastic producers and consumer goods companies lobbied to defeat or water down legislation on plastic bans or quotas, while promoting voluntary initiatives that align with their interests (Auty, 2024). In the EU's circular economy policy debates, there have been reports of certain member states and industry groups pushing back on high recycling targets or stricter rules when they felt their economic interests would be jeopardized (Becque et al., 2016). This underscores a simple truth: those controlling significant economic resources or jobs can often exercise a "veto" or at least a brake on policy shifts.

To address power asymmetries, political economy analysis suggests several tactics. One is to build countervailing alliances; for example, unite the voices of multiple smaller beneficiaries of CE (recyclers, green businesses, local governments that favor sustainability) into a coalition that can collectively lobby for reform, thus balancing the influence of a few big players. Indeed, Becque et al. (2016) recommend to "build alliances with leading individuals" and even with traditionally neutral or opposed actors, turning them into supporters by finding common cause. Another tactic is framing and public opinion. If the broader public can be convinced of the need for CE (for instance, through media exposure of waste crises or by linking CE to national pride in innovation), then even powerful lobbies may find it costly to be seen as obstructing a popular cause. In democracies, public sentiment can shift the balance. In more closed political systems, appeal might be made to the leadership's legacy concerns or international reputation. There is also the approach of compensation or co-optation such as using policy design to ensure that powerful stakeholders do not all end up losers.

For example, if the oil industry fears losing profits from plastics, maybe policies can encourage them to invest in chemical recycling or bio-plastics, giving them a stake in the new system (so-called "business model transition" for incumbents). This was seen in some renewable energy transitions where utilities were given roles in renewable generation so they would not block it entirely. Naturally, this has to be balanced against not giving away the store, co-opting incumbents should not mean designing weak policies, but smart sequencing can help, such as gradual phase-outs that give industries time to adapt rather than immediate bans (Haider & Rao, 2010).

Ultimately, tackling power asymmetries often requires political will at the highest levels, because it can mean confronting influential interests. This is where the role of visionary leadership or strong public mandates comes in. Historical transformations like environmental regulations in the 1970s or anti-trust actions earlier show that it is possible to curb corporate power for public good, but it requires mobilizing sufficient political capital. A political economy approach arms reformers with knowledge about where that capital must be spent and what backlash to expect, so they can prepare accordingly.

2. **Institutional path dependency and policy lock-in.** Another fundamental challenge is that existing institutions, whether they are laws, regulations, infrastructure systems, or market structures, often create a self-reinforcing logic that locks in the linear model. This is often referred to as path dependency. Past decisions shape present options. For example, decades of urban planning favoring single-use zoning and car-centric transport lock in higher material and energy use (suburban sprawl makes it harder to have circular systems like product-sharing or efficient public transport). Legal codes might classify waste in ways that make reuse legally difficult (e.g., something once labeled "waste" might face regulatory hurdles to be reintroduced as input). Subsidies for natural resource extraction or fossil energy, still prevalent in many parts of the world, artificially reduce the cost of linear production, thereby discouraging the use of recycled or alternative materials. This constitutes a form of financial lock-in that reinforces the dominance of unsustainable practices. Additionally, public procurement regulations often prioritize the lowest immediate cost, creating a barrier to the adoption of circular products which may entail higher upfront expenditures but offer lower total costs over their lifecycle. These kinds of institutionalized rules and practices create inertia.

Organizations, including government bureaucracies and firms, get used to doing things a certain way and have routines built around them. Changing these requires not just a decree but often detailed adjustments and overcoming internal resistance from those who are comfortable with the status quo (Kirchherr et al., 2017).

Policy lock-in also occurs when earlier policies created constituencies or expectations that are hard to reverse. For instance, if a government promised cheap energy and achieved it by subsidizing electricity (often generated from linear processes), removing that subsidy to reflect true costs or to fund circular initiatives might meet public anger, people plan their budgets around cheap power, industries build business models on it. Similarly, if a city signed a 30-year contract with a waste management company to supply a certain tonnage of waste to an incinerator (a common practice), the city might face financial penalties if it now tries to divert waste to recycling and does not meet the incinerator quota, a lock-in that punishes moving to circularity. As one analysis put it, "the linear economy exhibits strong path dependency and systemic inertia, making a transition to circularity inherently challenging" (Sustainability Directory, 2025). Addressing institutional lock-in often involves a mix of incremental and disruptive strategies. Incrementally, governments can start by reforming the most obviously counterproductive incentives. For example, gradually phasing out subsidies for virgin resources, introducing "green budgeting" to shift public funds toward circular activities, or revising waste regulations to legally redefine certain wastes as secondary materials to ease reuse. These are technical but important changes. More disruptively, sometimes new institutions might need to be created to bypass the locked-in ones. For instance, if municipal waste systems are tied up in bad contracts, a parallel system of community recycling or deposit-return schemes might be started by other actors (maybe at regional or national scale) to create a new dynamic that eventually forces renegotiation of old arrangements. In the energy sector, the rise of independent renewable power producers introduced competition into a field once locked to utilities. In waste, innovative social enterprises doing local circular initiatives can similarly challenge incumbents. From a policy perspective, governments can encourage such innovation niches essentially creating alternative models that, if successful, can be scaled up and supplant the old (Haider & Rao, 2010).

However, unlocking path dependencies often has upfront costs and requires careful management of transition. For example, as mentioned earlier, if a city has too much incineration capacity, it may need to renegotiate contracts or find alternate uses (like waste import or repurposing facilities) to avoid financial ruin while ramping up recycling. Political economy analysis helps by anticipating these snags so they can be addressed as part of policy design rather than coming as nasty surprises. It may also highlight opportunities where lock-ins are weakening, e.g. a long-term contract coming up for renewal, or an outdated law due for revision those become strategic moments to intervene. On a positive note, institutions can also be harnessed to lock-in good practices. A goal of CE policy should be not just to break old lock-ins but to create new lock-ins that favor circularity, for example, enshrining circular economy targets in law (making it hard for future governments to backslide), or investing in infrastructure (like circular materials hubs, repair cafes, remanufacturing parks) that then form a new normal. Over time, as circular practices become embedded, they develop their own constituencies and feedback loops, which then defend and expand them. This is essentially the theory of change behind many transitions (Poole, 2011).

3. **Stakeholder resistance and social acceptance.** While much of the discussion often centers on elite interests or industries, another critical challenge is the reaction of ordinary stakeholders (consumers, workers, communities) to circular economy policies. Any significant transition will ask people to change behavior or may affect their livelihoods, and if these social dimensions are mishandled, even the best-intentioned policies can falter. For instance, policies to encourage product longevity and repair might mean consumers cannot find ultra-cheap disposable goods as easily or might have to pay a bit more upfront for durable products. This could cause discontent if people do not understand the long-term benefits or if they feel their choices are being restricted. Workers in extractive or waste disposal industries might fear job losses from a shift to circular practices

(e.g., less mining if recycling increases, or less landfilling if waste is reduced). Small businesses might worry about new regulations or reporting requirements adding burden. Thus, beyond organized lobbyists, grassroots resistance or simply lack of buy-in can be an obstacle. Examples are plentiful where public backlash has slowed environmental measures from protests against pay-by-weight waste schemes or landfill taxes (when seen as just higher bills), to yellow-vest type protests in France partly sparked by eco-taxes seen as unfair (Serrat, 2017).

The political economy insight here is to pay attention to perceptions of fairness and the distribution of costs and benefits among the general population. If a CE policy is perceived to impose high costs on the average person for nebulous benefits, it will face resistance. Conversely, if it can be designed (or at least communicated) as bringing tangible benefits to most people (cleaner neighbourhoods, new job opportunities in recycling, savings from reusing items, etc.) it stands a better chance. Hence the importance of social impact analysis (like PSIA) as discussed, to identify who might be adversely affected and find ways to alleviate that. It's also crucial to involve stakeholders early. If citizens and communities have a voice in shaping CE initiatives, their concerns can be addressed and they are more likely to support the outcomes. Sometimes opposition comes simply from feeling excluded or not understanding the rationale. Public education campaigns, deliberative forums (like citizens' assemblies on climate and circular economy, which some countries have tried), and pilot programs that allow people to experience circular solutions can build acceptance. People might be wary of a policy in abstract, but more welcoming if they see it in action improving their lives or locality (Serrat, 2017).

One particular stakeholder dynamic to note is that not everyone currently benefits equally from the linear economy, and so not everyone will benefit equally from a circular one either if left to market forces. For instance, cheap throwaway products may benefit consumers in the short term, but the negative effects (pollution, waste) often hit other groups or the environment. Conversely, a circular economy might have economy-wide benefits, but if, e.g. durable goods cost more, low-income households might feel a pinch unless policies account for that (through subsidies or second-hand markets or service models that reduce upfront costs). The equity dimension is thus key. A failure to ensure a just transition, where the burdens of change do not fall disproportionately on those least able to bear them, can create justifiable resistance. Thus, proactive measures like job retraining programs, social safety nets for disrupted workers, and affordability schemes for sustainable products are not just morally right but politically smart to preempt opposition (Keblowski et al., 2020).

It's also worth noting that "stakeholder resistance" can stem from habits and cultural values, not only material interests. People might simply be used to certain ways of consuming (e.g. the convenience of single-use items or fast fashion) and resist change out of habit or skepticism.

Political economy intersects with psychology and culture here. Overcoming this requires changing mindsets, something that likely involves education, social marketing, and time. Younger generations often have different values and may embrace circular practices more readily, so part of the transition is generational. In the interim, policies may use nudges and incentives: making the sustainable choice the default easiest choice (e.g. deposit-refund systems make returning bottles simple and rewarding) or harnessing social norms (publicizing how many neighbors are participating in a recycling program to encourage others) (Haider & Rao, 2010).

A successful CE transition must therefore be people-centred. It is not just an industrial restructuring; it is a societal change in how resources are valued and used. Addressing stakeholder concerns, ensuring fairness, and actively engaging citizens can convert potential resistance into support. Indeed, some circular economy initiatives can be very popular if framed well, for example, the idea of repairing and sharing often resonates with community values and can be marketed as a return to common-sense practices of the past (which counters the narrative of "sacrifice" with one of "wisdom" or "thrift"). In sum, the challenge is to manage the politics not only between government and business, but also between government and society, and even within society among different groups. Political economy analysis, especially tools like PSIA and power analysis at community level, helps identify these dynamics so policy can be tailored accordingly.

4. **Ideational and cognitive lock-ins (narratives and mindsets).** Beyond concrete interests and institutions, a subtler but equally significant challenge lies in the realm of ideas, the prevailing economic narratives, ideologies, and cognitive frameworks that guide decision-makers and public perceptions. The dominant economic paradigm of the last decades has been one of growth through consumption, efficiency defined narrowly in terms of GDP output, and a faith in technological fixes without major lifestyle or structural changes. The circular economy concept itself is a challenge to some of these entrenched ideas. It calls for rethinking progress in terms of quality and regeneration rather than sheer quantity of goods, and it emphasizes systemic change over incremental tinkering. However, if policymakers and influencers are still in the grip of traditional thinking, for example, the belief that environmental regulation inevitably hampers economic growth, or the assumption that markets will naturally solve resource scarcities without government intervention, they may be intellectually resistant to the CE concept.

In some cases, CE might be misunderstood as merely "recycling more" rather than a holistic transformation, leading to half-hearted policies that do not capture the full benefit (Auty, 2024). One narrative lock-in is the idea of the linear economy as normal and circular as exceptional. Many current laws, education curricula in economics and business, and media discourses treat take-make-dispose as the default and talk about circular initiatives as niche experiments. This framing can marginalize CE efforts or cast doubt on their scalability. Another cognitive bias is short-termism, politicians and even businesses often focus on short-term results (electoral cycles, quarterly reports) and discount long-term benefits or costs. Circular economy investments often have upfront costs with longer-term payoffs (e.g. designing a product for longevity might cost more now but save costs and create value over years). If decision-makers are mentally discounting the future too heavily, they underinvest in circular approaches (Auty, 2024).

To overcome ideational barriers, a political economy approach would stress the importance of shifting discourse and building new narratives. As Polanyi (2001) famously described in historical context, society's perspective on the economy has undergone transformations and a new "great transformation" in thinking may be needed to embrace sustainability. Strategies include elevating alternative indicators of well-being (so success is not just GDP growth but maybe resource productivity, circular material use rate, etc.) and highlighting examples that break the old mold (like countries or companies thriving with circular models, to show that prosperity and circularity can go hand in hand). It's also about education and capacity-building. Economists, engineers, and managers trained in linear thinking may need re-training or exposure to circular economy principles to incorporate them into their work. This is happening slowly as CE courses and government guides proliferate, but it requires intentional push so that tomorrow's civil servants and business leaders think differently from yesterday's (Keblowski et al., 2020). Furthermore, narratives of fear vs. opportunity need balancing. If the CE is seen mainly as a threat (to jobs, to convenience, to profits), it will scare off support. Emphasizing innovation, modernity, and competitive advantage can reframe CE as an opportunity. For instance, countries or firms can adopt the narrative: "We want to be a leader in the industries of the future, and circular economy is the future, those who move first will reap the rewards." This narrative jujitsu can win over skeptics who might otherwise only see cost. Indeed, many governments have latched onto CE partly for its economic development promise (resource efficiency, reduced import dependence, new markets), which is a useful alignment of sustainability and economic narrative.

At the same time, one must manage the risk of greenwashing narratives, some might co-opt the CE buzzword without intent of deep change, which can dilute the concept. By examining real forces and incentives, political economy analysis can help understand when a narrative is being used constructively and when it is being used deceptively (Becque et al., 2016).

In summary, the battle for a circular economy is fought not just in the halls of legislatures or boardrooms, but also in the realm of public imagination and accepted wisdom. Changing minds is a gradual but crucial process. It involves education, demonstration, and the proliferation of new ideas. A heartening sign is that concepts like zero waste, sharing economy, repair culture, and regenerative design have gained significant traction in public discourse in recent years. The more these become mainstream, the easier it gets for bold CE policies to be politically acceptable. Thus, part of innovative CE policy making is storytelling and vision-casting. Painting a compelling picture of what a circular future looks like (e.g., cleaner cities, resilient supply chains, innovative jobs, harmony with nature) to inspire buy-in. Polanyi's (2001) idea that economies are embedded in society reminds that ultimately the values of society will shape the economy, so promoting the values of stewardship, interdependence and long-term thinking is an integral part of the transition.

5. **Multi-level governance and policy coherence issues.** Circular economy policies often involve multiple levels of governance (local, national, and international) and multiple sectors, raising coordination challenges. A city might implement a circular initiative (e.g. a plastic bag ban), but if national policy does not support it (or if an adjacent city does not, leading to cross-jurisdictional issues) the impact is limited. Similarly, one country's efforts can be undermined by global trade (e.g., if it bans certain waste, but then ends up exporting it to less regulated markets, simply shifting the problem). International political economy comes into play with questions like trade rules, extended producer responsibility across borders (who takes responsibility for a product made in country A, consumed in B, dumped in C?), and technology transfer for circular innovations. Ensuring policy coherence, that environmental, industrial, trade, and education policies all align to support circular goals rather than work at cross purposes, is a governance challenge. From a political economy standpoint, this often comes down to whether there is a strong coordinating center (like a national CE task force with authority) and whether powerful ministries (like finance or industry) are on board with the agenda.

If not, one department's efforts might be counteracted by another's decisions. Innovative approaches some countries have tried include embedding circular economy into the highest-level strategies (so all ministries must incorporate it) and creating cross-ministerial budgets and indicators (Kirchherr et al., 2017).

In dealing with multi-level issues, a concept from political economy is the importance of vertical and horizontal integration. Vertically, aligning local initiatives with national frameworks and vice versa, perhaps through pilot projects that inform national policy, or national legislation that empowers and resources local action. Horizontally, ensuring different branches of government (environment, economy, labor, etc.) collaborate, maybe via interdepartmental committees or joint programs. It is easy to say but hard to do, because bureaucratic politics and turf wars are real. This again comes to leadership and incentive alignment sometimes an external pressure (like an EU directive or an international agreement) can prod domestic coordination by creating a common goal. Political economy analysis might advise leveraging such external commitments to overcome internal fragmentation.

In conclusion, by identifying a set of recurring challenges (spanning material interests, institutional configurations, social dynamics, ideational constraints, and governance coordination) political economy analysis does not offer a pessimistic outlook but rather a realistic and diagnostic framework that highlights where innovation is most urgently required. Its primary value lies in its capacity to direct attention toward feasible solutions. For each challenge identified, there are corresponding strategies for mitigation or resolution, many of which have been addressed throughout the preceding discussion. Accordingly, innovative CE policy-making is unlikely to be achieved through isolated interventions, such as the introduction of a recycling law or a circular public procurement guideline, alone. Instead, it necessitates a comprehensive package of measures. These may include worker retraining programs to address stakeholder concerns, revisions to subsidies and legal frameworks to dismantle institutional lock-ins, coalition-building efforts and strategic public communication to navigate power asymmetries and contested narratives, and reforms in governance structures to enhance institutional capacity and accountability. The political economy perspective, in this sense, broadens the conception of "policy" to encompass not only its substantive content but also the processes and institutional architectures through which it is developed and implemented.

It encourages policymakers to adopt a proactive and anticipatory stance: to identify potential sources of resistance in advance and engage relevant actors early, to forecast implementation challenges and resolve them strategically, and to create enabling conditions that ensure the long-term viability and legitimacy of circular economy reforms. It is precisely this integrated and systemic approach that is likely to distinguish successful CE transitions from those that falter.

TOWARD INNOVATIVE AND INTEGRATED POLICY SOLUTIONS

Given the array of challenges and frameworks discussed, what might innovative policy making for the circular economy actually look like in practice? Drawing on the political economy perspective, it would involve crafting policies that are not only technically sound but also politically savvy, inclusive, and adaptive. Here are a few key principles and examples of what this type of policy design entails:

- **Policy mixes with carrots, sticks, and support measures:** Rather than relying on single instruments, innovative CE policy packages combine regulatory mandates (the "sticks") with economic incentives (the "carrots") and enabling support. For instance, a package to curb plastic waste might ban certain unnecessary single-use plastics (regulation), impose a levy on other disposable items (economic disincentive), while simultaneously funding R&D for alternatives and offering grants to companies for developing refill/reuse systems (support). This mix serves a dual purpose, it pushes actors away from the linear norm and also helps them move into the circular alternative. Critically, it also addresses political resistance by providing a "helping hand" to stakeholders in meeting the new requirements (Becque et al., 2016). Companies that might oppose a ban could be less hostile if they have access to support for switching materials or redesigning products. Consumers facing a new fee might accept it if they see improved circular services or infrastructure making sustainable choices easier. The political economy logic is that by lowering the cost of compliance and increasing the cost of non-compliance, while maintaining fairness, one can better align stakeholders' incentives with the policy goals.
- **Sequencing and pacing reforms strategically:** Not everything must (or can) be done at once. Innovative policy design will consider what sequence of actions builds momentum. For example, starting with "low-hanging fruit" can demonstrate success and create constituencies for further change. A city might initially focus on a popular measure like food waste composting (which visibly reduces landfill load and gives community gardens fertilizer) before taking on harder issues like construction waste or consumer product rules. Early wins can shift expectations and norms, a concept from political economy where initial reforms change the calculus of future reforms by altering stakeholders' expectations or by proving that change is possible. Conversely, sequencing also means anticipating backlash, perhaps "let sleeping giants sleep" by not provoking powerful opponents until necessary (Becque et al., 2016). If a certain industry is not actively opposing a CE policy, there is no need to gratuitously antagonize them. The policy can fly under their radar or be framed in a way that does not trigger them until it is established enough that reversal is hard. This kind of tactical patience is a political art. For instance, a government might avoid tackling a very powerful industry in the first phase of CE strategy, focusing on others first. By the time it circles back

to that industry, alternatives might be more developed and public awareness higher, so the final push is more achievable.

- **Coalition-building and participatory governance:** A theme throughout has been that involving stakeholders not just as targets of policy but as partners in policy development yields more durable outcomes. Innovative CE policy processes often create multi-stakeholder councils or platforms (including businesses, NGOs, academia, local authorities, and sometimes citizen representatives) to co-create roadmaps and monitor progress. This echoes the idea of "collaborative governance", which can be slower in the formulation stage, but tends to produce greater buy-in and smoother implementation. For example, the Netherlands' circular economy planning has involved sectoral "Green Deals" where government facilitates voluntary agreements among companies, municipalities, and others to take specific circular actions, which are then scaled up. While voluntary approaches alone may not suffice, when combined with eventual regulation, they ease the path by allowing experimentation and consensus-building first. Such coalitions also serve as a counter-force to narrower lobbies, a broad alliance of different actors all supporting CE can provide political cover for policymakers to take bold steps. Additionally, engaging labor unions and workers in planning transitions (to ensure job issues are handled) can preempt social conflict (Poole, 2011).
- **Embedding circular economy into broader economic strategy:** Instead of treating CE as an environmental silo, innovative policy would integrate it into industrial policy, innovation policy, skills development, and regional development plans. This mainstreaming makes circular economy a cross-cutting priority. For instance, a government might include circular economy criteria in its public procurement across all departments (so that the education ministry buys circular furniture for schools, defense ministry adopts circular procurement for equipment, etc.), which not only creates market demand for circular products but signals that CE is a government-wide ethos. Or in innovation policy, allocate grants specifically for circular design and engineering solutions, thereby stimulating entrepreneurship in that area. The political economy advantage of embedding CE in economic strategy is that it then gets championed not only by environment ministers but also by finance, trade, and industry ministers as a source of competitiveness and resilience. It reframes the narrative from "environmental cost" to "economic opportunity and modernization", attracting broader political support. China, for example, integrated circular economy into its five-year plans as part of its economic restructuring, which meant it was pushed by top-level economic planners, not just environmental agencies (Keblowski et al., 2020).

- **Adaptive policy and feedback loops:** Innovative policy-making recognizes the inherent uncertainty associated with complex systemic transitions such as the shift toward a CE and therefore incorporates mechanisms for continuous learning and adaptation. This may take the form of pilot initiatives accompanied by rigorous monitoring and evaluation, phased implementation strategies that allow for iterative refinement based on stakeholder feedback, or the inclusion of sunset clauses and scheduled review points to ensure that policies remain responsive and relevant over time. From a political economy perspective, such adaptive mechanisms are particularly valuable, as they serve to mitigate perceived risks for stakeholders. Knowing that corrective processes are embedded within the policy framework can increase initial buy-in by reassuring actors that ineffective or counterproductive measures can be revised. Moreover, this approach supports the principle of responsiveness as articulated in the CAR framework as societal preferences, political conditions or environmental realities evolve, policies can be recalibrated accordingly. An illustrative example would be a government pledging to revisit a newly enacted CE regulation after two years, engaging both industry representatives and civil society actors in the review process to address any unforeseen impacts.

Such commitments can help reduce early resistance by providing institutionalized avenues for dialogue and adjustment, thereby enhancing the legitimacy and durability of reform efforts (Haider & Rao, 2010).

- **Leveraging technology and data for governance:** The digital revolution offers new tools (big data, blockchain, IoT) that can help with transparency and enforcement in circular economy, which in turn addresses political economy issues like accountability and information asymmetry. For example, using digital tracking of waste and materials can expose illegal dumping or inefficiencies, empowering regulators and communities with evidence. It can also build trust, if citizens have an app that shows where their recycled items go and how it benefits the city, they may be more engaged. Technology is not a panacea, but innovative policies can incorporate tech to strengthen implementation credibility. Some countries have open data portals on waste statistics or real-time monitoring of air/water quality, similarly one can imagine material flow accounts being made public to track progress. Transparency itself can shift power, as it's harder for interest groups to argue against action when data openly shows a problem or a solution's impact (Becque et al., 2016).

Throughout all these approaches, a unifying thread is integration, integrating different policy tools, integrating stakeholders in decision-making, integrating CE into the broader policy landscape, and integrating feedback into the policy cycle. Such holistic, inclusive strategies are naturally informed by political economy thinking and they recognize the need to deal with interests, ideas, institutions in tandem, not isolation.

CONCLUSION

This study has examined "Innovative Policy Making for the Circular Economy" through the lens of political economy, asserting that the transition to a circular economy constitutes not only a technical or managerial endeavour but also a deeply political and institutional project. It began by identifying the limitations of conventional policy models, which often presume that market mechanisms or straightforward policy levers will seamlessly facilitate the circular economy transition. In reality, however, such models tend to overlook the complex web of power relations, vested interests, and institutional inertia that sustain the linear economic paradigm (Becque et al., 2016).

To address these deficiencies, the study investigated conceptual frameworks rooted in political economy, such as Sector Governance Analysis, Drivers of Change, and Power Analysis, demonstrating how each can offer critical insights when applied to the design of circular economy policies.

Through the application of these analytical frameworks, several key themes have emerged. Drawing on Polanyi's (2001) insights, the analysis underscored that economic systems, whether linear or circular, are deeply embedded within broader social and political structures. Efforts to transform economic models without engaging these foundational structures are therefore likely to encounter significant obstacles. As emphasized by Serrat (2017), political economy analysis centers on the practical dynamics of "who gets what, when, how, and why", focusing on the distribution of power and incentives among actors, the roles of institutions, and the normative values that shape decision-making. These are precisely the kinds of questions that must be addressed in the context of CE transitions, where divergent stakeholder interests and evolving societal norms around consumption and waste complicate the reform landscape. Frameworks such as Sector Governance Analysis and the Political Economy of Policy Reform approach provide tools for identifying sector-specific and process-oriented strategies that accommodate political constraints while advancing CE reforms. The Drivers of Change framework draws attention to the structural conditions and overarching political climate that can either enable or constrain circular initiatives. Power Analysis illuminates the often asymmetric relationships between incumbents and emerging actors, as well as between state institutions and civil society, thereby highlighting the need to empower marginalized voices and carefully manage entrenched interests. The CAR framework reinforces the notion that even the most technically sound CE policies may falter in the absence of institutional capacity, clear lines of accountability, and responsiveness to stakeholder needs. Finally, the CEL framework demonstrates the critical role of evidence in informing policy, as well as the mechanisms through which knowledge is translated into political action. Collectively, these frameworks offer a multidimensional understanding of the political and institutional dynamics that shape the prospects for successful circular economy transitions.

Bringing these threads together, a political economy perspective does not offer a simple formula for circular economy transition, rather, it offers a critical toolkit and mindset. It urges policymakers, scholars, and practitioners to continually ask: "What are the interests at play? Where are the power imbalances? How will the institutional context shape outcomes? Who needs to be on board (or at least not vehemently opposed) to make this policy work? Why might this good idea fail in practice and how can we prevent that?" By asking these questions early and often, policy-makers can design more innovative and resilient strategies. For example, instead of just legislating a recycling target and hoping for the best, a political economy-informed approach would simultaneously engage industry in the solution, educate and involve the public, secure funding for necessary infrastructure, and put in place accountability mechanisms, aligning the political and economic factors with the environmental goal (Becque et al., 2016).

One of the core contributions of political economy to CE governance, as articulated in this study is the emphasis on integrated thinking. CE challenges cut across traditional silos, they involve environmental science, economics, engineering, but also politics, sociology, and ethics. Political economy, by its nature, bridges the economic and the political, the formal and informal, the technical and the social. It therefore serves as a valuable integrative framework. By applying this, it can be predicted that a brilliant technical plan may fail due to social opposition or, conversely, that a modest technical change that cleverly seizes political opportunities may succeed. This broader systems awareness is crucial in managing something as complex as the transformation of our economic model.

For the field of management and organization studies, which was referenced at the outset, incorporating political economy insights can greatly enrich analysis and practice. Management scholars often study how organizations innovate for sustainability, implement circular business models, or collaborate in supply chains for better environmental outcomes. What a political economy lens adds is the understanding that these organizational efforts do not happen in a vacuum. They are enabled or constrained by the broader policy environment, power dynamics, and institutional context. For instance, a company's bold circular business model might fail not because the model is flawed, but because current regulations or market incentives penalize it relative to linear competitors.

By recognizing that, managers can become more savvy in lobbying for policy change or in forming industry coalitions to shift the playing field. Likewise, organization theorists examining institutional change can draw from political economy theories about how coalitions for change form, or why path dependency is so strong, thereby better explaining why some firms succeed in spearheading circular practices and others do not. Integrating these perspectives fosters a more holistic approach to innovation for sustainability, one that combines technological and managerial creativity with political and institutional strategy.

In practical terms, as businesses and governments work together on CE initiatives, an appreciation of political economy can encourage more fruitful partnerships. Businesses can support governments in designing workable policies (offering data and pilots), and governments can support businesses through clear signals and stable frameworks, each understanding the other's constraints and incentives. This synergy is vital. A circular economy cannot be built by policy alone nor by business alone, it requires co-evolution of both. The political economy viewpoint essentially says align the interests, rules, and narratives such that doing the right thing (circular practices) is also the path of least resistance or greatest reward for all key actors. That might sound idealistic, but the analyses in this study show concrete ways to move in that direction, from adjusting incentives and accountability to nurturing pro-circular coalitions and shifting norms.

REFERENCES

Auty, L. D. (2024). *The Political Economy of Reuse Organizing for Reform and Transformation of the Make-and-waste Economy*. Faculty of Social Sciences, Lund University.

Becque, R., Roy, N., & Hamza-Goodacre, D. (2016). *The Political Economy of the Circular Economy*. Climate Works Foundation.

Bjuremalm, H. (2006). *Power analysis – Experiences and challenges*. Swedish International Development Cooperation Agency (SIDA).

Castles, S., Cubas, M. A., Kim, C., Koleth, E., Ozkul, D., & Williamson, R. (2011). *Karl Polanyi's great transformation as a framework for understanding neo-liberal globalisation*. University of Sydney. http://sydney.edu.au/arts/transformation_migration/downloads/STIM_WP1_Final.pdf

Collinson, S. (2003). *Power, livelihoods and conflict: Case studies in political economy analysis for humanitarian action* (Humanitarian Policy Group Report 13). Overseas Development Institute.

Department for International Development (DFID). (2009). *Political economy analysis how to note*. https://gsdrc.org/docs/open/PO58.pdf

Edelmann, D. (2009). *Analysing and managing the political dynamics of sector reforms: A sourcebook on sector-level political economy approaches*. Overseas Development Institute. https://odi.org/en/publications/analysing-and-managing-the-political-dynamics-of-sector-reforms/

Fritz, V., Kaiser, K., & Levy, B. (2009). *Problem-driven governance and political economy analysis: Good practice framework*. World Bank. DOI: 10.1596/16777

Haider, H., & Rao, S. (2010). *Political and social analysis for development policy and practice: An overview of five approaches*. Governance and Social Development Resource Centre.

Harris, D., Kooy, M., & Jones, L. (2011). *Analysing the governance and political economy of water and sanitation service delivery*. Overseas Development Institute. https://odi.org/en/publications/analysing-the-governance-and-political-economy-of-water-and-sanitation-service-delivery/

Keblowski, W., Lambert, D., & Bassens, D. (2020). Circular economy and the city: An urban political economy agenda. *Culture and Organization*, *26*(2), 142–158. DOI: 10.1080/14759551.2020.1718148

Kirchherr, J., Hekkert, M., Bour, R., Huijbrechtse-Truijens, A., Kostense-Smit, E., & Muller, J. (2017). *Breaking the Barriers to the Circular Economy. Deloitte*. Utrecht University.

Mcloughlin, C. (2012). *Political Economy Analysis: Topic Guide*. GSDRC.

Polanyi, K. (2001). *The Great Transformation: The Political and Economic Origins of Our Time*. Beacon Press.

Poole, A. (2011). *How-to notes: Political economy assessments at sector and project levels*. Government of Canada, GAC in Projects.

Poulton, C. (2012) Democratisation and the Political Economy of Agricultural Policy in Africa, FAC Working Paper 43, Brighton: Future Agricultures Consortium.

Serrat, O. (2011). *Political economy analysis for development effectiveness*. Asian Development Bank. http://digitalcommons.ilr.cornell.edu/intl/186/

Serrat, O. (2017). Political Economy Analysis for Development Effectiveness. In *Knowledge Solutions* (pp. 207–222). Springer. DOI: 10.1007/978-981-10-0983-9_21

Strange, S. (1970). International economics and international relations: A case of mutual neglect. *International Affairs*, *46*(2), 304–315. DOI: 10.2307/2613829

Sustainability Directory. (2025, April 24). What Are the Key Barriers to Circular Economy Adoption? URL: https://climate.sustainability-directory.com/question/what-are-the-key-barriers-to-circular-economy-adoption/

The World Bank. (2012). *Operationalizing political economy: Urban bus operations in Dhaka*. https://documents.worldbank.org/en/publication/documents-reports/documentdetail/693780BRI0P1080Bus0Operations0final

Underhill, G. R. D. (2000). State, market, and global political economy: Genealogy of an (inter) discipline. *International Affairs*, *76*(4), 805–824. DOI: 10.1111/1468-2346.00166

Unsworth, S., & Williams, G. (2011). *Using Political Economy Analysis to improve EU Development Effectiveness*. URL: https://thepolicypractice.com/using-political-economy-analysis-improve-development-effectiveness-unsworth-and-williams-2011

Chapter 6
Invisible Waste:
Information Pollution and Circular Economy Policy

Lina Shouman
https://orcid.org/0000-0001-8952-4924
Lebanese International University, Lebanon

ABSTRACT

This thematic paper addresses the growing challenge of information pollution, or "infollution," characterized by the overproduction, duplication, and inaccuracy of digital content that impairs decision-making, affects trust, and burdens technology infrastructure. The circular economy (CE) has traditionally focused on the responsible management of physical resources, yet its principles can be adapted to address the challenges posed by infollution. This study suggests a framework that applies CE strategies, like data minimization, reuse, recycling, sharing, and quality enhancement as effective mitigation strategies to the information ecosystem. By recognizing data as a resource with value across its lifecycle, organizations may boost knowledge flows, decrease redundancy, and improve information quality. The integration of CE principles into data management leads to cleaner digital environments, enhanced operational efficiency, and more sustainable knowledge practices. This strategy not only minimizes the detrimental consequences of infollution but also supports global sustainability goals for the digital era.

INTRODUCTION

The idea of sustainability has significantly influenced corporate management techniques in recent years. Within this context, the circular economy models, which seek to lower resource consumption and waste generation, have gained attention

DOI: 10.4018/979-8-3373-3852-1.ch006

in support of sustainable development (Gupta et al., 2019). A fundamental change in organizational operations, the circular economy aligns economic processes with environmental sustainability (Jabbour et al., 2019) and encourages the creation of novel business models that improve economic, social, and environmental performance (Stahel, 2016; Teixeira et al., 2016).

Although circular economy (CE) frameworks have historically concentrated on material, energy, and waste-related resources, the advent of digital transformation has brought forth a new, frequently undetectable type of waste: information pollution, or "infollution", which this chapter frames as a parallel to material waste in CE. According to Van Bavel et al. (2021) and Orman (1984), this term describes the excessive, redundant, outdated, or misleading information that is generated and disseminated through digital systems. Much like physical waste damages the environment and depletes resources, information waste undermines organizational performance, distorts decision-making, and raises environmental costs due to excessive data storage and energy consumption,

The concepts of the circular economy—reduction, reuse, and recycling—provide novel framework for addressing information overload. Through the application of the three "R's"—reduce, reuse, and recycle—the CE seeks to maximize the use of already-existing resources. By prolonging the usable lives of products in this way, waste may be effectively utilized and a more environmentally friendly manufacturing model can be developed over time (Madaan et al., 2024). These same principles are increasingly applied to digital resources, prompting businesses to investigaet cross-industry digital networks that foster transparency, shared value, and sustainable data practices in place of exclusively using vertically integrated IT systems to manage resources (Moghrabi et al., 2023; Camarinha-Matos et al., 2019). Information stewardship is in line with environmental and organizational performance when information flows are redesigned to prevent duplication (Drössler et al., 2018), improve information quality (Graf & Antoni, 2021), and filter and prioritize pertinent data (Bergström et al., 2010). To ensure their survival and competitive edge in today's world, organizations must deal with information pollution (Iqbal et al., 2019). Consequently, organizational decision-makers play a crucial role in selecting suitable software, upholding transparency, and establishing internal guidelines for information management (Arnold et al., 2023).

This challenge continues to grow in scale and complexity. According to studies, the amount of information in companies doubles every two years and increases by 35–50% annually (Beath et al., 2012). Employees are burdened by this data overload, which also impairs decision-making, uses more energy, and may even put them in danger legally (Swar et al., 2017). Furthermore, the problems brought on by information pollution are becoming more complicated as it can take several interrelated forms that mutually reinforce one another. These forms include redundant data, low-quality data, false narratives, and irrelevant communication. Effective information processing is hampered by a number of factors, such as a lack of information literacy, an increase in duplicate and redundant content, a lack of prior knowledge, complicated tasks, language obstacles, and time limits (Bawden & Robinson, 2020; Hiltz & Plotnick, 2013).

In addition to these factors, a variety of systemic causes have exacerbated the issue of modern information pollution. Among these is the constant production of enormous amounts of data, especially in fiercely competitive fields like academia where quantity frequently triumphs over quality. Disseminating large volumes of copied or unverified information has become easier due to the simplicity of the content production and sharing processes on digital platforms. Additionally, information overload and fragmentation have resulted from the exponential growth of information channels, which include social networks, websites, email, and traditional media. The complexity is increased by the availability of enormous historical data repositories and the ubiquity of contradictory or inconsistent information. Lastly, users frequently lack effective methods for evaluating, comparing, or analyzing sources, and comprehension and retrieval are hampered by unclear information structures (Stanley, 2021).

The phenomenon of information overload, which occurs when the amount of incoming data exceeds a person's ability to process it, is closely related to infollution. Information overload, as seen from an organizational standpoint, is when the volume of incoming data surpasses the ability to process it effectively. Cognitive exhaustion, misunderstandings, and decreased productivity are the outcomes of this. The sheer amount of data frequently causes problems for people, especially when they lack the knowledge or support networks necessary to handle it efficiently. To characterize the psychological and professional consequences of this situation, terms like "infobesity" and "information anxiety" have been developed (Stanley, 2021). The impact of information overload on organizational effectiveness is further exacerbated by factors such as limited information processing capacity, poor organizational skills, inefficient time usage, and a reluctance to delegate tasks, as further identified by Rajabzadeh et al. (2011).

Alongside strategies inspired by the circular economy, technological solutions were developed to help alleviate these problems. Artificial intelligence developments have produced filtering and summarization algorithms that try to reduce the cognitive strain caused by an abundance of information (Kaufhold et al., 2020). Additionally, new tools like emotion-aware recommendation engines, which take into account the emotional impact of information when customizing digital content to user needs, have become possible due to advancements in recommender systems (Batmaz et al., 2019; Costa & Macedo, 2013; Rasmussen Pennington, 2016).

Infollution is still underexplored in the literature on information systems and the circular economy, despite the issue's increasing importance (Iqbal et al., 2018). In order to fill this gap, this chapter provides a thematic review of the newly developed idea of information pollution from the perspective of circular economy policy. The origins, motivators, and organizational effects of infollution are examined, and methods for incorporating information governance into circular models are suggested. The chapter offers practical insights for policy and practice by extending the circular economy theory to digital ecosystems and framing information pollution as a hindrance to sustainable development.

1. CONCEPTUALIZING INFORMATION POLLUTION

The problem of infollution has grown in importance as digital technologies play a bigger role in contemporary society. In order to better comprehend the impact of information pollution on society, this section defines it, lists its salient features, and places it within a variety of theoretical frameworks. By providing a conceptual framework, it prepares the ground for investigating the relationship between information pollution and sustainability issues and the potential benefits of policy frameworks, especially those based on the ideas of the circular economy.

1.1 Definition and Origins of Information Pollution

Information pollution or infollution is the term used to describe situations where low-value content, such as redundant, irrelevant, or erroneous material, deteriorates the information supply (Orman, 1984). Infollution describes the dissemination of irrelevant, low-value, or redundant information that interferes with social interactions and decision-making. It shows up as information overload, which depletes people's cognitive abilities, leading to indecision and a distraction from important details. Infollution is ethereal, invisible, and frequently passes unnoticed without mental exhaustion or critical thought. It can be created purposefully or unconsciously by ICT (Hassan et al., 2019). It also covers cases of misinformation and disinformation[1]. Scholars have lately broadened the discussion to encompass malinformation, which is the intentional exploitation of accurate information to do harm (Wardle & Derakhshan, 2017). The information landscape is further complicated by the emergence of conspiracy theories, which are narratives that link important social and political events to covert conspiracies hatched by influential people (Douglas et al., 2019).

According to Zhao et al. (2019), social media and digital libraries are two significant disruptive sources of information pollution. Aljukhadar and Senecal (2017) claim that these platforms and other online information sources play a major role in the growth of information pollution. The problem is made worse by the continuous flow of data across social media platforms and the frequently erroneous or out-of-date content available in digital libraries. As García-Marco (2011) points out, the spread of contaminated content is greatly aided by the declining quality of information, especially with regard to obsolescence and inaccuracy.

People play two roles in this process: they are both information creators and, in the event of information pollution, polluters (Uğraş, 2015; Berkan, 2012). Individuals directly contribute to the deterioration of digital ecosystems by creating and sharing offensive or harmful content. According to Cho and Lee (2020), some academics refer to negative internet occurrences like cyberbullying and violent content as "digital pollutants." This polluting habit causes a number of harmful effects, including as mental exhaustion and detrimental effects on decision-making processes.

Disinformation, or the intentional dissemination of false information, is one of the many types of information pollution that has recently emerged as a particularly significant factor disrupting political life (Bimber & Gil de Zúñiga, 2020). The extensive effects of information pollution are further highlighted by the fact that the quick dissemination of inaccurate or misleading information, particularly on social media platforms, has a significant impact on public opinion, election procedures, and policies (Bakdash et al., 2018). Even though the phrase information pollution had been used before, it became well-known when online usability specialist Jakob Nielsen (2003) raised concerns about the possible drawbacks of democratized content generation in his critical analysis of the phenomena.

The many forms of information pollution covered above can be arranged into a two-dimensional taxonomy to improve conceptual clarity, as indicated in Table 1. This taxonomy makes a distinction between unintentional forms, which include redundant duplication, poorly maintained content, and increase in the quantity of information (Belabbes et al., 2023), and intentional forms, which include misinformation, disinformation, malinformation, and cyberbullying (Rezayi et al., 2018). Additionally, it distinguishes between infrastructural pollution, which affects technological systems and resources (e.g., redundant archived data, inefficient data storage, and excessive energy consumption), and cognitive pollution, which overloads or distorts human information processing (e.g., spam, manipulative messaging, and information overload).

Table 1. Forms of information pollution

Type of infollution	Cognitive Pollution	Infrastructural Pollution
Intentional	Disinformation, misinformation, malinformation, cyberbullying, manipulative messaging	Coordinated server overload
Unintentional	Outdated or inaccurate information, excessive duplication, spam, poorly structured data	Redundant archived data, inefficient storage formats, unnecessary replication of large files

Source(s): Authors 'own (2025)

1.2 Theoretical Perspectives and Frameworks

Several theoretical perspectives have been used to examine the idea of information pollution. While Cognitive Load Theory (Sweller, 1988) emphasizes the cognitive strain caused by excessive information, Information Ecology (Nardi & O'Day, 1999) emphasizes the interconnection of information systems and their influence on users. Similarly, McLuhan's 1964 book Media Ecology explores how media technologies influence human perception and communication. When taken as a whole, these frameworks offer a comprehensive understanding of the effects of information pollution and overload on people and organizations, demonstrating that the problem is not just the sheer amount of data but also its poor quality, inconsistency, and propensity for disinformation.

These viewpoints highlight the fact that information pollution is more than just a numerical problem; rather, it is a reflection of more serious issues stemming from the deterioration of informational ecosystems. Prior information science research has focused heavily on information quality (IQ), with discussions centered on its essential components, including objectivity, completeness, accuracy, and presentation (Hilligoss & Rieh, 2008; Lee et al., 2002; Liu, 2004; Rieh & Danielson, 2007; Wang & Strong, 1996). According to Media Ecology, technologies such as social media and news platforms intended to improve communication can also spread false information, making the information ecosystem more polluted (Colombo, 2022).

Similarly, Cognitive Load Theory demonstrates that people's capacity to make decisions might be hampered by an overload of information that is either irrelevant or conflicting (Sweller, 1994).

Despite the enormous amount of information that is currently available, assessing its quality is still difficult. Information overload (IO) has thus become a more prevalent problem. According to a representative poll in Germany, information overload was actually cited by 22.5% of respondents as one of their main sources of stress (Meyer et al., 2021). IO's increase can be explained by a few significant changes, including the shift from an industrial to an information-driven economy (MacDonald et al., 2011) and the emergence of social media platforms (Koroleva et al., 2010). Because of the vast array of content available on social media, the increasing number of information sources, and the constant barrage of irrelevant content and unsolicited adverts (Fu et al., 2020), IO has flourished in this environment.

Poor-quality information deteriorates decision-making, leading to inefficiencies, uncertainty, and societal mistrust (all characteristics of invisible waste), much like how physical pollution harms natural ecosystems. In this context, "invisible waste" refers to the accumulation of poor-quality, misleading, and redundant digital content that deteriorates organizational, social, and cognitive settings.

The problems of information overload have been exacerbated by this change in the information landscape, which has been mostly caused by social media and digital technology (Stanley, 2021). It has become more challenging to weed out noise and false information, particularly on social media, due to the decentralization of information in news reporting and the accessibility made possible by digital platforms (Holton & Chyi, 2012; Kaufhold et al., 2020). High levels of exposure and stress associated with information overload are caused by this environment, which also makes it easier for fake news to proliferate and complicates journalistic methods (Schmitt et al., 2018). Social media, blogs, and websites are examples of emerging information and communication technologies that have greatly lowered barriers to content access and sharing, frequently leading to people receiving unwanted material (Aljukhadar & Senecal, 2017). Information pollution is also distributed by a variety of outlets, such as print media, which disseminate content without following explicit advertising restrictions (Boerman & van Reijmersdal, 2016).

The outburst of unwanted, unverified, and poorly categorized digital content is comparable to the unchecked spread of garbage in industrial settings, which begs the question of whether information should be governed by the same rules as environmental sanitation. The widespread availability of information presents both significant challenges and valuable opportunities for learning, creativity, innovation, and improved performance (Iqbal et al., 2018). In addition to raising the expenses of information gathering, dissemination, and storage, an oversupply of data also leads to skewed and inefficient decision-making. The abundance of inconsistent and low-quality data from multiple sources has made processing this influx more challenging Thus, many organizations find it difficult to control what is now known as information pollution. Since decision-makers must designate funds to reduce information waste, this problem entails organizational, societal, and economic ramifications.

In the context of Industry 4.0, information pollution is becoming more widely acknowledged as a pressing concern. Industry 4.0 is the general term used to describe the transition of businesses to digital form. Cloud-based manufacturing, radio frequency identification (RFID), Internet of Things (IoT), Internet of Service

(IoS), enterprise resource planning (ERP), and social product development are just a few of the technologies that are part of Industry 4.0 (Baur & Wee, 2015; Fonseca, 2018; Georgakopoulos et al., 2016; Kube & Rinn, 2014; Lasi et al., 2014; Lin et al., 2015; Lom et al., 2016; Lu, 2017; Singer, 2015). In the era of disruptive digital technologies, Iqbal et al. (2018) draw attention to the paucity of study in this field and stress the pressing need to create efficient solutions to combat information pollution (Iqbal & Nawaz, 2021). This offers a significant lens for evaluating whether the concepts of the circular economy—such as design for clarity, reuse, and closed-loop systems—can be modified to deal with the increasing magnitude of digital content being produced and consumed.

Concerns have recently been raised by researchers on the detrimental impacts of information overload, which is seen to be the digital counterpart of the pollution that industrial activities produce in the environment. Social media's participation during the COVID-19 epidemic has been characterized by new terminology such as "disinfomedic" and "infodemic." These broader conceptions underscore the potential harm to persons living in a "mediated reality constructed out of fake news, misinformation, rumors, and lies" (Deuze, 2020). Social media and the internet have become popular, extensive, and easy-to-use channels for disseminating information in real time. They act as open forums for sharing feelings and thoughts, expressing opinions, exchanging knowledge, and having public conversations. These platforms have become extremely popular and have a growing user base across all age and demographic categories particularly in the age of the digital economy, when technology is considered to "mediate time," (Jung & Kowalski, 2021). But a crucial question is whether the content that circulates on these platforms every second, influencing the lives, attitudes, and perceptions of billions of people is validated, authenticated, and held to quality standards (Meel & Vishwakarma, 2020). Regulation of information pollution is just as important as that of environmental toxins because this issue is at the heart of its policy consequences.

As digital material becomes more widely available, competition for users' attention, a resource growing ever more limited in the so-called "attention economy", intensifies (Wu, 2018). It is crucial to comprehend these informational risks before visualizing how circular economy frameworks could address them, change digital practices, and guide sustainable policy responses.

1.3 Effects of information pollution

Despite not being a recent phenomenon, information pollution has significantly increased in scope and velocity in recent years (Talwar et al., 2019). Subjective, low-quality, and misleading content has spread quickly due to developments in information and communication technologies, especially the emergence of social media platforms. Nowadays, major hazards to public health, societal well-being, institutional trust, and cognitive environments arise from the widespread dissemination of contaminated information.

- *Economic/social effect*

Information pollution, especially misinformation, has a significant financial cost. Previous studies and papers have attempted to calculate the monetary losses brought on by the dissemination of poor-quality and misleading content. In the context of the circular economy (CE), where false information can hinder efforts to maximize resource usage, discourage investment in eco-friendly innovations, and impede progress toward sustainability, this problem becomes even more pressing. Greenwashing, the practice of businesses making exaggerated claims about their environmental advantages, is a type of strategic information pollution that damages consumer confidence, alters markets, and reduces support for truly circular solutions.

According to a 2019 research (Cavazos, 2019) by cybersecurity analysts and economists, fake news alone caused almost $78 billion in losses worldwide in a single year. The industries most impacted were stock market volatility and losses ($39 billion), financial misinformation in the United States ($17 billion), and public health and reputation management expenses ($9 billion per year). Complementary findings from the Economic Policy Institute's (Carson, 2018; Shierholz & Zipperer, 2017) highlightde how American retirement savings lose $17 billion annually as a result of receiving false advice from biased financial advisors. To counteract the financial drivers of online information pollution, activist and nonprofit organizations have joined forces. For instance, the activist network Sleeping Giants, which has chapters across several nations, was successful in getting more than 820 businesses, such as AT&T, BMW, and Visa, to stop placing advertisements on extreme and unreliable news outlets like Breitbart News (Braun et al., 2019).

Similarly, to help adtech companies defund sources of information pollution, the Global Disinformation Index (GDI)[2] publishes risk assessments of media outlets. Legal action has also begun to play a role in addressing the consequences of disinformation. In late 2022, the families of Sandy Hook Elementary School victims won two major defamation cases against conspiracy theorist Alex Jones, who falsely claimed the massacre of 20 children and six staff members at a Connecticut school had been staged. This case marks a notable legal precedent in the fight against harmful disinformation. Jones was ordered to pay a total of $1.49 billion in damages (Bulgakova, 2024).

All things considered, these instances show that the social and financial harm brought about by information pollution frequently totals billions of dollars every year, presenting serious threats to societal well-being, financial stability, and public confidence. These financial and social expenses have the potential to postpone or impede CE-related activities like extended producer responsibility, circular procurement, and green investment.

- *Cognitive overload*

Because information pollution and cognitive overload are closely related, information pollution also has the negative consequence of contributing to cognitive overload. Information overload emphasizes the cognitive effects of processing such enormous volumes of stuff, especially in digital environments, whereas information pollution refers to the spread of unnecessary, deceptive, or superfluous data. This is especially important in the context of the circular economy (CE), where people and organizations may find it difficult to make informed decisions and adopt sustainable behaviors due to the complexity of sustainable practices and the deluge of information.

According to research, working memory's capacity to process information at any given time is known as cognitive load, and it is restricted (Sweller, 2011). This cognitive threshold is frequently exceeded when people are exposed to too much information, particularly through social media, which makes it challenging to efficiently assimilate and retain knowledge (Sweller, 2011). Though it was first used to study education and learning (Sweller 2011; Zen et al., 2010), Cognitive Load Theory (CLT) has more recently been used to study how people cope with the deluge of digital content that can overstimulate the brain's processing capacity (Laato et al., 2020; Islam et al., 2020).

People who are overloaded frequently have lower levels of social trust, less self-control, and are more likely to make poor decisions because they are unable to properly evaluate the information they are receiving (Samson & Kostyszyn, 2015). Unintentionally spreading contaminated content is one example of this careless behavior (Laato et al., 2020; Islam et al., 2020). Users are less inclined to carefully consider what they consume as information overload increases, which raises the possibility of disseminating inaccurate or misleading information (Bermes, 2021). Excessive content causes psychological stress that inhibits critical thinking and verification efforts (Whelan et al., 2020), increasing vulnerability to information pollution. Moreover, exhaustion has been linked to information overload (Whelan et al., 2020), which hinders users' capacity to assess the veracity of the material they come across (Laato et al., 2020). Cognitive overload is also the driving force behind social media fatigue, a more general problem that has been connected to this fatigue (Xiao & Mou, 2019). Previous research has established a clear link between this kind of fatigue and a rise in the dissemination of false information (Talwar et al., 2019).

Rajabzadeh et al. (2011) described a number of behavioral and cognitive symptoms resulting from short-term memory saturation and overstimulation, while also documenting additional psychological impacts of information overload, a consequence of information pollution. These consist of:

- Difficulty focusing due to the brain's struggle to process the overwhelming influx of information.
- An ongoing feeling of urgency, which reflects the need to process information fast.
- Multilateral conduct, in which people try to do several things at once, frequently without success.
- Enhanced irritability, characterized by sensitivity and mood swings.
- Cognitive shutdown, which occurs when extreme familiarity or overstimulation leading to mental exhaustion or brief stop in processing information.

These symptoms highlight the more profound effects of information pollution on cognition, particularly in settings where there is an abundance of excessive or poor-quality digital content.

- *Productivity and Decision-Making Paralysis*

In addition to straining cognitive resources, information pollution impairs strategic decision-making and organizational productivity, two essential elements of a healthy circular economy. Employee focus and productivity are regularly undermined by disruptive information and communication technologies, which have grown to be major causes of workplace distraction (Karr-Wisniewski & Lu, 2010; Zha et al., 2019). Workers are interrupted six times a day on average by unsolicited or irrelevant information, which hinders their ability to focus and makes their decisions of lower quality (Swar et al., 2017). The deluge of available data impedes development and negatively affects worker satisfaction. These consequences are not limited to individuals; organizations may also be subject to legal action (Swar et al., 2017). In order to optimize supply chains, execute reverse logistics, and fulfill sustainability reporting obligations, companies aiming for circularity rely on fast reliable information. These procedures are hampered by contaminated or overly abundant information, which compromises the long-term transformation plans and operational agility that are key to CE models.

Employee performance and job satisfaction are adversely affected by inaccurate or overly detailed information (Edmunds & Morris, 2000). Therefore, to remain robust and maintain a competitive edge in today's information-intensive economy, firms must face the problems presented by information pollution. According to Bewick and Corrall (2010), ensuring access to high-quality information that enhances organizational performance is the foremost priority in combating information pollution.

A byproduct of information pollution, information overload (IO) has a variety of internal and external effects that can seriously hinder decision-making, productivity, and general efficiency. These impacts can take many different forms, from poor teamwork and serious organizational errors to cognitive strain and decreased creativity.

People's cognitive abilities and general well-being are the main internal effects of information overload (IO). IO results in:

- Emotional and cognitive exhaustion, including lower creativity (Rötzel & Fehrenbacher, 2019), trouble focusing (Koltay, 2017), and problems learning and solving problems (Green, 2011; Sabeeh & Ismail, 2013). The mental burden of knowledge overload is further compounded by emotional exhaustion, which includes detrimental effects on wellbeing (Jackson & Farzaneh, 2012; Tan & Kuo, 2019) and disengagement from work.
- Reduced focus and attention difficulties (Koltay, 2017), making it difficult to focus on tasks or take in important details due to an abundance of information.
- The overwhelming amount of data makes it hard to identify trustworthy sources or develop confidence in decision-making, which leads to a lower level of trust in information and others (Furner & Zinko, 2017).
- Increased cognitive load, which causes mental exhaustion and impairs efficient problem-solving by placing additional demands on working memory (Lauri & Virkus, 2019; Rötzel & Fehrenbacher, 2019).
- Task abandonment and ceased learning, in which people may completely stop looking for or processing information as a result of the excessive mental strain that IO causes (Swar et al., 2017).

The emotional exhaustion and internal cognitive pressure brought on by IO are not limited to individuals. The detrimental consequences on organizational performance and collaboration are exacerbated by these individual effects, which swiftly transfer into low productivity, inability to make decisions, and task abandonment at the organizational level (Swar et al., 2017; Wild et al., 2012).

Information overload (IO) has external effects on people's performance as well as the world at large. Among these repercussions are:

- Poor decision-making, as excessive information makes it hard to prioritize and comprehend, resulting in poor decisions (Aikat & Remund, 2012).

- Reduced productivity and task abandonment, as an abundance of information leads to disengagement and impairs concentration on critical tasks (Swar et al., 2017; Wild et al., 2012).
- Reduced collaboration as information overload makes it difficult to communicate and operate as a team (Koroleva et al., 2010; Rötzel & Fehrenbacher, 2019).
- Financial loss as a result of IO-induced inefficiency and poor decision-making (Rötzel & Fehrenbacher, 2019).

Organizations must act quickly to address information pollution, as evidenced by the increasing prevalence of information overload. In addition to endangering cognitive health, failing to do so compromises decision-making, teamwork, and efficiency, all of which are essential for preserving a competitive edge in a world that prioritizes digitalization. Organizations must put in place strong information management procedures that prioritize pertinent, high-quality data, expedite communication, and protect staff members from the negative impacts of information overload in order to reduce these risks. Adopting these solutions is essential to long-term organizational growth and the success of circular economy models.

2. DEFINING THE CIRCULAR ECONOMY

Sustainability and the Circular Economy (CE) are becoming more and more popular among academics, businesspeople, and legislators (Geissdoerfe et al., 2017). Many obstacles still stand in the way of implementing sustainable measures, despite increased interest (Bey et al., 2013). With the goal of achieving a win-win situation from both an economic and value-creation standpoint, CE is becoming a prominent strategic response to the twin problems of resource scarcity and waste generation (Homrich et al., 2018).

British environmental economists David W. Pearce and R. Kerry Turner first codified the idea of CE in their 1989 book Economics of Natural Resources and the Environment. They underlined that society at the time lacked sufficient systems to handle the trash brought on by patterns of consumption (Su et al., 2013). The importance of CE has greatly increased in the modern era, leading legislators to consider public concerns before passing and enforcing relevant laws (Pan et al., 2015).

CE has connections to many other disciplines and themes. For example, it conceptually links to sustainability (Homrich et al., 2018), industrial ecology (Lewandowski, 2016), eco-design (MacArthur et al., 2015), cleaner production (Geng et al., 2010), eco-innovation (Castellani et al., 2014), closed economies (Geng & Doberstein, 2008), ecological loops (Haas et al., 2015), and product-service systems (Tukker, 2015).

It also introduces new perspectives on waste and resource management (Blomsma & Brennan, 2017). Beyond its technical uses, CE can also be seen as a political and strategic objective to replace the conventional linear economic model—which is often characterized as "take, make, use, dispose"—with a regenerative circular model that maximizes resource efficiency and reduces externalized waste (Gregson et al., 2015; Geng et al., 2016).

2.1 Circular economy in policy and practice

According to Berg et al. (2018), the circular economy (CE) is now widely recognized as a crucial framework for promoting environmental sustainability and addressing long-term ecological issues. Governments, businesses, and academic institutions have all expressed a great deal of interest in it (Geissdoerfer et al., 2017; Suárez-Eiroa et al., 2019). By reimagining the design, use, and recovery of products and materials, CE provides workable solutions to resource depletion, pollution, biodiversity loss, and unsustainable land use.

Through the creation of focused policies that encourage circular processes across industries, nations like China, the Netherlands, and Finland have taken the initiative to embrace CE concepts (Zhu et al., 2019; Hartley et al., 2020). According to Bleischwitz et al. (2022) and Taghipour et al. (2022), fostering circular practices requires appropriate policies. Additionally, Govindan and Hasanagic (2018) point out that different policy tools are designed to assist distinct CE supply chain segments. For instance, extensive policy frameworks that regulate CE practices from product design to manufacture, consumption, and waste management have been adopted by both the European Union and China (McDowall et al., 2017). These programs show how CE helps achieve more general sustainability objectives.

The European Green Deal, a comprehensive growth plan, was unveiled by the European Commission (EC) in December 2019, aiming to transform the European Union (EU) into a more equitable and prosperous society with a modern, resource-efficient, and competitive economy. Decoupling economic growth from resource usage and achieving net-zero greenhouse gas emissions throughout the Union by 2050 are two of the agreement's main goals (European Commission, 2019). The shift to a clean and circular economy (CE), which will necessitate a 25-year transformation of industrial sectors and their value chains, is a top goal within this strategy (Tóth, 2019). The EC reinforced this commitment by stressing on the urgency of taking action within the next five years. It introduced a new CE Action Plan in March 2020 with the goal of making Europe cleaner and more competitive (European Commission, 2020).

The European Commission's first circularity communication in 2014 marked the official start of the EU's involvement in CE (European Commission, 2014).

The 2015 CE Action Plan (European Commission, 2015), the 2018 CE Monitoring Framework (European Commission, 2018), and a 2019 implementation report on the initial action plan (European Commission, 2019) were among the policy tools that followed. According to Smol et al. (2015), the CE model encourages a change from the linear "take–make–dispose" system to a circular one in which waste is turned into a resource. In this transformation, the management of mineral resources is essential. In addition to promoting recycling and recovery from waste streams, the EC advises optimizing the efficiency of raw material use. As stressed in the 2018 CE monitoring framework, it also emphasizes the necessity of keeping an eye on how member states handle these resources (European Commission, 2018).

By 2050, about 70% of the global population are expected to live in cities that already significantly contribute to global environmental pollution through high resource consumption and carbon emissions (Arora et al., 2020; Wang et al., 2019). Urban regions must address the intricate and interrelated socioeconomic and environmental issues highlighted by the Sustainable Development Goals (SDGs) as they grow to accommodate population increase. Accordingly, attaining the SDGs requires improving urban sustainability (Bian et al., 2020; Shah et al., 2020). This entails tackling problems including climate change, reducing ecological effects, and increasing resource utilization efficiency (de Morais et al., 2021; Zhang et al., 2019).

The need for materials and energy keeps growing as a result of industrialization, economic growth, urbanization, and rising living standards. Environmental targets, including a 50% decrease in CO_2 emissions, are unlikely to be achieved without further interventions, despite hopeful predictions about technological advancements (Fang et al., 2017; Kim et al., 2018). Therefore, in order to achieve SDG Goal 11: "Sustainable Cities and Communities," comprehensive and systemic solutions that go beyond just technical approaches are desperately needed (Márquez & Rutkowski, 2020; Tseng et al., 2018). Improving resource efficiency and controlling municipal and other types of waste are important ways to accomplish this and lessen the environmental impact of urban areas (Márquez & Rutkowski, 2020; Suárez-Eiroa et al., 2019; Xavier et al., 2021).

Through symbiotic techniques that maximize the flow of materials and energy, the circular economy (CE) offers a comprehensive strategy to rethink urban systems and lessen the ecological impacts of cities (Joensuu et al., 2020; Bjørnbet et al., 2021; Schöggl et al., 2020). In response, a number of cities, including Shanghai, Tokyo, Amsterdam, and San Francisco, have recently implemented progressive programs like "eco-cities," "circular cities," and "zero-waste cities." These initiatives are being led by trailblazing practitioners and policymakers (Wang et al., 2019; Fratini et al., 2019; Xavier et al., 2021; Schöggl et al., 2020). Advanced recycling systems, industrial symbiosis, and life cycle management techniques that improve resource and energy circulation reduce waste output in these ideal urban models (de Morais et al., 2021; Abou Taleb & Al Farooque, 2021; Friant et al., 2021; Roy, 2021).

Although the circular economy has long recognized the value of reduction, reuse, and recycling in the management of material resources, their application to the management of information in digital ecosystems is still in the early stages. However, a number of studies examine different methods for preventing or lessening information overload, emphasizing strategies like enhancing personal information management, organizing teamwork, and defining organizational responsibilities like choosing the right software and enforcing transparency guidelines (Arnold et al., 2023).

2.2 Information as a Pillar of Circular Economy Implementation

Although resource cycles and material flows are essential to the concept of the Circular Economy (CE), little is known about how information either facilitates or hinders these movements. Information is the glue holding circular plans together in the digital era, directing choices about value chain optimization, waste reduction, product design, and resource usage. However, information itself can turn into waste if it is not managed purposefully. In order to fully realize the potential of a circular model, it is imperative to treat information as a crucial sustainability asset. This section examines how information, its quality, management, and misuse impact the application of CE principles.

The Circular Economy (CE) has drawn more attention from academics and decision-makers as a viable approach to severing the link between economic growth and trash generation and resource consumption (Lieder & Rashid, 2016; MacArthur, 2013). Businesses can preserve the competitiveness of their value chains while promoting sustainability by fully embracing CE principles. But there are a number of obstacles in the way of the shift to a circular economy (Bressanelli, 2019). Because digital technologies can facilitate the redesign of products, business models, consumption patterns, and value chains to incorporate CE techniques, the digital era presents potential to address these difficulties (Bressanelli et al., 2021; Cagno et al., 2021). Circular approaches, such as lifetime evaluations (Edelen & Ingwersen, 2018), digital product passports (Jensen et al., 2023), and real-time material flow tracking (Cagno et al., 2021), all depend on high-quality data. To find chances for recycling, remanufacturing, and reuse, these systems rely on reliable, interoperable data.

Despite its potential for integration, information pollution is a new type of waste that is mostly ignored by current CE frameworks. Unchecked creation, redundancy, and poor curation of information provide a serious but little-considered sustainability concern in an increasingly digital economy. Few, if any, scholars have looked at how the data produced by digital economies might actually hinder or harm circular initiatives, despite the fact that many have analyzed the positive contributions of digital technologies like the Internet of Things (IoT) and Big Data to furthering the CE. It is critical to start seeing our information space as a component of the larger environment and to put policies in place to protect it from pollution and overload.

Applying this conventional "clean-up" method to digital data presents special difficulties. The Comprehensive Environmental Response, Compensation, and Liability Act of 1980 (CERCLA) is an example of how environmental rules frequently seek to clean up hazardous waste after it has been released; however, there is no comparable system for digital waste. Data cannot be cleanly removed or contained way physical items can. With only a keystroke or a line of code, it can be replicated indefinitely and for almost no cost. It exists outside of defined boundaries. It's really hard to manage once it's out there. Therefore, rather than depending solely on cleanup tactics, digital regulation needs to move toward proactive harm mitigation and post-event responsibility.

The CE's sustainability ideals must be fully embraced by taking into account digital ecosystems in addition to material flows. Similar to tangible items, information has a lifespan that includes production, dissemination, usage, and obsolescence. In order to apply CE principles to information, systems must be designed with informational quality, longevity, accuracy, reuse, and ethical disposal as top priorities. For example, circular thinking in the digital age could promote the production of high-quality, context-aware information, backed by strong metadata and archival standards, just like circular design in manufacturing stresses durability and repairability. Digital systems could incorporate features for reusing correct information while discarding out-of-date, redundant, or deceptive content, just like CE encourages recycling and upcycling.

2.3 Digital Technologies Driving Circular Economy Innovation

Digital technology breakthroughs are revolutionizing sectors and are essential to the circular economy (CE). This section examines how the adoption of CE and sustainable development are being fueled by new digital breakthroughs, especially those related to Industry 4.0.

There are significant financial and environmental benefits when moving toward a circular economy (CE), which is aided by the 10Rs framework (Refuse, Reduce, Reuse, Repair, Refurbish, Remanufacture, Repurpose, Recycle, Recover, Redesign) (Bag et al., 2021a). However, the unavailability of cutting-edge technologies (Jabbour et al., 2020a) and the uncertainty surrounding the financial rewards of investing in such advances (Piscitelli et al., 2020; Abdul-Hamid et al., 2020) frequently hinder practical adoption. In this regard, new Industry 4.0 (I4.0) technologies have been essential for promoting collaborative economic models and speeding up the implementation of CE (Jabbour et al., 2020b).

Smart factory components, cyber-physical system integration, environmentally conscious product design, life cycle assessment, and advanced machine learning algorithms are all included in Industry 4.0, which is characterized by the integration of digital tools to increase organizational efficiency (Yadav et al., 2020). These technologies improve supply chain coordination, boost resilience, increase resource efficiency, reduce processing times and product costs, and improve industrial resource utilization (Fatorachian & Kazemi, 2018). I4.0, which offers substantial environmental advantages as well as commercial value, has thus emerged as a key component of industrial transformation (Fettermann et al., 2018).

By supporting the reuse of waste materials, restoration of old items, and production of remanufactured goods, I4.0 technologies directly promote CE practices (Sun et al., 2012). For instance, by lowering transaction costs, enhancing supply chain communication, reducing waste, and decreasing carbon emissions, blockchain technology supports CE (Upadhyay et al., 2021).

Effective CE practices are made possible in Indonesia by the Internet of Things (IoT), which is essential to the management of commercial trash collection, transportation, and processing (Fatimah et al., 2020). Similarly, big data, IT infrastructure, and human capital are recognized as crucial I4.0 elements in South Africa that advance circular economy outcomes and sustainable production (Bag et al., 2021b). According to qualitative research conducted in Estonia, big data analytics and additive manufacturing significantly improve the adoption of CE practices at every level (Prause & Atari, 2017). Globally, research involving CE project leaders across Europe, America, Asia, and Africa indicates that I4.0 technologies significantly lower emissions, waste production, and material and energy consumption (Laskurain-Iturbe et al., 2021). Robotics and additive manufacturing have the most effects among these technologies. Industry 4.0 is a crucial facilitator for developing circular economy activities and attaining environmental sustainability, according to a thorough literature study (Lopes de Sousa Jabbour et al., 2018).

IoT, 3D printing, big data analytics, virtual reality (VR), augmented reality (AR), and other digital technologies are driving the Fourth Industrial Revolution and are well known for upending traditional patterns of production and consumption (Bressanelli et al., 2018). Commercial mainframe computers started the digitization process in the 1960s, and the introduction of personal computers in the mid-1980s accelerated it. This led to improvements in digital design and automated manufacturing (Sturgeon, 2021; Gereffi et al., 2005). Over time, global positioning, Internet connectivity, and portable computing have become essential components of the digital economy, and their widespread use has been made possible by the growth and cost reduction of information and communication technologies (ICTs) (Sturgeon, 2021). In addition to promoting creativity in less developed areas, these digital technologies increase productivity and worldwide connectedness among customers, employees, businesses, and ancillary sectors. Therefore, new ICTs, digital knowledge, and Internet-related data form the foundation of the digital economy, which is influencing all facets of industrial and social life globally (Zhen et al., 2021; Pimenova, 2021).

According to Despeisse et al. (2017), digital technologies are essential for advancing CE in businesses. For example, IoT enables businesses to track materials (Lewandowski, 2016), recycle scrap items (Pagoropoulos et al., 2017), and manage product consumption, status, and location in real time (Baines et al., 2013). These capabilities help businesses make the shift to circular economy models (Pialot et al., 2017). Digital information greatly increases efficiency in storage, sales, and delivery across a variety of industries, technologies, equipment, products, and services by utilizing data from process analysis and large-scale data processing in the digital economy (Ugli & Ugli, 2020). Nevertheless, achieving the United Nations Sustainable Development Goals (SDGs) remains challenging; estimates suggest that pandemic-related failures could jeopardize the attainment of two-thirds of the 169 targets by 2030 (Naidoo & Fisher, 2020).

The circular economy requires new talents to enable its development as digital transformation progresses and sustainability demands rise (Miehe et al., 2019). Digital technologies' potential to promote CE advancement is becoming more and more clear (Pialot et al., 2017), but research on the intersection of digital technologies and the circular economy is still in its infancy and is developing quickly (Pagoropoulos et al., 2017).

All things considered, the combination of Industry 4.0 technologies and the ideas of the circular economy presents encouraging avenues for achieving both economic efficiency and environmental sustainability. To completely comprehend and maximize the integration of these digital technologies within circular systems, more research is required.

3. MITIGATION STRATEGIES: TOWARD CLEANER INFORMATION ECOSYSTEMS

3.1 Technological Interventions for Managing Information Overload

Technological tools have become both contributors to and solutions for information overload as digital ecosystems grow increasingly complex. This section examines the ways in which these tools, specifically information architecture and semantic technologies, can help manage the problem of excess information.

By transferring more of the responsibility for information search and filtering to intelligent software agents, organizations can employ a well-known technological strategy for reducing information overload (IO). Incorporating concepts like the "semantic web," which envision web environments enhanced with built-in intelligence to address the shortcomings of current search engine technologies, is crucial to these initiatives, according to bibliometric studies (Olson et al., 2015). Despite the tremendous advancements in semantic web technologies, there are still uncharted areas for their use (Ristoski & Paulheim, 2016). However, the design and capability of information architectures, systems that establish significant semantic and contextual links based on user objectives and behavior, inherently limit the efficacy of such technological interventions (Davis, 2010).

One of the main causes of IO is information that is inaccurate and poorly organized. Users' capacity to digest information can be greatly improved by enhancing clarity, coherence, and presentation through improved selection, organization, and formatting (Eppler & Mengis, 2008; Blummer & Kenton, 2014). This demonstrates the critical role of information architects in reducing information overload. The idea of findability, which is the art and science of making knowledge easily discoverable by browsing, searching, or inquiring, is a fundamental component of information architecture (Morville, 2005). True findability entails integrating intelligence into content structures to reduce irrelevant results and expedite access, even though search tools play a role. Effective content retrieval relies on striking a balance between search precision (finding just relevant results) and recall (finding all relevant results) (Frappaolo & Keldsen, 2012).

Information architecture's continued relevance is questioned by some critics despite changing user capabilities. However, Hinton (2009) and Davis (2012) contend that all structures need careful design, whether they are used for personal or professional purposes. Information systems that evolve naturally are more likely to fail if they are not guided. As a result, IO mitigation supports the overarching goal of information architecture, which is to create user-friendly, socially useful information environments (Dillon, 2002).

To accomplish this, information architects need to have a thorough understanding of the socio-technical contexts in which they work as well as users, especially those who are burdened by IO (Davis, 2011, 2012). This entails addressing the complexity and volume of modern digital content by moving beyond surface-level design (Morville, 2005).

Users' informational demands and tasks should be given priority in mitigation techniques, which shouldn't be solely technological or cultural (Surla, 2007). The process of informing, or information-as-process, is especially pertinent in this context, as Buckland (1991) highlighted, because information architecture is concerned with interaction dynamics (Martin et al., 2010).

Lastly, there may be interesting avenues for integrating document architecture with information architecture. Because digital documents fall into distinct genres that influence their use and structure, any changes to these genres call for a reassessment of architectural principles. By doing so, information practices can be improved and new techniques to reduce IO symptoms can be provided (Francke, 2009).

3.2 Behavioral Strategies for Countering Misinformation

Protecting the information space involves far more than merely regulating content or suspending accounts. A wide range of information pollution prevention strategies are available to address the problem of limited viewpoint (Kozyreva et al., 2024). A summary of these tools' varying degrees of efficacy and scalability is provided in Table 2 below.

Table 2. Key Tools and Measures to Address Information Pollution

Intervention / Mechanism	Purpose / Intended Function	Impact and Scalability	Challenges / Limitations
Content moderation and deplatforming	Eliminating false or deceptive information and suspending related accounts.	Effective in limiting the spread of misinformation in the short term but requires significant resource allocation from the platform.	Might not be popular with the public and could be seen as censorship; only reactive in nature.
Debunking and factchecking	Providing factual evidence and logical explanations to show why a piece of information is incorrect or misleading.	Efficient in controlling circulation quickly but demands substantial resources.	May diminish trust in media and reduce belief in reliable information; reactive and its effectiveness may decline over time.
Accuracy-nudging	Encouraging people to consider the accuracy of a post or headline.	Scalable, especially with platform collaboration, though its immediate impact is limited.	Can lose effectiveness over time; may only be useful in specific contexts or for certain political or partisan groups
Pre-bunking	Raising awareness about how misinformation spreads.	Produces a strong impact by preventing misinformation before it spreads, with moderate scalability.	Requires periodic updates or reinforcement; effectiveness can vary based on the medium.

Source: Adapted and revised from Kozyreva et al. (2024)

Machine learning and neural network approaches are the main tools used in automated content labeling to help with content moderation (Alaphilippe et al., 2019; Gorwa et al., 2020). The overall objective is to classify content into problematic groups, including possible misinformation, or to compare uploads against databases of previously detected hazardous content, however the precise techniques vary (Thorne & Vlachos, 2018; Guo et al., 2022). Research on the efficacy of content warnings, including those on alcohol or smoking, identifies a number of crucial information processing phases (Conzola & Wogalter, 2001). First, the label must capture users' attention and hold it long enough for them to absorb all the relevant details. The label's content must then be understandable, albeit users' preexisting attitudes and beliefs may influence comprehension. Lastly, the label needs to motivate people to follow the advice. Notably, Bode and Vraga (2018) discovered that peer-provided social corrections and automated corrections were equally successful in lowering misinformation, indicating that uptake of corrections does not always require direct human engagement.

Addressing incorrect claims through fact-based corrections or exposing deceptive tactics is a widespread practice known as debunking misinformation (Cook et al., 2017; Vraga & Bode, 2020). To refute material, platforms such as Meta integrate human and automated efforts (Guo et al., 2022; Thorne & Vlachos, 2018). According to Lewandowsky et al. (2020), effective debunking should state the facts in an explicit manner, warn against false information, clarify why it is incorrect, and reaffirm the truth. Although there were early worries about "backfire effects," new research indicates that these are uncommon and that disproving false information often lowers belief in it (Swire-Thompson et al., 2020; Wood & Porter, 2019). Debunking is difficult, though, because incorrect ideas frequently endure in spite of corrections (Ecker et al., 2020), corrections seldom reach people in misinformation echo chambers (Zollo et al., 2017), and acceptance is dependent on the reliability of the source (Benegal & Scruggs, 2018). Effectiveness may also be restricted by political concerns and platform control (Coleman, 2018; Nyhan, 2017). Although debunking yields inconsistent outcomes when compared to prebunking, it is nevertheless a crucial technique in the control of misinformation (Brashier et al., 2021; Jolley & Douglas, 2017). Prebunking is an educational strategy that aims to help people become more adept at spotting and avoiding false information before they come across it. This proactive strategy, which is founded on the inoculation hypothesis (Compton, 2013; McGuire, 1961), entails exposing people to a weaker version of deceptive arguments together with a preemptive refutation and a warning about possible manipulation (Compton et al., 2021). Prebunking can be done actively via interactive games like the Bad News Game, which teaches players about typical disinformation strategies, or passively with texts or videos (Basol et al., 2020; Roozenbeek & van der Linden, 2019). Prebunking attempts to "vaccinate" people against incorrect information by fostering psychological resistance beforehand, in contrast to debunking and fact-checking, which are reactive and take place after misinformation has spread (Unver, 2020) (McPhedran et al., 2023).

According to research, inoculation treatments may reduce vulnerability to false information about issues like climate change (van der Linden et al., 2017), COVID-19 (Basol et al., 2021), and extremist propaganda (Braddock, 2022; Hughes et al., 2021). They also typically have moderate effects on increasing resistance to persuasion (Banas & Rains, 2010). Nonetheless, there are still issues: prebunking's efficacy depends on voluntary participation, and its influence could be restricted if the false information is quite distinct from the inoculation's content (Roozenbeek et al., 2022). Furthermore, certain interventions run the risk of undermining credibility if the source is viewed as unreliable (Traberg et al., 2022) and fostering a generalized mistrust about all news, even reliable information (Guess et al., 2020; Modirrousta-Galian & Higham, 2022). Despite these drawbacks, prebunking, which stops the spread of false information before it happens, presents a viable alternative to conventional debunking techniques.

According to Thaler and Sunstein (2009), nudges are small adjustments to the architecture of choices that affect behavior without limiting options or incentives. Their goal is to change behavior rather than develop abilities. Sharing false information on social media is frequently associated with users' lack of attention to accuracy (Pennycook & Rand, 2019). Researchers have created "accuracy nudges" to help individuals think about correctness before sharing content in order to remedy this. One way to prevent false sharing is to invite users to pause and consider news headlines (Fazio, 2020; Rathje et al., 2022). Nudges, like Twitter's prompt asking users if they have read an article before retweeting, are simple to employ, affordable, non-intrusive, and scalable. Nudges, however, tend to be less successful outside of lab settings (DellaVigna & Linos, 2022) and can backfire by inciting opposition (Mosleh et al., 2021). According to Kozyreva et al. (2020), low-cost nudges can ethically reduce support for more demanding solutions.

There are two primary nudge types that have been researched:

- Accuracy Primes: these techniques gently remind readers to share responsibly by asking them to assess the veracity of a non-political headline. Numerous studies demonstrate that these primes enhance the quality of sharing; nonetheless, the effects are modest, sporadic, and quickly deteriorate over time (Pennycook & Rand, 2022; Roozenbeek et al., 2021). Political beliefs also affect the effectiveness; conservatives, who are more likely to believe false information to be true, find it less successful (Pretus et al., 2022; Rathje et al., 2022).
- Social-Norm Nudges: their main goal is to draw attention to the social norms around the sharing of honest content. Although the results are still preliminary and have not been thoroughly examined in real-world contexts (Epstein et al., 2021), these techniques have demonstrated potential in lowering the inclination to spread false information and believe in conspiracies (Andı & Akesson, 2020; Cookson et al., 2021).

Overall, prebunking, debunking, boosting, and nudging provide alternative behavioral strategies to counter false information. Nudging helps people make better decisions, pre-bunking and boosting concentrate on fostering resilience in advance, and debunking deals with misleading information reactively. When combined, these tactics provide a comprehensive defense against false information, although further study is required to increase their practicality. Various national governments have taken different approaches to managing the swift changes that come with digitization. Three broad governance approaches for sustainable digitalization were identified at an OECD Ministerial Meeting in Paris in June 2017: (i) an industry-driven, laissez-faire model; (ii) a proactive, preemptive regulatory strategy; and (iii) a stewardship or "active surveillance" approach, in which governments conduct continuous oversight to reduce risks and foster innovation.

With little government involvement, the laissez-faire approach depends on industry self-regulation and market forces. It is expected of both individuals and businesses to autonomously manage and navigate digitalization processes. Although this approach encourages innovation and open markets, it does not centrally regulate acceptable practices, making it susceptible to cyberattacks and escalating social injustices. Additionally, it runs the risk of increasing corporate influence at the expense of public policy objectives and national sovereignty (Ostrom, 2000; Böhme et al., 2015).

The precautionary approach, on the other hand, places more emphasis on risk mitigation and regulation prior to the widespread adoption of new digital technologies. By establishing guidelines for data management, system architecture, and software usage, governments proactively address any permanent consequences. Although this strategy protects vital infrastructure and vulnerable groups, it may inhibit free enterprise and impede economic growth. Furthermore, the speed at which digital dangers are developing may surpass the speed at which regulations react, which could lower competitiveness in international marketplaces (Aradau, 2016; Stirling, 2006).

By promoting active government participation only when required, the stewardship model aims to strike a balance between innovation and risk management. To track advancements in digitalization, create best practices, and address new dangers, agencies work with business, academia, and civil society. Cybersecurity defense organizations entrusted with detecting and thwarting cybercrime are among the examples. While tackling sustainability issues, this collaborative governance promotes flexibility and creativity (Sylvain, 2021; Barben et al., 2008).

Together, these governance techniques show the variety of approaches that governments might take to make digital spaces safer and cleaner. A more robust framework for handling the intricate social, economic, and security challenges presented by digitalization may be provided by combining aspects of each strategy, even though no single strategy is without trade-offs.

3.3 Infollution, CE and Mitigation Strategies

The production, distribution, and handling of information have all undergone radical change as a result of information technology, which is thought to be a significant contributor to information pollution (Pandita, 2014). Few studies have explicitly addressed CE principles' significance in improving storage efficiency and data lifecycle management, even though previous research has looked at them within larger sustainability contexts. Organizations can reduce unnecessary data accumulation, improve efficiency, and support sustainable data governance by implementing the CE principles of reducing, reusing, recycling, and optimizing resources. Digital ecosystems benefit from the alignment of CE principles, which guarantee that data is managed properly, is value, and is accessible throughout its lifecycle.

To successfully apply CE principles to data management, firms need to create organized methods that maximize data governance, collection, storage, and reuse. Traditionally applied to physical resources, the CE model (Yap, 2005) provides a framework for maximizing data use, reducing waste, and improving efficiency. The following are important data management techniques that are in line with CE (Mufida et al., 2025):

- Data minimization: reducing unnecessary data collection and storage
- Data reuse: utilizing current datasets in different applications
- Data recycling: transforming irrelevant data into useful formats
- Data sharing: promoting collaboration to avoid duplication
- Data quality and standardization: improving integration by ensuring accuracy and structured formats
- Data lifecycle management: managing data from collection to disposal.
- Data privacy and security: putting compliance, anonymization, and encryption into practice.
- Data governance and compliance: establishing guidelines for the ethical and controlled usage of data.

The conceptual framework for integrating circular economy (CE) ideas into dealing with infollution is depicted in Figure 1.

Figure 1. Conceptual framework: CE Strategies for Mitigating Infollution

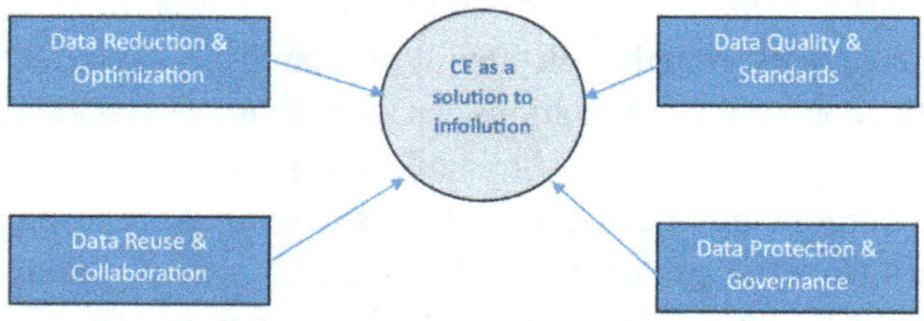

Figure 1. Conceptual framework: CE Strategies for Mitigating Infollution

There are advantages and disadvantages to incorporating CE address infollution. Adoption is hampered by a number of factors, such as privacy concerns, interoperability problems, and opposition to new governance models, even if CE tactics improve data efficiency, reduce redundant storage, and encourage sustainability.

Advanced governance structures and technological innovation are necessary to ensure data security while promoting reuse (Bressanelli et al., 2018).

4. FUTURE DIRECTIONS AND POLICY RECOMMENDATIONS

Addressing information pollution needs to be a key component of sustainability discussions and circular economy projects as the digital ecosystem grows. Quantifying digital waste and its systemic effects on cognitive load, decision-making, and the usage of environmental resources should be the focus of future studies. This entails creating uniform measures to quantify information pollution and incorporating them into evaluations of sustainability.

Bray (2008) advocates for a change in professional practice rather than just concentrating on creating new technological solutions. Information professionals should actively replace low-quality information with better alternatives, stay away from tools that encourage task-switching, and treat cognitive bandwidth and human attention as limited resources that need to be preserved. This viewpoint is consistent with the research conducted by Iqbal et al. (2019, 2020) and Iqbal and Nawaz (2021), who expand on the seminal studies of Orman and Nielsen to examine how information pollution impairs wellbeing and productivity in knowledge-based work contexts.

Multiple levels of interventions are needed to address information overload (IOL). By restricting excessive smartphone use and using defensive apps that monitor and regulate online time, people can restore control over their digital environments on an individual basis. Employees in businesses can gain from training that improves their ability to use collaboration and communication tools effectively (Soucek & Moser, 2010). Some technology solutions, though, can have drawbacks. Generative AI models, for instance, can lower IOL through features like intelligent search and summarization, but they also run the danger of making the issue worse by producing fake material, spreading false information, and strengthening algorithmic biases (De Freitas et al., 2023).

Three key domains—science, education, and legislation—need to coordinate their response. In order to foster cooperative projects spanning the social sciences, computer science, and communication studies, more funding should first be allocated to multidisciplinary research on information ecology and multilevel IOL. Second, information ecology should be incorporated early in school curricula to promote digital responsibility, much like environmental education encouraged behavioral changes in waste recycling. Lastly, legislators ought to start investigating the viability of a global regulatory framework known as the "Clean Information Act," which would aim to lessen information pollution and promote healthier digital ecosystems. This idea is modeled after the UK's 1956 Clean Air Act.

Based on current research and global developments, four key policy recommendations proposed by Sinanoglu and Breuer (2024) emerge:

1. To counteract information pollution, diversify and implement a wide range of digital tools. More neutral, scalable, and preventative methods should replace the current focus on politically charged content moderation. Pre-bunking, real-time detection, and automatic alarms are examples of techniques that can be used with little human moderation, which makes them less biased and more sustainable.
2. Carefully assess and modify interventions. Information pollution has no universal solution. Initial promising tools, such algorithmic flagging or pre-bunking, may lose their efficacy over time or work differently in various media or cultural contexts. When scaling these instruments, policymakers should take a measured, evidence-based approach, ideally backed by adaptive policies, context-specific research, and iterative testing. AI has the potential to help these treatments reach a wider audience, but its application needs to be supported by strong oversight procedures.
3. Make long-term investments in community resilience and media literacy. Programs for digital literacy that enhance critical thinking and content discernment should be given top priority by governments and foreign development partners. In order to combat digital misinformation, build resistance to disinformation efforts, and reduce social tensions both online and offline, offline activities like school-based education and local dialogue forums are crucial.
4. Create a global information integrity regulatory framework. Multisectoral and international cooperation is necessary to address global information pollution, especially when it comes to large technological businesses that influence digital ecosystems. Independent monitoring, public accountability, and openness should be prioritized in a new regulatory framework. A suitable forum for advancing such cooperative governance initiatives and creating globally standardized criteria for cleaner information environments is provided by the forthcoming Global Digital Compact, which will be negotiated at the UN Summit of the Future.

In addition to the four core recommendations by Sinanoglu and Breuer (2024), several broader policy directions deserve consideration:

- Encouraging cross-sectoral and multilateral collaboration. All pertinent parties, including governments, academia, civil society, and most importantly, the private sector, must take the initiative to establish a transnational regulatory framework for a secure and welcoming digital environment. Global coordination and shared accountability must be the cornerstones of digital cooperation.

- Extending the perspective on policy. Moderation of problematic information is a specific emphasis of current tactics. In order to scale up detection and prevention methods without introducing new biases, future approaches should prioritize content-neutral interventions and make use of AI capabilities. Such tools need to be thoroughly assessed for ethical use and openness.
- Avoiding one-size-fits-all solutions and consider context sensitivity. Tools that work well for one group or area might not work well for another. Only after thorough local testing and research to comprehend the cultural, social, and political ramifications should national policy integration take place.
- Committing to systemic, long-term change. There are no quick fixes when it comes to combating information pollution. Strong support for independent media, pluralistic information ecosystems, and the incorporation of information literacy into educational institutions are examples of holistic approaches that are required to increase societal resilience. Information ecology must now be acknowledged as a cornerstone of civic education and democratic sustainability, much like environmental literacy has been a major curriculum topic.

5. REFERENCES

Abdul-Hamid, A. Q., Ali, M. H., Tseng, M. L., Lan, S., & Kumar, M. (2020). Impeding challenges on industry 4.0 in circular economy: Palm oil industry in Malaysia. *Computers & Operations Research, 123*, 105052. DOI: 10.1016/j.cor.2020.105052

Abou Taleb, M., & Al Farooque, O. (2021). Towards a circular economy for sustainable development: An application of full cost accounting to municipal waste recyclables. *Journal of Cleaner Production, 280*, 124047. DOI: 10.1016/j.jclepro.2020.124047

Aikat, D. D., & Remund, D. (2012). Of time magazine, 24/7 media, and data deluge: The evolution of information overload theories and concepts. *Information overload: An international challenge for professional engineers and technical communicators*, 13-40.

Alaphilippe, A., Gizikis, A., Hanot, C., & Bontcheva, K. (2019). *Automated tackling of disinformation: Major challenges ahead.* European Parliament.

Aljukhadar, M., & Senecal, S. (2017). Communicating online information via streaming video: The role of user goal. *Online Information Review, 41*(3), 378–397. DOI: 10.1108/OIR-06-2016-0152

Andı, S., & Akesson, J. (2020). Nudging away false news: Evidence from a social norms experiment. *Digital Journalism (Abingdon, England), 9*(1), 106–125. DOI: 10.1080/21670811.2020.1847674

Aradau, C. (2016). Risk,(in) security and international politics. In *Routledge handbook of risk studies* (pp. 290-298). Routledge.

Arnold, M., Goldschmitt, M., & Rigotti, T. (2023). Dealing with information overload: A comprehensive review. *Frontiers in Psychology, 14*, 1122200. DOI: 10.3389/fpsyg.2023.1122200 PMID: 37416535

Arnold, M., Goldschmitt, M., & Rigotti, T. (2023). Dealing with information overload: A comprehensive review. *Frontiers in Psychology, 14*, 1122200. DOI: 10.3389/fpsyg.2023.1122200 PMID: 37416535

Arora, M., Raspall, F., Cheah, L., & Silva, A. (2020). Buildings and the circular economy: Estimating urban mining, recovery and reuse potential of building components. *Resources, Conservation and Recycling, 154*, 104581. DOI: 10.1016/j.resconrec.2019.104581

Bag, S., Gupta, S., & Kumar, S. (2021a). Industry 4.0 adoption and 10R advance manufacturing capabilities for sustainable development. *International Journal of Production Economics, 231*, 107844. DOI: 10.1016/j.ijpe.2020.107844

Bag, S., Yadav, G., Dhamija, P., & Kataria, K. K. (2021b). Key resources for industry 4.0 adoption and its effect on sustainable production and circular economy: An empirical study. *Journal of Cleaner Production, 281*, 125233. DOI: 10.1016/j.jclepro.2020.125233

Baines, T., & Lightfoot, , H. (2013). Servitization of the manufacturing firm: Exploring the operations practices and technologies that deliver advanced services. *International Journal of Operations & Production Management, 34*(1), 2–35. DOI: 10.1108/IJOPM-02-2012-0086

Bakdash, J., Sample, C., Rankin, M., Kantarcioglu, M., Holmes, J., Kase, S., & Szymanski, B. (2018, April). The future of deception: Machine-generated and manipulated images, video, and audio? In *2018 International Workshop on Social Sensing (SocialSens)* (pp. 2-2). IEEE. DOI: 10.1109/SocialSens.2018.00009

Banas, J. A., & Rains, S. A. (2010). A meta-analysis of research on inoculation theory. *Communication Monographs, 77*(3), 281–311. DOI: 10.1080/03637751003758193

Barben, D., Fisher, E., Selin, C., & Guston, D. H. (2008). 38 anticipatory governance of nanotechnology: foresight, engagement, and integration. *The handbook of science and technology studies, 979.*

Basol, M., Roozenbeek, J., Berriche, M., Uenal, F., McClanahan, W. P., & Linden, S. V. D. (2021). Towards psychological herd immunity: Cross-cultural evidence for two prebunking interventions against COVID-19 misinformation. *Big Data & Society, 8*(1), 20539517211013868. DOI: 10.1177/20539517211013868

Basol, M., Roozenbeek, J., & Van der Linden, S. (2020). Good news about bad news: Gamified inoculation boosts confidence and cognitive immunity against fake news. *Journal of cognition, 3*(1), 2.Fazio, L. (2020). Pausing to consider why a headline is true or false can help reduce the sharing of false news. *Harvard Kennedy School Misinformation Review, 1*(2).

Batmaz, Z., Yurekli, A., Bilge, A., & Kaleli, C. (2019). A review on deep learning for recommender systems: Challenges and remedies. *Artificial Intelligence Review, 52*(1), 1–37. DOI: 10.1007/s10462-018-9654-y

Baur, C., & Wee, D. (2015). Manufacturing's next act. *McKinsey & company, 6*, 1-5.

Bawden, D., & Robinson, L. (2020). Information overload: An introduction. In *Oxford research encyclopedia of politics.*

Belabbes, M. A., Ruthven, I., Moshfeghi, Y., & Rasmussen Pennington, D. (2023). Information overload: A concept analysis. *The Journal of Documentation, 79*(1), 144–159. DOI: 10.1108/JD-06-2021-0118

Benegal, S. D., & Scruggs, L. A. (2018). Correcting misinformation about climate change: The impact of partisanship in an experimental setting. *Climatic Change, 148*(1), 61–80. DOI: 10.1007/s10584-018-2192-4

Bergström, J., Dahlström, N., Henriqson, E., & Dekker, S. (2010). Team coordination in escalating situations: An empirical study using mid-fidelity simulation. *Journal of Contingencies and Crisis Management, 18*(4), 220–230. DOI: 10.1111/j.1468-5973.2010.00618.x

Berkan, R. (2012). Information pollution & doomsday consequence. *SEJ: Search Engine Journal.*

Bermes, A. (2021). Information overload and fake news sharing: A transactional stress perspective exploring the mitigating role of consumers' resilience during COVID-19. *Journal of Retailing and Consumer Services, 61*, 102555. DOI: 10.1016/j.jretconser.2021.102555

Bewick, L., & Corrall, S. (2010). Developing librarians as teachers: A study of their pedagogical knowledge. *Journal of Librarianship and Information Science, 42*(2), 97–110. DOI: 10.1177/0961000610361419

Bey, N., Hauschild, M. Z., & McAloone, T. C. (2013). Drivers and barriers for implementation of environmental strategies in manufacturing companies. *CIRP Annals, 62*(1), 43–46. DOI: 10.1016/j.cirp.2013.03.001

Bian, Y., Dong, L., Liu, Z., & Zhang, L. (2020). A sectoral eco-efficiency analysis on urban-industrial symbiosis. *Sustainability (Basel), 12*(9), 3650. DOI: 10.3390/su12093650

Bimber, B., & Gil de Zúñiga, H. (2020). The unedited public sphere. *New Media & Society, 22*(4), 700–715. DOI: 10.1177/1461444819893980

Bjørnbet, M. M., Skaar, C., Fet, A. M., & Schulte, K. Ø. (2021). Circular economy in manufacturing companies: A review of case study literature. *Journal of Cleaner Production, 294*, 126268. DOI: 10.1016/j.jclepro.2021.126268

Blomsma, F., & Brennan, G. (2017). The emergence of circular economy: A new framing around prolonging resource productivity. *Journal of Industrial Ecology, 21*(3), 603–614. DOI: 10.1111/jiec.12603

Blummer, B., & Kenton, M., J. (. (2014). Reducing patron information overload in academic libraries. *College & Undergraduate Libraries, 21*(2), 115–135. DOI: 10.1080/10691316.2014.906786

Bode, L., & Vraga, E. K. (2018). See something, say something: Correction of global health misinformation on social media. *Health Communication, 33*(9), 1131–1140. DOI: 10.1080/10410236.2017.1331312 PMID: 28622038

Böhme, R., Christin, N., Edelman, B., & Moore, T. (2015). Bitcoin: Economics, technology, and governance. *The Journal of Economic Perspectives, 29*(2), 213–238. DOI: 10.1257/jep.29.2.213

Braddock, K. (2022). Vaccinating against hate: Using attitudinal inoculation to confer resistance to persuasion by extremist propaganda. *Terrorism and Political Violence, 34*(2), 240–262. DOI: 10.1080/09546553.2019.1693370

Brashier, N. M., Pennycook, G., Berinsky, A. J., & Rand, D. G. (2021). Timing matters when correcting fake news. *Proceedings of the National Academy of Sciences of the United States of America, 118*(5), e2020043118. DOI: 10.1073/pnas.2020043118 PMID: 33495336

Braun, J. A., Coakley, J. D., & West, E. (2019). Activism, advertising, and far-right media: The case of sleeping giants. *Media and Communication, 7*(4), 68–79. DOI: 10.17645/mac.v7i4.2280

Bray, D. A. (2008). Information pollution, knowledge overload, limited attention spans, and our responsibilities as IS professionals. In *Global Information Technology Management Association (GITMA) World Conference-June*.

Bressanelli, G., Adrodegari, F., Perona, M., & Saccani, N. (2018). Exploring how usage-focused business models enable circular economy through digital technologies. *Sustainability (Basel), 10*(3), 639. DOI: 10.3390/su10030639

Bressanelli, G., Adrodegari, F., Perona, M., & Saccani, N. (2018). Exploring how usage-focused business models enable circular economy through digital technologies. *Sustainability (Basel), 10*(3), 639. DOI: 10.3390/su10030639

Bressanelli, G., Perona, M., & Saccani, N. (2019). Challenges in supply chain redesign for the Circular Economy: A literature review and a multiple case study. *International Journal of Production Research, 57*(23), 7395–7422. DOI: 10.1080/00207543.2018.1542176

Bressanelli, G., Pigosso, D. C., Saccani, N., & Perona, M. (2021). Enablers, levers and benefits of Circular Economy in the Electrical and Electronic Equipment supply chain: A literature review. *Journal of Cleaner Production*, *298*, 126819. DOI: 10.1016/j.jclepro.2021.126819

Buckland, M. K. (1991). Information as thing. *Journal of the American Society for Information Science*, *42*(5), 351–360. DOI: 10.1002/(SICI)1097-4571(199106)42:5<351::AID-ASI5>3.0.CO;2-3

Bulgakova, D. (2024). Doxing: the Sandy Hook case study.

Cagno, E., Neri, A., Negri, M., Bassani, C. A., & Lampertico, T. (2021). The role of digital technologies in operationalizing the circular economy transition: A systematic literature review. *Applied Sciences (Basel, Switzerland)*, *11*(8), 3328. DOI: 10.3390/app11083328

Camarinha-Matos, L. M., Fornasiero, R., Ramezani, J., & Ferrada, F. (2019). Collaborative networks: A pillar of digital transformation. *Applied Sciences (Basel, Switzerland)*, *9*(24), 5431. DOI: 10.3390/app9245431

Carson, R. (2018). *R.: Retirement savers are losing $17 billion a year from fake news and conflicts of interest.*

Castellani, V., Sala, S., & Mirabella, N. (2014). Beyond the throwaway society: A life cycle-based assessment of the environmental benefit of reuse. *Integrated Environmental Assessment and Management*, *11*(3), 373–382. DOI: 10.1002/ieam.1614 PMID: 25557152

Cavazos, R. (2019). The economic cost of bad actors on the Internet. *Techical Report.*

Cho, D. J., & Lee, J. (2020). *Fighting against "infollution" that contaminates our children's minds and their thoughts.*

Coleman, S. (2018). The elusiveness of political truth: From the conceit of objectivity to intersubjective judgement. *European Journal of Communication*, *33*(2), 157–171. DOI: 10.1177/0267323118760319

Colombo, F. (2022). A Media Ecology for a Platform Society. *CHANGING MEDIA CHANGING WORLD IN A*, 162.

Compton, J. (2013). Inoculation theory. *The SAGE handbook of persuasion: Developments in theory and practice, 2*, 220-237.

Compton, J., van der Linden, S., Cook, J., & Basol, M. (2021). Inoculation theory in the post-truth era: Extant findings and new frontiers for contested science, misinformation, and conspiracy theories. *Social and Personality Psychology Compass*, *15*(6), e12602. DOI: 10.1111/spc3.12602

Conzola, V. C., & Wogalter, M. S. (2001). A communication–human information processing (C–HIP) approach to warning effectiveness in the workplace. *Journal of Risk Research*, *4*(4), 309–322. DOI: 10.1080/13669870110062712

Cook, J., Lewandowsky, S., & Ecker, U. K. (2017). Neutralizing misinformation through inoculation: Exposing misleading argumentation techniques reduces their influence. *PLoS One*, *12*(5), e0175799. DOI: 10.1371/journal.pone.0175799 PMID: 28475576

Cookson, D., Jolley, D., Dempsey, R. C., & Povey, R. (2021). A social norms approach intervention to address misperceptions of anti-vaccine conspiracy beliefs amongst UK parents. *PLoS One*, *16*(11), e0258985. DOI: 10.1371/journal.pone.0258985 PMID: 34767581

Costa, H., & Macedo, L. (2013). Emotion-based recommender system for overcoming the problem of information overload. In *Highlights on Practical Applications of Agents and Multi-Agent Systems: International Workshops of PAAMS 2013, Salamanca, Spain, May 22-24, 2013.* [Springer Berlin Heidelberg.]. *Proceedings*, *11*, 178–189.

Davis, N. (2010). *The function of information architecture. DSIA Portal of Information Architecture*. Methodbrain.

Davis, N. (2012). IA strategy: Addressing the signatures of information overload.

De Freitas, J., Agarwal, S., Schmitt, B., & Haslam, N. (2023). Psychological factors underlying attitudes toward AI tools. *Nature Human Behaviour*, *7*(11), 1845–1854. DOI: 10.1038/s41562-023-01734-2 PMID: 37985913

de Morais, L. H. L., Pinto, D. C., & Cruz-Jesus, F. (2021). Circular economy engagement: Altruism, status, and cultural orientation as drivers for sustainable consumption. *Sustainable Production and Consumption*, *27*, 523–533. DOI: 10.1016/j.spc.2021.01.019

DellaVigna, S., & Linos, E. (2022). RCTs to scale: Comprehensive evidence from two nudge units. *Econometrica*, *90*(1), 81–116. DOI: 10.3982/ECTA18709

Despeisse, M., Baumers, M., Brown, P., Charnley, F., Ford, S. J., Garmulewicz, A., Knowles, S., Minshall, T. H. W., Mortara, L., Reed-Tsochas, F. P., & Rowley, J. (2017). Unlocking value for a circular economy through 3D printing: A research agenda. *Technological Forecasting and Social Change, 115*, 75–84. DOI: 10.1016/j.techfore.2016.09.021

Deuze, M. (2020). The role of media and mass communication theory in the global pandemic. *Communication today, 11*(2), 4-16.

Dillon, A. (2002). Information architecture in JASIST: Just where did we come from?.

Douglas, K. M., Uscinski, J. E., Sutton, R. M., Cichocka, A., Nefes, T., Ang, C. S., & Deravi, F. (2019). Understanding conspiracy theories. *Political Psychology, 40*(S1), 3–35. DOI: 10.1111/pops.12568

Drössler, S., Steputat, A., Schubert, M., Günther, N., Staudte, R., Kofahl, M., Hegewald, J., & Seidler, A. (2018). Information overload by digital media at the workplace: Systematic review of qualitative studies. *Zentralblatt für Arbeitsmedizin, Arbeitsschutz und Ergonomie, 68*(2), 77–88. DOI: 10.1007/s40664-018-0267-8

Ecker, U. K., Lewandowsky, S., & Chadwick, M. (2020). Can corrections spread misinformation to new audiences? Testing for the elusive familiarity backfire effect. *Cognitive Research: Principles and Implications, 5*(1), 1–25. DOI: 10.1186/s41235-020-00241-6 PMID: 32844338

Edelen, A., & Ingwersen, W. W. (2018). The creation, management, and use of data quality information for life cycle assessment. *The International Journal of Life Cycle Assessment, 23*(4), 759–772. DOI: 10.1007/s11367-017-1348-1 PMID: 29713113

Edmunds, A., & Morris, A. (2000). The problem of information overload in business organisations: A review of the literature. *International Journal of Information Management, 20*(1), 17–28. DOI: 10.1016/S0268-4012(99)00051-1

Eppler, M. J., & Mengis, J. (2008). The Concept of Information Overload-A Review of Literature from Organization Science, Accounting, Marketing, MIS, and Related Disciplines (2004) The Information Society: An International Journal, 20 (5), 2004, pp. 1–20. *Kommunikationsmanagement im Wandel: Beiträge aus 10 Jahren= mcminstitute*, 271-305.

Epstein, Z., Berinsky, A. J., Cole, R., Gully, A., Pennycook, G., & Rand, D. G. (2021). Developing an accuracy-prompt toolkit to reduce COVID-19 misinformation online.

European Commission. (2014). *Communication No. 398, 2014. Towards a Circular Economy: A Zero Waste Programme for Europe; (COM no. 398, 2014)*. Commission of European Communities.

European Commission. (2015). *Communication No. 614, 2015. Closing the Loop—An EU Action Plan for the Circular Economy; (COM no. 614, 2015)*. Commission of European Communities.

European Commission. (2018). *Communication No. 29, 2018. Monitoring Framework for the Circular Economy; (COM no. 29, 2018)*. Commission of European Communities.

European Commission. (2019). *Communication No. 640, 2019. The European Green Deal; (COM no. 640, 2019)*. Commission of European Communities.

European Commission. (2019). *Report from the Commission to the European Parliament, the Council, the European Economic and Social Committee and the Committee of the Regions on the Implementation of the Circular Economy Action Plan; (COM No. 190, 2019)*. Commission of European Communities.

European Commission. (2020). *Communication No. 98, 2020. A New Circular Economy Action Plan for a Cleaner and More Competitive Europe; (COM no. 98, 2020)*. Commission of European Communities.

Fang, K., Dong, L., Ren, J., Zhang, Q., Han, L., & Fu, H. (2017). Carbon footprints of urban transition: Tracking circular economy promotions in Guiyang, China. *Ecological Modelling*, *365*, 30–44. DOI: 10.1016/j.ecolmodel.2017.09.024

Fatimah, Y. A., Govindan, K., Murniningsih, R., & Setiawan, A. (2020). Industry 4.0 based sustainable circular economy approach for smart waste management system to achieve sustainable development goals: A case study of Indonesia. *Journal of Cleaner Production*, *269*, 122263. DOI: 10.1016/j.jclepro.2020.122263

Fatorachian, H., & Kazemi, H. (2018). A critical investigation of Industry 4.0 in manufacturing: Theoretical operationalisation framework. *Production Planning and Control*, *29*(8), 633–644. DOI: 10.1080/09537287.2018.1424960

Fettermann, D. C., Cavalcante, C. G. S., Almeida, T. D. D., & Tortorella, G. L. (2018). How does Industry 4.0 contribute to operations management?. *Journal of industrial and Production Engineering, 35*(4), 255-268.

Fonseca, L. M. (2018, March). Industry 4.0 and the digital society: concepts, dimensions and envisioned benefits. In *Proceedings of the international conference on business excellence* (Vol. 12, No. 1, pp. 386-397). Bucharest, Romania: Sciendo. DOI: 10.2478/picbe-2018-0034

Francke, H. (2009). Towards an architectural document analysis. *Journal of Information Architecture*, *1*(1), 19–44. DOI: 10.55135/1015060901/091.001/3.003

Frappaolo, C., & Keldsen, D. (2012). *Findability. The Art and Science of Making Content Easy to Find. MarketIQ. Intelligence Quarterly Q2 2008. Silver Spring, MD: AIIM, 2009.*

Fratini, C. F., Georg, S., & Jørgensen, M. S. (2019). Exploring circular economy imaginaries in European cities: A research agenda for the governance of urban sustainability transitions. *Journal of Cleaner Production, 228*, 974–989. DOI: 10.1016/j.jclepro.2019.04.193

Friant, M. C., Vermeulen, W. J., & Salomone, R. (2021). Analysing European Union circular economy policies: Words versus actions. *Sustainable Production and Consumption, 27*, 337–353. DOI: 10.1016/j.spc.2020.11.001

Fu, S., Li, H., Liu, Y., Pirkkalainen, H., & Salo, M. (2020). Social media overload, exhaustion, and use discontinuance: Examining the effects of information overload, system feature overload, and social overload. *Information Processing & Management, 57*(6), 102307. DOI: 10.1016/j.ipm.2020.102307

Furner, C. P., & Zinko, R. A. (2017). The influence of information overload on the development of trust and purchase intention based on online product reviews in a mobile vs. web environment: An empirical investigation. *Electronic Markets, 27*(3), 211–224. DOI: 10.1007/s12525-016-0233-2

García-Marco, F. J. (2011). Libraries in the digital ecology: Reflections and trends. *The Electronic Library, 29*(1), 105–120. DOI: 10.1108/02640471111111460

Geissdoerfer, M., Savaget, P., Bocken, N. M., & Hultink, E. J. (2017). The Circular Economy–A new sustainability paradigm? *Journal of Cleaner Production, 143*, 757–768. DOI: 10.1016/j.jclepro.2016.12.048

Geng, Y., & Doberstein, B. (2008). Developing the circular economy in China: Challenges and opportunities for achieving'leapfrog development'. *International Journal of Sustainable Development and World Ecology, 15*(3), 231–239. DOI: 10.3843/SusDev.15.3:6

Geng, Y., Fujita, T., Park, H. S., Chiu, A. S., & Huisingh, D. (2016). Recent progress on innovative eco-industrial development. *Journal of Cleaner Production, 114*, 1–10. DOI: 10.1016/j.jclepro.2015.09.051

Geng, Y., Xinbei, W., Qinghua, Z., & Hengxin, Z. (2010). Regional initiatives on promoting cleaner production in China: A case of Liaoning. *Journal of Cleaner Production, 18*(15), 1502–1508. DOI: 10.1016/j.jclepro.2010.06.028

Georgakopoulos, D., Jayaraman, P. P., Fazia, M., Villari, M., & Ranjan, R. (2016). Internet of Things and edge cloud computing roadmap for manufacturing. *IEEE Cloud Computing*, *3*(4), 66–73. DOI: 10.1109/MCC.2016.91

Gereffi, G., Humphrey, J., & Sturgeon, T. (2005). The governance of global value chains. *Review of International Political Economy*, *12*(1), 78–104. DOI: 10.1080/09692290500049805

Gorwa, R., Binns, R., & Katzenbach, C. (2020). Algorithmic content moderation: Technical and political challenges in the automation of platform governance. *Big Data & Society*, *7*(1), 2053951719897945. DOI: 10.1177/2053951719897945

Graf, B., & Antoni, C. H. (2021). The relationship between information characteristics and information overload at the workplace-a meta-analysis. *European Journal of Work and Organizational Psychology*, *30*(1), 143–158. DOI: 10.1080/1359432X.2020.1813111

Green, A. (2011). Information overload in healthcare management: How the READ Portal is helping healthcare managers. *Journal of the Canadian Health Libraries Association/Journal de l'Association des bibliothèques de la santé du Canada*, *32*(3), 173-176.

Gregson, N., Crang, M., Fuller, S., & Holmes, H. (2015). Interrogating the circular economy: The moral economy of resource recovery in the EU. *Economy and Society*, *44*(2), 218–243. DOI: 10.1080/03085147.2015.1013353

Guess, A. M., Lerner, M., Lyons, B., Montgomery, J. M., Nyhan, B., Reifler, J., & Sircar, N. (2020). A digital media literacy intervention increases discernment between mainstream and false news in the United States and India. *Proceedings of the National Academy of Sciences of the United States of America*, *117*(27), 15536–15545. DOI: 10.1073/pnas.1920498117 PMID: 32571950

Guo, Z., Schlichtkrull, M., & Vlachos, A. (2022). A survey on automated fact-checking. *Transactions of the Association for Computational Linguistics*, *10*, 178–206. DOI: 10.1162/tacl_a_00454

Gupta, S., Chen, H., Hazen, B. T., Kaur, S., & Gonzalez, E. D. S. (2019). Circular economy and big data analytics: A stakeholder perspective. *Technological Forecasting and Social Change*, *144*, 466–474. DOI: 10.1016/j.techfore.2018.06.030

Haas, W., Krausmann, F., Wiedenhofer, D., & Heinz, M. (2015). How circular is the global economy?: An assessment of material flows, waste production, and recycling in the European Union and the world in 2005. *Journal of Industrial Ecology*, *19*(5), 765–777. DOI: 10.1111/jiec.12244

Hassan, S. H., Mohamed, N., Ahmad, N. H., Halim, H. A., & Ramayah, T. (2019). Conceptualizing Perceived Infollution Processing and Management and Its Consequence on Employee Well-Being. European Proceedings of Social and Behavioural Sciences.

Hilligoss, B., & Rieh, S. Y. (2008). Developing a unifying framework of credibility assessment: Construct, heuristics, and interaction in context. *Information Processing & Management*, *44*(4), 1467–1484. DOI: 10.1016/j.ipm.2007.10.001

Hiltz, S. R., & Plotnick, L. (2013, May). Dealing with information overload when using social media for emergency management: Emerging solutions. In *ISCRAM*.

Hinton, A. (2009). The machineries of context. *Journal of Information Architecture*, *1*(1), 37–47. DOI: 10.55135/1015060901/091.001/4.004

Holton, A. E., & Chyi, H. I. (2012). News and the overloaded consumer: Factors influencing information overload among news consumers. *Cyberpsychology, Behavior, and Social Networking*, *15*(11), 619–624. DOI: 10.1089/cyber.2011.0610 PMID: 23020743

Homrich, A. S., Galvão, G., Abadia, L. G., & Carvalho, M. M. (2018). The circular economy umbrella: Trends and gaps on integrating pathways. *Journal of Cleaner Production*, *175*, 525–543. DOI: 10.1016/j.jclepro.2017.11.064

Hughes, B., Goldberg, B., Jereza, R., & West, J. J. (2021). Inoculating against persuasion by scientific racism propaganda: The moderating roles of propaganda form and subtlety.

Iqbal, Q., Ahmad, N. H., & Nawaz, R. (2020). Perceived information pollution: Conceptualization, measurement, and nomological validity. *Online Information Review*, *44*(3), 705–722. DOI: 10.1108/OIR-10-2018-0322

Iqbal, Q., Hassan, S. H., & Ahmad, N. H. (2018). The assessment of perceived information pollution in banking sector: A scale development and validation study. *Business Information Review*, *35*(2), 68–76. DOI: 10.1177/0266382118772891

Iqbal, Q., & Nawaz, R. (2021). Rife information pollution (infollution) and virtual organizations in industry 4.0: within reality causes and consequences. In *Research Anthology on Digital Transformation, Organizational Change, and the Impact of Remote Work* (pp. 1578-1592). IGI Global.

Iqbal, Q., & Nawaz, R. (2021). Rife information pollution (infollution) and virtual organizations in industry 4.0: within reality causes and consequences. In *Research Anthology on Digital Transformation, Organizational Change, and the Impact of Remote Work* (pp. 1578-1592). IGI Global.

Iqbal, Q., Yang, S., Nawaz, R., & Iqbal, K. (2019). A multi-dimensional construct of perceived information pollution in the era of rife infollution. *VINE Journal of Information and Knowledge Management Systems*, *49*(2), 162–180. DOI: 10.1108/VJIKMS-10-2018-0093

Islam, A. N., Laato, S., Talukder, S., & Sutinen, E. (2020). Misinformation sharing and social media fatigue during COVID-19: An affordance and cognitive load perspective. *Technological Forecasting and Social Change*, *159*, 120201. DOI: 10.1016/j.techfore.2020.120201 PMID: 32834137

Jabbour, C. J. C., de Sousa Jabbour, A. B. L., Sarkis, J., & Godinho Filho, M. (2019). Unlocking the circular economy through new business models based on large-scale data: An integrative framework and research agenda. *Technological Forecasting and Social Change*, *144*, 546–552. DOI: 10.1016/j.techfore.2017.09.010

Jabbour, C. J. C., Fiorini, P. D. C., Wong, C. W., Jugend, D., Jabbour, A. B. L. D. S., Seles, B. M. R. P., & da Silva, H. M. R. (2020b). First-mover firms in the transition towards the sharing economy in metallic natural resource-intensive industries: Implications for the circular economy and emerging industry 4.0 technologies. *Resources Policy*, *66*, 101596. DOI: 10.1016/j.resourpol.2020.101596

Jabbour, C. J. C., Seuring, S., de Sousa Jabbour, A. B. L., Jugend, D., Fiorini, P. D. C., Latan, H., & Izeppi, W. C. (2020a). Stakeholders, innovative business models for the circular economy and sustainable performance of firms in an emerging economy facing institutional voids. *Journal of Environmental Management*, *264*, 110416. DOI: 10.1016/j.jenvman.2020.110416 PMID: 32217311

Jackson, T. W., & Farzaneh, P. (2012). Theory-based model of factors affecting information overload. *International Journal of Information Management*, *32*(6), 523–532. DOI: 10.1016/j.ijinfomgt.2012.04.006

Jensen, S. F., Kristensen, J. H., Adamsen, S., Christensen, A., & Waehrens, B. V. (2023). Digital product passports for a circular economy: Data needs for product life cycle decision-making. *Sustainable Production and Consumption*, *37*, 242–255. DOI: 10.1016/j.spc.2023.02.021

Joensuu, T., Edelman, H., & Saari, A. (2020). Circular economy practices in the built environment. *Journal of Cleaner Production*, *276*, 124215. DOI: 10.1016/j.jclepro.2020.124215

Jolley, D., & Douglas, K. M. (2017). Prevention is better than cure: Addressing anti-vaccine conspiracy theories. *Journal of Applied Social Psychology*, *47*(8), 459–469. DOI: 10.1111/jasp.12453

Jung, B., & Kowalski, T. (2021). Restructuring Time Use Under COVID-19 Pandemics. *International Journal of Inspiration & Resilience Economy*, *5*(1), 22–31.

Karr-Wisniewski, P., & Lu, Y. (2010). When more is too much: Operationalizing technology overload and exploring its impact on knowledge worker productivity. *Computers in Human Behavior*, *26*(5), 1061–1072. DOI: 10.1016/j.chb.2010.03.008

Kaufhold, M. A., Rupp, N., Reuter, C., & Habdank, M. (2020). Mitigating information overload in social media during conflicts and crises: Design and evaluation of a cross-platform alerting system. *Behaviour & Information Technology*, *39*(3), 319–342. DOI: 10.1080/0144929X.2019.1620334

Kendeou, P., Robinson, D. H., & McCrudden, M. T. (2019). Misinformation and disinformation in education: An introduction. *Misinformation and fake news in education*, 1-4.

Kim, H. W., Dong, L., Choi, A. E. S., Fujii, M., Fujita, T., & Park, H. S. (2018). Co-benefit potential of industrial and urban symbiosis using waste heat from industrial park in Ulsan, Korea. *Resources, Conservation and Recycling*, *135*, 225–234. DOI: 10.1016/j.resconrec.2017.09.027

Koltay, T. (2017). Information overload in a data-intensive world. *Understanding information: From the big bang to big data*, 197-217.

Koroleva, K., Krasnova, H., & Günther, O. (2010). 'stop spamming me!'-exploring information overload on facebook.

Kozyreva, A., Lewandowsky, S., & Hertwig, R. (2020). Citizens versus the internet: Confronting digital challenges with cognitive tools. *Psychological Science in the Public Interest*, *21*(3), 103–156. DOI: 10.1177/1529100620946707 PMID: 33325331

Kozyreva, A., Lorenz-Spreen, P., Herzog, S. M., Ecker, U. K., Lewandowsky, S., Hertwig, R., Ali, A., Bak-Coleman, J., Barzilai, S., Basol, M., Berinsky, A. J., Betsch, C., Cook, J., Fazio, L. K., Geers, M., Guess, A. M., Huang, H., Larreguy, H., Maertens, R., & Wineburg, S. (2024). Toolbox of individual-level interventions against online misinformation. *Nature Human Behaviour*, *8*(6), 1044–1052. DOI: 10.1038/s41562-024-01881-0 PMID: 38740990

Kube, G., & Rinn, T. (2014). Industry 4.0-The next revolution in the industrial sector. *ZKG International*, *67*(11), 30–32.

Laato, S., Islam, A. N., Islam, M. N., & Whelan, E. (2020). What drives unverified information sharing and cyberchondria during the COVID-19.

Lasi, H., Fettke, P., Kemper, H. G., Feld, T., & Hoffmann, M. (2014). Industry 4.0. *Business & Information Systems Engineering*, *6*(4), 239–242. DOI: 10.1007/s12599-014-0334-4

Laskurain-Iturbe, I., Arana-Landín, G., Landeta-Manzano, B., & Uriarte-Gallastegi, N. (2021). Exploring the influence of industry 4.0 technologies on the circular economy. *Journal of Cleaner Production*, *321*, 128944. DOI: 10.1016/j.jclepro.2021.128944

Lauri, L., & Virkus, S. (2019). Information overload of academic staff in higher education institutions in Estonia. In *Information Literacy in Everyday Life: 6th European Conference, ECIL 2018, Oulu, Finland, September 24–27, 2018, Revised Selected Papers 6* (pp. 347-356). Springer International Publishing. DOI: 10.1007/978-3-030-13472-3_33

Lazer, D. M., Baum, M. A., Benkler, Y., Berinsky, A. J., Greenhill, K. M., Menczer, F., Metzger, M. J., Nyhan, B., Pennycook, G., Rothschild, D., Schudson, M., Sloman, S. A., Sunstein, C. R., Thorson, E. A., Watts, D. J., & Zittrain, J. L. (2018). The science of fake news. *Science*, *359*(6380), 1094–1096. DOI: 10.1126/science.aao2998 PMID: 29590025

Lee, Y. W., Strong, D. M., Kahn, B. K., & Wang, R. Y. (2002). AIMQ: A methodology for information quality assessment. *Information & Management*, *40*(2), 133–146. DOI: 10.1016/S0378-7206(02)00043-5

Lewandowski, M. (2016). Designing the business models for circular economy—Towards the conceptual framework. *Sustainability (Basel)*, *8*(1), 43. DOI: 10.3390/su8010043

Lewandowsky, S., Cook, J., Ecker, U., Albarracin, D., Amazeen, M. A., Kendeou, P., ... & Zaragoza, M. S. (2020). The Debunking Handbook 2020: Downloads and Translations.

Lieder, M., & Rashid, A. (2016). Towards circular economy implementation: A comprehensive review in context of manufacturing industry. *Journal of Cleaner Production*, *115*, 36–51. DOI: 10.1016/j.jclepro.2015.12.042

Lin, F., Chen, C., Zhang, N., Guan, X., & Shen, X. (2015). Autonomous channel switching: Towards efficient spectrum sharing for industrial wireless sensor networks. *IEEE Internet of Things Journal*, *3*(2), 231–243. DOI: 10.1109/JIOT.2015.2490544

Liu, Z. (2004). Perceptions of credibility of scholarly information on the web. *Information Processing & Management*, *40*(6), 1027–1038. DOI: 10.1016/S0306-4573(03)00064-5

Lom, M., Pribyl, O., & Svitek, M. (2016, May). Industry 4.0 as a part of smart cities. In *2016 Smart Cities Symposium Prague (SCSP)* (pp. 1-6). IEEE. DOI: 10.1109/SCSP.2016.7501015

Lopes de Sousa Jabbour, A. B., Jabbour, C. J. C., Godinho Filho, M., & Roubaud, D. (2018). Industry 4.0 and the circular economy: A proposed research agenda and original roadmap for sustainable operations. *Annals of Operations Research*, *270*(1-2), 273–286. DOI: 10.1007/s10479-018-2772-8

Lu, Y. (2017). Industry 4.0: A survey on technologies, applications and open research issues. *Journal of Industrial Information Integration*, *6*, 1–10. DOI: 10.1016/j.jii.2017.04.005

MacArthur, E. (2013). *Towards the circular economy, economic and business rationale for an accelerated transition*. Ellen MacArthur Foundation.

MacArthur, E., Zumwinkel, K., & Stuchtey, M. R. (2015). Growth within: a circular economy vision for a competitive Europe. *Ellen MacArthur Foundation, 100*.

MacDonald, J., Bath, P., & Booth, A. (2011). Information overload and information poverty: Challenges for healthcare services managers? *The Journal of Documentation*, *67*(2), 238–263. DOI: 10.1108/00220411111109458

Madaan, G., Singh, A., Mittal, A., & Shahare, P. (2024). Reduce, reuse, recycle: Circular economic principles, sustainability and entrepreneurship in developing ecosystems. *Journal of Small Business and Enterprise Development*, *31*(6), 1041–1066. DOI: 10.1108/JSBED-01-2023-0009

Márquez, A. J. C., & Rutkowski, E. W. (2020). Waste management drivers towards a circular economy in the global south–The Colombian case. *Waste Management (New York, N.Y.)*, *110*, 53–65. DOI: 10.1016/j.wasman.2020.05.016 PMID: 32447195

Martin, A., Dmitriev, D., & Akeroyd, J. (2010). A resurgence of interest in Information Architecture. *International Journal of Information Management*, *30*(1), 6–12. DOI: 10.1016/j.ijinfomgt.2009.11.008

McGuire, W. J. (1961). Resistance to persuasion conferred by active and passive prior refutation of the same and alternative counterarguments. *Journal of Abnormal and Social Psychology*, *63*(2), 326–332. DOI: 10.1037/h0048344

McLuhan, M. (1964). *Understanding Media, The Extensions of Man*. Massachusetts Institute of Technology.

McPhedran, R., Ratajczak, M., Mawby, M., King, E., Yang, Y., & Gold, N. (2023). Psychological inoculation protects against the social media infodemic. *Scientific Reports*, *13*(1), 5780. DOI: 10.1038/s41598-023-32962-1 PMID: 37031339

Meel, P., & Vishwakarma, D. K. (2020). Fake news, rumor, information pollution in social media and web: A contemporary survey of state-of-the-arts, challenges and opportunities. *Expert Systems with Applications*, *153*, 112986. DOI: 10.1016/j.eswa.2019.112986

Meyer, B., Zill, A., Dilba, D., & Voermans, S. (2021). *Entspann dich*. TK-Stressstudie.

Miehe, R., Fischer, E., Berndt, D., Herzog, A., Horbelt, J., Full, J., Bauernhansl, T., & Schenk, M. (2019). Enabling bidirectional real time interaction between biological and technical systems: Structural basics of a control oriented modeling of biology-technology-interfaces. *Procedia CIRP*, *81*, 63–68. DOI: 10.1016/j.procir.2019.03.012

Modirrousta-Galian, A., & Higham, P. A. (2022). How effective are gamified fake news interventions? Reanalyzing existing research with signal detection theory. *PsyArxiv Preprints*.

Moghrabi, I. A., Bhat, S. A., Szczuko, P., AlKhaled, R. A., & Dar, M. A. (2023). Digital transformation and its influence on sustainable manufacturing and business practices. *Sustainability (Basel)*, *15*(4), 3010. DOI: 10.3390/su15043010

Morville, P. (2005). *Ambient findability: What we find changes who we become*. O'Reilly Media, Inc.

Mosleh, M., Martel, C., Eckles, D., & Rand, D. (2021, May). Perverse downstream consequences of debunking: Being corrected by another user for posting false political news increases subsequent sharing of low quality, partisan, and toxic content in a Twitter field experiment. In *proceedings of the 2021 CHI Conference on Human Factors in Computing Systems* (pp. 1-13). DOI: 10.1145/3411764.3445642

Mufida, M. K., Snoun, A., Sarkis, J., Ait El-Cadi, A., Delot, T., & Trépanier, M. (2025). Circular Economy Practices for Data Management. *Engineering Proceedings*, *97*(1), 34.

Naidoo, R., & Fisher, B. (2020). Reset sustainable development goals for a pandemic world. *Nature*, *583*(7815), 198–201. DOI: 10.1038/d41586-020-01999-x PMID: 32632244

Nardi, B. A., & O'Day, L. (1999). Information Ecology.

Nielsen, J. (2003). IM, Not IP (Information Pollution) A steady dose of realtime interruptions is toxic to anyone's health. *ACM Queue; Tomorrow's Computing Today*, *1*(8), 76–75. DOI: 10.1145/966712.966731

Nyhan, B. (2017). Why the fact-checking at Facebook needs to be checked. *New York Times*.

Olson, N., Nolin, J. M., & Nelhans, G. (2015). Semantic web, ubiquitous computing, or internet of things? A macro-analysis of scholarly publications. *The Journal of Documentation*, *71*(5), 884–916. DOI: 10.1108/JD-03-2013-0033

Orman, L. (1984). Fighting information pollution with decision support systems. *Journal of Management Information Systems*, *1*(2), 64–71. DOI: 10.1080/07421222.1984.11517704

Ostrom, E. (2000). Collective action and the evolution of social norms. *The Journal of Economic Perspectives*, *14*(3), 137–158. DOI: 10.1257/jep.14.3.137

Pagoropoulos, A., Pigosso, D. C., & McAloone, T. C. (2017). The emergent role of digital technologies in the Circular Economy: A review. *Procedia CIRP*, *64*, 19–24. DOI: 10.1016/j.procir.2017.02.047

Pan, S. Y., Du, M. A., Huang, I. T., Liu, I. H., Chang, E. E., & Chiang, P. C. (2015). Strategies on implementation of waste-to-energy (WTE) supply chain for circular economy system: A review. *Journal of Cleaner Production*, *108*, 409–421. DOI: 10.1016/j.jclepro.2015.06.124

Pandita, R. (2014). Information pollution, a mounting threat: Internet a major causality. *Journal of Information Science Theory and Practice*, *2*(4), 49–60. DOI: 10.1633/JISTaP.2014.2.4.4

Pearce, D. W., & Turner, R. K. (1989). *Economics of natural resources and the environment*. Johns Hopkins University Press. DOI: 10.56021/9780801839863

Pennycook, G., & Rand, D. G. (2019). Lazy, not biased: Susceptibility to partisan fake news is better explained by lack of reasoning than by motivated reasoning. *Cognition*, *188*, 39–50. DOI: 10.1016/j.cognition.2018.06.011 PMID: 29935897

Pennycook, G., & Rand, D. G. (2022). Accuracy prompts are a replicable and generalizable approach for reducing the spread of misinformation. *Nature Communications*, *13*(1), 2333. DOI: 10.1038/s41467-022-30073-5 PMID: 35484277

Pialot, O., Millet, D., Bisiaux, J., & Upgradable, P. S. S. (2017). Clarifying a new concept of sustainable consumption/production based on upgradability. *Journal of Cleaner Production*, *141*, 538–550. DOI: 10.1016/j.jclepro.2016.08.161

Pimenova, E. M. (2021). Specificity of sustainability assessment for industrial enterprise functioning in the digital economy. In *Engineering economics: Decisions and solutions from Eurasian perspective* (pp. 3–10). Springer International Publishing. DOI: 10.1007/978-3-030-53277-2_1

Piscitelli, G., Ferazzoli, A., Petrillo, A., Cioffi, R., Parmentola, A., & Travaglioni, M. (2020). Circular economy models in the industry 4.0 era: A review of the last decade. *Procedia Manufacturing*, *42*, 227–234. DOI: 10.1016/j.promfg.2020.02.074

Prause, G., & Atari, S. (2017). On sustainable production networks for Industry 4.0. *Entrepreneurship and Sustainability Issues*, *4*(4), 421–431. DOI: 10.9770/jesi.2017.4.4(2)

Pretus, C., Servin-Barthet, C., Harris, E., Brady, W., Vilarroya, O., & Van Bavel, J. (2022). The role of political devotion in sharing partisan misinformation.

Rajabzadeh, A., Nejadirani, F., Soroodian, R., & Kermani, R. A. (2011). Informational overload; roots and consequences. *Australian Journal of Basic and Applied Sciences*, *5*(12), 353–359.

Rasmussen Pennington, D. (2016). "The most passionate cover I've seen": Emotional information in fan-created U2 music videos. *The Journal of Documentation*, *72*(3), 569–590. DOI: 10.1108/JD-07-2015-0086

Rathje, S., Roozenbeek, J., Traberg, C. S., Van Bavel, J. J., & Svd, L. (2022). Letter to the editors of Psychological Science: Meta-analysis reveals that accuracy nudges have little to no effect for US conservatives: Regarding Pennycook et al.(2020).

Rezayi, S., Balakrishnan, V., Arabnia, S., & Arabnia, H. R. (2018, December). Fake news and cyberbullying in the modern era. In *2018 International Conference on Computational Science and Computational Intelligence (CSCI)* (pp. 7-12). IEEE. DOI: 10.1109/CSCI46756.2018.00010

Rieh, S. Y., & Danielson, D. R. (2007). Credibility: A multidisciplinary framework.

Ristoski, P., & Paulheim, H. (2016). Semantic Web in data mining and knowledge discovery: A comprehensive survey. *Journal of Web Semantics*, *36*, 1–22. DOI: 10.1016/j.websem.2016.01.001

Roozenbeek, J., Freeman, A. L., & Van Der Linden, S. (2021). How accurate are accuracy-nudge interventions? A preregistered direct replication of Pennycook et al.(2020). *Psychological Science*, *32*(7), 1169–1178. DOI: 10.1177/09567976211024535 PMID: 34114521

Roozenbeek, J., Van Der Linden, S., Goldberg, B., Rathje, S., & Lewandowsky, S. (2022). Psychological inoculation improves resilience against misinformation on social media. *Science Advances, 8*(34), eabo6254. DOI: 10.1126/sciadv.abo6254 PMID: 36001675

Roy, M. (2021). Chapter 7-circular economy: a new sustainable management paradigm. *Sustainable development strategies*, 189-214.

Sabeeh, Z. A., & Ismail, Z. (2013, November). Effects of information overload on productivity in enterprises: a literature review. In *2013 International Conference on Research and Innovation in Information Systems (ICRIIS)* (pp. 210-214). IEEE. DOI: 10.1109/ICRIIS.2013.6716710

Samson, K., & Kostyszyn, P. (2015). Effects of cognitive load on trusting behavior–an experiment using the trust game. *PLoS One, 10*(5), e0127680. DOI: 10.1371/journal.pone.0127680 PMID: 26010489

Schmitt, J. B., Debbelt, C. A., & Schneider, F. M. (2018). Too much information? Predictors of information overload in the context of online news exposure. *Information Communication and Society, 21*(8), 1151–1167. DOI: 10.1080/1369118X.2017.1305427

Schöggl, J. P., Stumpf, L., & Baumgartner, R. J. (2020). The narrative of sustainability and circular economy-A longitudinal review of two decades of research. *Resources, Conservation and Recycling, 163*, 105073. DOI: 10.1016/j.resconrec.2020.105073

Shah, I. H., Dong, L., & Park, H. S. (2020). Tracking urban sustainability transition: An eco-efficiency analysis on eco-industrial development in Ulsan, Korea. *Journal of Cleaner Production, 262*, 121286. DOI: 10.1016/j.jclepro.2020.121286

Shierholz, H., & Zipperer, B. (2017). Here is what's at stake with the conflict of interest ('fiduciary') rule.

Sinanoglu, S., & Breuer, A. (2024). *Countering information pollution to protect democracy* (No. 29/2024). IDOS Policy Brief.

Singer, P. (2015). Are you ready for Industry 4.0? *Solid State Technology, 58*(8), 2–2.

Smol, M., Kulczycka, J., Henclik, A., Gorazda, K., & Wzorek, Z. (2015). The possible use of sewage sludge ash (SSA) in the construction industry as a way towards a circular economy. *Journal of Cleaner Production, 95*, 45–54. DOI: 10.1016/j.jclepro.2015.02.051

Soucek, R., & Moser, K. (2010). Coping with information overload in email communication: Evaluation of a training intervention. *Computers in Human Behavior, 26*(6), 1458–1466. DOI: 10.1016/j.chb.2010.04.024

Stahel, W. R. (2016). The circular economy. *Nature, 531*(7595), 435–438. DOI: 10.1038/531435a PMID: 27008952

Stanley, O. E. (2021). Information overload: Causes, symptoms, consequences and solutions. *Asian Journal of Information Science and Technology, 11*(2), 1–6. DOI: 10.51983/ajist-2021.11.2.2887

Stirling, A. (2006). Precaution, foresight and sustainability: reflection and reflexivity in the governance of science and technology. In *Reflexive governance for sustainable development*. Edward Elgar Publishing. DOI: 10.4337/9781847200266.00020

Sturgeon, T. J. (2021). Upgrading strategies for the digital economy. *Global Strategy Journal, 11*(1), 34–57. DOI: 10.1002/gsj.1364

Su, B., Heshmati, A., Geng, Y., & Yu, X. (2013). A review of the circular economy in China: Moving from rhetoric to implementation. *Journal of Cleaner Production, 42*, 215–227. DOI: 10.1016/j.jclepro.2012.11.020

Suárez-Eiroa, B., Fernández, E., Méndez-Martínez, G., & Soto-Oñate, D. (2019). Operational principles of circular economy for sustainable development: Linking theory and practice. *Journal of Cleaner Production, 214*, 952–961. DOI: 10.1016/j.jclepro.2018.12.271

Sun, M., Li, J., Yang, C., Schmidt, G. A., Bambacus, M., Cahalan, R., Huang, Q., Xu, C., Noble, E., & Li, Z. (2012). A web-based geovisual analytical system for climate studies. *Future Internet, 4*(4), 1069–1085. DOI: 10.3390/fi4041069

Surla, S. M. (2007). An information architecture approach to building a much better digital library. *Bulletin of the American Society for Information Science, 33*(6), 41–43. DOI: 10.1002/bult.2007.1720330612

Swar, B., Hameed, T., & Reychav, I. (2017). Information overload, psychological ill-being, and behavioral intention to continue online healthcare information search. *Computers in Human Behavior, 70*, 416–425. DOI: 10.1016/j.chb.2016.12.068

Sweller, J. (1988). Cognitive load during problem solving: Effects on learning. *Cognitive Science, 12*(2), 257–285. DOI: 10.1207/s15516709cog1202_4

Sweller, J. (1994). Cognitive load theory, learning difficulty, and instructional design. *Learning and Instruction, 4*(4), 295–312. DOI: 10.1016/0959-4752(94)90003-5

Sweller, J. (2011). Cognitive load theory. [). Academic Press.]. *Psychology of Learning and Motivation, 55*, 37–76. DOI: 10.1016/B978-0-12-387691-1.00002-8

Swire-Thompson, B., DeGutis, J., & Lazer, D. (2020). Searching for the backfire effect: Measurement and design considerations. *Journal of Applied Research in Memory and Cognition*, *9*(3), 286–299. DOI: 10.1016/j.jarmac.2020.06.006 PMID: 32905023

Sylvain, F. R. A. C. C. O. L. A. (2021). OECD Science, Technology and Innovation Outlook 2021-Perspectivas de la OCDE sobre.

Talwar, S., Dhir, A., Kaur, P., Zafar, N., & Alrasheedy, M. (2019). Why do people share fake news? Associations between the dark side of social media use and fake news sharing behavior. *Journal of Retailing and Consumer Services*, *51*, 72–82. DOI: 10.1016/j.jretconser.2019.05.026

Tan, W. K., & Kuo, P. C. (2019). The consequences of online information overload confusion in tourism.

Teixeira, A. A., Jabbour, C. J. C., de Sousa Jabbour, A. B. L., Latan, H., & De Oliveira, J. H. C. (2016). Green training and green supply chain management: Evidence from Brazilian firms. *Journal of Cleaner Production*, *116*, 170–176. DOI: 10.1016/j.jclepro.2015.12.061

Thaler, R. H., & Sunstein, C. R. (2009). *Nudge: Improving decisions about health, wealth, and happiness*. Penguin.

Thorne, J., & Vlachos, A. (2018). Automated fact checking: Task formulations, methods and future directions. *arXiv preprint arXiv:1806.07687.*

Tóth, G. (2019). Circular economy and its comparison with 14 other business sustainability movements. *Resources*, *8*(4), 159. DOI: 10.3390/resources8040159

Traberg, C. S., Roozenbeek, J., & van der Linden, S. (2022). Psychological inoculation against misinformation: Current evidence and future

Tseng, M. L., Chiu, A. S., & Liang, D. (2018). Sustainable consumption and production in business decision-making models. *Resources, Conservation and Recycling*, *128*, 118–121. DOI: 10.1016/j.resconrec.2017.02.014

Tukker, A. (2015). Product services for a resource-efficient and circular economy–a review. *Journal of Cleaner Production*, *97*, 76–91. DOI: 10.1016/j.jclepro.2013.11.049

Ugli, R. D. J., & Ugli, K. A. M. (2020). The Concept of Digital Economy in Modern Life and Its Application to Life. *JournalNX*, *6*(05), 118–121.

Uğraş, T. (2015). Bilgi tüketicileri ve üreticileri. In Gülseçen, S. (Ed.), *Bilgi yönetimi, Bilgi Türeticileri, Büyük Veri, İnovasyon ve Kurumsal Zeka* (pp. 17–29). Papatya Bilim Üniversite Yayıncılığı.

Unver, A. (2020). *Fact-checkers and fact-checking in Turkey*. EDAM Research Reports.

Upadhyay, A., Mukhuty, S., Kumar, V., & Kazancoglu, Y. (2021). Blockchain technology and the circular economy: Implications for sustainability and social responsibility. *Journal of Cleaner Production, 293*, 126130. DOI: 10.1016/j.jclepro.2021.126130

Van Bavel, J. J., Harris, E. A., Pärnamets, P., Rathje, S., Doell, K. C., & Tucker, J. A. (2021). Political psychology in the digital (mis) information age: A model of news belief and sharing. *Social Issues and Policy Review, 15*(1), 84–113. DOI: 10.1111/sipr.12077

Van der Linden, S., Leiserowitz, A., Rosenthal, S., & Maibach, E. (2017). Inoculating the public against misinformation about climate change. *Global Challenges (Hoboken, NJ), 1*(2), 1600008. DOI: 10.1002/gch2.201600008 PMID: 31565263

Vraga, E. K., & Bode, L. (2020). Defining misinformation and understanding its bounded nature: Using expertise and evidence for describing misinformation. *Political Communication, 37*(1), 136–144. DOI: 10.1080/10584609.2020.1716500

Wang, R. Y., & Strong, D. M. (1996). Beyond accuracy: What data quality means to data consumers. *Journal of Management Information Systems, 12*(4), 5–33. DOI: 10.1080/07421222.1996.11518099

Wang, Y., Ren, H., Dong, L., Park, H. S., Zhang, Y., & Xu, Y. (2019). Smart solutions shape for sustainable low-carbon future: A review on smart cities and industrial parks in China. *Technological Forecasting and Social Change, 144*, 103–117. DOI: 10.1016/j.techfore.2019.04.014

Wardle, C., & Derakhshan, H. (2017). *Information disorder: Toward an interdisciplinary framework for research and policymaking* (Vol. 27). Council of Europe.

Wardle, C., & Derakhshan, H. (2017). *Information disorder: Toward an interdisciplinary framework for research and policymaking* (Vol. 27). Council of Europe.

Whelan, E., Islam, A. N., & Brooks, S. (2020). Applying the SOBC paradigm to explain how social media overload affects academic performance. *Computers & Education, 143*, 103692. DOI: 10.1016/j.compedu.2019.103692

Wild, U., Laumer, S., & Kroenke, A. (2012). The bipartite influence of information overload on user resistance to knowledge management systems.

Wood, T., & Porter, E. (2019). The elusive backfire effect: Mass attitudes' steadfast factual adherence. *Political Behavior*, *41*(1), 135–163. DOI: 10.1007/s11109-018-9443-y

Wu, T. (2018). Blind spot: The attention economy and the Law. *Antitrust Law Journal*, *82*, 771.

Xavier, L. H., Giese, E. C., Ribeiro-Duthie, A. C., & Lins, F. A. F. (2021). Sustainability and the circular economy: A theoretical approach focused on e-waste urban mining. *Resources Policy*, *74*, 101467. DOI: 10.1016/j.resourpol.2019.101467

Xiao, L., & Mou, J. (2019). Social media fatigue-Technological antecedents and the moderating roles of personality traits: The case of WeChat. *Computers in Human Behavior*, *101*, 297–310. DOI: 10.1016/j.chb.2019.08.001

Yadav, G., Luthra, S., Jakhar, S. K., Mangla, S. K., & Rai, D. P. (2020). A framework to overcome sustainable supply chain challenges through solution measures of industry 4.0 and circular economy: An automotive case. *Journal of Cleaner Production*, *254*, 120112. DOI: 10.1016/j.jclepro.2020.120112

Yap, N. T. (2005). Towards a Circular Economy. Greener Management International, (50).

Zha, X., Liu, K., Yan, Y., Yan, G., Guo, J., Cao, F., & Wang, Y. (2019). Comparing digital libraries with social media from the dual route perspective. *Online Information Review*, *43*(4), 617–634. DOI: 10.1108/OIR-11-2017-0344

Zhang, C., Hu, M., Dong, L., Gebremariam, A., Miranda-Xicotencatl, B., Di Maio, F., & Tukker, A. (2019). Eco-efficiency assessment of technological innovations in high-grade concrete recycling. *Resources, Conservation and Recycling*, *149*, 649–663. DOI: 10.1016/j.resconrec.2019.06.023

Zhen, Z., Yousaf, Z., Radulescu, M., & Yasir, M. (2021). Nexus of digital organizational culture, capabilities, organizational readiness, and innovation: Investigation of SMEs operating in the digital economy. *Sustainability (Basel)*, *13*(2), 720. DOI: 10.3390/su13020720

Zollo, F., Bessi, A., Del Vicario, M., Scala, A., Caldarelli, G., Shekhtman, L., Havlin, S., & Quattrociocchi, W. (2017). Debunking in a world of tribes. *PLoS One*, *12*(7), e0181821. DOI: 10.1371/journal.pone.0181821 PMID: 28742163

ENDNOTES

1 Misinformation involves the unintentional spread of incorrect information by individuals who believe what they are sharing is accurate. In contrast, disinformation is the deliberate dissemination of false content by individuals who are aware of its inaccuracy and aim to mislead others (Kendeou et al., 2019). A specific category of disinformation is fake news, defined as "fabricated information that mimics news media content in form but not in organizational process or intent" (Lazer et al., 2018, p. 1094). While information pollution is often illustrated through digital content like spam emails, the current emphasis is on its circulation through both modern and traditional media platforms, as well as through communications from influential or authoritative figures.

2 https://www.disinformationindex.org

Chapter 7

The Impact of Corporate Finance on the Circular Economy

Nada Mallah Boustani
https://orcid.org/0000-0003-2252-0149
Saint Joseph University, Lebanon

ABSTRACT

This chapter explores the role of corporate finance in enabling the circular economy (CE), positioning financial decision-making as key to long-term transformation. It examines how capital budgeting, risk management, and investment strategies can either advance or hinder circular practices. Grounded in stakeholder, resource-based, and institutional theories, the chapter assesses how finance can internalize environmental externalities, value intangibles, and support uncertain long-term investments. Using a qualitative approach, it draws on academic literature, sustainability reports, and case studies (e.g., Philips, Schneider Electric, Interface Inc.) to show real-world applications. It highlights tools like green bonds, lifecycle costing, and performance-based financing, while noting structural barriers. Adapting finance to CE requires shifting financial logic, adopting new metrics (e.g., Total Cost of Ownership, Environmental P&L), and supportive policies. The chapter contributes to academic and managerial understanding of finance's role in circular value creation.

INTRODUCTION

The circular economy (CE) is a paradigm shift from the traditional linear model of production and consumption—extract, manufacture, use, dispose—to a more sustainable model that's all about resource efficiency, waste reduction and value

DOI: 10.4018/979-8-3373-3852-1.ch007

retention throughout product and material lifecycles. In the face of environmental degradation, climate change and resource scarcity the CE framework is a compelling vision for resilient and regenerative growth. For companies looking to get to circular, corporate finance is not just a support function but a strategic driver of change.

Finance departments traditionally focus on maximising shareholder value, often through short term profit maximisation and cost minimisation. But aligning business strategies with CE principles requires rethinking those priorities. Corporate finance must internalise environmental and social externalities, value intangible assets like circular innovation and brand reputation and support investments with longer term horizons and uncertain returns. Financial models must adapt to include lifecycle costs, environmental risks and evolving regulatory requirements and incentive structures must reward circular performance.

Now, financial decision-making in the form of capital budgeting, risk assessment, investment policies, and access to finance instruments could either speed up or slow down a company's transition toward circularity. Awareness of this interconnection is crucial for academics and practitioners alike. The financial equilibrium of a company, how it measures itself, and the instruments it deploys in raising capital all affect the implementation and success of circular strategies.

Within this chapter lies an examination of the interactions between corporate finance and the circular economy and the way financial regulations, instruments, and governance structures may support circular-based projects. Both theoretical and practical examples are thus used to point out the ongoing transformation of financial methods toward sustainability orientation. The chapter's structure will follow this format: it first introduces the conceptual framework that links corporate finance to CE theory. Then, it elaborates on selected financial tools, such as capital budgeting, life cycle costing, and sustainability instruments. It then continues with corporate cases (i.e., Philips, Schneider Electric, and Interface Inc.) to evidence concrete applications of circular financial models. Thereafter, it engages in issues concerning reporting formats and communication with stakeholders-a strategic orientation for companies that want to reorganize their financial systems along CE lines being presented in conclusion. The approach of the chapter is qualitative and descriptive. It is drawn upon academic research, financial reports, and sustainability disclosures, as well as case analyses of companies that have integrated circular economy approaches into their financial operations. All in all, the study aims to reveal trends, highlight innovations, and offer actionable insights into how corporate finance can become a catalyst for circular change.

This chapter takes a qualitative and descriptive approach, focusing on a thorough study of academic literature, sustainability reports, company disclosures, and global policy frameworks. Empirical support is provided by case studies of Philips, Schneider Electric, and Interface Inc., while financial modeling techniques (such as the NPV, WACC) are tailored to CE-specific requirements. Journal publications (2019-2025), white papers, and organizational ESG financial reports are among the data sources.

THEORETICAL FOUNDATIONS AND LITERATURE REVIEW

This section is divided to two major subsections, one related to the foundations of corporate finance and circular economy and the second subsection relates to literature gaps, barriers and drivers.

Corporate Finance and the Circular Economy

First the theoretical foundation of corporate finance has been built on Modigliani and Miller (1958) who assumed capital structure neutrality in ideal markets. But now we have new models that incorporate environmental, social and governance (ESG) factors. Stakeholder theory bridges the gap by expanding financial goals beyond shareholders to include broader societal implications, institutional theory provides a framework to understand how normative forces push companies to use sustainability aligned financial tools. This conceptual progression from classical finance theory to ESG integrated models is the intellectual foundation for circular finance.

Corporate finance needs to adapt to the circular economy (CE) which is about resource efficiency, waste reduction and long-term value creation. To incorporate CE principles means to modify existing financial structures to include environmental and social considerations and long-term economic consequences instead of only short-term financial gains.

Corporate finance has always dealt with optimal capital structure, investment evaluation, cost of capital and maximize shareholder value.

But the establishment of CE requires a change in the CFDs definition.

Capital Budgeting: Decisions should incorporate environmental externalities and long-term lifecycle costs.

Risk Management: Climate, regulatory and resource risks require new valuation models.

Return on Investment (ROI): Financial measures must grow to include environmental and societal returns, not solely economic gain.

A theoretical triangulation clarifies the ways by which corporate finance might promote the circular economy. Stakeholder theory emphasizes the importance of considering broader societal and environmental implications, in addition to shareholder returns, when making financial decisions. Resource-based theory views CE capabilities (such as eco-design or closed-loop logistics) as strategic assets that must be funded. Institutional theory analyzes the growing demand on businesses to conform to emerging sustainability norms and standards, which has resulted in financial innovation such as ESG bonds and CE-focused portfolios. The convergence of these theories emphasizes the significance of integrating financial mechanisms with environmental stewardship, long-term planning, and stakeholder legitimacy (table 1 below).

Table 1. Theoretical Lenses Supporting Circular Economy Finance: Key Concepts and Implications

Theory	*Its relevance to CE Finance*	*Financial Implications*
Stakeholder Theory	Expands value beyond shareholders	Need for inclusive ROI metrics, ESG-aligned KPIs
Resource-Based View	Circular capabilities as competitive advantage	Investment in eco-design, recycling infrastructure
Institutional Theory	Institutional pressure drives CE adoption	Green bonds, sustainability-linked loans, disclosures

Literature review

To supplement the theoretical foundations outlined earlier, this section examines academic and institutional contributions defining the subject of circular finance. It examines the transition from traditional finance to ESG-integrated models, identifies structural barriers to circular finance adoption, investigates regulatory drivers such as taxonomies and disclosure mandates, and discusses the role of blended finance and public guarantees in derisking and scaling circular investments.

The research on circular economy (CE) financing shows a dynamic interaction between sustainability imperatives and changing financial logic. In his section we shed the light on major academic, legislative, and institutional contributions to demonstrate how the integration of ESG principles, risk reframing, and financial innovation is redefining the role of corporate finance in the CE transition.

Modigliani and Miller (1958) and other classical corporate finance models make assumptions about market efficiency, rational actors, and neutrality in capital structure decisions. These theories, while important, are becoming more inadequate when applied to sustainability-oriented projects, which frequently involve long time horizons, intangible value creation, and non-linear returns.

Modern literature is calling for a wider framework. Bebbington and Unerman (2018) suggest we redefine finance to include planetary boundaries and intergenerational equity. Busch et al. (2022) show how ESG (Environmental, Social and Governance) considerations now impact both cost of capital and investment decisions. Recent developments include sustainability-adjusted WACC, multi-capital performance measures and lifecycle financial planning.

Despite the growing interest, there are still systemic barriers to CE finance. Rizos et al. (2016) and Kirchherr et al. (2018) show the gap between environmental goals and economic viability. Investors see CE business models as high risk because of uncertain ROI and lack of historical benchmarks. Credit assessments are hindered by information asymmetry, especially for small and medium sized companies (SMEs).

Another issue is the misalignment of linear financial metrics and circular value creation. Traditional capital budgeting methods like NPV and ROI struggle to capture externalities like avoided emissions or resource regeneration. This creates a gap between environmental performance and financial viability which often penalizes circular initiatives in internal investment decisions.

Policy frameworks and regulatory instruments are becoming more and more important in climate finance. The EU Taxonomy of Sustainable Activities (European Commission, 2020) sets out the rules for what is "green" or "sustainable" financing for both investors and issuers. The Corporate Sustainability Reporting Directive (CSRD) requires more environmental disclosure which means more transparency and investor accountability. Beyond Europe there is also global momentum. ASEAN countries, China and Latin American jurisdictions are creating their own green taxonomies (OECD, 2023). These regulations shape the capital markets by setting standards for green bonds, sustainability-linked loans (SLLs) and ESG ratings, making circular finance a compliance opportunity rather than a niche problem.

Blended finance is becoming a risk management tool and a way to unlock more capital. Institutions like the International Finance Corporation (IFC) and the United Nations Environment Program (UNEP) have tested instruments that combine public and private funding streams

These include first-loss guarantees, concessional loans, and technical assistance, all of which attempt to reduce the risk of circular initiatives, particularly in emerging markets (IFC, 2023).

Public-private partnerships (PPPs), development banks, and climate funds can also help raise patient capital for circular infrastructure and industrial innovation. By bearing early-stage risks or providing catalytic subsidies, these actors help test CE business models and attract mainstream investors.

REIMAGINING THE CORE OBJECTIVES OF CORPORATE FINANCE

Capital Allocation and Risk Assessment

Corporate finance must undergo a transformative shift to support the transition from a linear economic model, based on take, make, and dispose, to a circular economy (CE), which emphasizes resource efficiency, waste minimization, regeneration of natural systems, and long-term value creation. Traditional financial decision-making structures, guided by short-term profitability and shareholder value maximization, are increasingly inadequate in the face of emerging environmental, social, and governance (ESG) challenges. To remain relevant and sustainable, corporate finance must evolve to integrate the principles of CE, embedding environmental and social externalities into financial strategies, risk assessment, and performance evaluation (Munteanu 2024).

Classical corporate finance focuses on:

- Determining the optimal capital structure (debt vs. equity financing),
- Evaluating investments through capital budgeting techniques,
- Calculating the cost of capital (Weighted Average Cost of Capital - WACC),
- Maximizing shareholder wealth through value-creating activities.

In a CE framework, these objectives are redefined to incorporate a triple bottom line: economic, environmental, and social returns. This holistic approach requires financial managers to adjust their metrics, tools, and time horizons (Tantia, V., & Sukanya, 2024)

Capital Budgeting in the Circular Economy

Capital budgeting remains central to investment decision-making. However, in a CE, traditional techniques such as Net Present Value (NPV) and Internal Rate of Return (IRR) must be reinterpreted.

We will begin by defining some Circular Finance Terms (as a small glossary):

NPV (Net Present Value): Calculates today's value of future cash flows. In CE, it should include savings from eco-efficiency or avoided waste.

WACC (Weighted Average Cost of Capital): The average cost a company pays for capital (debt + equity). CE projects may lower WACC through green bonds.

Shadow Pricing: Assigns a monetary value to non-market goods (like clean air). Used in CE to account for environmental benefits in investment decisions.

TCO (Total Cost of Ownership): A financial estimate that includes all direct and indirect costs of a product over its lifecycle.

Blended ROI: A metric that includes financial, environmental, and social returns on investment

Standard NPV formula:

$$NPV = \sum_{t=0}^{n} \left(\frac{CF_t}{(1+r)^t}\right) - C_0$$

In a CE-oriented project, CF_t should reflect not only financial returns but also quantified environmental and social benefits...

Where:

- CF_t = Cash flow at time t,
- r = Discount rate (typically the WACC),
- C_0 = Initial investment,
- n = Project duration.

In a CE-oriented project, CF_t should reflect not only financial returns but also quantified environmental and social benefits, such as:

- Cost savings from resource efficiency (e.g., closed-loop production),
- Revenue from recycled materials or extended product lifecycles,
- Avoided regulatory fines and carbon taxes,
- Reputation and brand value from sustainable practices.

Shadow pricing, which assigns economic value to non-market assets like clean air or biodiversity, can be used to monetise these externalities and include them in the adjusted net present value. For instance:

$$NPV_{CE} = \sum_{t=0}^{n} \left(\frac{CF_t + Et + St}{(1+r)^t}\right) - C_0$$

Where:

- E_t = Environmental benefit at time t,
- S_t = Social benefit at time t.

Similarly, because CE investments have high upfront costs and long-term gains, they frequently have extended payback periods that should be taken into account by IRR (Nunden, 2022).

Cost of Capital Adjustments

In CE-aligned finance, the Weighted Average Cost of Capital (WACC), which is commonly employed as a hurdle rate in capital budgeting, should likewise be re-examined. Conventionally:

$$WACC = \left(\frac{E}{V}\right) r_{e+} \left(\frac{D}{V}\right) r_d \left(1 - T\right)$$

Where:

- E = Market value of equity,
- D = Market value of debt,
- $V=E+D$ = Total value,
- r_e = Cost of equity,
- r_d = Cost of debt,
- T = Corporate tax rate.

r_e and r_d must be modified to account for sustainability risks and opportunities:

- Premiums or discounts for environmental risk,
- Lower cost of capital from green financing instruments (e.g., green bonds),
- Access to impact investors or ESG-aligned capital with lower return expectations.

For instance, when a company issues green bonds, demand from investors who care about environmental, social, and governance issues may cause the cost of debt (r_d) to drop. This would lower the overall weighted average cost of capital (WACC) and make sustainable projects more appealing (figure 1).

Figure 1.How CE Modifies Capital Budgeting Decisions

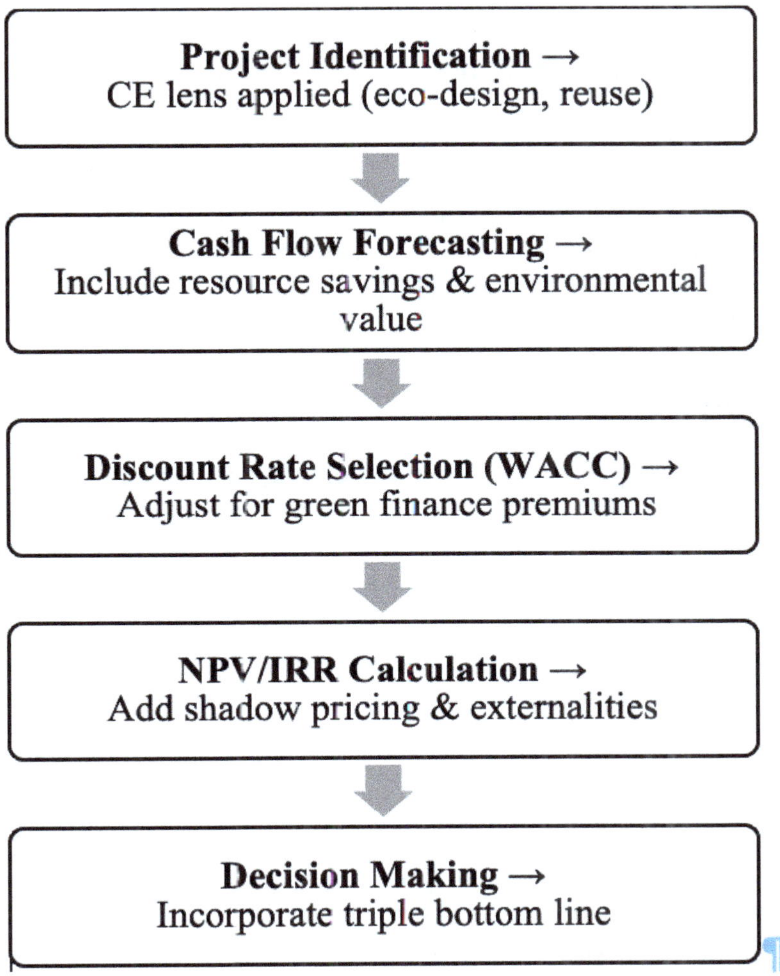

This figure visually maps how capital budgeting, risk management, and performance metrics interact with environmental and governance dimensions to drive CE-aligned financial decision-making.

Risk Management in the CE Framework

Traditional financial risk management evaluates market, credit, and operational risks. However, in the context of the CE, firms must incorporate environmental, regulatory, and resource-based risks:

Climate risk: Exposure to physical risks (e.g., floods) and transition risks (e.g., carbon pricing),
Resource scarcity: Dependence on finite inputs increases vulnerability to supply chain disruption,
Regulatory risk: Potential for stricter environmental regulations, extended producer responsibility laws.

These require new valuation models and tools such as:

Scenario analysis (e.g., different carbon pricing futures),
Real options analysis to value managerial flexibility in uncertain environments,
Monte Carlo simulations to assess variability in eco-design and product recovery rates.

For example, a CE firm might use Value at Risk (VaR) adjusted for environmental volatility:

$$VaR = \mu - z \cdot \sigma$$

Where:

- μ = Expected return on the CE investment,
- z = Z-score based on confidence level,

σ = Standard deviation, including environmental uncertainties.

Beyond ROI: Measuring Integrated Returns

Return on Investment (ROI) has traditionally been expressed as:

$$ROI = \frac{Net\ Profit}{Investment} \times 100$$

However, in CE projects, net profit should encompass a broader array of benefits. The emergence of Integrated Reporting (IR) and Triple Bottom Line (TBL) accounting encourages firms to report on:

Economic Value Added (EVA),

Environmental Return on Investment (EROI),

Social Return on Investment (SROI).

A composite metric, Blended ROI, can be introduced:

$$Blended\ ROI = \frac{NP + EV + SV}{IC}$$

Where:

- NP = Net profit,
- EV = Environmental value,
- SV = Social value,
- IC = Investment cost.

These measures reflect how circular strategies such as remanufacturing, upcycling, product-service systems (PSS), and take-back schemes yield tangible benefits not visible in traditional ROI metrics (Nevatia,2022).

Policy Incentives and Financial Innovation

Policymakers are increasingly providing tax incentives, subsidies, and grant funding for CE initiatives. Financial managers must integrate these into project appraisals and evaluate the cost-benefit impact of compliance vs. non-compliance with environmental legislation.

Additionally, financial innovation is supporting CE through:

Green bonds and sustainability-linked loans,

Impact investing vehicles,

Circular asset-backed securities.

These instruments can reduce the cost of capital and unlock capital for CE-aligned business models, especially when supported by robust environmental, social, and governance (ESG) reporting (Krystallis et al., 2025)

Corporate finance plays a foundational role in enabling the circular economy. By reimagining capital budgeting, integrating environmental and social risks, recalibrating cost of capital, and redefining ROI to reflect holistic value creation, financial decision-makers can align capital allocation with sustainability imperatives. The evolution of finance towards circularity is not just a strategic option—it is a necessary response to the systemic risks and opportunities of the 21st century.

Embracing this transformation positions firms to thrive in a regenerative, low-carbon, and inclusive economic future.

Adapting Financial Principles for the Circular Economy

Capital Budgeting and Investment Appraisal: Hence, investment decision must incorporate environmental externalities, lifecycle costs, and resource efficiency along with immediate financial returns. This often implies higher initial investment and more complex structuring of the business, more so for smaller companies (De Souza Mello Gonçalves et al., 2023; Saarinen & Aarikka-Stenroos, 2023; Aranda-Usón et al., 2019).

Risk Management: New risk models are needed to address climate, regulatory and resource risks in CE projects. Financial institutions and investors are developing specialized criteria and instruments (e.g. green bonds, CE focused funds) to evaluate and support circular business models (Kumar et al., 2024a; Saarinen & Aarikka-Stenroos, 2023; Ozili, 2021).

Return on Investment (ROI): Financial metrics are evolving to include environmental and social returns alongside traditional economic gains. Empirical evidence shows that CE practices can improve ROI, gross profit margin, and shareholder returns, especially over time and in larger or high-tech firms (Shavkatov et al., 2024; Munteanu et al., 2024; Chen et al., 2023).

By 2024, various market developments are intensifying the convergence of corporate finance and the circular economy. The global green bond market surpassed $1.8 trillion (Climate Bonds Initiative, 2024), indicating a growing investor interest for sustainability-linked financial securities. ESG investment now accounts for more than 36% of all professionally managed assets (GSIA, 2023), requiring firms to disclose CE practices. Furthermore, laws like the EU Taxonomy and CSRD incorporate CE measures into compliance and reporting structures. These financial developments are changing risk-return assumptions and bringing market incentives in line with circular performance (table 2 below).

Table 2. Key Financial Drivers and Market Trends Supporting Circular Economy Adoption (2024)

Financial Driver	*Market Trend (by 2024)*	*Implication for CE*
ESG Investment Growth	36% of global assets under management	Incentivizes CE-aligned disclosures
Green Bond Expansion	$1.8 trillion cumulative issuance	New capital for eco-projects
Regulatory Compliance	EU Taxonomy, CSRD enforcement	Drives financial reporting on circular KPIs

Financial Drivers, Barriers, and Innovations

As of 2024, various market changes are hastening the integration of corporate finance and the circular economy. The global green bond market has topped $1.8 trillion in total issuance (Alliance, 2018), as investors demand greater transparency in ESG-linked performance. Simultaneously, ESG-aligned assets now represent more than 36% of overall assets under professional management (CBI, 2024). These developments are bolstered by legal obligations like the EU Taxonomy and CSRD, which require businesses to connect disclosures and financial plans with sustainable goals. These trends provide both pressure and opportunity on corporate finance to accelerate CE adoption.

Small and medium-sized firms (SMEs) confront unique challenges in implementing circular economy practices, particularly in terms of obtaining green financing and managing complex regulatory requirements. These constraints are exacerbated in the Global South, where CE funding networks are still emerging. The integration of specific policy instruments, concessional funds, and blended finance models is crucial for SMEs to participate in circular transitions. Case studies from emerging countries, such as Kenya and Brazil, demonstrate how novel microfinance and cooperative models can improve financial availability for decentralized circular projects (Taera and Lakner 2025; Moser and Gonzalez 2015).

Drivers: Availability of funds, quality of internal financial resources and public subsidies stimulate CE adoption in companies (Aranda-Usón et al., 2019; Saarinen & Aarikka-Stenroos, 2023). Financial innovation—green loans, pay-for-performance mechanisms and fintech—aligns financial incentives with sustainability goals (Kumar et al., 2024b; Ozili, 2021).

Barriers: High upfront costs, limited access to finance for small businesses and perceived riskiness of CE investments due to novelty and complexity (De Souza Mello Gonçalves et al., 2023; Saarinen & Aarikka-Stenroos, 2022; Fang et al., 2024).

Role of Financial Institutions: Banks and insurers benefit from CE through loan diversification, responsible banking and new insurance products and support broader sustainability goals (Ozili, 2021).

Table 3.Key Financial Drivers and Market Trends Supporting Circular Economy Adoption (2024)

Financial Driver	Market Trend (2024)	*Implication for CE*
ESG Investment Growth	36% of global assets under management	Incentivizes CE-aligned disclosures
Green Bond Expansion	$1.8 trillion cumulative issuance	New capital for eco-projects
Regulatory Compliance	EU Taxonomy, CSRD enforcement	Standardizes CE reporting and financial metrics

CE challenges traditional metrics like Net Present Value (NPV) and Internal Rate of Return (IRR) which often undervalue circular projects due to long payback periods and uncertain returns. Total Cost of Ownership (TCO) and Environmental Profit and Loss (EP&L) statements are gaining ground (Lacy et al., 2015; WBCSD, 2020). Integrating circular economy principles into corporate finance means re-thinking investment, risk and performance metrics to capture long-term sustainable value. To remove obstacles and accelerate the shift to a circular, resource-efficient economy, financial innovation and supportive policies are essential.

Corporate Finance and the Circular Economy

Financial governance is essential for transforming circular plans into capital allocation. Board oversight structures, sustainability committees, and ESG-linked executive remuneration schemes are increasingly employed to incorporate CE measures into financial decision-making. Linking sustainability KPIs to performance incentives enhances strategic consistency and departmental responsibility. This convergence of governance and finance strengthens CE investments' legitimacy and long-term credibility.

By giving businesses the tools, incentives and innovation they need to go circular, corporate finance plays a key role in the circular economy. The factors that allow businesses to move from linear to circular and reap the economic and environmental benefits are financial innovation, funding and supportive financial institutions.

MECHANISMS AND DRIVERS

Financial Innovation Organisations can incorporate environmental, social and governance (ESG) and circular economy (CE) principles into their strategy with the help of green bonds, green loans, pay-for-performance schemes and CE focused investment funds. Circular finance is being enabled by fintech, AI and machine learning (Kumar et al.b, 2024).

Access to Financial Resources: The amount and quality of public subsidies and internal funds encourage businesses to go CE (Aranda-Usón et al., 2019).

Financial Institutions' Role: Responsible banking, lending to circular businesses and loan diversification are good for banks and other financial institutions. They support circular businesses through special insurance and collaborative funding (Ozili, 2021; Goovaerts & Verbeek, 2018).

Business Impact

Financial Performance: CE adoption is linked to better financial outcomes: higher ROI, profit margins and shareholder returns. This is stronger in larger firms and high-tech sectors and over time (Feng & Goli, 2023; Palea et al., 2023; Shavkatov et al., 2024).

Stock Market and Credit: Companies with strong CE performance are rewarded by the stock market, creditors are more attentive to CE practices especially after major policy milestones like the Paris Agreement (Palea et al., 2023).

Operational Efficiency: CE strategies like eco-design, recycling and waste reduction enhance operational efficiency and are key to financial gains (Palea et al., 2023; Shavkatov et al., 2024).

Table 4. Financial Mechanisms and Their Effect on Performance and Adoption of the Circular Economy

Financial Mechanism/Driver	*Impact on CE Adoption and Performance*
Green bonds, loans, CE funds	Accelerate CE integration and ESG alignment
Public subsidies	Stimulate CE initiatives, especially for SMEs
Financial institution engagement	Enables transition, offers new profit opportunities
Internal financial resource quality	Supports advanced CE activities

Barriers and Considerations

Barriers: High upfront costs, business size (especially for micro and small firms), complex business structuring and perceived risks can hinder CE financing (Saarinen & Aarikka-Stenroos, 2023; De Souza Mello Gonçalves et al., 2023; Dewick et al.,

2020).Monitoring: Clear investment standards are needed to ensure circular finance delivers real sustainability and not just a buzzword (Dewick et al., 2020).

Corporate finance is a key enabler of the circular economy, delivering both environmental and financial benefits through innovation, resource allocation and institutional support. But overcoming barriers and robust monitoring are key to maximise the impact of finance on circular economy transitions.

Capital for Circular Projects

In a circular economy companies must invest in:

- Renewable energy and clean tech
- Reverse logistics and recycling infrastructure
- Product design for durability and modularity

Capital allocation for circular projects in a circular economy requires new approaches to investment planning, project assessment and financial decision making. Effective capital allocation frameworks must balance economic returns with sustainability goals, prioritize long-term value and support the unique requirements of circular initiatives.

Key Principles for Capital Allocation

Distinct Planning Stages: Circular projects need early-phase planning that includes decision gates and methods tailored to circularity, such as life cycle assessment (LCA) monetization, selective disassembly and optimization for adaptive reuse vs new construction (Sanchez & Haas, 2018).

Portfolio Selection Frameworks: Organizations should use multi-criteria decision tools that integrate both financial and sustainability metrics (e.g. LCA), and adjust investment portfolios to align with strategic sustainability targets and financial constraints (Donat & Souza, 2023).

Allocation Approaches: Different LCA allocation methods (e.g. cut-off, Circular Footprint Formula, 50:50, linearly degressive) distribute environmental impacts differently across product life cycles, and influence which circular economy principles are incentivized. The linearly degressive approach is promising for both open and closed-loop systems (Malabi et al., 2020).

Practical Implementation Strategies

Green Budgeting and Dedicated Portfolios: Establishing green budgeting processes and dedicated sustainability investment portfolios ensures capital is directed towards circular assets and projects (Donat & Souza, 2023).

Cleaner Production as a Stepping Stone: For SMEs, implementing cleaner production projects can be an initial, cost-effective way to demonstrate circularity and become eligible for external funding (Stasiuk-Piekarska et al., 2024).

Dynamic Programming for Capital Allocation: Advanced capital allocation models, such as dynamic programming, can optimize investment decisions under budget constraints and project interdependencies, for more complex circular project portfolios (Nemhauser & Ullmann, 1969).

Table 5. Analytical Instruments for Assessing Circular Economy Initiatives: Objective, Advantages, and Uses

Approach/Tool	Purpose/Benefit	Details and Application
Life Cycle Assessment (LCA)	Quantifies environmental impacts over multiple cycles	LCA is a standardized methodology that evaluates the environmental impacts associated with all stages of a product's life—from raw material extraction to disposal. In project assessments, it is used to identify high-impact phases, improve design choices, and compare alternatives based on sustainability outcomes. It supports decision-making in industries like manufacturing, construction, and energy by revealing trade-offs in environmental footprints.
Multi-Attribute Utility Theory (MAUT)	Balances economic and sustainability criteria	MAUT is a decision-support framework that enables the assessment of complex projects based on multiple criteria—such as cost, environmental performance, social impact, and risk. It assigns weights to each attribute according to stakeholder preferences and provides a composite utility score. This helps in selecting the most balanced and sustainable alternative, especially when trade-offs between goals are involved.
Cleaner Production Projects (CPP)	Initial assessment and funding eligibility for SMEs	CPPs are structured programs aimed at minimizing waste and resource consumption through process improvements. For small and medium-sized enterprises (SMEs), these projects are vital for identifying entry points for environmental upgrades, compliance with regulations, and access to green funding mechanisms. Early-stage assessments focus on feasibility and potential environmental and economic benefits, enabling better alignment with national or regional sustainability goals.

Capital allocation for circular projects requires new frameworks that integrate sustainability and financial performance, use advanced assessment tools and support both large organizations and SMEs. Early planning, dedicated investment portfolios and innovative assessment methods are essential to enable the transition to a circular economy.

This requires significant upfront capital and a willingness to prioritize long-term benefits. Corporate finance must evolve to support:

Green budgeting processes

Dedicated sustainability investment portfolios

Capital expenditure (CAPEX) allowances for circular assets

If we consider the case of Philips and the "Pay-per-Lux" Circular Business Model, we can state that:

Philips, a multinational firm best recognized for its breakthroughs in lighting and healthcare technologies, has been a trailblazer in circular economy ideas. The "Pay-per-Lux" paradigm, which turned lighting from a product to a service, is a prime illustration of this. Rather than selling lighting equipment to clients, Philips kept ownership of the systems and charged users for the illumination delivered over time (measured in lux). This marked a significant shift in business strategy and financial planning.

The company's capital planning must be adjusted as a result of the transition away from traditional sales. Rather of calculating profitability through one-time sales, Philips developed frameworks that took into consideration recurring revenue, maintenance duties, and long-term asset management.

This included investing in smart technology, sensors, and digital infrastructure to track and maintain lighting performance. Environmentally it encouraged the building of lighting systems that were durable, repairable and recyclable so reducing waste and increasing resource efficiency. The result was not just a lower environmental impact but also cost savings for the client who avoided big upfront investments and got energy efficient solutions tailored to their needs.

Plus, by providing lighting as a service Philips established deeper, more continuous relationships with their clients. These partnerships increased customer satisfaction and retention, reinforced brand loyalty and opened new opportunities for innovation and cross sector collaboration.

According to the Ellen MacArthur Foundation (2020) this is an example of how circular economy strategies can align sustainability with long term profitability and how companies can reposition themselves as service providers rather than product manufacturers.

Table 6. Comparative Analysis of Business Models and Circular Economy Assessment Techniques

Criterion	Life Cycle Assessment (LCA)	Multi-Attribute Utility Theory (MAUT)	Cleaner Production Projects (CPP)	Philips – Pay-per-Lux Model
Core Focus	Environmental impact across product life cycle	Balanced evaluation of multiple decision criteria	Initial sustainability assessment and funding for SMEs	Business model transformation via service-based lighting
Methodology Type	Analytical/quantitative, lifecycle-based	Decision analysis with weighted attributes	Diagnostic and eligibility-oriented	Service-oriented circular economy strategy
Financial Implications	Identifies cost-saving and eco-efficiency opportunities	Supports resource allocation across conflicting objectives	Supports SMEs in accessing green funding	Shifts revenue to recurring streams; reduced client capital cost
Environmental Outcome	Promotes low-impact design and resource efficiency	Weighs environmental factors in decisions	Encourages pollution prevention and eco-efficiency	Reduces waste, promotes reuse and recycling of equipment
Innovation in Practice	Supports sustainable design and policy	Applied in sustainability-oriented strategic planning	Entry-level eco-innovation for SMEs	Reimagines ownership; incentivizes durability and efficiency
Stakeholder Engagement	Used by designers, engineers, and environmental analysts	Involves decision-makers and stakeholders	Engages SMEs, regulators, and funding bodies	Builds long-term relationships with clients through service
Limitations	Can be data- and resource-intensive	Subjective weight assignment can bias results	May lack scalability for large enterprises	Requires upfront investment and system monitoring infrastructure

ACCESS TO CIRCULAR FINANCE INSTRUMENTS

Integrating Corporate Finance with Circular Economy (CE) Goals

You need the right tools to make the transition to a circular economy. Circular finance mechanisms are key to aligning business models with sustainability goals.

These make businesses put social and environmental goals into their main financial plan to create financial and ecological value.

Businesses need to match their financial strategy with sustainability goals to go circular. To drive ecological and financial value and integrate social and environmental goals into business models corporate finance must use circular finance mechanisms

Finance in Circular Economy

Financial innovation, such as pay-for-performance schemes, green bonds, green loans, and CE-focused investment funds, helps businesses incorporate environmental, social, and governance (ESG) and the circular economy (CE) into their decision-making processes and hasten the transition to sustainable business models (Kumar et al., 2024a; Sarra, 2020; Munteanu et al., 2024).

As instruments to promote circular finance, remove obstacles, and enhance CE practices, fintech, artificial intelligence, and machine learning are becoming more and more popular (Kumar et al., 2024).

Corporate Finance and Circular Economy

Strategic Planning: Incorporating circular economy principles into corporate sustainability strategies, particularly in areas such as supply chain, cost management, and product design, is leading to more sustainable economic outcomes and a smaller environmental impact (Munteanu et al., 2024; Barros et al., 2021; Stewart & Niero, 2018).

Reporting and Transparency: Most companies mention CE in their sustainability reports but only a few set targets and indicators, so CE integration in corporate finance and reporting is still superficial and inconsistent (Opferkuch et al., 2022; Stewart & Niero, 2018).

Performance Metrics: There is growing focus on linking CE practices to financial performance but standardized metrics and reporting is underdeveloped (Munteanu et al., 2024; Opferkuch et al., 2022).

Circular Economy and Sustainable Development Goals (SDGs)

CE practices support several SDGs, especially those related to clean water, clean energy, economic growth, responsible consumption and life on land. But there are trade-offs, like decent work and safe environments vs recycling practices which require careful financial and strategic management (Schroeder et al., 2019; Velenturf & Purnell, 2021).

Green bonds are specifically projects that want to help the environment, such as renewable energy infrastructure, trash reduction, and eco-design efforts. On the other hand, sustainability-linked loans are even more eco-friendly by associating loan conditions, like interest rates, with ESG criteria already established. Impact investments go one step further, setting out to create actual outcomes that can be witnessed and that are of an environmental and social nature, while at the same time providing economic rewards to investors that have both profit and purpose as their goals.

One of the best examples of this is Schneider Electric, which is the number one company in the world that deals with energy management and automation. The corporation used green bonds to cover the cost of a range of actions such as increasing energy efficiency and implementing eco-design in its operations and product lines.

Importantly, Schneider Electric established a sustainability-linked financing system that does a lot more than just connect its overall financial strategy to the objectives of the circular economy. A total integration of the impact areas is the next step in the ecological innovation chain and a cross-functional team of finance, sustainability, operations, and R&D departments is the key to success and ensures the financial strategy is green rather than branding it as such a division of corporate social responsibility apart from financial one (Cronin, 2025).This coordination gives more obvious advantages. This alignment provides tangible benefits. Empirical studies suggest that enterprises dedicated to circular and ESG-aligned models have a lower cost of capital, as investors prefer assets that adhere to sustainability standards (Friede et al., 2015; Clark et al., 2015). This reflects itself in improved credit ratings, increased demand for green securities, and access to specialist financing markets.

Circular finance mechanisms are not just funding tools; they are levers for systemic change that reward companies for embedding sustainability into financial logic and decision-making. Corporate finance is key to the transition to a circular economy by using innovative financial instruments and integrating sustainability into core strategies. While progress is made, deeper integration, transparent reporting and advanced financial tools are needed to fully unlock the ecological and financial benefits of circular business models.

Table 7. Comparative Matrix: Corporate Impact and Circular Finance Instruments

Instrument	Definition/Purpose	Corporate Example	Strategic Benefit	Circular Outcome
Green Bonds	Debt instruments to fund environmentally friendly projects	Schneider Electric	Enables large-scale green investment with transparency	Finances eco-design and energy efficiency initiatives
Sustainability-Linked Loans	Loans with rates tied to ESG performance metrics	Schneider Electric (SLL framework)	Incentivizes corporate ESG compliance and performance	Aligns financial KPIs with CE indicators across departments
Impact Investment	Capital focused on measurable social/ environmental impact alongside returns	Broad sectoral use (e.g., SMEs, NGOs)	Attracts value-driven investors; fosters innovation	Funds circular solutions in waste, water, and energy sectors
Integrated CE Finance	Holistic integration of finance with CE across governance, policy, and strategy	Schneider Electric	Institutionalizes sustainability within financial management	Strengthens CE culture and interdepartmental alignment
Investor Behavior Impact	Favorability of ESG-aligned firms by capital markets	General trend (Friede et al., 2015)	Reduces cost of capital; increases asset liquidity	Encourages long-term CE commitment and transparent ESG reporting

RISK MANAGEMENT AND CIRCULAR STRATEGY

The strategies conducted by companies in terms of Circular finance and circular economy (CE) are becoming essential tools for the firms enabling the management of various risks including regulatory, resource and reputational risks. The firms can integrate the CE principles into financial planning and supply chain management to increase resilience, reduce exposure to disruptions and improve sustainability outcomes. In the subsections below, we will present key risk types in CE strategies.

Key Risk Types in Circular Strategies

Regulatory Risk

Due to fragmented legal frameworks and evolving regulations especially around hazardous substances in waste streams and REACH regulation, companies are facing many problems. Therefore, risk management tools and policy frameworks are needed to manage risks from material reuse and recycling (Bodar et al., 2018; De Lima & Seuring, 2023).Moreover, the lack of political support and incentives and inadequate regulatory frameworks are major barriers to CE adoption especially in developing countries (Hassan et al., 2023; Dulia et al., 2021).

Furthermore, companies operating in multiple jurisdictions need to overcome CE-related regulatory inconsistencies, complicating compliance and increasing legal risk. Thereofre, investment in circular technologies and procedures may be deterred by this legal uncertainty. Many companies are creating internal compliance departments and pushing for standardised international standards to address this (De Lima & Seuring, 2023).

Extended producer responsibility (EPR) regulations which puts the cost of post-consumer waste treatment on producers increases regulatory risk. This pressure requires re-evaluating lifespan assessments and cost structures in capital planning (Krstić et al., 2024).

Resource Risk

One major problem is the availability and volatility of raw materials. Recycling and remanufacturing are two CE strategies that can reduce dependence on external suppliers and supply chain disruptions by providing domestic or alternative sources of critical materials (De Lima & Seuring, 2023; Krstić et al., 2024; Ethirajan et al., 2021; Gaustad et al., 2018).

Risks include unstable prices for virgin and recycled materials and uncertainty around quality, availability and delivery of secondary resources (De Lima & Seuring, 2023; Krstić et al., 2024; Dulia et al., 2021). Furthermore, lack of infrastructure for collection or reverse logistics may make it difficult for companies to recover and reintegrate commodities. Investing in supplier interaction and traceability systems has become essential to financial planning to mitigate this (Gaustad et al., 2018).

Another source of resource risk is technological obsolescence since scalability is limited by outdated recycling or remanufacturing techniques. Financial models must include capital investment for R&D, technology upgrades and equipment retrofitting to ensure compliance with evolving CE standards (Toxopeus et al., 2021).

Reputational Risk

A company's reputation can be damaged by consumer backlash against unsustainable practices and degradation of recycled products. Consumer trust depends on high standards for circular product design and transparency (Krstić et al., 2024; Dulia et al., 2021; Ethirajan et al., 2021).

Corporate responsibility is highlighted by social media exposure, stakeholder engagement and ESG reporting. Perceived "greenwashing" which erodes stakeholder confidence and market value can result from inadequate explanation of CE goals and achievements (Ethirajan et al., 2021).

Furthermore, if a company is seen to be lagging behind in its CE commitments, B2B partnerships may be at risk. Reputation management has become a financial priority along with capital access and equity cost as institutional investors are looking for circularity indicators in ESG assessments (Toxopeus et al., 2021).

Risk Management Approaches

Risk Identification and Prioritisation: Companies can identify and rank the most critical risks such as supply chain complexity, resource availability and technological challenges with the help of multi-criteria decision-making models and expert evaluations (Hassan et al., 2023; Krstić et al., 2024; Dulia et al., 2021; Ethirajan et al., 2021).

Risk prediction can be enhanced through scenario analysis and stress testing using circular indicators. Tools for analysing financial vulnerability under different CE adoption scenarios and identifying the most vulnerable projects or materials were developed by Aranda-Usón et al. (2019).Furthermore, materiality assessments according to TCFD and GRI frameworks are gaining ground as a way to identify CE related risks that are financially material. This approach enables strategic capital allocation and integrates sustainability into enterprise risk management (Toxopeus et al., 2021).

Mitigation Strategies: Interfirm cooperation and circular product design are two examples of mitigation strategies.

Financial risk management, flexibility and information sharing are coping mechanisms (De Lima & Seuring, 2023; Krstić et al., 2024).

Resource related risks are being reduced through CE compliant procurement standards, advance contracts for recycled materials and supplier diversification. Similar to this, digital systems that align supply and demand for secondary materials remove uncertainties around quality (Gaustad et al., 2017).

Integrated alternatives in circular projects like the ability to switch materials or increase recycling capacity offer practical flexibility from a financial perspective. Financial models that provide a more accurate valuation under uncertainty like Black-Scholes model or binomial trees can be used to assess these (Toxopeus et al., 2021).

Financial Planning: For CE projects funding availability, internal financial resources and government subsidies are key. By connecting, forecasting future cash flows and creating standardised circular assets companies can also access bank financing (Gaustad et al., 2018; Aranda-Usón et al., 2019; Toxopeus et al., 2021).

Circular initiatives are being financed through sustainability linked loans and green bonds. According to Aranda-Usón et al. (2019) capital costs may be impacted by performance based triggers related to waste reduction, recyclability or reuse targets.

Additionally, integrated capital budgeting methods like Environmental Net Present Value (ENPV) and Adjusted Net Present Value (ANPV) are needed. For a more comprehensive assessment of circular investments Krstić et al. (2024) provide models that account for carbon pricing, environmental externalities and policy incentives.

BENEFITS AND LIMITATIONS

In addition to financial savings, energy conservation and corporate social responsibility CE strategies can reduce regulatory, resource and reputational risks (Ethirajan et al., 2021; Gaustad et al., 2018).But it's not without risks.

Case of Interface Inc.: Integrating Circularity into Core Financial Models

Interface Inc., a global pioneer in modular carpet production, exemplifies how industrial companies may connect their business processes with circular economy (CE) concepts while employing novel finance structures to internalize environmental costs. The transformation of the company was manifested with the decision to become a sustainable company that does not leave a negative impact on the environment (which was called "Mission Zero") and has since grown into a commitment to restoring the climate starting with their Climate Take Back™ campaign. There are two key principles of Interface's circular business model. The first is that the products must be designed in a way so that raw material extraction will be minimized and recycled and biomaterial will be the primary resources in the production. The second is that waste must be less while no external resources prom the supply chain.

One of the remarkable novelties in the new concept is the implementation of carbon pricing and waste valuation in Interface's internal financial models. By taking into account carbon and landfill waste as a source of cost, the direct costs of polluting the environment are internalized thereby strictly following the environmental rules as per the traditional accounting rules. These initiatives of the firm had a policy impact on the strategic process and a number of positive strategic outcomes. One of them is that the company is in a good position to lead the market as well as have less of a burden with environmental concerns in the future by aligning themselves with the stricter regulation. Another one is that this action allows the company to supply the financial, technical, and social data that the investors and stakeholders, particularly those interested in the ESG performance, seek and require. And the last one is that it causes a cross-functional collaboration among sustainability, finance, procurement, and R&D, where a culture of awareness for the environment through creative and innovative methods can thrive. Furthermore, by using eco-costing Interface, manufacturers can better determine the total lifecycle cost of their products, and design teams can prioritize materials and methods with reduced environmental impact. This increases brand equity, customer loyalty, and long-term profitability.

Interface's experience demonstrates that incorporating circularity into financial systems, such as internal carbon pricing, can generate a compelling business case for sustainability by combining environmental ambition with long-term economic stability.

COMPARATIVE MATRIX: CIRCULAR ECONOMY INTEGRATION IN BUSINESS MODELS

Table 8. Business Case Studies on Financial Innovation for the Implementation of the Circular Economy

Company	Circular Strategy	Financial Innovation	Outcome
Philips	Shifted to "Pay-per-Lux" lighting-as-a-service model	New capital budgeting for service-based models	Increased customer retention; long-term savings (Ellen MacArthur Foundation, 2020)
Schneider Electric	Financed eco-projects via green bonds and SLL framework	Linked interest rates to ESG targets and performance	Embedded CE goals in corporate finance; reduced capital costs
Interface Inc.	Adopted closed-loop production with recycled inputs	Introduced internal carbon/waste pricing and eco-costing	Mitigated regulatory risk; improved supply chain resilience and ESG scores

Integrating circular finance and CE strategies into risk management allows companies to better manage regulatory, resource and reputational risks. While these approaches offer significant resilience and sustainability benefits, successful implementation requires risk identification, supportive regulation and strategic planning.

CORPORATE GOVERNANCE AND STRATEGIC PLANNING

Corporate governance and strategic planning are converging with circular economy (CE) principles as companies seek to be more sustainable, access capital and stay competitive long-term. Integrating CE into governance and strategic frameworks is seen as key to economic, environmental and social benefits.

Circular Economy in Corporate Strategy

Embedding CE into corporate strategy allows companies to go beyond traditional KPIs, circular supply chains, eco-innovation and industrial symbiosis as core business levers (Maranesi & Giovanni, 2020; Zlotnik, 2021).

Strategic planning that internalizes circularity principles helps organisations achieve more sustainable economic results and reduce environmental impacts (Barros et al., 2021; Zlotnik, 2021).

CE models in corporate strategy is linked to increased resilience especially in response to global risks and economic crises (Zlotnik, 2021).

Governance Structures and Oversight

CE governance requires strong public leadership and active stakeholder involvement, often through network governance (Cramer, 2022). Board oversight and formal governance mechanisms are key to aligning CE goals with overall business objectives and strategic coherence (Maranesi & Giovanni, 2020; Cramer, 2022; Gennari & Cassano, 2020).

CE in governance frameworks helps with resource management, risk mitigation and compliance with sustainability standards (Gennari & Cassano, 2020; Zlotnik, 2021).

Strategic Planning Tools and Implementation

Formal strategic planning tools and stakeholder engagement are essential for knowledge sharing, CE integration, and a commitment to circularity (Ferrari et al., 2025; Abu-Bakar & Charnley, 2024).

Structured CE roadmapping that integrates sustainability science and systems thinking can help transform long-term CE goals into KPIs and strategic initiatives (Abu-Bakar & Charnley, 2024).

Circular thinking benefits several key business domains impacted by CE, including supply chain, logistics, cost control, research and development, and environmental management (Barros et al., 2021).

KEY BARRIERS AND RECOMMENDATIONS

Table 9. Barriers to the Adoption of the Circular Economy, Both Internal and External

Barrier Type	Examples
Internal	Risk aversion, short-term focus, lack of knowledge
External	Technology, market, legislative, societal factors

To overcome these barriers, comprehensive management frameworks and strategic recommendations for internal and external challenges are required (Takacs et al., 2022).

Reporting and Communication

As companies adopt the circular economy (CE), they must be careful about how they report on their environmental and social performance if they want to be accountable, win over stakeholders and attract investors who care about sustainability. With integrated reporting (IR) and corporate social responsibility (CSR) reports, a company can explain its CE objective, track its progress and show how circular practices deliver long term value creation.

Integrated reports, unlike financial reports, provide a narrative that links financial success to environmental, social and governance (ESG) metrics. This allows companies to show how circular practices – like resource recirculation, waste reduction, decarbonisation and product redesign – are embedded in their business plans and operational decisions.

According to Fortunati et al. (2020) the growth of non-financial disclosure standards like GRI, SASB and the EU's Corporate Sustainability Reporting Directive (CSRD) has increased the standardisation and impact of CE reporting on stakeholder perception.

By showing openness and forward thinking, companies that disclose circular goals, material flows, KPIs and lifecycle impacts increase their brand value and market differentiation. Publishing circular targets encourages departmental accountability and continuous improvement which in turn benefits internal alignment.

Furthermore, lending and investment decisions are increasingly influenced by CE reporting. Non-financial disclosures are being scrutinised by impact investors and financial institutions to evaluate opportunities and risks.

Companies that communicate CE integration are seen as more innovative, resilient and aligned with global sustainability agendas like the UN SDGs and the EU Green Deal.

In short, effective CE reporting is a communication tool that communicates business purpose, builds trust and enables new forms of green finance and collaboration. It goes beyond compliance. By making circular strategy visible, measurable and comparable across industries it also facilitates stakeholder communication.

Governance and corporate finance interact when determining CE goals and distributing incentives:

- Sustainability KPIs tied to executive compensation
- Integrated reporting frameworks (GRI, SASB, TCFD)
- Board oversight of circular economy goals

Companies that embed CE in their governance structures are better placed to access capital and maintain strategic coherence. Integrating circular economy principles into corporate governance and strategic planning is key to sustainability, resilience and long-term value. Effective governance structures, strategic planning tools and transparent reporting are the enablers while overcoming internal and external barriers is the challenge. Companies that embed CE into their core strategies and governance frameworks are better placed to access capital, manage risks and maintain strategic coherence in a rapidly changing business landscape.

BARRIERS TO FINANCIAL INTEGRATION OF CIRCULAR ECONOMY

Despite the growing interest in CE, there are many barriers to its financial integration. Main obstacles are short term financial perspectives, inadequate valuation tools, limited internal expertise and unclear or inconsistent regulations. Overcoming these challenges requires cross functional collaboration and stakeholder engagement throughout the value chain.

Main Financial Barriers

Short termism in Financial Markets: Financial markets focus on immediate returns and circular investments which have longer payback periods struggle to get funding (De Souza Mello Gonçalves et al., 2023; De La Cuesta-González & Morales-García, 2022; Saarinen & Aarikka-Stenroos, 2022; Manoharan et al., 2022).

Inadequate Valuation Tools: Traditional financial assessment methods don't capture the full value or risk profile of circular business models and therefore underinvest (De La Cuesta-González & Morales-García, 2022; Saarinen & Aarikka-Stenroos, 2022; Kumar et al., 2024; Manoharan et al., 2022).

High Initial Investment and Risk: Circular economy projects require significant upfront capital and are perceived as riskier due to their novelty and lack of established benchmarks especially for SMEs (Gonçalves et al., 2022; De La Cuesta-González & Morales-García, 2022; Saarinen & Aarikka-Stenroos, 2022; Manoharan et al., 2022; Ormazabal et al., 2018).

Limited Internal Capacity: Many finance departments lack the expertise or resources to evaluate and manage circular investments (Ritzén & Sandström, 2017; Saarinen & Aarikka-Stenroos, 2023; Manoharan et al., 2022).

Regulatory and Policy Uncertainty: Inconsistent or unclear regulations, fragmented policies and lack of supportive incentives create uncertainty and discourage investment (De La Cuesta-González & Morales-García, 2022; Kumar et al.a, 2024; Tuboalabo et al., 2024; Grafström & Aasma, 2021; Trevisan et al., 2023).

Additional Barriers

Table 10. Classification of Technological, Cultural, and Structural Obstacles to the Integration of the Circular Economy

Barrier Type	Description
Structural & Operational	Complexity of integrating CE into existing business models and supply chains
Attitudinal & Cultural	Resistance to change, lack of awareness, and limited knowledge
Technological & Logistical	Challenges in material recovery, recycling, and digital transformation

Engagement with stakeholders along the value chain and cross-functional alignment from procurement to treasury are necessary to overcome these limitations. In summary, financial integration in the circular economy is hindered by short term thinking, lack of tools, internal capacity gaps and regulatory uncertainty. To overcome these barriers supportive policy frameworks, collaborative internal efforts and financial innovation are needed.

POLICY AND INSTITUTIONAL SUPPORT

Policy and institutional support is key for corporate finance to drive the circular economy (CE). International frameworks and government incentives like the EU Circular Economy Action Plan, the UN Sustainable Development Goals (SDGs), the OECD/G20 guidelines impact the legal and financial environment for circularity. Green financing is promoted, sustainability standards are set and public private partnerships are encouraged. Government incentives and international policy frameworks are needed for corporate finance to support CE.

- EU Circular Economy Action Plan: **Green financing and CE taxonomies.**
- UN SDGs: **Especially Goals 9, 12 and 13.**

OECD and G20 guidelines: **Sustainable infrastructure and financing.**

Key International Policy Frameworks

EU Circular Economy Action Plan: The EU has been instrumental in promoting circular practices through the establishment of laws, regulations, and infrastructure. It encourages CE taxonomies, green finance, and technological innovation, especially in sectors like waste management and construction. However, policy fragmentation and end-of-pipe solutions remain challenges, so more systemic and coherent approaches are needed (Losa, 2025; Mhatre et al., 2021; Friant et al., 2021).

UN SDGs (Goals 9, 12, 13): CE strategies are closely linked to SDGs, especially those on responsible consumption and production, industry innovation and climate action. CE contributes most to SDGs 8, 12 and 13 by minimising waste, resource efficiency and sustainable growth. The alignment between CE and SDGs is strongest when policies support regenerative production, product longevity and clean end-of-life solutions (Friant et al., 2020; Ogunmakinde et al., 2022; Sharma et al., 2021; Ortiz-De-Montellano et al., 2023; Rodríguez-Antón et al., 2022).OECD and G20 Guidelines: Developed countries in the G20, with environmental policies and economic incentives (subsidies, tax exemptions, financing) do better in advancing SDG 12 through CE practices. These guidelines set sustainability standards and promote best practices (Campoli et al., 2025).

Government Incentives and Green Finance

Green Finance and Foreign Investment: Green finance policies including subsidies, tax incentives and targeted investments significantly promote CE by supporting innovation, recycling and sustainable business models. Green foreign financing has a measurable impact on CE outcomes such as increased recycling rates and CE related patents (Campoli et al., 2025; Ha, 2025; Kumar et al., 2023b).

Public-Private Partnerships (PPPs): To mobilise corporate finance and scale up circular initiatives, the public and private sectors must collaborate with fiscal incentives and explicit ESG disclosure requirements (Losa, 2025; Mhatre et al., 2021; Kumar et al., 2023b).

Challenges and Gaps

Policy fragmentation: Widespread adoption of CE is hampered by inconsistent and disjointed policies, particularly in the EU. Long-term, cross-sectoral, and more integrated policy frameworks are required (Losa, 2025; Friant et al., 2021).

Legal and Knowledge Barriers: Uncertain legal frameworks, imprecise definitions, and a lack of knowledge about CE and green finance deter investors and impede advancement (Kumar et al., 2023b).

Table 11. Effect on the Circularity Table and Corporate Finance

Policy Tool	Impact on CE Adoption
Green finance incentives	Boosts innovation, recycling, patents
Tax exemptions/subsidies	Encourages sustainable investments
PPPs and ESG requirements	Mobilizes private sector finance
International guidelines	Sets standards, shares best practices

International policy frameworks and government incentives are key to corporate finance supporting the circular economy. Though policy fragmentation and knowledge gaps persist, guidance is provided by the EU Action Plan, UN SDGs, and OECD/G20 guidelines. Circularity and sustainability are fuelled by green finance, public-private partnerships, and unambiguous regulatory standards.

PPPs, fiscal incentives and clearer ESG disclosure requirements can further mobilize corporate finance for circularity.

DISCUSSION

Corporate finance and the circular economy are moving from an idea to a reality. This paper has shown that companies like Philips, Interface, Schneider Electric, and Interface Inc. are already testing new financing models – pay-per-use services, recycled input integration, green bonds and integrated reporting – that combine profitability with sustainability.

A key takeaway from these cases is the importance of internal coherence between strategy, operations and finance. For example, Philips' shift to a service-based lighting model ("Pay-per-Lux") required new investment appraisal tools and coordination across departments. Interface Inc.'s use of carbon pricing embedded into financial models allowed for a proper valuation of long-term ecological risks. Schneider Electric's green bond issuance showed how CE outcomes can be monetized and aligned with investor expectations through transparent sustainability-linked frameworks.

But challenges remain. Many companies still use outdated appraisal frameworks that discount environmental externalities. Regulatory uncertainty, lack of standardised CE metrics and limited institutional capacity in sustainable finance also hinder widespread adoption. Overcoming these barriers requires strategic leadership, innovative financial design and collaborative ecosystems that incentivise systemic change.

In the future the financial sector will determine the pace and scale of circular transitions. Banks, asset managers and insurance companies are already integrating climate risk into their pricing models and regulatory mandates like the EU Taxonomy are forcing companies to think holistically about value creation.

In summary, corporate finance is both a lever and a test for circular transformation. By making circularity a core financial and strategic priority companies can future-proof their business models, meet stakeholder expectations and contribute to global sustainability goals.

Despite increased academic and practical attention on CE financing, significant research gaps persist. First, there is a lack of sector-specific comparisons of CE-related return on investment (ROI). Second, empirical research into the cost of capital differences between circular and linear projects is limited. Third, there is limited information on how financial institutions change credit scoring or risk assessments based on circularity indicators. Future research should look at these areas to help inform evidence-based policy and financial innovation. While the literature on circular finance is expanding, significant research gaps persist.

CONCLUSION AND RECOMMENDATIONS

The integration of circular economy principles into corporate finance is not a compliance trend but a strategic necessity. Businesses must alter their financial models to remain competitive and resilient in the face of global economic restrictions, environmental laws, and shifting customer expectations. When corporate finance is focused on sustainability and circularity, it becomes a long-term value generation driver. Companies that use novel financial tools, approach investment decisions from a lifecycle perspective, and match incentives with sustainability goals will be better positioned to flourish in the circular economy. These strategic actions improve internal efficiencies and risk management while also increasing external legitimacy and market trust. The business case for circular finance is robust and growing, including cost reductions through resource efficiency and lower capital costs via green finance instruments.

Recommendations

1. Integrate Life Cycle Assessment (LCA) with Capital Budgeting.

Financial assessments should look beyond short-term profitability indicators and include all environmental costs and benefits throughout the product or project lifecycle. This highlights the hidden hazards and long-term worth of circular inventions.

2. Integrate circular KPIs into financial planning and executive incentives.

Linking executive salary and departmental performance assessments to circular results (waste reduction, material reuse, product longevity) enables top-level strategy alignment and responsibility.

3. Consider ESG-linked financial instruments.

Companies should investigate and implement circular financing instruments such as green bonds, sustainability-linked loans (SLLs), and blended finance. These instruments not only provide access to financing but also attract mission-aligned investors.

4. Develop internal capabilities for sustainable finance.

Building internal competence in ESG reporting, impact valuation, and sustainable investment research is critical. Capacity-building initiatives, as well as collaborations with academic and policy organizations, can help finance departments adopt circular thinking.

5. Collaborate for Systemic Impact.

Companies must collaborate with authorities, supply chain partners, financial institutions, and civil society to break down systemic hurdles and expand circular economy models. Policy advocacy and engagement in global frameworks (such as CSRD and TNFD) can strengthen leadership and coherence.

REFERENCES

Abu-Bakar, H., & Charnley, F. (2024). Developing a strategic methodology for circular economy roadmapping: A theoretical framework. *Sustainability (Basel), 16*(15), 6682. DOI: 10.3390/su16156682

Alliance, G. S. I. (2018, April). *Global sustainable investment review*.

Aranda-Usón, A., Portillo-Tarragona, P., Marín-Vinuesa, L. M., & Scarpellini, S. (2019). Financial resources for the circular economy: A perspective from businesses. *Sustainability (Basel), 11*(3), 888. DOI: 10.3390/su11030888

Barros, M. V., Salvador, R., do Prado, G. F., de Francisco, A. C., & Piekarski, C. M. (2021). Circular economy as a driver to sustainable businesses. *Cleaner Environmental Systems, 2*, 100006. DOI: 10.1016/j.cesys.2020.100006

Bebbington, J., & Unerman, J. (2018). Achieving the United Nations Sustainable Development Goals: An enabling role for accounting research. *Accounting, Auditing & Accountability Journal, 31*(1), 2–24. DOI: 10.1108/AAAJ-05-2017-2929

Bodar, C., Spijker, J., Lijzen, J., Waaijers-van der Loop, S., Luit, R., Heugens, E., Janssen, M., Wassenaar, P., & Traas, T. (2018). Risk management of hazardous substances in a circular economy. *Journal of Environmental Management, 212*, 108–114. DOI: 10.1016/j.jenvman.2018.02.014 PMID: 29428645

Busch, T., Johnson, M., & Pioch, T. (2022). Corporate carbon performance data: Quo vadis? *Journal of Industrial Ecology, 26*(1), 350–363. DOI: 10.1111/jiec.13008

Campoli, J. S., Kodama, T. K., Nagano, M. S., & Burnquist, H. L. (2025). Advancing circular economy: G20 nations' path towards 12th sustainable development goal. *Circular Economy and Sustainability, 5*(1), 1–24. DOI: 10.1007/s43615-024-00415-0

Chen, P., & Dagestani, A. A. (2023). What lies about circular economy practices and performance? Fresh insights from China. *Journal of Cleaner Production, 416*, 137893. DOI: 10.1016/j.jclepro.2023.137893

Clark, G. L., Feiner, A., & Viehs, M. (2015). From the stockholder to the stakeholder: How sustainability can drive financial outperformance. *Available at SSRN* 2508281.

Climate Bonds Initiative. (2024). https://www.climatebonds.net/data-insights/publications/quarterly-market-update-q1-2024

Cramer, J. (2022). Effective governance of circular economies: An international comparison. *Journal of Cleaner Production, 343*, 130874. DOI: 10.1016/j.jclepro.2022.130874

Cronin, S. (2025). Schneider Electric Case Study. In *Examining Net Zero: Creating Solutions for a Greener Society and Sustainable Economic Growth* (pp. 77–85). Emerald Publishing Limited. DOI: 10.1108/978-1-83608-574-420251008

De La Cuesta-González, M., & Morales-García, M. (2022). Does finance as usual work for circular economy transition? A financiers and SMEs qualitative approach. *Journal of Environmental Planning and Management*, *65*(13), 2468–2489. DOI: 10.1080/09640568.2021.1972798

De Lima, F. A., & Seuring, S. (2023). A Delphi study examining risk and uncertainty management in circular supply chains. *International Journal of Production Economics*, *258*, 108810. DOI: 10.1016/j.ijpe.2023.108810

Dewick, P., Bengtsson, M., Cohen, M. J., Sarkis, J., & Schröder, P. (2020). Circular economy finance: Clear winner or risky proposition? *Journal of Industrial Ecology*, *24*(6), 1192–1200. DOI: 10.1111/jiec.13025

Donat, G. C., & de Souza, J. S. (2023). Circular economy investments: A portfolio selection framework. https://doi.org/DOI: 10.14488/IJCIEOM2023_FULL_0032_37736

Dulia, E. F., Ali, S. M., Garshasbi, M., & Kabir, G. (2021). Admitting risks towards circular economy practices and strategies: An empirical test from supply chain perspective. *Journal of Cleaner Production*, *317*, 128420. DOI: 10.1016/j.jclepro.2021.128420

Ellen MacArthur Foundation. (2020). Financing the circular economy: Capturing the opportunity.

Ethirajan, M., Arasu, M. T., Kandasamy, J., Kek, V., Nadeem, S. P., & Kumar, A. (2021). Analysing the risks of adopting circular economy initiatives in manufacturing supply chains. *Business Strategy and the Environment*, *30*(1), 204–236. DOI: 10.1002/bse.2617

Fang, F., Parida, S., & Sarkis, J. (2024). Private financing and the circular economy. *Resources, Conservation and Recycling*, *205*, 107581. DOI: 10.1016/j.resconrec.2024.107581

Feng, X., & Goli, A. (2023). Enhancing business performance through circular economy: A comprehensive mathematical model and statistical analysis. *Sustainability (Basel)*, *15*(16), 12631. Advance online publication. DOI: 10.3390/su151612631

Ferrari, A. G., Jugend, D., Armellini, F., & Seles, B. M. R. P. (2025). Opportunities and challenges of strategic planning in the context of circular economy: An exploratory analysis. *Management of Environmental Quality*, *36*(3), 833–854. Advance online publication. DOI: 10.1108/MEQ-05-2024-0183

Fortunati, S., Martiniello, L., & Morea, D. (2020). The strategic role of the corporate social responsibility and circular economy in the cosmetic industry. *Sustainability (Basel), 12*(12), 5120. DOI: 10.3390/su12125120

Friant, M. C., Vermeulen, W. J., & Salomone, R. (2021). Analysing European Union circular economy policies: Words versus actions. *Sustainable Production and Consumption, 27*, 337–353. DOI: 10.1016/j.spc.2020.11.001

Friede, G., Busch, T., & Bassen, A. (2015). ESG and financial performance: Aggregated evidence from more than 2000 empirical studies. *Journal of Sustainable Finance & Investment, 5*(4), 210–233. DOI: 10.1080/20430795.2015.1118917

Gaustad, G., Krystofik, M., Bustamante, M., & Badami, K. (2018). Circular economy strategies for mitigating critical material supply issues. *Resources, Conservation and Recycling, 135*, 24–33. DOI: 10.1016/j.resconrec.2017.08.002

Gennari, F., & Cassano, R. (2020). Circular economy and strategic risk. *Symphonya. Emerging Issues in Management*, 136-148. https://doi.org/DOI: 10.4468/2020.1.11gennari.cassano

Gonçalves, B. D. S. M., Carvalho, F. L. D., & Fiorini, P. D. C. (2022). Circular economy and financial aspects: A systematic review of the literature. *Sustainability (Basel), 14*(5), 3023. DOI: 10.3390/su14053023

Goovaerts, L., & Verbeek, A. (2018). Sustainable banking: finance in the circular economy. *Investing in Resource Efficiency: The Economics and Politics of Financing the Resource Transition*, 191-209. https://doi.org/.DOI: 10.1007/978-3-319-78867-8_9

Grafström, J., & Aasma, S. (2021). Breaking circular economy barriers. *Journal of Cleaner Production, 292*, 126002. DOI: 10.1016/j.jclepro.2021.126002

Ha, L. T. (2025). Circular Economy in European Countries: The Required Link for Green Foreign Financing Investment Policy. *Circular Economy and Sustainability, 5*(3), 1–30. DOI: 10.1007/s43615-024-00494-z

Hassan, M. S., Ali, Y., Petrillo, A., & De Felice, F. (2023). Risk assessment of circular economy practices in construction industry of Pakistan. *The Science of the Total Environment, 868*, 161418. DOI: 10.1016/j.scitotenv.2023.161418 PMID: 36642278

IFC. (2023). *Blended Finance for Sustainable Development* https://www.ifc.org/en/what-we-do/sector-expertise/blended-finance

Interface. (2020). *Sustainability Highlights Report.*

Kirchherr, J., Piscicelli, L., Bour, R., Kostense-Smit, E., Muller, J., Huibrechtse-Truijens, A., & Hekkert, M. (2018). Barriers to the circular economy: Evidence from the European Union (EU). *Ecological Economics, 150*, 264–272. DOI: 10.1016/j.ecolecon.2018.04.028

Krstić, M., Agnusdei, L., Palmi, P., & Baležentis, T. (2024). Enabling organizations to strategically manage risks in circular supply chains. *Business Strategy and the Environment, 33*(6), 5996–6009. DOI: 10.1002/bse.3793

Krystallis, I., Cardin, M., & de Neufville, R. (2025). Designing Flexibility for Strategic Decision-Making in Infrastructure Projects, Real Options, and Managing Uncertainty. *IEEE Transactions on Engineering Management.*

Kumar, B., Kumar, A., Sassanelli, C., & Kumar, L. (2024). Exploring the role of finance in driving circular economy and sustainable business practices. *Journal of Cleaner Production, 144480*. Advance online publication. DOI: 10.1016/j.jclepro.2024.144480

Kumar, B., Kumar, L., Kumar, A., Kumari, R., Tagar, U., & Sassanelli, C. (2024). Green finance in circular economy: A literature review. *Environment, Development and Sustainability, 26*(7), 16419–16459. DOI: 10.1007/s10668-023-03361-3 PMID: 37362997

Lacy, P., & Rutqvist, J. (2015). *Waste to wealth: The circular economy advantage* (Vol. 91). Palgrave Macmillan.

Losa, R. (2025). Public policies on circular economy: A systematic review. *Ecological Economics, 228*, 108452. DOI: 10.1016/j.ecolecon.2024.108452

Malabi Eberhardt, L. C., van Stijn, A., Nygaard Rasmussen, F., Birkved, M., & Birgisdottir, H. (2020). Development of a life cycle assessment allocation approach for circular economy in the built environment. *Sustainability (Basel), 12*(22), 9579. DOI: 10.3390/su12229579

Manoharan, S., Pulimi, V. S. K., Kabir, G., & Ali, S. M. (2022). Contextual relationships among drivers and barriers to circular economy: An integrated ISM and DEMATEL approach. *Sustainable Operations and Computers, 3*, 43–53. DOI: 10.1016/j.susoc.2021.09.003

Maranesi, C., & De Giovanni, P. (2020). Modern circular economy: Corporate strategy, supply chain, and industrial symbiosis. *Sustainability (Basel), 12*(22), 9383. DOI: 10.3390/su12229383

Mhatre, P., Panchal, R., Singh, A., & Bibyan, S. (2021). A systematic literature review on the circular economy initiatives in the European Union. *Sustainable Production and Consumption*, *26*, 187–202. DOI: 10.1016/j.spc.2020.09.008

Modigliani, F., & Miller, M. H. (1958). The cost of capital, corporation finance and the theory of investment. *The American Economic Review*, *48*(3), 261–297.

Moser, R. M. B., & Gonzalez, L. (2015). Microfinance and climate change impacts: The case of Agroamigo in Brazil. *RAE*, *55*(4), 397–407. DOI: 10.1590/S0034-759020150404

Munteanu, I., Ionescu-Feleagă, L., & Ionescu, B. . (2024). Financial Strategies for Sustainability: Examining the Circular Economy Perspective. *Sustainability (Basel)*, *16*(20), 8942. DOI: 10.3390/su16208942

Nemhauser, G. L., & Ullmann, Z. (1969). Discrete dynamic programming and capital allocation. *Management Science*, *15*(9), 494–505. DOI: 10.1287/mnsc.15.9.494

Nevatia, V. (2022). Sovereign Green Bonds: Reducing Climate Capital Costs in Emerging Markets. *Available at SSRN* 4983252. DOI: 10.2139/ssrn.4983252

Nunden, N., Abbana, S., Marimuthu, F., & Sentoo, N. (2022). An assessment of management skills on capital budgeting planning and practices: Evidence from the small and medium enterprise sector. *Cogent Business & Management*, *9*(1), 2136481. DOI: 10.1080/23311975.2022.2136481

OECD. (2023). *Green Finance and Investment: Global Taxonomies and ESG Regulation*. https://www.oecd.org/en/publications/green-finance-and-investment_24090344.html

Ogunmakinde, O. E., Egbelakin, T., & Sher, W. (2022). Contributions of the circular economy to the UN sustainable development goals through sustainable construction. *Resources, Conservation and Recycling*, *178*, 106023. DOI: 10.1016/j.resconrec.2021.106023

Opferkuch, K., Caeiro, S., Salomone, R., & Ramos, T. B. (2022). Circular economy disclosure in corporate sustainability reports: The case of European companies in sustainability rankings. *Sustainable Production and Consumption*, *32*, 436–456. DOI: 10.1016/j.spc.2022.05.003

Ormazabal, M., Prieto-Sandoval, V., Puga-Leal, R., & Jaca, C. (2018). Circular economy in Spanish SMEs: Challenges and opportunities. *Journal of Cleaner Production*, *185*, 157–167. DOI: 10.1016/j.jclepro.2018.03.031

Ortiz-de-Montellano, C. G. S., Samani, P., & van der Meer, Y. (2023). How can the circular economy support the advancement of the Sustainable Development Goals (SDGs)? A comprehensive analysis. *Sustainable Production and Consumption, 40*, 352–362. DOI: 10.1016/j.spc.2023.07.003

Ozili, P. K. (2021). Circular economy, banks, and other financial institutions: What's in it for them? *Circular Economy and Sustainability*, *1*(3), 787–798. DOI: 10.1007/s43615-021-00043-y

Palea, V., Santhià, C., & Miazza, A. (2023). Are circular economy strategies economically successful? Evidence from a longitudinal panel. *Journal of Environmental Management*, *337*, 117726. DOI: 10.1016/j.jenvman.2023.117726 PMID: 36933534

Ritzén, S., & Sandström, G. Ö. (2017). Barriers to the Circular Economy–integration of perspectives and domains. *Procedia CIRP*, *64*, 7–12. DOI: 10.1016/j.procir.2017.03.005

Rizos, V., Behrens, A., Van der Gaast, W., Hofman, E., Ioannou, A., Kafyeke, T., Flamos, A., Rinaldi, R., Papadelis, S., Hirschnitz-Garbers, M., & Topi, C. (2016). Implementation of circular economy business models by small and medium-sized enterprises (SMEs): Barriers and enablers. *Sustainability (Basel)*, *8*(11), 1212. DOI: 10.3390/su8111212

Rodríguez-Antón, J. M., Rubio-Andrada, L., Celemín-Pedroche, M. S., & Ruíz-Peñalver, S. M. (2022). From the circular economy to the sustainable development goals in the European Union: An empirical comparison. *International Environmental Agreement: Politics, Law and Economics*, *22*(1), 67–95. DOI: 10.1007/s10784-021-09553-4 PMID: 34744532

Saarinen, A., & Aarikka-Stenroos, L. (2023). Financing-related drivers and barriers for circular economy business: Developing a conceptual model from a field study. *Circular Economy and Sustainability*, *3*(3), 1187–1211. DOI: 10.1007/s43615-022-00222-5

Sanchez, B., & Haas, C. (2018). Capital project planning for a circular economy. *Construction Management and Economics*, *36*(6), 303–312. DOI: 10.1080/01446193.2018.1435895

Sarra, J. (2020). Sustainable Finance and the Move to a Circular Economy. *From Ideas to Action*, 249-294. https://doi.org/DOI: 10.1093/oso/9780198852308.003.0008

Schroeder, P., Anggraeni, K., & Weber, U. (2019). The relevance of circular economy practices to the sustainable development goals. *Journal of Industrial Ecology*, *23*(1), 77–95. DOI: 10.1111/jiec.12732

Sharma, H. B., Vanapalli, K. R., Samal, B., Cheela, V. S., Dubey, B. K., & Bhattacharya, J. (2021). Circular economy approach in solid waste management system to achieve UN-SDGs: Solutions for post-COVID recovery. *The Science of the Total Environment, 800*, 149605. DOI: 10.1016/j.scitotenv.2021.149605 PMID: 34426367

Shavkatov, N., Abdurakhimova, D., Sherkuziyeva, N., Omonov, S., & Rakhmedova, M. (2024). *Circular economy practices and their effect on corporate financial performance*. Economic Annals-XXI., DOI: 10.21003/ea.V207-01

Stasiuk-Piekarska, A., Hordyńska, M., & Michalska, M. (2024). The Usefulness of Cleaner Production Projects as an Element of the Initial Assessment of the Circularity of SMEs in the Context of Obtaining Funds Supporting the Implementation of the Circular Economy. *Sustainability (Basel), 16*(12), 4951. DOI: 10.3390/su16124951

Stewart, R., & Niero, M. (2018). Circular economy in corporate sustainability strategies: A review of corporate sustainability reports in the fast-moving consumer goods sector. *Business Strategy and the Environment, 27*(7), 1005–1022. DOI: 10.1002/bse.2048

Taera, E. G., & Lakner, Z. (2025). Sustainable Finance: Bridging Circular Economy Goals and Financial Inclusion in Developing Economies. *WORLD (Oakland, Calif.), 6*(2), 44. DOI: 10.3390/world6020044

Takacs, F., Brunner, D., & Frankenberger, K. (2022). Barriers to a circular economy in small-and medium-sized enterprises and their integration in a sustainable strategic management framework. *Journal of Cleaner Production, 362*, 132227. DOI: 10.1016/j.jclepro.2022.132227

Tantia, V., & Sukanya, R. (2024). Reinventing the Business Model to Navigate the Evolving Business Landscape. In *ESG and Ecosystem Services for Sustainability* (pp. 259–282). IGI Global. DOI: 10.4018/979-8-3693-3771-4.ch010

Taxonomy, E. U. (2020). EU taxonomy for sustainable activities. *Available at: EU taxonomy for sustainable activities–European Commission (europa. eu).*

Toxopeus, H., Achterberg, E., & Polzin, F. (2021). How can firms access bank finance for circular business model innovation? *Business Strategy and the Environment, 30*(6), 2773–2795. DOI: 10.1002/bse.2893

Trevisan, A. H., Lobo, A., Guzzo, D., de Vasconcelos Gomes, L. A., & Mascarenhas, J. (2023). Barriers to employing digital technologies for a circular economy: A multi-level perspective. *Journal of Environmental Management, 332*, 117437. DOI: 10.1016/j.jenvman.2023.117437 PMID: 36801533

Tuboalabo, A., Buinwi, U., Okatta, C. G., Johnson, E., & Buinwi, J. A. (2024). Circular economy integration in traditional business models: Strategies and outcomes. *Finance & Accounting Research Journal*, *6*(6), 1105–1123. DOI: 10.51594/farj.v6i6.1245

Velenturf, A. P., & Purnell, P. (2021). Principles for a sustainable circular economy. *Sustainable Production and Consumption*, *27*, 1437–1457. DOI: 10.1016/j.spc.2021.02.018

World Business Council for Sustainable Development (WBCSD). (2020). *Circular Transition Indicators v2.0*.

Zlotnik, M. (2021). Circular economy as a part of the organizational corporate strategy. *Management and Entrepreneurship in Ukraine: the stages of formation and problems of development*, 183-192. https://doi.org/DOI: 10.23939/smeu2021.01.183

Chapter 8
The Role of Neuroscience in Building Sustainable Brands Within the Circular Economy Framework

Fatma Gülşah Dizar
https://orcid.org/0009-0000-2568-5171
Istinye University, Turkey

ABSTRACT

This study examines the strategic role of neuroscience in developing strong and sustainable brands through implementing cognitive, emotional and sensory insights into marketing strategies. Based on this, this study focuses as well as investigates how neuromarketing methods such as EEG, fMRI, GSR, eye tracking and facial coding enable the scientific measurement of unconscious consumer responses and how these responses turn into a marketing strategies to achieve sustainable brand loyalty among the consumers. In order to achieve this aim, in this study, first of all theoretical background will be formed. Accordingly, Kahneman's System 1 and System 2 framework and Krishna's sensory marketing approach will be touched upon to understand how consumers behave and their decision making processes work. Following to this, in this study, the theoretical discussion will be supported by the Hayat Kimya's Molfix brand' case study. Analyzes showed that eye-tracking and EEG analyzes revealed critical insights about attention, emotional activation, comprehension and memory retention. Based on the findings revisions made by the company and accordingly, significant improvements were achieved in brand loyalty among the consumers. The results demonstrate that neuroscience supported mar-

DOI: 10.4018/979-8-3373-3852-1.ch008

keting strategies develop better communication with the consumers and contributes to significant improvements in long-term consumer loyalty. Such approaches also support the long-term sustainability of brands in competitive markets.

1. INTRODUCTION

This study examines the strategic role of neuroscience in developing strong and sustainable brands by applying cognitive, emotional, and sensory insights to marketing strategies.

The reptilian brain's greatest strength is its ability to process visual stimuli without using the visual cortex. Therefore, we prefer images over words and experiences over descriptions (Morin, 2011). With this understanding, packaging and advertising that incorporate visual and emotional associations have been shown to be more successful in triggering sustainable consumer behavior (Vital, 2021). Based on this understanding, this study examines how neuromarketing methods such as EEG, fMRI, GSR, eye tracking, and facial coding enable the scientific measurement of unconscious consumer responses and how these responses are translated into marketing strategies to foster sustainable brand loyalty among consumers. To achieve this goal, this study will first establish a theoretical background. Accordingly, Kahneman's System 1 and System 2 frameworks, along with Krishna's sensory marketing approach, will be explored to understand how consumers behave and how their decision-making processes operate. Subsequently, this study will support the theoretical discussion with a case study of Hayat Kimya's Molfix brand.

The case study will explore the use of neuroscientific tools to optimize the packaging design and advertising content for Molfix's " New Generation Ducted Diaper". These studies, conducted using EEG and eye tracking, will examine the impact of optimizing packaging and advertising content on the brand and its impact on sustainable brand loyalty.

2. THEORETICAL FOUNDATIONS

2.1. Kahneman's Dual-System Theory

Daniel Kahneman (2011) demonstrated that decision-making processes are strongly influenced by intuitive and emotional elements. Kahneman explains the functioning of the human mind within the framework of two distinct systems: System 1 and System 2. This theory facilitates the analysis of consumer behavior and provides a theoretical foundation for neuromarketing research.

System 1 is fast, effortless, automatic, intuitive and largely emotional. A consumer may see a product in a store, like it, and purchase it spontaneously; such decisions are typically governed by System 1. System 2, in contrast, encompasses slower, analytical, conscious and logical mental processes (Kahneman, 2011).

Figure 1. (a) Illustration of the categorical view of automatic and controlled processes as applied to brain function. The positions of the arrows illustrate the conflation of bottom-up processing with automaticity, and top-down processing with control. (b) Illustration of what is implied by a dual-system view, in which regions of the brain are assigned to one of two systems. (Spunt, 2015)

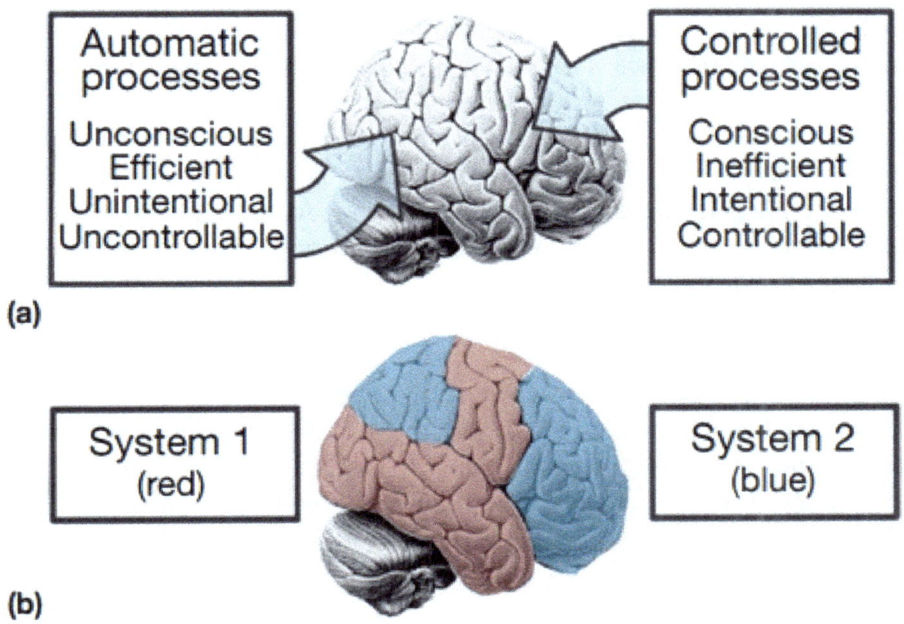

Decisions such as product comparisons, price-performance evaluations, or long-term benefit analyses are processed through this system. However, the majority of consumer purchasing decisions are made under the influence of System 1 (Kahneman, 2011).

The emotional and physiological responses triggered by System 1 can be observed, particularly through techniques such as EEG, facial coding, and GSR. This method makes it possible to determine which scenes in an ad evoke greater attention or empathy in consumers. This information allows brands to optimize their emotional engagement strategies. When combined with neuromarketing techniques, Kahneman's theory focuses on what consumers are saying and reveals how they are feeling.

2.2. Krishna's Sensory Marketing Approach

Krishna (2012) defines sensory marketing as the influence of sensory inputs on consumer perception and behavior. This approach suggests that marketing strategies should not only focus on visual and auditory elements but also incorporate the less frequently used senses such as touch, taste, and smell. Emphasizing that the human brain functions through an integrated system of multisensory perception, Krishna asserts that a successful brand experience can be built through multi-sensory stimulation.

The primary goal of sensory marketing is to make consumer interactions with a product or service richer, more meaningful, and more memorable. For example, a hotel chain can influence consumer behavior not only through its brand logo or pricing policy, but also through the distinctive scent in the lobby, the background music playing in the space and the overall atmosphere created by its interior design.

Neuroscience provides important insights into how such multisensory experiences are processed in the brain and which senses have the strongest impact on decision-making. Methods such as functional magnetic resonance imaging (fMRI) and electroencephalography (EEG) measure the neural correlates of sensory stimuli, while facial coding and galvanic skin response (GSR) analyses assess the emotional impact of these stimuli.

According to Krishna's approach, brand experiences created through the senses increase both brand awareness and loyalty. A unique sonic logo, tactile packaging design, or distinctive scent not only facilitate brand recognition but also strengthen the bond between the brand and the consumer by creating an emotional impact. Therefore, sensory marketing should be considered an integral element of sustainable brand strategies.

2.3. Integration of Consumer Decision-Making and Neuroscience

Theories explaining consumer behavior play a critical role in establishing a scientific basis for marketing strategies. In this context, Ajzen's Theory of Planned Behavior (TPB) and McGuire's Information Processing Model offer comprehensive explanatory frameworks for understanding the cognitive dimensions of consumer decision-making processes (Ajzen, 1991; McGuire, 1976).

Ajzen's theory suggests that an individual's behavior is shaped by three fundamental components: personal attitudes, perceived social norms, and perceived behavioral control (Ajzen, 1991). This framework assumes that behavior is planned, rational, and predictable.

However, in today's marketing landscape, a significant portion of consumer decisions is made through automatic, fast, and emotional systems. At this point, Kahneman's (2011) System 1 and System 2 model becomes relevant. While System 1 governs quick and intuitive responses, System 2 represents more deliberate and analytical thinking. Neuromarketing techniques allow for the concrete observation of how these two systems operate in response to brand stimuli.

McGuire's Information Processing Model posits that a message delivered to the consumer passes through stages such as attention, comprehension, persuasion, and recall (McGuire, 1976). Neuromarketing applications have demonstrated that consumers are affected not only cognitively but also emotionally during these stages. For instance, EEG can be used to measure attention levels, GSR to assess emotional arousal, and facial coding to detect micro-expressions on the face.

For sustainable brands, integrating these theoretical models with neuroscientific data is highly valuable. Consumers' responses to sustainability messages are not limited to conscious declarations but also include subconscious emotional and intuitive reflections. (Nilashi et al., 2020). In this regard, neuromarketing serves as a complementary measurement and analysis tool to planned behavior and information processing theories, enhancing the effectiveness of sustainability-driven brand strategies.

2.4. Neuroethics and Consumer Privacy

While the advanced technologies offered by neuromarketing enable the analysis of consumer behavior at a subconscious level, they also raise ethical concerns (Lee, Broderick & Chamberlain, (2007). Consumer privacy is a fundamental principle in preserving personal boundaries within marketing activities. The use of techniques such as EEG, fMRI, GSR, and Eye Tracking without informed consent or proper disclosure can lead to unethical practices (Stanton, Sinnott-Armstrong & Huettel, 2017).

Neuroethics is an ethical framework that prioritizes the rights, autonomy, and privacy of individuals during the collection, interpretation, and use of neuroscientific data. Ignoring this ethical framework in marketing practices may harm a brand's image in the long term. Especially for brands that position themselves as sustainable, ethical transparency is not merely a requirement but a strategic advantage (Illes & Bird, 2006).

It is essential to clearly communicate criteria such as informed consent, data security, and intended use when collecting consumers' neurophysiological data. Otherwise, the trust relationship between the consumer and the brand may be damaged. This can lead to backlash and mistrust rather than fostering sustainable brand loyalty (Plassmann, Ramsøy, & Milosavljevic, 2012).

In conclusion, although neuromarketing practices play a significant role in building sustainable brands, it is imperative that these practices be carried out within ethical guidelines. Neuroethical principles help establish a trust-based relationship with consumers and protect the long-term reputation of the brand (Vecchiato et al., 2011).

3. MARKETING STRATEGIES, AND SUSTAINABILITY

3.1. The Concept of Sustainability and Its Interpretation in the Context of Brands

The concept of sustainability, in general, refers to the balanced management of environmental, social, and economic resources to meet the needs of current and future generations (Brundtland Report, 1987).

In the business world, sustainability is addressed multidimensionally, not only in terms of profit maximization but also by fulfilling social responsibilities, reducing environmental impacts, and creating long-term value. Therefore, sustainability is both an ethical responsibility and a strategic imperative that provides brands with a competitive advantage.

In the marketing context, sustainability aims to establish long-term relationships with consumers based on trust and to integrate the brand's value with social benefits. In line with these objectives, it appears that practices such as environmentally friendly production processes, recyclable packaging, ethical supply chain management, and social impact projects have become decisive factors in consumers' brand preferences. Thus, sustainable brands do more than merely offer products or services—they create a meaningful universe aligned with the consumer's value system.

Neuromarketing provides the opportunity to measure how effectively this meaningful universe is established. Emotional and cognitive reactions to sustainability messages can be analysed through techniques such as EEG, GSR, facial coding, and heart rate monitoring. In this way, brands can scientifically test which messages truly foster empathy and trust (Plassmann et al., 2012).

Sustainability supports the value-oriented approach that is increasingly influential in consumer behavior, strengthens emotional attachment, and fosters lasting brand loyalty. Therefore, sustainability must be placed at the center of marketing strategies—it should not remain merely as a discourse in corporate reports but be actively shared with consumers as a core value.

3.2. Brand Sustainability and Emotional Bonding

A sustainable brand is defined not only by high environmental or economic performance, but also by its ability to establish a long-term, emotionally grounded bond with consumers (Keller, 2003). Such bonds enable consumers not only to prefer the brand but also to feel a sense of belonging, adopt its values, and become active advocates (Benito-León, Domínguez-González & Rodríguez, 2023). Therefore, brand sustainability requires the management of not only operational processes but also psychological and neuroscientific consumer interactions.

Neuroscientific methods offer an objective way to measure whether a brand is able to establish emotional bonds with consumers. Frequently used techniques in this context include:

EEG (Electroencephalography): Measures consumers' real-time brainwave responses to brand messages or visuals, analyzing levels of attention, interest, and emotional arousal.

Eye Tracking: Tracks which elements of an advertisement or package the consumer focuses on and for how long, providing insights into attention levels, visual engagement, and navigation effectiveness. Sustainability symbols, eco-labels, or social responsibility messages can be analyzed through this method.

GSR (Galvanic Skin Response): Detects stress, excitement, or empathy levels by measuring electrical conductivity through the skin.

Facial Coding: Automatically classifies positive or negative emotional reactions through micro-expressions on the face.

Heart Rate Monitoring: Evaluates whether sustainability messages generate excitement, focus, or relaxation in the consumer.

The impact of sustainability-themed campaigns on consumers can be tested using these techniques to enhance the effectiveness of brand messaging. For instance, a brand's "recyclable packaging" message may remain at an informational level for the consumer, but when supported with effective emotional triggers, it can create a much stronger connection (Krishna, 2012).

The following factors are critical to the success of sustainable brand strategies:

- Value-Based Communication: Brand messages should focus not only on product features but also on environmental and social responsibilities.
- Consistency: There must be alignment between what the brand says about sustainability and what it actually does.
- Emotional Harmony: Messages must resonate emotionally with the consumer's value system.
- Generating Empathy: Creating empathy toward the brand promotes long-term loyalty.

Sustainability and emotional attachment should be viewed as two interdependent core components. Neuroscientific measurement techniques offer a scientific opportunity to test the effectiveness of this relationship, making them an indispensable tool for the long-term success of brands (Plassmann et al., 2012; Kahneman, 2011).

3.3. The Role of Emotions in Brand Loyalty

Brand loyalty is defined as the consumer's repeated and voluntary preference for a brand, and one of the most decisive factors behind this preference is the emotional bond (Ariely & Berns, 2010). It is frequently emphasized in contemporary marketing literature that consumers develop loyalty not only because they are satisfied, but because they emotionally identify with the brand (Oliver, 1999). Loyalty, in this sense, is not merely a rational evaluation but a form of attachment woven with emotions.

The effect of emotions on brand loyalty can be analyzed more concretely through neuroscientific techniques (Aytekin & Kahraman, 2014). For instance, micro facial expressions recorded while watching an advertisement via facial coding, moments of heightened attention and emotional reaction measured through EEG, and levels of emotional arousal detected via GSR, provide scientific data on what the consumer actually feels beyond verbal expressions (Plassmann et al., 2012).

There is a strong connection between brand loyalty and sustainability. A sustainable brand strategy approaches the consumer not only with products or services, but also with ethical values, social responsibility, and environmental awareness. These types of brands establish meaningful emotional connections with consumers—not just functional ones. In this context, emotional loyalty becomes the cornerstone of sustainable brand strategies. Sustainable brands build long-term relationships of trust and attachment, thereby extending the brand's life and encouraging brand advocacy (Keller, 2003).

It is a known fact that brand loyalty is based not only on rational factors such as price, quality, or ease of use, but also on emotional stimuli. Neuroscience plays a key role in mapping and measuring this emotional dimension. By uncovering consumers' unconscious responses, it optimizes brand communication, product design, and campaign effectiveness, helping brands build stronger emotional connections with consumers and increase brand management efficiency (Hurzhyi, Popliuiko, Vasylyuk-Zaitseva, & Kobets, 2023). For brands that develop strategies based on values such as sustainability, creating and maintaining emotional attachment is no longer a choice but an essential component of sustainability.

4. HAYAT KIMYA AND ITS BRANDS

Molfix was launched in Turkey in 1998 and quickly became one of Hayat Kimya's leading diaper brands. With its focus on consumer needs, innovative product development, and commitment to sustainability, the brand has gained a strong market share in Turkey as well as in Europe, Africa, the Middle East and Asia (İstanbul Sanayi Odası, 2022).

Its growth is driven by diversification of the products, innovation and applying sustainability practices rooted from social responsibility. Molfix offers dermatologically tested, breathable and comfortable products designed to protect babies' skin health. The brand's slogan which is "As comfortable as a mother's lap," reflects its focus on comfort as a core value (Hayat Kimya, 2022).

As part of its environmental sustainability efforts Molfix uses recyclable packaging and invests in technologies to lower its carbon footprint during production. Its facilities use integrated systems to save energy and water and they follow environmentally friendly production policies. In social sustainability Molfix runs projects to raise awareness among mothers and create a positive social impact. The "Happy Babies, Happy Mothers" campaign provides education and support on health, hygiene and baby care. The "Life Link" project, aimed at supporting premature babies, offers medical help, emotional support, equipment and psychosocial assistance to mothers. These initiatives are closely connected to the principles of sustainable development (Hayat Kimya, 2022).

Hayat Kimya also uses neuroscience-based research to better understand consumer behavior and create effective strategies. In its Neuroscience Laboratory, the company applies methods such as EEG (Electroencephalography), GSR (Galvanic Skin Response), Eye Tracking and Facial Coding to design communication strategies tailored for its brands. These techniques help increase emotional connection between the brand and consumers, improve the impact of scientifically developed marketing materials and strengthen both brand awareness and loyalty.

5. CASE STUDY: NEUROSCIENTIFIC APPROACH AND SUSTAINABLE BRAND SUCCESS

5.1. Scope and Purpose of the Research

Rapidly evolving consumer expectations and intense competitive pressure have revealed that in the fast-moving consumer goods (FMCG) sector, it is no longer sufficient for brands to merely offer functional benefits. Today's consumers make purchasing decisions not only through rational evaluations but also through a combination of emotional, cognitive, and intuitive processes (Kahneman, 2011). In this context, the scientific measurement capabilities provided by neuromarketing techniques offer a strategic advantage for brands aiming to establish a deeper bond with consumers.

The primary objective of this study was to assess consumer perception of the packaging and advertising elements of Molfix's "New Generation Ducted Diaper" using objective data. This assessment was conducted using neuroscientific measurement techniques such as EEG (Electroencephalography) and Eye Tracking. The study consisted of pre-tests and post-tests for both the packaging and the advertising. Each study group consisted of 18 mothers, aged 20-40, from the ABC1C2 group, with babies aged 0-36 months and responsible for brand decision-making. Each participating consumer was interviewed for 15 minutes after the neurometric measurement. The neurophysiological data obtained from consumers during the study enabled analysis of how the packaging design and advertising triggered fundamental cognitive processes such as attention, emotional activation, comprehension, and memory retention.

The research is based on two pillars: Packaging Design and Commercial:

1. Packaging Design Research:

This phase of the research evaluated the degree to which Molfix product packaging captured consumer attention, the perception of intended messages, and the overall emotional impact. Neuroscience technologies can help businesses design and develop more successful products that meet consumer needs by examining consumers' physiological and neurophysiological responses to external features, such as a product's label. Attention can be defined as the ability to focus on specific aspects of the environment while ignoring other information (Venkatraman et al., 2015). Specifically, in neuromarketing, attention refers to the degree to which consumers focus on a stimulus. This is a prerequisite for information processing and, therefore, plays a key role in consumer decision-making (Varela et al., 2014; Krucien et al., 2017; García-Madariaga et al., 2019).

The research design for this phase involved randomly displaying different dummys images alongside the Molfix design. A pretest and a posttest were conducted with two separate groups of 18 consumers representing the target audience. Pretest results revealed that the current design lost attention in certain areas and lacked message cohesion. Eye-tracking analyses measured the visibility of slogans and product icons, fixation points, and gaze duration, while electroencephalography (EEG) data examined emotional responses and comprehension. Based on these findings, the packaging design was revised, and the final version demonstrated significant improvements in attention, message perception, and emotional engagement (Plassmann et al., 2012; Krishna, 2012).

2. TV Commercial Research:

Following the packaging research, Molfix advertising scenarios were pretested with an animated version and then posttested with the original film. A group of 18 consumers were recruited for the pretest and an additional group of 18 consumers for the posttest. The research design consisted of a series of seven different commercials, including the Molfix commercial. The commercials were shown to consumers in a random order. Neuroscientific methods such as EEG and eye tracking were used to measure consumers' attention levels and emotional responses, particularly during scenes with the theme "As Comfortable as a Mother's Lap." Findings showed that positive emotions increased in scenes featuring mother-child interactions, while attention levels decreased in some scenes. Following revisions based on this data, significant increases were achieved in empathy, trust, and liking scores (Kringelbach et al., 2008; Liu et al., 2024).

One of the most striking aspects of the study is the use of neuroscientific tools that measure the unconscious dimensions of consumer responses, rather than relying solely on traditional testing methods. The findings, evaluated within the framework of Daniel Kahneman's System 1 and System 2 model, provide a clear understanding of how intuitive decisions are shaped at initial touchpoints such as packaging and advertising (Kahneman, 2011). Optimizing these two touchpoints with neuroscientific data is seen as a strategic success in terms of building emotional closeness and long-term brand loyalty.

This case study demonstrates that neuroscientific methods in marketing communications are not a passing trend but a fundamental tool for developing sustainable, consumer-centric, and needs-focused brand strategies. Neuroscience can also help brands understand consumer behavior at both conscious and unconscious levels, strengthening the emotional bond between brand and consumer, fostering brand loyalty, and enhancing the effectiveness of marketing strategies (Hussein and Ozad, 2023, p. 2044). In other words, in-depth analysis of the unconscious influences of packaging and advertising enables brands to establish more empathetic, meaningful, and lasting relationships with their target audiences.

5.1.1 Molfix's Existing Packaging Design: A Neuroscience-Supported Approach

Rapidly changing consumer expectations, shopping behaviors shaped by digitalization, and increasing competition require fast-moving consumer goods (FMCG) brands to differentiate not only functionally but also emotionally. In this context, neuromarketing techniques that go beyond traditional research methods and analyze the unconscious dimensions of consumer responses have become a strategic transformation tool for brands (Plassmann et al., 2012; Lee et al., 2007).

Molfix, one of Hayat Kimya's leading brands, approached its packaging redesign not merely as a visual update but as a scientifically grounded communication strategy aimed at building emotional connection with consumers. Through data gathered from EEG and Eye-Tracking techniques, the brand was able to identify which elements of the packaging captured the most attention, where emotional activation occurred, and to what extent the brand was encoded into memory.

In light of this neuroscientific data, the placement of the slogan on the package was revised, product features were iconized, and the mother-baby theme was emphasized more effectively. The color palette, font choices, and visual hierarchy were redesigned to align with the emotional connotations of consumers. In accordance with Krishna's (2012) concept of sensory marketing, a new packaging language was developed under the premise that multi-sensory engagement with consumers enhances brand trust and loyalty.

The new Molfix packaging design is not only visually striking but also cognitively accessible and emotionally engaging. This approach, aligned with Keller's (2003) model of brand associations and brand equity, succeeded in creating a stronger and more sustainable brand impression in consumers' minds.

5.1.2 Initial Packaging Design and Pre-Test Findings

In the first phase of the research, the tested Molfix packaging design presented a classic layout that emphasized the brand's core functional messages and supported brand recognition. The overall layout highlighted key elements such as the brand logo, product type, and quantity. The central visual featuring a mother and baby was intended to create an emotional bond with the consumer.

Figure 2. Molfix packaging design

When this layout was analyzed using Eye-Tracking technology, it was observed that consumers' gazes were concentrated on the middle and lower edges of the packaging; however, the central visual area did not attract the expected level of visual attention. In particular, emotionally evocative messages such as the slogan failed to generate sufficiently sustained focus. Additionally, the functional benefit information of the product did not receive adequate visual attention. These findings indicate that the visual hierarchy needs to be reconsidered.

Figure 3. Heatmap image of Molfix packaging design

EEG data further supports these observations. During the time consumers examined the packaging, the measured levels of attention and emotional engagement remained generally moderate. It was particularly noted that the mother-and-baby image offered areas for improvement in triggering the intended empathic connection. These results demonstrate, as emphasized in Krishna's (2012) sensory marketing approach, that product packaging must serve not only an informative function but also evoke emotional associations. The visual attention distribution and brain activity findings revealed that some elements of the current packaging design require a more strategic reorganization to improve the consumer interaction (Reimann et al., 2010; Rojas et al., 2024; García-Madariaga et al., 2019).

Therefore, it was planned that the packaging would be redesigned in light of the neuroscientific findings to enhance both visual integrity and the effectiveness of message delivery.

The initial packaging design used in the first phase presented a conventional structure that emphasized the product's functional attributes and incorporated the brand's core visual elements. However, Eye-Tracking analyses showed that the slogan and product benefits were not sufficiently perceived by consumers; attention was dispersed toward the corners of the packaging, and the focus on the central area remained low.

5.1.3 Design Revision: Balancing Emotional and Functional Aspects

Following the pre-test phase, significant revisions were made to the Molfix packaging based on the EEG and Eye-Tracking findings. Notably, the slogan "As comfortable as a mother's embrace" was repositioned to a more central and prominent location on the packaging to improve message recognition. This revision not only increased the packaging's visibility but also strengthened its emotional impact (Keller, 2003). Furthermore, the doll's posture was updated to a warmer, more affectionate version that made direct eye contact with the consumer, aiming to strengthen the emotional connection.

Figure 4. Renewed design of Molfix packaging

Eye-tracking analysis showed that the revised packaging version showed a more consistent gaze sequence. Particular attention was paid to the slogan and product feature icons. Heatmap data indicated that consumer gaze focused on emotional touchpoints, such as the slogan and the baby's face, resulting in more effective information transfer.

EEG data revealed that the new design generated greater activation in the frontal cortex, particularly in regions associated with attention and focus. While the average attention score increased, mental effort levels indicated that consumers processed/understood the content more easily. This suggests that information is encoded more effectively in the consumer's mind, both functionally and emotionally (Plassmann et al., 2012).

Figure 5. Heatmap image of the renewed design of Molfix packaging

The qualitative interview findings included in the report also support these neurophysiological results. Most participants stated that they found the slogan memorable and warm, and that the overall appearance of the packaging felt more sincere and trustworthy compared to other brands. In particular, the soothing effect of blue tones, the smiling baby figure, and the association with a "mother's embrace" reinforced the emotional positioning of the brand. Additionally, icons symbolizing functional benefits such as "new generation channel technology" and "cotton-like softness" were strategically positioned and attracted consumer attention.

However, participants also provided aesthetic feedback regarding icon size inconsistencies and visual imbalance between symbols. Suggestions for improvement were reported accordingly. For example, some participants noted that increasing the color contrast of the icons, improving font readability, and presenting product content details more visibly would enhance the design. Based on this feedback, a simpler, more balanced, and information-optimized layout was adopted for the packaging.

As a result, the new packaging design developed in light of neuroscientific analyses achieved significant improvement not only in terms of visual aesthetics but also in the effective presentation of emotional and functional messages. This should be evaluated not only as an enhancement in aesthetic perception, but also as a strategic approach that deepens consumer-brand interaction and supports loyalty.

In this context, the contribution of neuromarketing plays a critical role in enabling the scientific understanding of consumer behavior and in guiding effective design decisions (Vecchiato et al., 2011, Kahneman, 2011; Krishna, 2012).

5.1.4 Commercialized Version of the Final Design: From Scientific Data to Consumer Shelf

Molfix 'Channelled New Generation Product' final packaging design reflects not only a visual and aesthetic transformation and change, but also a holistically optimized communication strategy in emotional, functional and cognitive dimensions. This packaging, revised in light of neuroscientific data and participant insights obtained during the research process, was restructured in alignment with unconscious consumer responses and directly transitioned into commercial implementation.

Figure 6. Final design of Molfix packaging

This approach demonstrates that packaging design, when viewed holistically, strengthens brand identity and communication effectiveness through emotional associations and cognitive impressions. Furthermore, it is consistent with literature suggesting that packaging functions as a strategic "silent communication tool" (Orth & Malkewitz, 2008; Underwood, 2003).

5.1.5 Characteristics of the Final Design Developed Through a Scientific Method

One of the most striking features of the newly developed packaging is the balanced presentation of emotional appeal and functional messages. The slogan "As comfortable as a mother's embrace" was centrally positioned, becoming the area with the highest gaze concentration, as observed in Eye-Tracking data. In EEG analyses, high frontal cortex activation in this region indicated that consumers found it both meaningful and emotionally compelling.

The baby's smiling expression used on the package was described by participants as "sympathetic and reassuring." This feature directly supported emotional satisfaction and increased the level of brand identification. A majority of participants identified the baby image as a strong brand identity element. In heatmap analyses, the baby's face, along with the slogan, had the highest fixation duration.

5.1.6 Effective Presentation of Functional Information

The product benefit icons (e.g., x3 absorbency, new generation channel technology) placed on the right side of the design were positioned more symmetrically and balanced compared to the initial version. Size disparities and color inconsistencies that previously distracted attention were minimized, and a visual hierarchy was established through equal and symmetrical placement of icons. This helped consumers more easily and accurately perceive the product features.

According to EEG data, a decrease in mental effort scores suggested that consumers processed the information more easily, while high attention scores indicated that the messages were effectively communicated (Plassmann et al., 2012).

5.1.7 Contribution of Qualitative Feedback to the Final Design

In qualitative interviews, participants particularly described the blue tones and soft transitions on the packaging as soothing. The reduction of visual clutter and simplification of messages enhanced the product's perception of professionalism and reliability (Pieters et al., 2010; Reber & Schwarz, 1999; Mugge, 2011; Ding et al., 2024). The expression "a design that reflects a motherly feeling" frequently appeared in consumer comments.

"The packaging feels warmer; the baby's smile makes me feel safe."

"The 'new generation' label and technological icons caught my attention; they make the diaper look innovative."

Such comments demonstrate that the findings from neuroscientific data were also supported by qualitative insights.

5.1.8 Memory Retention and Sustainable Brand Loyalty

Within Keller's (2003) Brand Resonance Model, the final design effectively integrates both informational (product features) and emotional (mother-baby theme) components. As such, it leaves a multidimensional trace in brand memory and contributes to the construction of both cognitive and emotional loyalty.

In the FMCG category, visual contact must not only be eye-catching but also capable of creating a repeatable and sustainable emotional bond (Lee et al., 2007). The Molfix packaging achieves long-term mental positioning by offering both functionality and emotional benefit.

5.1.9 Strategic Contribution of a Technology-Based Research Approach

This study demonstrates that neuroscientific approaches contribute to strategic brand positioning and long-term brand memory, extending beyond packaging and communication design. Plassmann et al. (2012) emphasize that neuromarketing sheds light on decision-making mechanisms by measuring consumers' emotional responses and recall processes, in addition to attention.

Hayat Kimya's EEG and eye-tracking-based revision processes implemented for its Molfix brand validated intuitive approaches, measurable user experience, and guided design decisions. This process strengthened the company's culture of innovation.

The company's neuroscience investments support its goals of creating sustainable value, fostering consumer empathy, and emotional connection across its entire brand portfolio, and offer the opportunity for multidimensional analysis based on unconscious decision-making dynamics (Kahneman, 2011; Lee et al., 2007). Furthermore, the integration of these methods into innovation processes provides a competitive advantage in terms of organizational learning, marketing agility, and data literacy.

5.2. Molfix Commercial Film Process: Neuroscientific Traces of Emotional Engagement

The shift from traditional research methods like surveys and focus groups to neuroscience-based approaches in understanding consumer behavior signals a significant paradigm shift in marketing. Analyzing consumer responses at the unconscious level, particularly in short-form communication media dominated by visual and auditory stimuli (such as TV commercials and digital marketing content), allows for more precise measurement of message effectiveness and, through revisions, for correct use (Plassmann et al., 2012; Vecchiato et al., 2011).

In this context, the advertisement developed by Hayat Kimya for the Molfix brand was tested not only against traditional marketing criteria but also with neurotechnological tools such as EEG (electroencephalography) and eye tracking. The commercial was systematically analyzed and developed using neuroscience methods, including both attentional tracking and emotional response assessment of the consumer.

Within the framework of Kahneman's (2011) System 1 and System 2 framework, the advertisement was designed to trigger intuitive, rapid, and emotional decision-making mechanisms. The emotional resonance created in the audience during the advertisement is aimed to include the meaningful universe associated with the brand along with the functional benefits of the product.

The theme "As comfortable as a mother's embrace" was selected as a deliberate emotional anchor, designed to generate high emotional resonance. Including emotional components such as baby health, trust, comfort, and affection, the theme aligns with the brand's values and directly appeals to the maternal instincts of the target audience.

In the pre-testing stage conducted with Eye-Tracking, viewers' eye movements were analyzed to scientifically map which scenes drew attention and where attention loss occurred. Simultaneously, EEG measurements revealed what kind of neurophysiological responses were triggered by these visual stimuli. These combined assessments allowed for the quantification of how the commercial was perceived not only visually, but also cognitively and emotionally (Guixeres et al., 2017; Teixeira et al., 2012).

As a result, this neuromarketing-based commercial film process by Hayat Kimya did more than just produce a communication tool—it constructed meaning maps in the consumer's mind on a scientific foundation. The emotional strength of the commercial directly contributed to long-term retention of brand messages, making this process a benchmark for sustainable brand communication (Keller, 2003).

5.2.1 Strategic Positioning and Emotional Theme of the Commercial

The commercial was shaped around the theme "as comfortable as a mother's embrace." This theme serves as an emotional anchor to reinforce brand identity and resonates with the maternal instincts of the target audience. The narrative here focuses on the baby's happiness, the warm family relationships where mother and father figures come together, and the comfort Molfix offers. The ad emphasizes both the product's functional benefits and its emotional value.

Family images, such as mother, father, and child, reinforce the perceived warmth of the brand, while highlighting functional benefit points reflecting comfort and protection reinforces the brand's perceived competence. Hedonic benefits increase loyalty by creating pleasure, while utilitarian benefits foster trust and satisfaction; furthermore, the baby schema activates the reward system, increasing attention and emotional involvement (Chitturi et al., 2008; Glocker et al., 2009; Kervyn et al., 2012).

5.2.2 Preliminary Testing Process and Scenario Analysis

The Molfix commercial, themed "As Comfortable as a Mother's Lap," was pre-tested before broadcast using neuroscientific measurement methods integrating EEG (electroencephalography) and eye-tracking technologies. In the study, conducted at Hayat Kimya's neuro-research laboratory, participants watched seven different animated commercials. EEG measured attention, interest, excitement, and mental effort levels, while eye-tracking measured focus points, gaze duration, and gaze intensity.

The research aimed to scientifically evaluate the ad's ability to capture attention, create emotional impact, and convey product perception. The appearance of renowned actor Kıvanç Tatlıtuğ in the opening scene significantly increased emotional engagement (Amos et al., 2008; Knoll & Matthes, 2017; Spry et al., 2011); eye-tracking data revealed a focus on the central elements of the screen, while EEG results showed high activation in the frontal cortex. The findings demonstrated that the ad successfully achieved its intended objectives of capturing attention and establishing an emotional connection.

Figure 7. Opening scene of Molfix advertising script

However, some weak points were also identified in the subsequent scenes of the scenario. Notably, the scenes featuring the mother figure showed a significant increase in viewer interest. When the mother entered through the door and approached the baby, both attention and mental effort levels increased meaningfully. This indicates that the target audience established a stronger emotional connection with the "mother figure", aligning with their cultural expectations (Robertson, 1995; Hofstede, 2001). Especially in markets like Turkey, where traditional family structures play a strong role, the emotional tone of the advertisement must align with prevailing cultural codes.

Figure 8. Values of Molfix advertising script

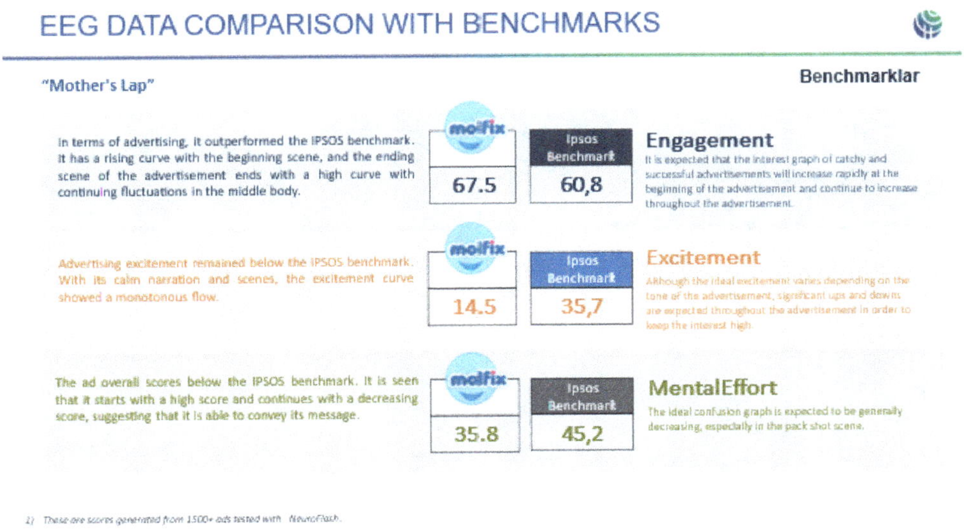

On the other hand, a decline in attention levels was observed in scenes where the father figure was prominent. Although the father-baby interaction conveyed a positive message, in-depth face-to-face interviews confirmed that viewers perceived these scenes as "incomplete" or "insufficient on their own." Some participants stated that the mother figure should have been more dominant in these parts, and that the "family" emphasis could have been communicated more strongly. This indicates that the advertisement needs to be re-evaluated through a lens of cultural sensitivity, particularly as part of its glocalization strategy (de Mooij, 2010).

Another area identified for improvement was the lack of sufficient emphasis on the product's technical features in the storyline. While participants appreciated the overall emotional tone of the advertisement, they felt that technical benefits of the diaper such as preventing rashes, being skin-friendly, or providing overnight dryness were not adequately communicated. This finding suggests that informational content, in addition to emotional resonance, enhances brand value in the consumer's mind (Keller, 2003).

Throughout the animatic film, the interest metric started high, showed partial declines in the middle sections, and rose again in the final scene. However, EEG data revealed that during the "pack shot" scene (the final frame showing the product), mental effort was low, and the slogan had limited impact on attention. Although the slogan "As comfortable as a mother's embrace" was linguistically strong, its potential impact was not fully realized due to a lack of synchronized visual support.

Figure 9. Graphical representation of Molfix advertising scenario values

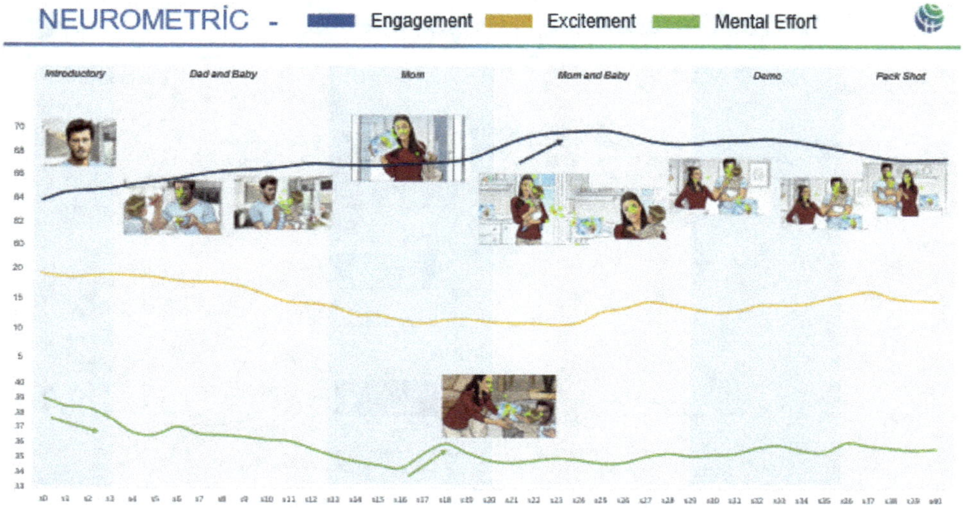

During the post-scenario interviews, some participants stated that the product remained in the background throughout the commercial, and they emphasized that certain scenes needed to be restructured in order to enhance brand visibility and improve slogan memorability. In particular, it was evaluated that the diaper appearing without branding and the mother's inability to engage in direct interaction with the baby undermined the emotional coherence of the advertisement.

In summary:

- The opening scene created high attention and emotional impact.
- Scenes featuring the mother figure increased both interest and cognitive processing.
- Scenes focusing on the father figure showed lower performance due to a lack of alignment with cultural codes.
- The insufficient communication of product benefits limited the strength of brand perception.
- The pack shot scene, although supported by the slogan, failed to create the desired effect.

This pre-test process has demonstrated how neuroscientific data can be utilized not only to optimize the creative aspects of an advertisement but also its strategic components. Therefore, this neuro-marketing supported evaluation served as a valuable guide for subsequent revisions of the commercial.

5.2.3 Analysis of the Final Commercial and Neurophysiological Findings

Following the findings obtained from the scenario tests, various structural and visual adjustments were made to the commercial. The final version of the advertisement was re-evaluated using EEG and Eye-Tracking tests conducted in Hayat Kimya's Neuro Research Laboratory. These tests measured the emotional impact of the commercial as well as the retention of product messages by the target audience using neurophysiological metrics.

Figure 10. Values of Molfix advertising

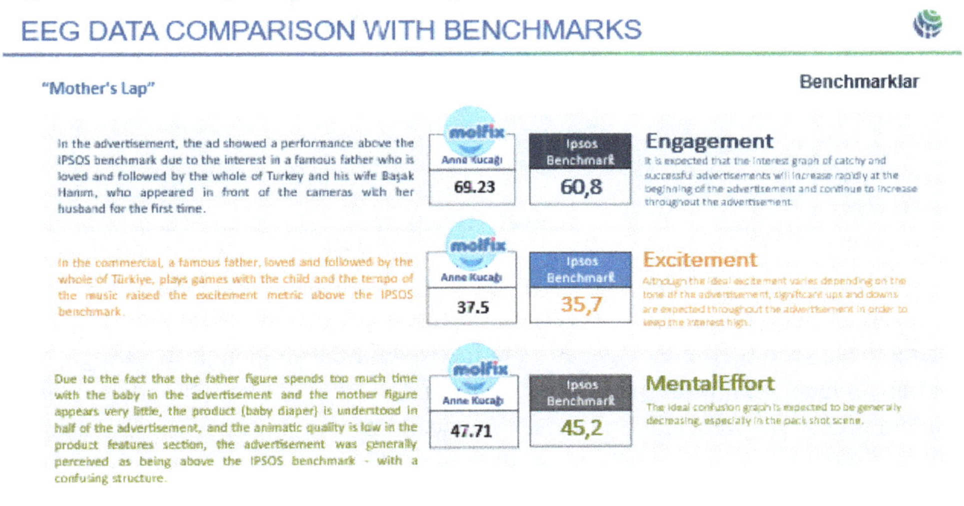

5.2.4 Emotional Engagement Through EEG and Eye-Tracking Data

In the final version of the commercial, significant increases were observed in both attention and emotional resonance levels, particularly in scenes where the theme of "as comforting as a mother's embrace" was emphasized both visually and audibly. EEG measurements showed notable increases in attention and excitement metrics during the scene where the mother enters from outside and holds the baby. This increase was associated with positive emotional responses and a sense of trust (Plassmann et al., 2012).

Figure 11. Graphical representation of Molfix advertising values

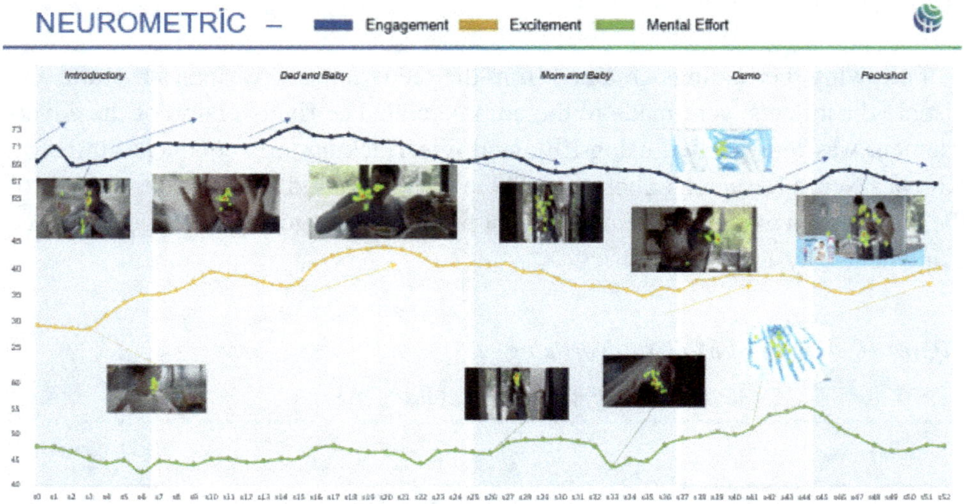

Similarly, the close-up of the product (packshot) at the end of the commercial and the simultaneous auditory/visual delivery of the slogan activated both the viewers' attention and comprehension processes. According to the Eye-Tracking findings, during these scenes, viewers' gazes were focused on the slogan, product logo, and the baby's face, with fixation durations reported to be above benchmark averages. The simultaneous presentation of the final scene of the commercial, "Packshot," with the verbal slogan is consistent with the multimedia principle that speech-eye coordination and memory are enhanced, with findings that multisensory integration improves performance, and with auditory-visual verbal redundancy enhances recall (Mayer, 2002; Shams & Seitz, 2008; Hinkin et al., 2014).

5.2.5 Audience Perception and Scenario Adaptations

In-depth interviews with participants revealed that the commercial was generally perceived as "evoking empathy" and "conducive to forming an emotional bond." Moreover, the elimination of certain narrative weaknesses identified in the earlier version contributed to this positive impact. For instance, while the dominance of the father figure in the first version created a sense of cultural mismatch among viewers, in the final version, the mother being placed in a more central role enhanced both the realism and emotional resonance of the commercial (Robertson, 1995).

Figure 12. An improved scene from the Molfix commercial

The presence of physical contact between the baby and the mother in the visuals, as well as the mother's warm and protective gaze towards the child, directly contributed to strengthening emotional resonance.

This finding aligns with Krishna's (2012) principle of "sensory consistency" emphasized in her sensory marketing model.

5.2.6 Product Presentation and Message Clarity

In the final version, the product presentation scenes were supported by simpler, clearer, and higher-quality visuals compared to the previous animatic version. Participants stated that the product features—especially technical benefits such as absorbency, comfort, and leakage protection—were clearly communicated and positively influenced their purchase intent. EEG data showed that mental effort decreased in these scenes and comprehension became easier.

In an advertisement or promotional film, clearly and concisely communicating product features—for example, absorbency, comfort, leakage protection, and cotton content—increases the ad's informational content and argumentative quality, thereby positively impacting credibility and purchase intention. This approach is expected to be matched by lower mental effort and easier comprehension when analyzed scene-by-scene with EEG technology within the advertisement (Abernethy & Franke, 1996; Areni & Lutz, 1988; Darley & Smith, 1993; Di Flumeri et al., 2018; Vecchiato et al., 2010).

Comments highlighted by participants included:

"The product is introduced more clearly, and the baby really looks comfortable."

"If the physical contact with the mother had been maintained throughout the ad, the impact would have been stronger."

5.2.7 Evaluation from a Neuromarketing Perspective

These findings support Keller's (2003) brand association model. The model suggests that emotional associations increase memorability and that positive images linked to the brand foster loyalty. The consistent presentation of metaphors ("mother's embrace", "happy baby") and emotional stimuli (music, close-up facial expressions) in the commercial confirms this process on a neuroscientific level.

Hayat Kimya's commercial stands out not only as attention-grabbing content but also as a holistic brand communication that touches both the mental and emotional worlds of consumers. Supported by EEG and Eye-Tracking data, this approach not only enhances the efficiency of advertising investments but also adds value to the brand's long-term image.

5.2.8 Consumer Perception and Reflections on Brand Communication

The conducted ad testing clearly revealed the emotional and cognitive effects of the advertisement on consumers. Participant feedback showed that the commercial was generally appreciated and created a positive brand perception among viewers. In particular, emotional themes such as "empathy," "mother's warmth," and "feeling understood" were found to be successfully communicated. Eye-Tracking analysis revealed that viewers intensely focused on emotionally intense scenes in the commercial—especially those involving mother-baby interaction and the delivery of brand messages. EEG measurements also indicated an increase in emotional resonance and attention levels during these scenes. These findings demonstrate that consumer decision-making processes are not purely rational but also contain strong emotional components.

The synchronously delivered audio and visual slogan at the end of the advertisement left a more lasting impression in consumer memory and reinforced the sense of trust associated with the product. All these neuroscientific findings indicate that the advertisement successfully achieved its goal of establishing an emotional connection and built a deeper relationship between the brand and the consumer.

When evaluated within the framework of Oliver's (1999) brand loyalty theory, it becomes clear that the advertisement is not only effective in generating short-term attention but also capable of building long-term emotional commitment. In this regard, the Molfix advertisement has evolved into not just a promotional tool but also a narrative platform that shapes brand personality.

5.2.9 The Contribution of Neuroscience-Supported Advertising to Sustainable Brand Strategies

Sustainable brand success is not only linked to environmental responsibility but also directly related to the ability to secure a place in the minds and hearts of consumers. Neuroscience-supported marketing approaches go beyond traditional methods and offer the opportunity to optimize subconscious consumer-brand connections. As seen in the case of Molfix, advertising strategies supported by EEG and Eye-Tracking methods demonstrate that it is possible to build a sustainable emotional relationship with the consumer.

The metaphors, facial expressions, scene transitions, and music used in the content not only enhanced emotional impact but also helped the brand gain a stronger place in the viewer's memory. In alignment with the cognitive-emotional sustainability model of Lee et al. (2007), this communication approach enables the brand to be remembered not just for its product features but also for its values and emotional promises.

Furthermore, with a narrative language that considers cultural codes and consumer habits, the advertisement ceased to be merely a media message and communicated with the consumer as an "empathetic partner." When assessed within the framework of Robertson's (1995) glocalization concept, this approach shows that the brand has developed a universal emotional language while remaining compatible with local values.

In conclusion, the Molfix example clearly demonstrates the contribution of neuroscientific approaches to sustainable brand strategies. It shows that advertising content combining emotional attachment, empathy, and cultural adaptation can support brand success in the long term.

5.2.10 Academic Evaluation and Learnings

The neuroscience-based research implemented in Molfix's packaging and advertising communication processes not only guided creative decisions but also contributed to the strategic brand-building process at an academic level. Analyses conducted using objective measurement techniques such as EEG (Electroencephalography) and Eye-Tracking went beyond traditional surveys or focus group studies and scientifically revealed what attracts attention in the consumer's mind, what creates emotional resonance, and what is retained in long-term memory.

Scenario, Advertisement, and Packaging Design Tests Serve as Strategic Guides

The pre-tests conducted for packaging design and advertising films provided not only aesthetic feedback but also served as strategic guidance in terms of attention distribution, comprehensibility, and emotional alignment. For instance, the low visual perception of the slogan and product benefits in the initial packaging design directed the redesign process. Similarly, in the advertisement film, the decrease in attention scores detected through EEG and Eye-Tracking data in scenes where the father figure was dominant triggered creative revisions in the context of cultural appropriateness.

Visual and Auditory Synchronization Increases Neurophysiological Impact

The synchronization of textual and visual elements on the packaging, as well as the harmony between sound/music and visuals in the advertisement, created a deeper processing experience in the consumer's mind. Especially in the final scene of the commercial, the simultaneous delivery of the slogan both audibly and visually was supported by increased activation in EEG data. This finding, when evaluated within Keller's (2003) brand association model, demonstrates the direct relationship between emotional impact and memorability.

Adapting to Cultural Codes Determines Success

Strategic decisions such as modifying the baby image on the packaging to establish eye contact or prioritizing the mother figure in the commercial indicate the importance of the socio-cultural context in which the consumer exists. In line with Robertson's (1995) theory of glocalization, brand messages that resonate with local values significantly increased their impact on viewers.

Subconscious Interactions Provide Critical Input

Neuromarketing methods provided significant advantages in interpreting subconscious processes by examining consumer behavior not only on a rational but also on an emotional and intuitive level. The intense gaze movements directed toward the baby's face on the packaging or the increased emotional activation during the hugging scene in the commercial supported the brand's strategy of increasing empathy. Such emotional reactions offer deep insights that are difficult to measure with classical methods but become visible through neuroscientific tools.

Sustainability Must Be Considered Alongside Emotional and Cognitive Continuity

The Molfix example demonstrates that being a sustainable brand is not limited to environmental responsibility but also includes aspects such as emotional continuity and cognitive memorability. This emotional continuity established through neuromarketing methods used in both packaging and advertising strengthened the consumer's loyalty to the brand (Lee et al., 2007). Especially the increase in metrics such as the "understands me" empathy indicator demonstrates that this bond has been built in a sustainable manner.

In light of this evaluation, it has been revealed that packaging and advertising processes can be rebuilt not only on creative but also scientific and cultural foundations; and that it is possible to establish a deeper, lasting, and trust-based relationship with the consumer. In this sense, neuromarketing has become not just a preference but an indispensable component of a competitive and sustainable brand strategy.

6. CONCLUSION

This study clearly reveals that neuroscience functions as a strategic lever in the process of creating a sustainable brand identity. In particular, traditional survey methods are not sufficient to overcome challenges such as building emotional bonds with consumers, creating brand loyalty, and strengthening brand associations. At this point, neuromarketing methods such as EEG and Eye Tracking enable brands to more effectively shape their marketing strategies by measuring consumers' subconscious responses.

The case study conducted on the Molfix brand presents a concrete example of this transformation. Through EEG and eye-tracking analyses applied in the packaging and advertising film development processes, Hayat Kimya was able to scientifically measure consumer attention and emotional responses, and accordingly optimize its communication materials.

The insights gained from these studies not only guided the creative process but also directly transformed the brand's positioning and perception. In this context, the brand's focus on product development, innovation, and the importance it attaches to research have ensured its success.

In light of the data provided by Ipsos, it is observed that this neuroscience-supported strategic approach has provided tangible contributions to the brand. Market growth increased by 19% in 2024. This indicates that the campaigns created not only awareness but also had a sales-based impact. The market share increased by 5 points compared to 2023, enhancing the brand's competitive power.

The TOM (Top of Mind) awareness rate rose from 24% to 30%, indicating a significant leap in brand recall power.

Significant increases were also observed in brand image indicators:

Trust metric increased from 36% to 42%;

High quality perception rose from 35% to 40%;

"Understands me" empathy perception climbed from 29% to 37%.

In addition to these findings, between 2022 and Q3 of 2024:

The performance parameter increased from 53 to 58;

The proximity parameter reached 68, up from 61.

All these indicators show that Molfix's sustainable brand strategy created not only perceptual but also behavioral outcomes and was able to build a long-term bond with the consumer.

In conclusion, the neuroscience-based approach supported by this book chapter offers a strong synergy at the intersection of creative communication, consumer behavior, and brand sustainability. Marketing practices supported by scientific methods have now become not only a tool to measure impact but also a fundamental condition to create it. In this regard, neuroscience and neuromarketing offer an indispensable roadmap for organizations that aim to build the sustainable brands of the future.

REFERENCES

Abernethy, A. M., & Franke, G. R. (1996). The information content of advertising: A meta-analysis. *Journal of Advertising*, *25*(2), 1–17. DOI: 10.1080/00913367.1996.10673496

Ajzen, I. (1991). The theory of planned behavior. *Organizational Behavior and Human Decision Processes*, *50*(2), 179–211. DOI: 10.1016/0749-5978(91)90020-T

Amos, C., Holmes, G., & Strutton, D. (2008). Exploring the relationship between celebrity endorser effects and advertising effectiveness: A quantitative synthesis of effect size. *International Journal of Advertising*, *27*(2), 209–234. DOI: 10.1080/02650487.2008.11073052

Areni, C. S., & Lutz, R. J. (1988). The role of argument quality in the Elaboration Likelihood Model. In Houston, M. J. (Ed.), *Advances in Consumer Research* (Vol. 15, pp. 197–203). Association for Consumer Research.

Ariely, D., & Berns, G. S. (2010). Neuromarketing: The hope and hype of neuroimaging in business. *Nature Reviews. Neuroscience*, *11*(4), 284–292. DOI: 10.1038/nrn2795

Aytekin, P., & Kahraman, A. (2014). A new research approach in marketing: Neuromarketing. Journal of Management [JMML]. *Marketing and Logistics*, *1*(1), 48–62.

Benito-León, J., Domínguez-González, C., & Rodríguez, J. (2023). Neuroscience applications in business: From brainwaves to consumer behavior. *Journal of Consumer Psychology*, *33*(1), 58–72. DOI: 10.1002/jcpy.1234

Brundtland, G. (1987). Report of the World Commission on Environment and Development: Our Common Future. United Nations General Assembly Document A/42/427.

Chitturi, R., Raghunathan, R., & Mahajan, V. (2008). Delight by design: The role of hedonic versus utilitarian benefits. *Journal of Marketing*, *72*(3), 48–63. DOI: 10.1509/JMKG.72.3.048

Darley, W. K., & Smith, R. E. (1993). Advertising claim objectivity: Antecedents and effects. *Journal of Marketing*, *57*(4), 100–113. DOI: 10.1177/002224299305700408

de Mooij, M. (2010). *Global marketing and advertising: Understanding cultural paradoxes* (3rd ed.). SAGE Publications.

Di Flumeri, G., Aricò, P., Borghini, G., Sciaraffa, N., & Babiloni, F. (2018). EEG-based mental workload neurometric. *Frontiers in Human Neuroscience, 12*, 509. DOI: 10.3389/fnhum.2018.00509

Ding, Y., Meng, X., & Sun, C. (2024). Simplicity matters: Unraveling the impact of minimalist packaging on green trust in daily consumer goods. *Sustainability (Basel), 16*(12), 4932. DOI: 10.3390/su16124932

García-Madariaga, J., Blasco López, M.-F., Moya Burgos, I., & Recuero Virto, N. (2019). Do isolated packaging variables influence consumers' attention and preferences? *Physiology & Behavior, 200*, 96–103. DOI: 10.1016/j.physbeh.2018.04.030

Glocker, M. L., Langleben, D. D., Ruparel, K., Loughead, J. W., Valdez, J. N., Griffin, M. D., Sachser, N., & Gur, R. C. (2009). Baby schema modulates the brain reward system in nulliparous women. *Proceedings of the National Academy of Sciences of the United States of America, 106*(22), 9115–9119. DOI: 10.1073/pnas.0811620106

Guixeres, J., Bigné, E., Ausín Azofra, J. M., Alcañiz Raya, M., Colomer Granero, A., Fuentes Hurtado, F., & Naranjo Ornedo, V. (2017). Consumer neuroscience-based metrics predict recall, liking and viewing rates in online advertising. *Frontiers in Psychology, 8*, 1808. DOI: 10.3389/fpsyg.2017.01808

Hayat Kimya. (2022). Kurumsal Tanıtım Raporu. https://www.hayat.com.tr

Hinkin, M. P., Harris, R. J., & Miranda, A. T. (2014). Verbal redundancy aids memory for filmed entertainment dialogue. *The Journal of Psychology, 148*(2), 161–176. DOI: 10.1080/00223980.2013.767774

Hofstede, G. (2001). *Culture's Consequences: Comparing Values, Behaviors, Institutions and Organizations across Nations*. SAGE.

Hurzhyi, N., Popliuiko, Y., Vasylyuk-Zaitseva, S., & Kobets, D. (2023). Harnessing neuromarketing techniques to enhance brand engagement. *Futurity of Social Sciences, 1*(4), 4–37.

Hussein, K. M. A. M., & Ozad, B. E. (2023). A systematic literature review on neuromarketing in branding, advertising and consumer behavior. *International Journal of Innovative Science and Research Technology, 8*(6), 2037–2045.

Illes, J., & Bird, S. J. (2006). Neuroethics: A modern context for ethics in neuroscience. *Trends in Neurosciences, 29*(9), 511–517. DOI: 10.1016/j.tins.2006.07.002

Istanbul Sanayi Odası [İSO]. (2022). Türkiye'nin 500 Büyük Sanayi Kuruluşu 2021. https://www.iso.org.tr

Kahneman, D. (2011). *Thinking, fast and slow*. Farrar, Straus and Giroux.

Keller, K. L. (2003). *Strategic brand management: Building, measuring, and managing brand equity* (2nd ed.). Prentice Hall.

Kervyn, N., Fiske, S. T., & Malone, C. (2012). Brands as intentional agents framework: How perceived intentions and ability can map brand perception. *Journal of Consumer Psychology*, *22*(2), 166–176. DOI: 10.1016/j.jcps.2011.09.006

Knoll, J., & Matthes, J. (2017). The effectiveness of celebrity endorsements: A meta-analysis. *Journal of the Academy of Marketing Science*, *45*(1), 55–75. DOI: 10.1007/s11747-016-0503-8

Kringelbach, M. L., Lehtonen, A., Squire, S., Harvey, A. G., Craske, M. G., Holliday, I. E., Green, A. L., Aziz, T. Z., Hansen, P. C., Cornelissen, P. L., & Stein, A. (2008). A specific and rapid neural signature for parental instinct. *PLoS One*, *3*(2), e1664. DOI: 10.1371/journal.pone.0001664

Krishna, A. (2012). An integrative review of sensory marketing: Engaging the senses to affect perception, judgment and behavior. *Journal of Consumer Psychology*, *22*(3), 332–351. DOI: 10.1016/j.jcps.2011.08.003

Lee, N., Broderick, A. J., & Chamberlain, L. (2007). What is 'neuromarketing'? A discussion and agenda for future research. *International Journal of Psychophysiology*, *63*(2), 199–204. DOI: 10.1016/j.ijpsycho.2006.03.007

Liu, Q., Zhu, S., Zhou, X., Liu, F., Becker, B., Kendrick, K. M., & Zhao, W. (2024). Mothers and fathers show different neural synchrony with their children during shared experiences. *NeuroImage*, *288*, 120529. DOI: 10.1016/j.neuroimage.2024.120529

Mayer, R. E. (2002). *Multimedia learning*. Cambridge University Press.

McGuire, W. J. (1976). Some internal psychological factors influencing consumer choice. *The Journal of Consumer Research*, *2*(4), 302–319. DOI: 10.1086/208643

Morin, C. (2011). Neuromarketing: The new science of consumer behavior. *Society*, *48*(2), 131–135. DOI: 10.1007/s12115-010-9408-1

Mugge, R. (2011). The effect of a business-like personality on the perceived performance quality of products. *International Journal of Design*, *5*(3), 67–76.

Nilashi, M., Yadegaridehkordi, E., Samad, S., Mardani, A., Ahani, A., Aljojo, N., Razali, N. S., & Tajuddin, T. (2020). Decision to adopt neuromarketing techniques for sustainable product marketing: A fuzzy decision-making approach. *Symmetry*, *12*(2), 305. DOI: 10.3390/sym12020305

Oliver, R. L. (1999). Whence consumer loyalty? *Journal of Marketing*, *63*(Special Issue), 33–44. DOI: 10.1177/00222429990634s105

Orth, U. R., & Malkewitz, K. (2008). Holistic package design and consumer brand impressions. *Journal of Marketing*, *72*(3), 64–81. DOI: 10.1509/JMKG.72.3.064

Pieters, R., Wedel, M., & Batra, R. (2010). The stopping power of advertising: Measures and effects of visual complexity. *Journal of Marketing*, *74*(5), 48–60. DOI: 10.1509/jmkg.74.5.048

Plassmann, H., Ramsøy, T. Z., & Milosavljevic, M. (2012). Branding the brain: A critical review and outlook. *Journal of Consumer Psychology*, *22*(1), 18–36. DOI: 10.1016/j.jcps.2011.11.010

Reber, R., & Schwarz, N. (1999). Effects of perceptual fluency on judgments of truth. *Consciousness and Cognition*, *8*(3), 338–342. DOI: 10.1006/ccog.1999.0386

Reimann, M., Zaichkowsky, J. L., Neuhaus, C., Bender, T., & Weber, B. (2010). Aesthetic package design: A behavioral, neural, and psychological investigation. *Journal of Consumer Psychology*, *20*(4), 431–441. DOI: 10.1016/j.jcps.2010.06.009

Robertson, R. (1995). Glocalization: Time-space and homogeneity-heterogeneity. In Featherstone, M., Lash, S., & Robertson, R. (Eds.), *Global modernities* (pp. 25–44). SAGE. DOI: 10.4135/9781446250563.n2

Rojas, J.-C., Contero, M., Vergara, M., & Higuera-Trujillo, J. L. (2024). Using event-related potentials to evidence the visual and semantic impact: A pilot study with N400 effect and food packaging. *Foods*, *13*(12), 1876. DOI: 10.3390/foods13121876

Shams, L., & Seitz, A. R. (2008). Benefits of multisensory learning. *Trends in Cognitive Sciences*, *12*(11), 411–417. DOI: 10.1016/j.tics.2008.07.006

Spry, A., Pappu, R., & Cornwell, T. B. (2011). Celebrity endorsement, brand credibility and brand equity. *European Journal of Marketing*, *45*(6), 882–909. DOI: 10.1108/03090561111119958

Spunt, R. P. (2015). Dual-Process Theories in Social Cognitive Neuroscience. In Toga, A. W. (Ed.), *Brain Mapping: An Encyclopedic Reference* (Vol. 3, pp. 211–215). Academic Press: Elsevier. DOI: 10.1016/B978-0-12-397025-1.00181-0

Stanton, S. J., Sinnott-Armstrong, W., & Huettel, S. A. (2017). Neuromarketing: Ethical implications of its use and potential misuse. *Journal of Business Ethics*, *144*(4), 799–811. DOI: 10.1007/s10551-016-3059-0

Teixeira, T., Wedel, M., & Pieters, R. (2012). Emotion-induced engagement in Internet video advertisements. *JMR, Journal of Marketing Research*, *49*(2), 144–159. DOI: 10.1509/jmr.10.0207

Underwood, R. L. (2003). The communicative power of product packaging: Creating brand identity via lived and mediated experience. *Journal of Marketing Theory and Practice*, *11*(1), 62–76. DOI: 10.1080/10696679.2003.11501933

Varela, P., Antúnez, L., Cadena, R. S., Giménez, A., and Ares, G. (2014). Attentional capture and importance of package attributes for consumers' perceived similarities and differences among products: A case study with breakfast cereal packages. Food Res. Int. 64, 701–710. doi: . foodres.2014.08.015DOI: 10.1016/j

Vecchiato, G., Astolfi, L., De Vico Fallani, F., Cincotti, F., Mattia, D., Salinari, S., & Babiloni, F. (2011). EEG correlates of sensorimotor integration and embodiment during the appreciation of virtual architectural environments. *Brain Research Bulletin*, *85*(5), 253–260. DOI: 10.1016/j.brainresbull.2010.12.003

Vecchiato, G., Astolfi, L., De Vico Fallani, F., Cincotti, F., Mattia, D., Salinari, S., Soranzo, R., & Babiloni, F. (2010). Changes in brain activity during the observation of TV commercials by using EEG, GSR and HR measurements. *Brain Topography*, *23*(2), 165–179. DOI: 10.1007/s10548-009-0127-0

Venkatraman, V., Dimoka, A., Pavlou, P. A., Vo, K., Hampton, W., Bollinger, B., Hershfield, H. E., Ishihara, M., & Winer, R. S. (2015). Predicting advertising success beyond traditional measures: New insights from neurophysiological methods and market response modeling. *JMR, Journal of Marketing Research*, *52*(4), 436–452. DOI: 10.1509/jmr.13.0593

Vidal-Raméntol, S. (2020). Neuromarketing and sustainability. *Advances in Social Sciences Research Journal*, *7*(12), 364–377. DOI: 10.14738/assrj.712.9360

Compilation of References

Abdul-Hamid, A. Q., Ali, M. H., Tseng, M. L., Lan, S., & Kumar, M. (2020). Impeding challenges on industry 4.0 in circular economy: Palm oil industry in Malaysia. *Computers & Operations Research, 123*, 105052. DOI: 10.1016/j.cor.2020.105052

Abernethy, A. M., & Franke, G. R. (1996). The information content of advertising: A meta-analysis. *Journal of Advertising, 25*(2), 1–17. DOI: 10.1080/00913367.1996.10673496

Abou Taleb, M., & Al Farooque, O. (2021). Towards a circular economy for sustainable development: An application of full cost accounting to municipal waste recyclables. *Journal of Cleaner Production, 280*, 124047. DOI: 10.1016/j.jclepro.2020.124047

Abu-Bakar, H., & Charnley, F. (2024). Developing a strategic methodology for circular economy roadmapping: A theoretical framework. *Sustainability (Basel), 16*(15), 6682. DOI: 10.3390/su16156682

Aghion, P., & Howitt, P. (1992). A model of growth through creative destruction. *Econometrica, 60*(2), 323–351. DOI: 10.2307/2951599

Agrawal, R., Agrawal, S., Samadhiya, A., Kumar, A., Luthra, S., & Jain, V. (2024). Adoption of green finance and green innovation for achieving circularity: An exploratory review and future directions. *Geoscience Frontiers, 15*(4), 101669. DOI: 10.1016/j.gsf.2023.101669

Aikat, D. D., & Remund, D. (2012). Of time magazine, 24/7 media, and data deluge: The evolution of information overload theories and concepts. *Information overload: An international challenge for professional engineers and technical communicators*, 13-40.

Ajzen, I. (1991). The theory of planned behavior. *Organizational Behavior and Human Decision Processes, 50*(2), 179–211. DOI: 10.1016/0749-5978(91)90020-T

Alaphilippe, A., Gizikis, A., Hanot, C., & Bontcheva, K. (2019). *Automated tackling of disinformation: Major challenges ahead*. European Parliament.

Alberich, J. P., Llorente-González, L. J., Ramezankhani, M. J., Bimpizas-Pinis, M., & Lowe, B. (2023). Using macroeconomic indicators to enact an ambitious circular economy. *Circular Economy and Sustainability*, *3*(3), 1515–1544. DOI: 10.1007/s43615-022-00232-3

Aldowaish, A., Kokuryo, J., Almazyad, O., & Goi, H. C. (2022). Environmental, social, and governance integration into the business model: Literature review and research agenda. *Sustainability (Basel)*, *14*(5), 2959. DOI: 10.3390/su14052959

Alghababsheh, M. (2024). Understanding whether, how and when circular supply chain management influences firm performance. *Business Strategy and the Environment*, *33*(7), 7139–7161. DOI: 10.1002/bse.3865

Aljukhadar, M., & Senecal, S. (2017). Communicating online information via streaming video: The role of user goal. *Online Information Review*, *41*(3), 378–397. DOI: 10.1108/OIR-06-2016-0152

Alliance, G. S. I. (2018, April). *Global sustainable investment review*.

Altenburg, T., & Rodrik, D. (2017). Green industrial policy: Accelerating structural change towards wealthy green economies. *Green Industrial Policy*, *1*, 2–20.

Amos, C., Holmes, G., & Strutton, D. (2008). Exploring the relationship between celebrity endorser effects and advertising effectiveness: A quantitative synthesis of effect size. *International Journal of Advertising*, *27*(2), 209–234. DOI: 10.1080/02650487.2008.11073052

Andersen, I. (2021, Feb 24). *United Nations Environment Programme*. Retrieved April 2025, from https://www.unep.org/news-and-stories/speech/circularity-transition-leaving-no-one-behind

Anderton, A. (2006). *Economics* (4th ed.). Pearson Education.

Andı, S., & Akesson, J. (2020). Nudging away false news: Evidence from a social norms experiment. *Digital Journalism (Abingdon, England)*, *9*(1), 106–125. DOI: 10.1080/21670811.2020.1847674

Andriof, J., & Waddock, S. (2002). Unfolding stakeholder engagement. In Andriof, J., Waddock, S., Husted, B., & Rahman, S. S. (Eds.), *Unfolding Stakeholder Thinking: Theory, Responsibility and Engagement* (pp. 19–42). Greenleaf. DOI: 10.9774/GLEAF.978-1-909493-28-5_3

Apple Inc. (2023). Environmental Progress Report. https://www.apple.com/environment/

Aradau, C. (2016). Risk,(in) security and international politics. In *Routledge handbook of risk studies* (pp. 290-298). Routledge.

Aranda-Usón, A., Portillo-Tarragona, P., Marín-Vinuesa, L. M., & Scarpellini, S. (2019). Financial resources for the circular economy: A perspective from businesses. *Sustainability (Basel)*, *11*(3), 888. DOI: 10.3390/su11030888

Areni, C. S., & Lutz, R. J. (1988). The role of argument quality in the Elaboration Likelihood Model. In Houston, M. J. (Ed.), *Advances in Consumer Research* (Vol. 15, pp. 197–203). Association for Consumer Research.

Ariely, D., & Berns, G. S. (2010). Neuromarketing: The hope and hype of neuroimaging in business. *Nature Reviews. Neuroscience*, *11*(4), 284–292. DOI: 10.1038/nrn2795

Arnold, M., Goldschmitt, M., & Rigotti, T. (2023). Dealing with information overload: A comprehensive review. *Frontiers in Psychology*, *14*, 1122200. DOI: 10.3389/fpsyg.2023.1122200 PMID: 37416535

Arora, M., Raspall, F., Cheah, L., & Silva, A. (2020). Buildings and the circular economy: Estimating urban mining, recovery and reuse potential of building components. *Resources, Conservation and Recycling*, *154*, 104581. DOI: 10.1016/j.resconrec.2019.104581

As You Sow. (2023). Decarbonize your portfolio [Investment report series]. https://www.asyousow.org

Auty, L. D. (2024). *The Political Economy of Reuse Organizing for Reform and Transformation of the Make-and-waste Economy*. Faculty of Social Sciences, Lund University.

Aytekin, P., & Kahraman, A. (2014). A new research approach in marketing: Neuromarketing. Journal of Management [JMML]. *Marketing and Logistics*, *1*(1), 48–62.

Bag, S., Gupta, S., & Kumar, S. (2021a). Industry 4.0 adoption and 10R advance manufacturing capabilities for sustainable development. *International Journal of Production Economics*, *231*, 107844. DOI: 10.1016/j.ijpe.2020.107844

Bag, S., Yadav, G., Dhamija, P., & Kataria, K. K. (2021b). Key resources for industry 4.0 adoption and its effect on sustainable production and circular economy: An empirical study. *Journal of Cleaner Production*, *281*, 125233. DOI: 10.1016/j.jclepro.2020.125233

Baines, T., & Lightfoot, , H. (2013). Servitization of the manufacturing firm: Exploring the operations practices and technologies that deliver advanced services. *International Journal of Operations & Production Management, 34*(1), 2–35. DOI: 10.1108/IJOPM-02-2012-0086

Bakdash, J., Sample, C., Rankin, M., Kantarcioglu, M., Holmes, J., Kase, S., & Szymanski, B. (2018, April). The future of deception: Machine-generated and manipulated images, video, and audio? In *2018 International Workshop on Social Sensing (SocialSens)* (pp. 2-2). IEEE. DOI: 10.1109/SocialSens.2018.00009

Baker, M., Berg, F., & Kölbel, J. F. (2022). *The sustainable corporate governance debate: Evidence from ESG ETFs*. European Corporate Governance Institute.

Banas, J. A., & Rains, S. A. (2010). A meta-analysis of research on inoculation theory. *Communication Monographs, 77*(3), 281–311. DOI: 10.1080/03637751003758193

Barben, D., Fisher, E., Selin, C., & Guston, D. H. (2008). 38 anticipatory governance of nanotechnology: foresight, engagement, and integration. *The handbook of science and technology studies, 979.*

Barro, R. J., & Sala-i-Martin, X. (2004). *Economic growth* (2nd ed.). MIT Press.

Barros, M. V., Salvador, R., do Prado, G. F., de Francisco, A. C., & Piekarski, C. M. (2021). Circular economy as a driver to sustainable businesses. *Cleaner Environmental Systems, 2*, 100006. DOI: 10.1016/j.cesys.2020.100006

Bartikowski, B., & Berens, G. (2020). Message Framing in CSR Communication: An Abstract. In Pantoja, F., Wu, S., & Krey, N. (Eds.), *Enlightened Marketing in Challenging Times* (pp. 175–176). Springer., DOI: 10.1007/978-3-030-42545-6_46

Bartikowski, B., & Berens, G. (2021). Attribute framing in CSR communication: Doing good and spreading the word – But how? *Journal of Business Research, 131*, 700–708. DOI: 10.1016/j.jbusres.2020.12.059

Basol, M., Roozenbeek, J., Berriche, M., Uenal, F., McClanahan, W. P., & Linden, S. V. D. (2021). Towards psychological herd immunity: Cross-cultural evidence for two prebunking interventions against COVID-19 misinformation. *Big Data & Society, 8*(1), 20539517211013868. DOI: 10.1177/20539517211013868

Basol, M., Roozenbeek, J., & Van der Linden, S. (2020). Good news about bad news: Gamified inoculation boosts confidence and cognitive immunity against fake news. *Journal of cognition, 3*(1), 2.Fazio, L. (2020). Pausing to consider why a headline is true or false can help reduce the sharing of false news. *Harvard Kennedy School Misinformation Review, 1*(2).

Batmaz, Z., Yurekli, A., Bilge, A., & Kaleli, C. (2019). A review on deep learning for recommender systems: Challenges and remedies. *Artificial Intelligence Review*, *52*(1), 1–37. DOI: 10.1007/s10462-018-9654-y

Baur, C., & Wee, D. (2015). Manufacturing's next act. *McKinsey & company, 6*, 1-5.

Bawden, D., & Robinson, L. (2020). Information overload: An introduction. In *Oxford research encyclopedia of politics*.

BBVA. (2023). *BBVA and Tiendas Ara now offer reverse factoring in Colombia with a social impact.* Retrieved May 2025, from https://www.bbva.com/en/sustainability/bbva-and-tiendas-ara-now-offer-reverse-factoring-in-colombia-with-a-social-impact/

BCG. (2023). Industrial sharing platforms: The $900 billion opportunity. https://www.bcg.com

Bebbington, J., & Unerman, J. (2018). Achieving the United Nations Sustainable Development Goals: An enabling role for accounting research. *Accounting, Auditing & Accountability Journal*, *31*(1), 2–24. DOI: 10.1108/AAAJ-05-2017-2929

Beckmann, C. S., Morsing, M., & Reisch, L. (2006). Strategic CSR Communication: An Emerging Field. In Morsing, M., & Beckmann, S. C. (Eds.), *Strategic CSR Communication*. DJOF Publishing.

Becque, R., Roy, N., & Hamza-Goodacre, D. (2016). *The Political Economy of the Circular Economy*. Climate Works Foundation.

Belabbes, M. A., Ruthven, I., Moshfeghi, Y., & Rasmussen Pennington, D. (2023). Information overload: A concept analysis. *The Journal of Documentation*, *79*(1), 144–159. DOI: 10.1108/JD-06-2021-0118

Benegal, S. D., & Scruggs, L. A. (2018). Correcting misinformation about climate change: The impact of partisanship in an experimental setting. *Climatic Change*, *148*(1), 61–80. DOI: 10.1007/s10584-018-2192-4

Benito-León, J., Domínguez-González, C., & Rodríguez, J. (2023). Neuroscience applications in business: From brainwaves to consumer behavior. *Journal of Consumer Psychology*, *33*(1), 58–72. DOI: 10.1002/jcpy.1234

Berg, F., Kölbel, J. F., & Rigobon, R. (2023). Aggregate confusion: The divergence of ESG ratings. MIT Sloan Research Paper No. 5822-21.

Bergström, J., Dahlström, N., Henriqson, E., & Dekker, S. (2010). Team coordination in escalating situations: An empirical study using mid-fidelity simulation. *Journal of Contingencies and Crisis Management, 18*(4), 220–230. DOI: 10.1111/j.1468-5973.2010.00618.x

Berkan, R. (2012). Information pollution & doomsday consequence. *SEJ: Search Engine Journal.*

Bermes, A. (2021). Information overload and fake news sharing: A transactional stress perspective exploring the mitigating role of consumers' resilience during COVID-19. *Journal of Retailing and Consumer Services, 61*, 102555. DOI: 10.1016/j.jretconser.2021.102555

Bewick, L., & Corrall, S. (2010). Developing librarians as teachers: A study of their pedagogical knowledge. *Journal of Librarianship and Information Science, 42*(2), 97–110. DOI: 10.1177/0961000610361419

Bey, N., Hauschild, M. Z., & McAloone, T. C. (2013). Drivers and barriers for implementation of environmental strategies in manufacturing companies. *CIRP Annals, 62*(1), 43–46. DOI: 10.1016/j.cirp.2013.03.001

Bian, Y., Dong, L., Liu, Z., & Zhang, L. (2020). A sectoral eco-efficiency analysis on urban-industrial symbiosis. *Sustainability (Basel), 12*(9), 3650. DOI: 10.3390/su12093650

Bimber, B., & Gil de Zúñiga, H. (2020). The unedited public sphere. *New Media & Society, 22*(4), 700–715. DOI: 10.1177/1461444819893980

Bjørnbet, M. M., Skaar, C., Fet, A. M., & Schulte, K. Ø. (2021). Circular economy in manufacturing companies: A review of case study literature. *Journal of Cleaner Production, 294*, 126268. DOI: 10.1016/j.jclepro.2021.126268

Bjuremalm, H. (2006). *Power analysis – Experiences and challenges.* Swedish International Development Cooperation Agency (SIDA).

BlackRock. (2023). Global Sustainable Investing Survey. https://www.blackrock.com/sustainability

BlackRock. (2023). iShares Global Clean Energy ETF (ICLN): Annual fund report. https://www.ishares.com

BlackRock. (2023). iShares Global Clean Energy ETF (ICLN): Prospectus. https://www.ishares.com

Blomsma, F., & Brennan, G. (2017). The emergence of circular economy: A new framing around prolonging resource productivity. *Journal of Industrial Ecology, 21*(3), 603–614. DOI: 10.1111/jiec.12603

Bloomberg, N. E. F. (2023). Green securitization market outlook. https://about.bnef.com

Bloomberg. (2023, June 15). UK gas networks bet big on hydrogen with £500m bond. https://www.bloomberg.com

Bloomberg. (2023, June 8). *ThreadUp's AI-powered resale engine drives valuation to $1.2B*. https://www.bloomberg.com

Bloomberg, N. E. F. (2023). *Global green bond market retrospective 2023*. Bloomberg Finance L.P.

Blummer, B., & Kenton, M., J. (. (2014). Reducing patron information overload in academic libraries. *College & Undergraduate Libraries, 21*(2), 115–135. DOI: 10.1080/10691316.2014.906785

Boas, F. R. V., & Machado, C. F. (2024). Chapter 9 - Social responsibility as a lever for the circular economy. *Circular Economy and Manufacturing*, 217-238. DOI: 10.1016/B978-0-443-14028-0.00011-6

Boatright, J. R. (1997). *Ethics and the Conduct of Business* (2nd ed.). Prentice-Hall.

Bocconi University. Ellen MacArthur Foundation; Intesa Sanpaolo. (2021). *The circular economy as a de-risking strategy and driver of superior risk-adjusted returns.* White paper. Retrieved from https://content.ellenmacarthurfoundation.org/m/244d98bd9b1a3cc5/original/The-circular-economy-as-a-de-risking-strategy-and-driver-of-superior-risk-adjusted-returns.pdf?_gl=1*1qidc3p*_ga*MjI1NjY2MTMwLjE3NDcwNTExMzE.*_ga_V32N675KJX*czE3NDcwNTExMjgkbzEkZzAkd

Bodar, C., Spijker, J., Lijzen, J., Waaijers-van der Loop, S., Luit, R., Heugens, E., Janssen, M., Wassenaar, P., & Traas, T. (2018). Risk management of hazardous substances in a circular economy. *Journal of Environmental Management, 212*, 108–114. DOI: 10.1016/j.jenvman.2018.02.014 PMID: 29428645

Bode, L., & Vraga, E. K. (2018). See something, say something: Correction of global health misinformation on social media. *Health Communication, 33*(9), 1131–1140. DOI: 10.1080/10410236.2017.1331312 PMID: 28622038

Böhme, R., Christin, N., Edelman, B., & Moore, T. (2015). Bitcoin: Economics, technology, and governance. *The Journal of Economic Perspectives*, *29*(2), 213–238. DOI: 10.1257/jep.29.2.213

Boulding, K. E. (1966). The economics of the coming spaceship Earth. In Jarrett, H. (Ed.), *Environmental quality in a growing economy* (pp. 3–14). Resources for the Future/Johns Hopkins University Press.

Braddock, K. (2022). Vaccinating against hate: Using attitudinal inoculation to confer resistance to persuasion by extremist propaganda. *Terrorism and Political Violence*, *34*(2), 240–262. DOI: 10.1080/09546553.2019.1693370

Branco, M. C., & Rodrigues, L. L. (2006). Corporate social responsibility and resource-based perspectives. *Journal of Business Ethics*, *69*(2), 111–132. DOI: 10.1007/s10551-006-9071-z

Brashier, N. M., Pennycook, G., Berinsky, A. J., & Rand, D. G. (2021). Timing matters when correcting fake news. *Proceedings of the National Academy of Sciences of the United States of America*, *118*(5), e2020043118. DOI: 10.1073/pnas.2020043118 PMID: 33495336

Braun, J. A., Coakley, J. D., & West, E. (2019). Activism, advertising, and far-right media: The case of sleeping giants. *Media and Communication*, *7*(4), 68–79. DOI: 10.17645/mac.v7i4.2280

Bray, D. A. (2008). Information pollution, knowledge overload, limited attention spans, and our responsibilities as IS professionals. In *Global Information Technology Management Association (GITMA) World Conference-June*.

Breakthrough Energy Ventures (BEV). (2023). Investment Portfolio. https://www.breakthroughenergy.org

Bressanelli, G., Adrodegari, F., Perona, M., & Saccani, N. (2018). Exploring how usage-focused business models enable circular economy through digital technologies. *Sustainability (Basel)*, *10*(3), 639. DOI: 10.3390/su10030639

Bressanelli, G., Perona, M., & Saccani, N. (2019). Challenges in supply chain redesign for the Circular Economy: A literature review and a multiple case study. *International Journal of Production Research*, *57*(23), 7395–7422. DOI: 10.1080/00207543.2018.1542176

Bressanelli, G., Pigosso, D. C., Saccani, N., & Perona, M. (2021). Enablers, levers and benefits of Circular Economy in the Electrical and Electronic Equipment supply chain: A literature review. *Journal of Cleaner Production*, *298*, 126819. DOI: 10.1016/j.jclepro.2021.126819

Brest, P. (2020). *The Strategic Value of Philanthropy*. Stanford University Press.

Brest, P., & Born, K. (2021). When Can Impact Investing Create Real Impact? *Stanford Social Innovation Review*.

Brundtland, G. (1987). Report of the World Commission on Environment and Development: Our Common Future. United Nations General Assembly Document A/42/427.

Buckland, M. K. (1991). Information as thing. *Journal of the American Society for Information Science*, *42*(5), 351–360. DOI: 10.1002/(SICI)1097-4571(199106)42:5<351::AID-ASI5>3.0.CO;2-3

Bulgakova, D. (2024). Doxing: the Sandy Hook case study.

Busch, T., Johnson, M., & Pioch, T. (2022). Corporate carbon performance data: Quo vadis? *Journal of Industrial Ecology*, *26*(1), 350–363. DOI: 10.1111/jiec.13008

Cadent Gas. (2023). Hydrogen transition bond framework. https://www.cadentgas.com

Cagno, E., Neri, A., Negri, M., Bassani, C. A., & Lampertico, T. (2021). The role of digital technologies in operationalizing the circular economy transition: A systematic literature review. *Applied Sciences (Basel, Switzerland)*, *11*(8), 3328. DOI: 10.3390/app11083328

Camarinha-Matos, L. M., Fornasiero, R., Ramezani, J., & Ferrada, F. (2019). Collaborative networks: A pillar of digital transformation. *Applied Sciences (Basel, Switzerland)*, *9*(24), 5431. DOI: 10.3390/app9245431

Campoli, J. S., Kodama, T. K., Nagano, M. S., & Burnquist, H. L. (2025). Advancing circular economy: G20 nations' path towards 12th sustainable development goal. *Circular Economy and Sustainability*, *5*(1), 1–24. DOI: 10.1007/s43615-024-00415-0

Carbon Brief. (2023). The state of voluntary carbon markets 2023. https://www.carbonbrief.org

Carroll, A. B. (1991). The Pyramid of Corporate Social Responsibility: Toward the Moral Management of Organizational Stakeholders. *Business Horizons*, *34*(July-August), 39–48. DOI: 10.1016/0007-6813(91)90005-G

Carson, R. (2018). *R.: Retirement savers are losing $17 billion a year from fake news and conflicts of interest.*

Castellani, V., Sala, S., & Mirabella, N. (2014). Beyond the throwaway society: A life cycle-based assessment of the environmental benefit of reuse. *Integrated Environmental Assessment and Management, 11*(3), 373–382. DOI: 10.1002/ieam.1614 PMID: 25557152

Castles, S., Cubas, M. A., Kim, C., Koleth, E., Ozkul, D., & Williamson, R. (2011). *Karl Polanyi's great transformation as a framework for understanding neo-liberal globalisation*. University of Sydney. http://sydney.edu.au/arts/transformation_migration/downloads/STIM_WP1_Final.pdf

Cavazos, R. (2019). The economic cost of bad actors on the Internet. *Techical Report*.

Chen, P., & Dagestani, A. A. (2023). What lies about circular economy practices and performance? Fresh insights from China. *Journal of Cleaner Production, 416*, 137893. DOI: 10.1016/j.jclepro.2023.137893

Chen, T. L., Kim, H., Pan, S. Y., Tseng, P. C., Lin, Y. P., & Chiang, P. C. (2020). Implementation of green chemistry principles in circular economy system towards sustainable development goals: Challenges and perspectives. *The Science of the Total Environment, 716*, 136998. DOI: 10.1016/j.scitotenv.2020.136998 PMID: 32044483

Chhatre, A., Lakhanpal, S., & Nelson, A. (2022). Community benefits from forest carbon credits: Evidence from Mozambique. World Development, *158*, 1-14. https://doi.org/DOI: 10.1016/j.worlddev.2022.105963

Chitturi, R., Raghunathan, R., & Mahajan, V. (2008). Delight by design: The role of hedonic versus utilitarian benefits. *Journal of Marketing, 72*(3), 48–63. DOI: 10.1509/JMKG.72.3.048

Cho, D. J., & Lee, J. (2020). *Fighting against "infollution" that contaminates our children's minds and their thoughts.*

Clark, G. L., Feiner, A., & Viehs, M. (2015). From the stockholder to the stakeholder: How sustainability can drive financial outperformance. *Available at SSRN* 2508281.

Clark, G. L., Feiner, A., & Viehs, M. (2022). *From the stockholder to the stakeholder: How sustainability can drive financial outperformance*. University of Oxford.

CleanTech Group. (2023). 2023 Global Cleantech 100 Report. https://www.cleantech.com

Climate Bonds Initiative. (2023). Green bond market summary: Annual report 2023. https://www.climatebonds.net

Climate Bonds Initiative. (2023). Green securitization state of the market.

Climate Bonds Initiative. (2023). Transition finance state of the market. https://www.climatebonds.net

Climate Bonds Initiative. (2024). https://www.climatebonds.net/data-insights/publications/quarterly-market-update-q1-2024

Coleman, S. (2018). The elusiveness of political truth: From the conceit of objectivity to intersubjective judgement. *European Journal of Communication*, *33*(2), 157–171. DOI: 10.1177/0267323118760319

Collinson, S. (2003). *Power, livelihoods and conflict: Case studies in political economy analysis for humanitarian action* (Humanitarian Policy Group Report 13). Overseas Development Institute.

Colombo, F. (2022). A Media Ecology for a Platform Society. *CHANGING MEDIA CHANGING WORLD IN A*, 162.

Compton, J. (2013). Inoculation theory. *The SAGE handbook of persuasion: Developments in theory and practice, 2*, 220-237.

Compton, J., van der Linden, S., Cook, J., & Basol, M. (2021). Inoculation theory in the post-truth era: Extant findings and new frontiers for contested science, misinformation, and conspiracy theories. *Social and Personality Psychology Compass*, *15*(6), e12602. DOI: 10.1111/spc3.12602

Conzola, V. C., & Wogalter, M. S. (2001). A communication–human information processing (C–HIP) approach to warning effectiveness in the workplace. *Journal of Risk Research*, *4*(4), 309–322. DOI: 10.1080/13669870110062712

Cook, J., Lewandowsky, S., & Ecker, U. K. (2017). Neutralizing misinformation through inoculation: Exposing misleading argumentation techniques reduces their influence. *PLoS One*, *12*(5), e0175799. DOI: 10.1371/journal.pone.0175799 PMID: 28475576

Cookson, D., Jolley, D., Dempsey, R. C., & Povey, R. (2021). A social norms approach intervention to address misperceptions of anti-vaccine conspiracy beliefs amongst UK parents. *PLoS One*, *16*(11), e0258985. DOI: 10.1371/journal.pone.0258985 PMID: 34767581

Costa, H., & Macedo, L. (2013). Emotion-based recommender system for overcoming the problem of information overload. In *Highlights on Practical Applications of Agents and Multi-Agent Systems: International Workshops of PAAMS 2013, Salamanca, Spain, May 22-24, 2013.* [Springer Berlin Heidelberg.]. *Proceedings*, *11*, 178–189.

CPC Central Committee. (2012). Decisions of the CPC Central Committee on Several Major Issues Concerning the Comprehensive Deepening of Reform adopted at the Third Plenum of the 18th CPC Congress.

Cramer, J. (2022). Effective governance of circular economies: An international comparison. *Journal of Cleaner Production, 343*, 130874. DOI: 10.1016/j.jclepro.2022.130874

Cronin, S. (2025). Schneider Electric Case Study. In *Examining Net Zero: Creating Solutions for a Greener Society and Sustainable Economic Growth* (pp. 77–85). Emerald Publishing Limited. DOI: 10.1108/978-1-83608-574-420251008

Cunha, F. A. F. S., Meira, E., & Orsato, R. J. (2021). Sustainable finance and investment: A review of trends and challenges in the Global South. *Journal of Cleaner Production, 312*, 127789. DOI: 10.1016/j.jclepro.2021.127789

da Silva, T. H., & Sehnem, S. (2025). The utilization of Industry 4.0 technologies to enhance the circular economy through the engagement of stakeholders in Brazilian food technology companies. *Business Strategy and the Environment, 34*(1), 129–161. DOI: 10.1002/bse.3954

Darley, W. K., & Smith, R. E. (1993). Advertising claim objectivity: Antecedents and effects. *Journal of Marketing, 57*(4), 100–113. DOI: 10.1177/002224299305700408

Dasgupta, P., & Weale, M. (1992). On measuring the quality of life. *World Development, 20*(1), 119–131. DOI: 10.1016/0305-750X(92)90141-H

Daumas, L. (2024). Financial stability, stranded assets and the low-carbon transition–A critical review of the theoretical and applied literatures. *Journal of Economic Surveys, 38*(3), 601–716. DOI: 10.1111/joes.12551

Davis, N. (2012). IA strategy: Addressing the signatures of information overload.

Davis, N. (2010). *The function of information architecture. DSIA Portal of Information Architecture.* Methodbrain.

Dawkins, C. J. (2004). *The public's views of Corporate Responsibility 2003.* MORI White Papers.

Day, R., & Woodward, T. (2009). CSR reporting and the UK financial services sector. *Journal of Applied Accounting Research, 10*(3), 159–175. DOI: 10.1108/09675420911006398

De Freitas, J., Agarwal, S., Schmitt, B., & Haslam, N. (2023). Psychological factors underlying attitudes toward AI tools. *Nature Human Behaviour, 7*(11), 1845–1854. DOI: 10.1038/s41562-023-01734-2 PMID: 37985913 de Hallgren, S. C., Julca, A., Lucio, J. P., Ferrufino, R., & Costa, H. S. P. (2024). New Economics for Sustainable Development: Circular Economy. https://www.un.org/sites/un2.un.org/files/circular_economy_14_march.pdf

De La Cuesta-González, M., & Morales-García, M. (2022). Does finance as usual work for circular economy transition? A financiers and SMEs qualitative approach. *Journal of Environmental Planning and Management*, *65*(13), 2468–2489. DOI: 10.1080/09640568.2021.1972798

De Lima, F. A., & Seuring, S. (2023). A Delphi study examining risk and uncertainty management in circular supply chains. *International Journal of Production Economics*, *258*, 108810. DOI: 10.1016/j.ijpe.2023.108810

de Mooij, M. (2010). *Global marketing and advertising: Understanding cultural paradoxes* (3rd ed.). SAGE Publications.

de Morais, L. H. L., Pinto, D. C., & Cruz-Jesus, F. (2021). Circular economy engagement: Altruism, status, and cultural orientation as drivers for sustainable consumption. *Sustainable Production and Consumption*, *27*, 523–533. DOI: 10.1016/j.spc.2021.01.019

DellaVigna, S., & Linos, E. (2022). RCTs to scale: Comprehensive evidence from two nudge units. *Econometrica*, *90*(1), 81–116. DOI: 10.3982/ECTA18709

Department for International Development (DFID). (2009). *Political economy analysis how to note*. https://gsdrc.org/docs/open/PO58.pdf

Despeisse, M., Baumers, M., Brown, P., Charnley, F., Ford, S. J., Garmulewicz, A., Knowles, S., Minshall, T. H. W., Mortara, L., Reed-Tsochas, F. P., & Rowley, J. (2017). Unlocking value for a circular economy through 3D printing: A research agenda. *Technological Forecasting and Social Change*, *115*, 75–84. DOI: 10.1016/j.techfore.2016.09.021

Desrochers, P. (2004). Industrial symbiosis: The case for market coordination. *Journal of Cleaner Production*, *12*(8–10), 1099–1110. DOI: 10.1016/j.jclepro.2004.02.008

Deuze, M. (2020). The role of media and mass communication theory in the global pandemic. *Communication today, 11*(2), 4-16.

Dewick, P., Bengtsson, M., Cohen, M. J., Sarkis, J., & Schröder, P. (2020). Circular economy finance: Clear winner or risky proposition? *Journal of Industrial Ecology*, *24*(6), 1192–1200. DOI: 10.1111/jiec 13025

Di Flumeri, G., Aricò, P., Borghini, G., Sciaraffa, N., & Babiloni, F. (2018). EEG-based mental workload neurometric. *Frontiers in Human Neuroscience, 12*, 509. DOI: 10.3389/fnhum.2018.00509

Dillon, A. (2002). Information architecture in JASIST: Just where did we come from?.

Dimson, E., Marsh, P., & Staunton, M. (2022). Responsible investing: The ESG-efficient frontier. Journal of Financial Economics, *145*(2), 1-24.

Ding, Y., Meng, X., & Sun, C. (2024). Simplicity matters: Unraveling the impact of minimalist packaging on green trust in daily consumer goods. *Sustainability (Basel), 16*(12), 4932. DOI: 10.3390/su16124932

Donaldson, T., & Preston, L. E. (1995). The stakeholder theory of the corporation: Concepts, evidence, and implications. *Academy of Management Review, 20*(1), 65–91. DOI: 10.2307/258887

Donat, G. C., & de Souza, J. S. (2023). Circular economy investments: A portfolio selection framework. https://doi.org/DOI: 10.14488/IJCIEOM2023_FULL_0032_37736

Douglas, K. M., Uscinski, J. E., Sutton, R. M., Cichocka, A., Nefes, T., Ang, C. S., & Deravi, F. (2019). Understanding conspiracy theories. *Political Psychology, 40*(S1), 3–35. DOI: 10.1111/pops.12568

Dow, J., Han, J., & Sangiorgi, F. (2024). The short-termism trap: Catering to informed investors with limited horizons. *Journal of Financial Economics, 159*, 103884. DOI: 10.1016/j.jfineco.2024.103884

Drössler, S., Steputat, A., Schubert, M., Günther, N., Staudte, R., Kofahl, M., Hegewald, J., & Seidler, A. (2018). Information overload by digital media at the workplace: Systematic review of qualitative studies. *Zentralblatt für Arbeitsmedizin, Arbeitsschutz und Ergonomie, 68*(2), 77–88. DOI: 10.1007/s40664-018-0267-8

Dulia, E. F., Ali, S. M., Garshasbi, M., & Kabir, G. (2021). Admitting risks towards circular economy practices and strategies: An empirical test from supply chain perspective. *Journal of Cleaner Production, 317*, 128420. DOI: 10.1016/j.jclepro.2021.128420

Easterlin, R. A. (1974). Does economic growth improve the human lot? Some empirical evidence. In David, P. A., & Reder, M. W. (Eds.), *Nations and households in economic growth* (pp. 89–125). Academic Press. DOI: 10.1016/B978-0-12-205050-3.50008-7

Easterlin, R. A. (1995). Will raising the incomes of all increase the happiness of all? *Journal of Economic Behavior & Organization*, *27*(1), 35–47. DOI: 10.1016/0167-2681(95)00003-B

Easterlin, R. A. (2000). The worldwide standard of living since 1800. *The Journal of Economic Perspectives*, *14*(1), 7–26. DOI: 10.1257/jep.14.1.7

Ecker, U. K., Lewandowsky, S., & Chadwick, M. (2020). Can corrections spread misinformation to new audiences? Testing for the elusive familiarity backfire effect. *Cognitive Research: Principles and Implications*, *5*(1), 1–25. DOI: 10.1186/s41235-020-00241-6 PMID: 32844338

Edelen, A., & Ingwersen, W. W. (2018). The creation, management, and use of data quality information for life cycle assessment. *The International Journal of Life Cycle Assessment*, *23*(4), 759–772. DOI: 10.1007/s11367-017-1348-1 PMID: 29713113

Edelmann, D. (2009). *Analysing and managing the political dynamics of sector reforms: A sourcebook on sector-level political economy approaches*. Overseas Development Institute. https://odi.org/en/publications/analysing-and-managing-the-political-dynamics-of-sector-reforms/

Edmunds, A., & Morris, A. (2000). The problem of information overload in business organisations: A review of the literature. *International Journal of Information Management*, *20*(1), 17–28. DOI: 10.1016/S0268-4012(99)00051-1

Eickhoff, H. (2024). The appeal of the circular economy revisited: On track for transformative change or enabler of moral licensing? *Humanities & Social Sciences Communications*, *11*(301), 301. Advance online publication. DOI: 10.1057/s41599-024-02815-x

Ellen MacArthur Foundation. (2020). Financing the circular economy: Capturing the opportunity.

Ellen MacArthur Foundation. (2020). *Financing the circular economy: Capturing the opportunity*. Ellen MacArthur Foundation. Retrieved from https://www.ellenmacarthurfoundation.org/financing-the-circular-economy-capturing-the-opportunity

Ellen MacArthur Foundation. (2023). Circular economy investment opportunities. https://ellenmacarthurfoundation.org

Ellen MacArthur Foundation. (2023). The circular design advantage: Economic benefits of durable products. https://ellenmacarthurfoundation.org

Eppler, M. J., & Mengis, J. (2008). The Concept of Information Overload-A Review of Literature from Organization Science, Accounting, Marketing, MIS, and Related Disciplines (2004) The Information Society: An International Journal, 20 (5), 2004, pp. 1–20. *Kommunikationsmanagement im Wandel: Beiträge aus 10 Jahren= mcminstitute*, 271-305.

Epstein, Z., Berinsky, A. J., Cole, R., Gully, A., Pennycook, G., & Rand, D. G. (2021). Developing an accuracy-prompt toolkit to reduce COVID-19 misinformation online.

Espuny, M., Reis, J. S., Giupponi, E. C., Rocha, A. B., Costa, A. C., Poltronieri, C. F., & Oliveira, O. J. (2025). The role of the triple helix model in promoting the circular economy: Government-led integration strategies and practical application. *Recycling*, *10*(2), 50. DOI: 10.3390/recycling10020050

Ethirajan, M., Arasu, M. T., Kandasamy, J., Kek, V., Nadeem, S. P., & Kumar, A. (2021). Analysing the risks of adopting circular economy initiatives in manufacturing supply chains. *Business Strategy and the Environment*, *30*(1), 204–236. DOI: 10.1002/bse.2617

European Commission (2020). Sustainable Europe Investment Plan/European Green Deal investment plan. Communication from the commission to the European Parliament, the European Council, the Council, the European Economic and Social Committee and the Committee of the Regions 21.

European Commission. (2014). *Communication No. 398, 2014. Towards a Circular Economy: A Zero Waste Programme for Europe; (COM no. 398, 2014).* Commission of European Communities.

European Commission. (2015). *Communication No. 614, 2015. Closing the Loop—An EU Action Plan for the Circular Economy; (COM no. 614, 2015).* Commission of European Communities.

European Commission. (2016). Resource Efficiency Scoreboard 2015. Brussels. *European Union, 2016*, 72.

European Commission. (2018). *Communication No. 29, 2018. Monitoring Framework for the Circular Economy; (COM no. 29, 2018).* Commission of European Communities.

European Commission. (2019) The European Green Deal, COM 640 final, 11 December. https://ec.europa.eu/info/sites/info/files/european-green-deal-communication_en.pdf

European Commission. (2019). *Communication No. 640, 2019. The European Green Deal; (COM no. 640, 2019).* Commission of European Communities.

European Commission. (2019). *Report from the Commission to the European Parliament, the Council, the European Economic and Social Committee and the Committee of the Regions on the Implementation of the Circular Economy Action Plan; (COM No. 190, 2019)*. Commission of European Communities.

European Commission. (2020). *Communication No. 98, 2020. A New Circular Economy Action Plan for a Cleaner and More Competitive Europe; (COM no. 98, 2020)*. Commission of European Communities.

European Commission. (2023). European green bond standard: Implementation report. https://ec.europa.eu

Fang, F., Parida, S., & Sarkis, J. (2024). Private financing and the circular economy. *Resources, Conservation and Recycling*, *205*, 107581. DOI: 10.1016/j.resconrec.2024.107581

Fang, K., Dong, L., Ren, J., Zhang, Q., Han, L., & Fu, H. (2017). Carbon footprints of urban transition: Tracking circular economy promotions in Guiyang, China. *Ecological Modelling*, *365*, 30–44. DOI: 10.1016/j.ecolmodel.2017.09.024

Farache, F., & Perks, K. J. (2010). CSR advertisements: A legitimacy tool? *Corporate Communications*, *15*(3), 235–248. DOI: 10.1108/13563281011068104

Fatimah, Y. A., Govindan, K., Murniningsih, R., & Setiawan, A. (2020). Industry 4.0 based sustainable circular economy approach for smart waste management system to achieve sustainable development goals: A case study of Indonesia. *Journal of Cleaner Production*, *269*, 122263. DOI: 10.1016/j.jclepro.2020.122263

Fatorachian, H., & Kazemi, H. (2018). A critical investigation of Industry 4.0 in manufacturing: Theoretical operationalisation framework. *Production Planning and Control*, *29*(8), 633–644. DOI: 10.1080/09537287.2018.1424960

Feng, X., & Goli, A. (2023). Enhancing business performance through circular economy: A comprehensive mathematical model and statistical analysis. *Sustainability (Basel)*, *15*(16), 12631. Advance online publication. DOI: 10.3390/su151612631

Ferrari, A. G., Jugend, D., Armellini, F., & Seles, B. M. R. P. (2025). Opportunities and challenges of strategic planning in the context of circular economy: An exploratory analysis. *Management of Environmental Quality*, *36*(3), 833–854. Advance online publication. DOI: 10.1108/MEQ-05-2024-0183

Fettermann, D. C., Cavalcante, C. G. S., Almeida, T. D. D., & Tortorella, G. L. (2018). How does Industry 4.0 contribute to operations management?. *Journal of industrial and Production Engineering*, *35*(4), 255-268.

Financial Times. (2022, March 15). "How Green Bonds Went Mainstream." https://www.ft.com

Financial Times. (2023). Sustainable investing review 2023. https://www.ft.com/reports/sustainable-investing

Financial Times. (2023, March 15). How Unilever's plastic pledge is reshaping packaging finance. https://www.ft.com

Financial Times. (2023, March 15). IKEA's circular business model pivot. https://www.ft.com

Financial Times. (2023, March 8). The contentious rise of transition bonds. https://www.ft.com

Finlayson, J. A. (2002). Living standards: How does British Columbia compare? *Polish Perspectives*, *9*(4), 1–4.

FIRST. (2023). Guide to sustainable REIT investing. https://www.first.org

Fonseca, L. M. (2018, March). Industry 4.0 and the digital society: concepts, dimensions and envisioned benefits. In *Proceedings of the international conference on business excellence* (Vol. 12, No. 1, pp. 386-397). Bucharest, Romania: Sciendo. DOI: 10.2478/picbe-2018-0034

Forbes. (2023, April 15). Circularise's blockchain solution tracks materials through supply chains. https://www.forbes.com

Fortunati, S., Martiniello, L., & Morea, D. (2020). The strategic role of the corporate social responsibility and circular economy in the cosmetic industry. *Sustainability (Basel)*, *12*(12), 5120. DOI: 10.3390/su12125120

Francke, H. (2009). Towards an architectural document analysis. *Journal of Information Architecture*, *1*(1), 19–44. DOI: 10.55135/1015060901/091.001/3.003

Frappaolo, C., & Keldsen, D. (2012). *Findability. The Art and Science of Making Content Easy to Find. MarketIQ. Intelligence Quarterly Q2 2008. Silver Spring, MD: AIIM, 2009.*

Fratini, C. F., Georg, S., & Jørgensen, M. S. (2019). Exploring circular economy imaginaries in European cities: A research agenda for the governance of urban sustainability transitions. *Journal of Cleaner Production*, *228*, 974–989. DOI: 10.1016/j.jclepro.2019.04.193

Freeman, R. E. (1984). *Strategic Management: A Stakeholder Approach*. Pitman.

Freeman, R. E., Harrison, J. S., Wicks, A. C., Parmar, B. L., & De Colle, S. (2010). *Stakeholder Theory. The State of the Art.* Cambridge University Press. DOI: 10.1017/CBO9780511815768

Friant, M. C., Vermeulen, W. J., & Salomone, R. (2021). Analysing European Union circular economy policies: Words versus actions. *Sustainable Production and Consumption*, *27*, 337–353. DOI: 10.1016/j.spc.2020.11.001

Friede, G., Busch, T., & Bassen, A. (2015). ESG and financial performance: Aggregated evidence from more than 2000 empirical studies. *Journal of Sustainable Finance & Investment*, *5*(4), 210–233. DOI: 10.1080/20430795.2015.1118917

Fritz, V., Kaiser, K., & Levy, B. (2009). *Problem-driven governance and political economy analysis: Good practice framework*. World Bank. DOI: 10.1596/16777

Frynas, J. (2005). The False Development Promise of Corporate Social Responsibility: Evidence from Multinational Oil Companies. *International Affairs*, *81*(3), 581–598. DOI: 10.1111/j.1468-2346.2005.00470.x

Furner, C. P., & Zinko, R. A. (2017). The influence of information overload on the development of trust and purchase intention based on online product reviews in a mobile vs. web environment: An empirical investigation. *Electronic Markets*, *27*(3), 211–224. DOI: 10.1007/s12525-016-0233-2

Fu, S., Li, H., Liu, Y., Pirkkalainen, H., & Salo, M. (2020). Social media overload, exhaustion, and use discontinuance: Examining the effects of information overload, system feature overload, and social overload. *Information Processing & Management*, *57*(6), 102307. DOI: 10.1016/j.ipm.2020.102307

Gagnon, B., Tanguay, X., Amor, B., & Imbrogno, A. F. (2022). Forest products and circular economy strategies: A Canadian perspective. *Energies*, *15*(3), 673. DOI: 10.3390/en15030673

García-Madariaga, J., Blasco López, M.-F., Moya Burgos, I., & Recuero Virto, N. (2019). Do isolated packaging variables influence consumers' attention and preferences? *Physiology & Behavior*, *200*, 96–103. DOI: 10.1016/j.physbeh.2018.04.030

García-Marco, F. J. (2011). Libraries in the digital ecology: Reflections and trends. *The Electronic Library*, *29*(1), 105–120. DOI: 10.1108/02640471111111460

Gates Foundation. (2023). Annual Goalkeepers Report. https://www.gatesfoundation.org

Gates, B. (2021). *How to avoid a climate disaster*. Knopf.

Gaustad, G., Krystofik, M., Bustamante, M., & Badami, K. (2018). Circular economy strategies for mitigating critical material supply issues. *Resources, Conservation and Recycling*, *135*, 24–33. DOI: 10.1016/j.resconrec.2017.08.002

Geissdoerfer, M., Savaget, P., Bocken, N. M., & Hultink, E. J. (2017). The Circular Economy–A new sustainability paradigm? *Journal of Cleaner Production*, *143*, 757–768. DOI: 10.1016/j.jclepro.2016.12.048

Geng, Y., & Doberstein, B. (2008). Developing the circular economy in China: Challenges and opportunities for achieving'leapfrog development'. *International Journal of Sustainable Development and World Ecology*, *15*(3), 231–239. DOI: 10.3843/SusDev.15.3:6

Geng, Y., Fujita, T., Park, H. S., Chiu, A. S., & Huisingh, D. (2016). Recent progress on innovative eco-industrial development. *Journal of Cleaner Production*, *114*, 1–10. DOI: 10.1016/j.jclepro.2015.09.051

Geng, Y., Xinbei, W., Qinghua, Z., & Hengxin, Z. (2010). Regional initiatives on promoting cleaner production in China: A case of Liaoning. *Journal of Cleaner Production*, *18*(15), 1502–1508. DOI: 10.1016/j.jclepro.2010.06.028

Gennari, F., & Cassano, R. (2020). Circular economy and strategic risk. *Symphonya. Emerging Issues in Management*, 136-148. https://doi.org/DOI: 10.4468/2020.1.11gennari.cassano

Gennari, F. (2024). Strategic risk-based approach for the circular economy. *European Journal of Business and Management Research*, *9*(3), 24–32. https://hdl.handle.net/11379/599545. DOI: 10.24018/ejbmr.2024.9.3.2294

Georgakopoulos, D., Jayaraman, P. P., Fazia, M., Villari, M., & Ranjan, R. (2016). Internet of Things and edge cloud computing roadmap for manufacturing. *IEEE Cloud Computing*, *3*(4), 66–73. DOI: 10.1109/MCC.2016.91

Gereffi, G., Humphrey, J., & Sturgeon, T. (2005). The governance of global value chains. *Review of International Political Economy*, *12*(1), 78–104. DOI: 10.1080/09692290500049805

Global Commission on the Economy and Climate. (2023). Unlocking the inclusive growth story of the 21st century. https://newclimateeconomy.report

Global Impact Investing Network (GIIN). (2022). Annual Impact Investor Survey.

Global Sustainable Investment Alliance (GSIA). (2021). Global Sustainable Investment Review 2020. https://www.gsi-alliance.org

Global Sustainable Investment Alliance. (2022). Global sustainable investment review 2022. https://www.gsi-alliance.org

Glocker, M. L., Langleben, D. D., Ruparel, K., Loughead, J. W., Valdez, J. N., Griffin, M. D., Sachser, N., & Gur, R. C. (2009). Baby schema modulates the brain reward system in nulliparous women. *Proceedings of the National Academy of Sciences of the United States of America, 106*(22), 9115–9119. DOI: 10.1073/pnas.0811620106

Gonçalves, B. D. S. M., Carvalho, F. L. D., & Fiorini, P. D. C. (2022). Circular economy and financial aspects: A systematic review of the literature. *Sustainability (Basel), 14*(5), 3023. DOI: 10.3390/su14053023

Goovaerts, L., & Verbeek, A. (2018). Sustainable banking: finance in the circular economy. *Investing in Resource Efficiency: The Economics and Politics of Financing the Resource Transition*, 191-209. https://doi.org/.DOI: 10.1007/978-3-319-78867-8_9

Gorwa, R., Binns, R., & Katzenbach, C. (2020). Algorithmic content moderation: Technical and political challenges in the automation of platform governance. *Big Data & Society, 7*(1), 2053951719897945. DOI: 10.1177/2053951719897945

Graf, B., & Antoni, C. H. (2021). The relationship between information characteristics and information overload at the workplace-a meta-analysis. *European Journal of Work and Organizational Psychology, 30*(1), 143–158. DOI: 10.1080/1359432X.2020.1813111

Grafström, J., & Aasma, S. (2021). Breaking circular economy barriers. *Journal of Cleaner Production, 292*, 126002. DOI: 10.1016/j.jclepro.2021.126002

Grand View Research. (2023). Waste management market analysis. https://www.grandviewresearch.com

Green Finance Institute. (2023). Innovations in asset-level sustainability data. https://www.greenfinanceinstitute.co.uk

Green, A. (2011). Information overload in healthcare management: How the READ Portal is helping healthcare managers. *Journal of the Canadian Health Libraries Association/Journal de l'Association des bibliothèques de la santé du Canada, 32*(3), 173-176.

GreenBiz. (2021, May). Retrieved from The Potential Impact of a Circular Economy: https://givingcompass.org/article/the-potential-impact-of-a-circular-economy

GreenBiz. (2023, April 12). Evrnu's $45M bet on fashion's circular future. https://www.greenbiz.com

Greenhouse Gas Protocol. (2023). *Carbon credit accounting guidelines*. World Resources Institute.

Gregson, N., Crang, M., Fuller, S., & Holmes, H. (2015). Interrogating the circular economy: The moral economy of resource recovery in the EU. *Economy and Society*, *44*(2), 218–243. DOI: 10.1080/03085147.2015.1013353

Guess, A. M., Lerner, M., Lyons, B., Montgomery, J. M., Nyhan, B., Reifler, J., & Sircar, N. (2020). A digital media literacy intervention increases discernment between mainstream and false news in the United States and India. *Proceedings of the National Academy of Sciences of the United States of America*, *117*(27), 15536–15545. DOI: 10.1073/pnas.1920498117 PMID: 32571950

Guixeres, J., Bigné, E., Ausín Azofra, J. M., Alcañiz Raya, M., Colomer Granero, A., Fuentes Hurtado, F., & Naranjo Ornedo, V. (2017). Consumer neuroscience-based metrics predict recall, liking and viewing rates in online advertising. *Frontiers in Psychology*, *8*, 1808. DOI: 10.3389/fpsyg.2017.01808

Guo, Z., Schlichtkrull, M., & Vlachos, A. (2022). A survey on automated fact-checking. *Transactions of the Association for Computational Linguistics*, *10*, 178–206. DOI: 10.1162/tacl_a_00454

Gupta, S., Chen, H., Hazen, B. T., Kaur, S., & Gonzalez, E. D. S. (2019). Circular economy and big data analytics: A stakeholder perspective. *Technological Forecasting and Social Change*, *144*, 466–474. DOI: 10.1016/j.techfore.2018.06.030

Haar, G. (2024). Transition to a Circular Economy. In *The Great Transition to a Green and Circular Economy* (pp. 89–126). Springer, Cham., DOI: 10.1007/978-3-031-49658-5_9

Haas, W., Krausmann, F., Wiedenhofer, D., & Heinz, M. (2015). How circular is the global economy?: An assessment of material flows, waste production, and recycling in the European Union and the world in 2005. *Journal of Industrial Ecology*, *19*(5), 765–777. DOI: 10.1111/jiec.12244

Hahn, T., Pinkse, J., Preuss, L., & Figge, F. (2015). Tensions in corporate sustainability: Towards an integrative framework. *Journal of Business Ethics*, *127*(2), 297–316. DOI: 10.1007/s10551-014-2047-5

Haider, H., & Rao, S. (2010). *Political and social analysis for development policy and practice: An overview of five approaches*. Governance and Social Development Resource Centre.

Ha, L. T. (2025). Circular Economy in European Countries: The Required Link for Green Foreign Financing Investment Policy. *Circular Economy and Sustainability*, *5*(3), 1–30. DOI: 10.1007/s43615-024-00494-z

Hannon Armstrong. (2023). Annual sustainability report. https://www.hannonarmstrong.com

Harris, D., Kooy, M., & Jones, L. (2011). *Analysing the governance and political economy of water and sanitation service delivery*. Overseas Development Institute. https://odi.org/en/publications/analysing-the-governance-and-political-economy-of-water-and-sanitation-service-delivery/

Harrison, R., Newholm, T., & Shaw, D. (2006). *The Ethical Consumer*. Sage Publications.

Harvard Business Review. (2023). The asset-light revolution. https://hbr.org

Harvard Business Review. (2023). The modular design revolution. https://hbr.org

Harvard Business Review. (2023, June 15). The new rules of impact investing. Harvard Business Review, 101(4), 56-67.

Harvard Management Company. (2021). *Harvard endowment sets 2050 net-zero goal*. https://www.hmc.harvard.edu_https://www.climatebonds.net

Hassan, S. H., Mohamed, N., Ahmad, N. H., Halim, H. A., & Ramayah, T. (2019). Conceptualizing Perceived Infollution Processing and Management and Its Consequence on Employee Well-Being. European Proceedings of Social and Behavioural Sciences.

Hassan, M. S., Ali, Y., Petrillo, A., & De Felice, F. (2023). Risk assessment of circular economy practices in construction industry of Pakistan. *The Science of the Total Environment*, *868*, 161418. DOI: 10.1016/j.scitotenv.2023.161418 PMID: 36642278

Hayat Kimya. (2022). Kurumsal Tanıtım Raporu. https://www.hayat.com.tr

Heeb, F., Kellers, A., & Kölbel, J. (2022). *Does ESG integration impact the real economy. A theory of change and review of current evidence.* Bern: Federal Office for the Environment (FOEN). Retrieved from https://www.csp.uzh.ch/dam/jcr:ac4406e3-ae17-43c0-8fa1-f967cd5abacb/BAFU%20Report_DIGITAL_pages.pdf

Hidalgo-Crespo, J., Riel, A., Golinska-Dawson, P., Peeters, J. R., Werner-Lewandowska, K., & Duflou, J. R. (2024). Facilitating circularity: Challenges and design guidelines of Product-as-a-Service (PaaS) business model offers for electrical and electronic equipment. *Procedia CIRP*, *128*, 567–572. DOI: 10.1016/j.procir.2024.03.037

Hilligoss, B., & Rieh, S. Y. (2008). Developing a unifying framework of credibility assessment: Construct, heuristics, and interaction in context. *Information Processing & Management*, *44*(4), 1467–1484. DOI: 10.1016/j.ipm.2007.10.001

Hiltz, S. R., & Plotnick, L. (2013, May). Dealing with information overload when using social media for emergency management: Emerging solutions. In *ISCRAM*.

Hinkin, M. P., Harris, R. J., & Miranda, A. T. (2014). Verbal redundancy aids memory for filmed entertainment dialogue. *The Journal of Psychology*, *148*(2), 161–176. DOI: 10.1080/00223980.2013.767774

Hinton, A. (2009). The machineries of context. *Journal of Information Architecture*, *1*(1), 37–47. DOI: 10.55135/1015060901/091.001/4.004

Hofstede, G. (2001). *Culture's Consequences: Comparing Values, Behaviors, Institutions and Organizations across Nations*. SAGE.

Holton, A. E., & Chyi, H. I. (2012). News and the overloaded consumer: Factors influencing information overload among news consumers. *Cyberpsychology, Behavior, and Social Networking*, *15*(11), 619–624. DOI: 10.1089/cyber.2011.0610 PMID: 23020743

Homrich, A. S., Galvão, G., Abadia, L. G., & Carvalho, M. M. (2018). The circular economy umbrella: Trends and gaps on integrating pathways. *Journal of Cleaner Production*, *175*, 525–543. DOI: 10.1016/j.jclepro.2017.11.064

Hong, T., Ou, J., Jia, F., Chen, L., & Yang, Y. (2023). Circular economy practices and corporate social responsibility performance: The role of sense-giving. *International Journal of Logistics*, *27*(11), 2208–2237. DOI: 10.1080/13675567.2023.2237914

Hughes, B., Goldberg, B., Jereza, R., & West, J. J. (2021). Inoculating against persuasion by scientific racism propaganda: The moderating roles of propaganda form and subtlety.

Hurzhyi, N., Popliuiko, Y., Vasylyuk-Zaitseva, S., & Kobets, D. (2023). Harnessing neuromarketing techniques to enhance brand engagement. *Futurity of Social Sciences*, *1*(4), 4–37.

Hussein, K. M. A. M., & Ozad, B. E. (2023). A systematic literature review on neuromarketing in branding, advertising and consumer behavior. *International Journal of Innovative Science and Research Technology*, *8*(6), 2037–2045.

Iannuzzi, A. P., Labini, S. S., & D'Apolito, E. (2023). Sustainability and the circular economy: the role of the financial sector and the response of Intesa Sanpaolo. In P. M. Falcone, E. Sica, & 1st (Ed.), *Sustainable Finance and the Global Health Crisis* (pp. 193-213). Routledge. DOI: 10.4324/9781003284703

IFC. (2023). *Blended Finance for Sustainable Development* https://www.ifc.org/en/what-we-do/sector-expertise/blended-finance

Illes, J., & Bird, S. J. (2006). Neuroethics: A modern context for ethics in neuroscience. *Trends in Neurosciences*, *29*(9), 511–517. DOI: 10.1016/j.tins.2006.07.002

Interface. (2020). *Sustainability Highlights Report.*

International Capital Market Association. (2022). Sustainability-linked bond principles. https://www.icmagroup.org

International Energy Agency (IEA). (2022). Special Report on Startups and Innovation. https://www.iea.org

International Energy Agency. (2023). Cleantech innovation and venture capital trends. https://www.iea.org

International Energy Agency. (2023). Financing clean energy transitions in industry. https://www.iea.org

International Finance Corporation. (2023). Scaling small-scale renewables through securitization. https://www.ifc.org

Intesa Sanpaolo. (2025). *Support to the Circular Economy.* Retrieved May 2025, from https://group.intesasanpaolo.com/en/sustainability/support-to-esg-transition/support-to-circular-economy

Iqbal, Q., & Nawaz, R. (2021). Rife information pollution (infollution) and virtual organizations in industry 4.0: within reality causes and consequences. In *Research Anthology on Digital Transformation, Organizational Change, and the Impact of Remote Work* (pp. 1578-1592). IGI Global.

Iqbal, Q., Ahmad, N. H., & Nawaz, R. (2020). Perceived information pollution: Conceptualization, measurement, and nomological validity. *Online Information Review*, *44*(3), 705–722. DOI: 10.1108/OIR-10-2018-0322

Iqbal, Q., Hassan, S. H., & Ahmad, N. H. (2018). The assessment of perceived information pollution in banking sector: A scale development and validation study. *Business Information Review*, *35*(2), 68–76. DOI: 10.1177/0266382118772891

Iqbal, Q., Yang, S., Nawaz, R., & Iqbal, K. (2019). A multi-dimensional construct of perceived information pollution in the era of rife infollution. *VINE Journal of Information and Knowledge Management Systems*, *49*(2), 162–180. DOI: 10.1108/VJIKMS-10-2018-0093

Islam, A. N., Laato, S., Talukder, S., & Sutinen, E. (2020). Misinformation sharing and social media fatigue during COVID-19: An affordance and cognitive load perspective. *Technological Forecasting and Social Change*, *159*, 120201. DOI: 10.1016/j.techfore.2020.120201 PMID: 32834137

Istanbul Sanayi Odası [İSO]. (2022). Türkiye'nin 500 Büyük Sanayi Kuruluşu 2021. https://www.iso.org.tr

IUCN. (1980). *World Conservation Strategy: Living Resource Conservation for Sustainable Development*. International Union for Conservation of Nature and Natural Resources. https://portals.iucn.org/library/efiles/documents/WCS-004.pdf

Jabbour, C. J. C., de Sousa Jabbour, A. B. L., Sarkis, J., & Godinho Filho, M. (2019). Unlocking the circular economy through new business models based on large-scale data: An integrative framework and research agenda. *Technological Forecasting and Social Change*, *144*, 546–552. DOI: 10.1016/j.techfore.2017.09.010

Jabbour, C. J. C., Fiorini, P. D. C., Wong, C. W., Jugend, D., Jabbour, A. B. L. D. S., Seles, B. M. R. P., & da Silva, H. M. R. (2020b). First-mover firms in the transition towards the sharing economy in metallic natural resource-intensive industries: Implications for the circular economy and emerging industry 4.0 technologies. *Resources Policy*, *66*, 101596. DOI: 10.1016/j.resourpol.2020.101596

Jabbour, C. J. C., Seuring, S., de Sousa Jabbour, A. B. L., Jugend, D., Fiorini, P. D. C., Latan, H., & Izeppi, W. C. (2020a). Stakeholders, innovative business models for the circular economy and sustainable performance of firms in an emerging economy facing institutional voids. *Journal of Environmental Management*, *264*, 110416. DOI: 10.1016/j.jenvman.2020.110416 PMID: 32217311

Jackson, T. W., & Farzaneh, P. (2012). Theory-based model of factors affecting information overload. *International Journal of Information Management*, *32*(6), 523–532. DOI: 10.1016/j.ijinfomgt.2012.04.006

Jensen, S. F., Kristensen, J. H., Adamsen, S., Christensen, A., & Waehrens, B. V. (2023). Digital product passports for a circular economy: Data needs for product life cycle decision-making. *Sustainable Production and Consumption*, *37*, 242–255. DOI: 10.1016/j.spc.2023.02.021

Joensuu, T., Edelman, H., & Saari, A. (2020). Circular economy practices in the built environment. *Journal of Cleaner Production*, *276*, 124215. DOI: 10.1016/j.jclepro.2020.124215

Jolley, D., & Douglas, K. M. (2017). Prevention is better than cure: Addressing anti-vaccine conspiracy theories. *Journal of Applied Social Psychology*, *47*(8), 459–469. DOI: 10.1111/jasp.12453

Journal of Cleaner Production. (2023). Advanced waste recovery technologies. https://www.sciencedirect.com

Journal of Cleaner Production. (2023). Bioleaching efficiency in e-waste recovery, 412(1), 1-12. https://doi.org/DOI: 10.1016/j.jclepro.2023.135000

Jung, B., & Kowalski, T. (2021). Restructuring Time Use Under COVID-19 Pandemics. *International Journal of Inspiration & Resilience Economy*, *5*(1), 22–31.

Kahneman, D. (2011). *Thinking, fast and slow*. Farrar, Straus and Giroux.

Kakwani, N. (1993). Performance in living standards: An international comparison. *Journal of Development Economics*, *41*(2), 307–336. DOI: 10.1016/0304-3878(93)90061-Q

Kanda, W., Klofsten, M., Bienkowska, D., Henry, M., & Hjelm, O. (2024). Challenges of circular new ventures: An empirical analysis of 70 cases. *Journal of Cleaner Production*, *442*, 141103. DOI: 10.1016/j.jclepro.2024.141103

Kandpal, V., Jaswal, A., Santibanez Gonzalez, E. D., & Agarwal, N. (2024). Circular economy principles: shifting towards sustainable prosperity. In *Sustainable energy transition: Circular economy and sustainable financing for environmental, social and governance (ESG) practices* (pp. 125–165). Springer, Cham., DOI: 10.1007/978-3-031-52943-6_4

Kandpal, V., Jaswal, A., Santibanez Gonzalez, E. D., & Agarwal, N. (2024). Sustainable energy transition, circular economy, and ESG practices. In *Sustainable Energy Transition: Circular Economy and Sustainable Financing for Environmental, Social and Governance (ESG) Practices* (pp. 1–51). Springer, Cham., DOI: 10.1007/978-3-031-52943-6_1

Kanwal, P., Yadav, A. K., & Dewasiri, N. J. (2025). Entrepreneurial orientation and green supply chain management (GSCM). In *Impacts of Entrepreneurial Orientation on Supply Chain Management* (pp. 197-236). IGI Global. DOI: 10.4018/979-8-3693-3386-0.ch008

Karim, R., Waaje, A., Roshid, M. M., & Yeamin, M. B. (2025). Turning the waste into wealth: Progressing toward global sustainability through the circular economy in waste management. In *Sustainable Waste Management in the Tourism and Hospitality Sectors* (pp. 507–552). IGI Global Scientific Publishing., DOI: 10.4018/979-8-3693-6110-8.ch019

Karr-Wisniewski, P., & Lu, Y. (2010). When more is too much: Operationalizing technology overload and exploring its impact on knowledge worker productivity. *Computers in Human Behavior*, *26*(5), 1061–1072. DOI: 10.1016/j.chb.2010.03.008

Kaufhold, M. A., Rupp, N., Reuter, C., & Habdank, M. (2020). Mitigating information overload in social media during conflicts and crises: Design and evaluation of a cross-platform alerting system. *Behaviour & Information Technology*, *39*(3), 319–342. DOI: 10.1080/0144929X.2019.1620334

Kaur, G., Uisan, K., Ong, K. L., & Lin, C. S. K. (2018). Recent trends in green and sustainable chemistry & waste valorisation: Rethinking plastics in a circular economy. *Current Opinion in Green and Sustainable Chemistry*, *9*, 30–39. DOI: 10.1016/j.cogsc.2017.11.003

Keblowski, W., Lambert, D., & Bassens, D. (2020). Circular economy and the city: An urban political economy agenda. *Culture and Organization*, *26*(2), 142–158. DOI: 10.1080/14759551.2020.1718148

Keller, K. L. (2003). *Strategic brand management: Building, measuring, and managing brand equity* (2nd ed.). Prentice Hall.

Kendeou, P., Robinson, D. H., & McCrudden, M. T. (2019). Misinformation and disinformation in education: An introduction. *Misinformation and fake news in education*, 1-4.

Kervyn, N., Fiske, S. T., & Malone, C. (2012). Brands as intentional agents framework: How perceived intentions and ability can map brand perception. *Journal of Consumer Psychology*, *22*(2), 166–176. DOI: 10.1016/j.jcps.2011.09.006

Kim, H. W., Dong, L., Choi, A. E. S., Fujii, M., Fujita, T., & Park, H. S. (2018). Co-benefit potential of industrial and urban symbiosis using waste heat from industrial park in Ulsan, Korea. *Resources, Conservation and Recycling*, *135*, 225–234. DOI: 10.1016/j.resconrec.2017.09.027

Kirchherr, J., Hekkert, M., Bour, R., Huijbrechtse-Truijens, A., Kostense-Smit, E., & Muller, J. (2017). *Breaking the Barriers to the Circular Economy. Deloitte.* Utrecht University.

Kirchherr, J., Piscicelli, L., Bour, R., Kostense-Smit, E., Muller, J., Huibrechtse-Truijens, A., & Hekkert, M. (2018). Barriers to the circular economy: Evidence from the European Union (EU). *Ecological Economics*, *150*, 264–272. DOI: 10.1016/j.ecolecon.2018.04.028

Kirchherr, J., Reike, D., & Hekkert, M. (2017). Conceptualizing the circular economy: An analysis of 114 definitions. *Resources, Conservation and Recycling*, *127*, 221–232. DOI: 10.1016/j.resconrec.2017.09.005

Knoll, J., & Matthes, J. (2017). The effectiveness of celebrity endorsements: A meta-analysis. *Journal of the Academy of Marketing Science*, *45*(1), 55–75. DOI: 10.1007/s11747-016-0503-8

Koch, N., Fuss, S., & Grosjean, G. (2021). Pricing carbon when costs are hidden. *Nature Climate Change*, *11*(3), 218–224. DOI: 10.1038/s41558-021-00988-w

Koltay, T. (2017). Information overload in a data-intensive world. *Understanding information: From the big bang to big data*, 197-217.

Korhonen, J., Honkasalo, A., & Seppälä, J. (2018). Circular economy: The concept and its limitations. *Ecological Economics*, *143*, 37–46. DOI: 10.1016/j.ecolecon.2017.06.041

Koroleva, K., Krasnova, H., & Günther, O. (2010). 'stop spamming me!'-exploring information overload on facebook.

Kotler, P., Armstrong, G., Saunders, J., & Wong, V. (1999). *Principles of Marketing* (2nd European edition). Prentice-Hall.

Kotler, P., & Lee, N. (2005). *Corporate Social Responsibility: Doing the Good for Your Company and Your Cause*. John Wiley & Sons.

Kozyreva, A., Lewandowsky, S., & Hertwig, R. (2020). Citizens versus the internet: Confronting digital challenges with cognitive tools. *Psychological Science in the Public Interest*, *21*(3), 103–156. DOI: 10.1177/1529100620946707 PMID: 33325331

Kozyreva, A., Lorenz-Spreen, P., Herzog, S. M., Ecker, U. K., Lewandowsky, S., Hertwig, R., Ali, A., Bak-Coleman, J., Barzilai, S., Basol, M., Berinsky, A. J., Betsch, C., Cook, J., Fazio, L. K., Geers, M., Guess, A. M., Huang, H., Larreguy, H., Maertens, R., & Wineburg, S. (2024). Toolbox of individual-level interventions against online misinformation. *Nature Human Behaviour*, *8*(6), 1044–1052. DOI: 10.1038/s41562-024-01881-0 PMID: 38740990

Krauss, J. E., Krüger, P., & Meyer, J. (2016). Sustainable finance prioritization: A global perspective on economic agents' strategies. *Environmental Economics and Policy Studies*, *18*(3), 405–423. DOI: 10.1007/s10018-016-0156-2

Kringelbach, M. L., Lehtonen, A., Squire, S., Harvey, A. G., Craske, M. G., Holliday, I. E., Green, A. L., Aziz, T. Z., Hansen, P. C., Cornelissen, P. L., & Stein, A. (2008). A specific and rapid neural signature for parental instinct. *PLoS One*, *3*(2), e1664. DOI: 10.1371/journal.pone.0001664

Krishna, A. (2012). An integrative review of sensory marketing: Engaging the senses to affect perception, judgment and behavior. *Journal of Consumer Psychology*, *22*(3), 332–351. DOI: 10.1016/j.jcps.2011.08.003

Krstić, M., Agnusdei, L., Palmi, P., & Baležentis, T. (2024). Enabling organizations to strategically manage risks in circular supply chains. *Business Strategy and the Environment*, *33*(6), 5996–6009. DOI: 10.1002/bse.3793

Krueger, P., Sautner, Z., & Starks, L. T. (2020). The importance of climate risks for institutional investors. *Review of Financial Studies*, *33*(3), 1067–1111. DOI: 10.1093/rfs/hhz137

Krystallis, I., Cardin, M., & de Neufville, R. (2025). Designing Flexibility for Strategic Decision-Making in Infrastructure Projects, Real Options, and Managing Uncertainty. *IEEE Transactions on Engineering Management*.

Kube, G., & Rinn, T. (2014). Industry 4.0-The next revolution in the industrial sector. *ZKG International*, *67*(11), 30–32.

Kuci, A., & Fogarassy, C. (2021). European Green Deal Policy for the Circular Economy: Opportunities and Challenges. *Hungarian Agricultural Engineering*, *39*(39), 65–73. DOI: 10.17676/HAE.2021.39.65

Kumar, B., Kumar, A., Sassanelli, C., & Kumar, L. (2024). Exploring the role of finance in driving circular economy and sustainable business practices. *Journal of Cleaner Production*, *144480*. Advance online publication. DOI: 10.1016/j.jclepro.2024.144480

Kumar, B., Kumar, L., Kumar, A., Kumari, R., Tagar, U., & Sassanelli, C. (2024). Green finance in circular economy: A literature review. *Environment, Development and Sustainability*, *26*(7), 16419–16459. DOI: 10.1007/s10668-023-03361-3

Laato, S., Islam, A. N., Islam, M. N., & Whelan, E. (2020). What drives unverified information sharing and cyberchondria during the COVID-19.

Lacy, P., & Rutqvist, J. (2015). *Waste to wealth: The circular economy advantage* (Vol. 91). Palgrave Macmillan.

Larivière, B., & Smit, E. G. (2022). People–planet–profits for a sustainable world: Integrating the triple-P idea in the marketing strategy, implementation and evaluation of service firms. *Journal of Service Management, 33*(4/5), 507–519. DOI: 10.1108/JOSM-01-2022-0033

Lasi, H., Fettke, P., Kemper, H. G., Feld, T., & Hoffmann, M. (2014). Industry 4.0. *Business & Information Systems Engineering, 6*(4), 239–242. DOI: 10.1007/s12599-014-0334-4

Laskurain-Iturbe, I., Arana-Landín, G., Landeta-Manzano, B., & Uriarte-Gallastegi, N. (2021). Exploring the influence of industry 4.0 technologies on the circular economy. *Journal of Cleaner Production, 321*, 128944. DOI: 10.1016/j.jclepro.2021.128944

Lauri, L., & Virkus, S. (2019). Information overload of academic staff in higher education institutions in Estonia. In *Information Literacy in Everyday Life: 6th European Conference, ECIL 2018, Oulu, Finland, September 24–27, 2018, Revised Selected Papers 6* (pp. 347-356). Springer International Publishing. DOI: 10.1007/978-3-030-13472-3_33

Lawrence, J. M. (2025). Impact of Environmental, Social, and Governance (ESG) and the Circular Economy (CE) on Financial Decision-Making. In *Fintech for ESG and the Circular Economy* (pp. 119-148). DOI: 10.1002/9781394234035.ch7

Lazer, D. M., Baum, M. A., Benkler, Y., Berinsky, A. J., Greenhill, K. M., Menczer, F., Metzger, M. J., Nyhan, B., Pennycook, G., Rothschild, D., Schudson, M., Sloman, S. A., Sunstein, C. R., Thorson, E. A., Watts, D. J., & Zittrain, J. L. (2018). The science of fake news. *Science, 359*(6380), 1094–1096. DOI: 10.1126/science.aao2998 PMID: 29590025

Lee, N., Broderick, A. J., & Chamberlain, L. (2007). What is 'neuromarketing'? A discussion and agenda for future research. *International Journal of Psychophysiology, 63*(2), 199–204. DOI: 10.1016/j.ijpsycho.2006.03.007

Lee, Y. W., Strong, D. M., Kahn, B. K., & Wang, R. Y. (2002). AIMQ: A methodology for information quality assessment. *Information & Management, 40*(2), 133–146. DOI: 10.1016/S0378-7206(02)00043-5

Lewandowski, M. (2016). Designing the business models for circular economy—Towards the conceptual framework. *Sustainability (Basel), 8*(1), 43. DOI: 10.3390/su8010043

Lewandowsky, S., Cook, J., Ecker, U., Albarracin, D., Amazeen, M. A., Kendeou, P., ... & Zaragoza, M. S. (2020). The Debunking Handbook 2020: Downloads and Translations.

Li, B., Wang, B., & Yu, J. (2023). *The Emerging Greenium*. The Brookings Institution., Retrieved from https://www.brookings.edu/wp-content/uploads/2023/05/GreenBonds_20230711.pdf

Lieder, M., & Rashid, A. (2016). Towards circular economy implementation: A comprehensive review in context of manufacturing industry. *Journal of Cleaner Production*, *115*, 36–51. DOI: 10.1016/j.jclepro.2015.12.042

Lindblom, C. K. (1994). The implications of organizational legitimacy for corporate social performance and disclosure. *In* Critical Perspectives on Accounting Conference, New York.

Lin, F., Chen, C., Zhang, N., Guan, X., & Shen, X. (2015). Autonomous channel switching: Towards efficient spectrum sharing for industrial wireless sensor networks. *IEEE Internet of Things Journal*, *3*(2), 231–243. DOI: 10.1109/JIOT.2015.2490544

Lin, L., & Hong, Y. (2022). Developing a green bonds market: Lessons from China. *European Business Organization Law Review*, *23*(1), 143–185. DOI: 10.1007/s40804-021-00231-1

Liu, Q., Zhu, S., Zhou, X., Liu, F., Becker, B., Kendrick, K. M., & Zhao, W. (2024). Mothers and fathers show different neural synchrony with their children during shared experiences. *NeuroImage*, *288*, 120529. DOI: 10.1016/j.neuroimage.2024.120529

Liu, Z. (2004). Perceptions of credibility of scholarly information on the web. *Information Processing & Management*, *40*(6), 1027–1038. DOI: 10.1016/S0306-4573(03)00064-5

Loan Market Association. (2023). Sustainability-linked loan principles. https://www.lma.eu.com

Loan Syndications & Trading Association. (2023). U.S. sustainability-linked loan market report. https://www.lsta.org

Lomax, G., Workman, M., & Lenton, T. (2023). Reframing carbon removals for net-zero policy. *Climate Policy*, *23*(2), 1–18.

Lom, M., Pribyl, O., & Svitek, M. (2016, May). Industry 4.0 as a part of smart cities. In *2016 Smart Cities Symposium Prague (SCSP)* (pp. 1-6). IEEE. DOI: 10.1109/SCSP.2016.7501015

Lopes de Sousa Jabbour, A. B., Jabbour, C. J. C., Godinho Filho, M., & Roubaud, D. (2018). Industry 4.0 and the circular economy: A proposed research agenda and original roadmap for sustainable operations. *Annals of Operations Research*, *270*(1-2), 273–286. DOI: 10.1007/s10479-018-2772-8

Losa, R. (2025). Public policies on circular economy: A systematic review. *Ecological Economics*, *228*, 108452. DOI: 10.1016/j.ecolecon.2024.108452

Luo, Y., Jiang, H., & Zeng, L. (2023). Linking Informative and Factual CSR Communication to Reputation: Understanding CSR Motives and Organizational Identification. *Sustainability (Basel)*, *15*(6), 5136. DOI: 10.3390/su15065136

Lu, Y. (2017). Industry 4.0: A survey on technologies, applications and open research issues. *Journal of Industrial Information Integration*, *6*, 1–10. DOI: 10.1016/j.jii.2017.04.005

MacArthur, E., Zumwinkel, K., & Stuchtey, M. R. (2015). Growth within: a circular economy vision for a competitive Europe. *Ellen MacArthur Foundation, 100.*

MacArthur, E. (2013). *Towards the circular economy, economic and business rationale for an accelerated transition.* Ellen MacArthur Foundation.

MacDonald, J., Bath, P., & Booth, A. (2011). Information overload and information poverty: Challenges for healthcare services managers? *The Journal of Documentation*, *67*(2), 238–263. DOI: 10.1108/00220411111109458

Madaan, G., Singh, A., Mittal, A., & Shahare, P. (2024). Reduce, reuse, recycle: Circular economic principles, sustainability and entrepreneurship in developing ecosystems. *Journal of Small Business and Enterprise Development*, *31*(6), 1041–1066. DOI: 10.1108/JSBED-01-2023-0009

Maignan, I., & Ferrell, O. C. (2004). Corporate Social Responsibility and Marketing: An Integrative Framework. *Journal of the Academy of Marketing Science*, *32*(1), 3–19. DOI: 10.1177/0092070303258971

Malabi Eberhardt, L. C., van Stijn, A., Nygaard Rasmussen, F., Birkved, M., & Birgisdottir, H. (2020). Development of a life cycle assessment allocation approach for circular economy in the built environment. *Sustainability (Basel)*, *12*(22), 9579. DOI: 10.3390/su12229579

Manoharan, S., Pulimi, V. S. K., Kabir, G., & Ali, S. M. (2022). Contextual relationships among drivers and barriers to circular economy: An integrated ISM and DEMATEL approach. *Sustainable Operations and Computers*, *3*, 43–53. DOI 10.1016/j.susoc.2021.09.003

Maranesi, C., & De Giovanni, P. (2020). Modern circular economy: Corporate strategy, supply chain, and industrial symbiosis. *Sustainability (Basel), 12*(22), 9383. DOI: 10.3390/su12229383

Márquez, A. J. C., & Rutkowski, E. W. (2020). Waste management drivers towards a circular economy in the global south–The Colombian case. *Waste Management (New York, N.Y.), 110*, 53–65. DOI: 10.1016/j.wasman.2020.05.016 PMID: 32447195

Martin, B. (2018). New Zealand goes beyond GDP. *Green Economy Coalition*. https://www.greeneconomycoalition.org/news-and-resources/new-zealand-goes-beyond-gdp

Martin, A., Dmitriev, D., & Akeroyd, J. (2010). A resurgence of interest in Information Architecture. *International Journal of Information Management, 30*(1), 6–12. DOI: 10.1016/j.ijinfomgt.2009.11.008

Mayer, R. E. (2002). *Multimedia learning*. Cambridge University Press.

McDonough, W., & Braungart, M. (2002). *Cradle to Cradle: Remaking The Way We Make Things*. Vintage.

McGuire, W. J. (1961). Resistance to persuasion conferred by active and passive prior refutation of the same and alternative counterarguments. *Journal of Abnormal and Social Psychology, 63*(2), 326–332. DOI: 10.1037/h0048344

McGuire, W. J. (1976). Some internal psychological factors influencing consumer choice. *The Journal of Consumer Research, 2*(4), 302–319. DOI: 10.1086/208643

McKinsey & Company. (2022). Philanthropy's Role in Energy Transition.

McKinsey & Company. (2022). The dawn of the climate tech boom. https://www.mckinsey.com

McKinsey & Company. (2023). Additive manufacturing in automotive: The circular opportunity. https://www.mckinsey.com

McKinsey & Company. (2023). Digital platforms for industrial symbiosis. https://www.mckinsey.com

Mcloughlin, C. (2012). *Political Economy Analysis: Topic Guide*. GSDRC.

McLuhan, M. (1964). *Understanding Media, The Extensions of Man*. Massachusetts Institute of Technology.

McPhedran, R., Ratajczak, M., Mawby, M., King, E., Yang, Y., & Gold, N. (2023). Psychological inoculation protects against the social media infodemic. *Scientific Reports, 13*(1), 5780. DOI: 10.1038/s41598-023-32962-1 PMID: 37031339

McWilliams, A., Siegel, S. D., & Wright, P. M. (2006). Corporate Social Responsibility: Strategic Implications. *Journal of Management Studies*, *43*(1), 1–18. DOI: 10.1111/j.1467-6486.2006.00580.x

Meel, P., & Vishwakarma, D. K. (2020). Fake news, rumor, information pollution in social media and web: A contemporary survey of state-of-the-arts, challenges and opportunities. *Expert Systems with Applications*, *153*, 112986. DOI: 10.1016/j.eswa.2019.112986

Melece, L. (2016). Challenges and opportunities of circular economy and green economy. *Engineering for Rural Development*, *25*, 1162–1169.

Meredith, S. (2023). The world's in a 'polycrisis'—and these countries want to quash it by looking beyond GDP. *CNBC*. https://www.cnbc.com/2022/12/26/well-being-these-countries-are-looking-beyond-gdp-and-economic-growth.html

Meyer, B., Zill, A., Dilba, D., & Voermans, S. (2021). *Entspann dich*. TK-Stressstudie.

Mhatre, P., Panchal, R., Singh, A., & Bibyan, S. (2021). A systematic literature review on the circular economy initiatives in the European Union. *Sustainable Production and Consumption*, *26*, 187–202. DOI: 10.1016/j.spc.2020.09.008

Microsoft. (2023). Sustainability report: Carbon removal portfolio. https://www.microsoft.com/sustainability

Miehe, R., Fischer, E., Berndt, D., Herzog, A., Horbelt, J., Full, J., Bauernhansl, T., & Schenk, M. (2019). Enabling bidirectional real time interaction between biological and technical systems: Structural basics of a control oriented modeling of biology-technology-interfaces. *Procedia CIRP*, *81*, 63–68. DOI: 10.1016/j.procir.2019.03.012

MIT Energy Initiative. (2022). Venture capital's role in energy transition. https://energy.mit.edu

Mitchell, R. K., Agle, B. R., & Wood, D. J. (1997). Toward a Theory of Stakeholder Identification and Salience: Defining the Principle of Who and What Really Counts. *Academy of Management Review*, *22*(4), 853–886. DOI: 10.2307/259247

Modigliani, F., & Miller, M. H. (1958). The cost of capital, corporation finance and the theory of investment. *The American Economic Review*, *48*(3), 261–297.

Modirrousta-Galian, A., & Higham, P. A. (2022). How effective are gamified fake news interventions? Reanalyzing existing research with signal detection theory. *PsyArxiv Preprints*.

Moghrabi, I. A., Bhat, S. A., Szczuko, P., AlKhaled, R. A., & Dar, M. A. (2023). Digital transformation and its influence on sustainable manufacturing and business practices. *Sustainability (Basel), 15*(4), 3010. DOI: 10.3390/su15043010

Morelli, G., Pozzi, C., Gurrieri, A. R., Mele, M., Costantiello, A., & Magazzino, C. (2024). The role of circular economy in EU entrepreneurship: A deep learning experiment. *Journal of Economic Asymmetries, 30*, e00372. DOI: 10.1016/j.jeca.2024.e00372

Morgan Stanley. (2023). Sustainable REITs: Performance and growth trends. https://www.morganstanley.com

Morin, C. (2011). Neuromarketing: The new science of consumer behavior. *Society, 48*(2), 131–135. DOI: 10.1007/s12115-010-9408-1

Morningstar. (2022). Sustainable Funds U.S. Landscape Report. https://www.morningstar.com

Morsing, M., & Schultz, M. (2006). Corporate Social Responsibility Communication: Stakeholder Information, Response and Involvement Strategies. *Business Ethics (Oxford, England), 15*(4), 323–338. DOI: 10.1111/j.1467-8608.2006.00460.x

Morsing, M., Schultz, M., & Nielsen, K. U. (2008). The 'Catch 22' of communicating CSR: Findings from a Danish study. *Journal of Marketing Communications, 14*(2), 97–111. DOI: 10.1080/13527260701856608

Morville, P. (2005). *Ambient findability: What we find changes who we become*. O'Reilly Media, Inc.

Moser, R. M. B., & Gonzalez, L. (2015). Microfinance and climate change impacts: The case of Agroamigo in Brazil. *RAE, 55*(4), 397–407. DOI: 10.1590/S0034-759020150404

Mosleh, M., Martel, C., Eckles, D., & Rand, D. (2021, May). Perverse downstream consequences of debunking: Being corrected by another user for posting false political news increases subsequent sharing of low quality, partisan, and toxic content in a Twitter field experiment. In *proceedings of the 2021 CHI Conference on Human Factors in Computing Systems* (pp. 1-13). DOI: 10.1145/3411764.3445642

MSCI. (2023). MSCI ESG Impact Metrics Methodology. https://www.msci.com

Mufida, M. K., Snoun, A., Sarkis, J., Ait El-Cadi, A., Delot, T., & Trépanier, M. (2025). Circular Economy Practices for Data Management. *Engineering Proceedings, 97*(1), 34.

Mugge, R. (2011). The effect of a business-like personality on the perceived performance quality of products. *International Journal of Design*, *5*(3), 67–76.

Munteanu, I., Ionescu-Feleagă, L., & Ionescu, B. . (2024). Financial Strategies for Sustainability: Examining the Circular Economy Perspective. *Sustainability (Basel)*, *16*(20), 8942. DOI: 10.3390/su16208942

Naidoo, R., & Fisher, B. (2020). Reset sustainable development goals for a pandemic world. *Nature*, *583*(7815), 198–201. DOI: 10.1038/d41586-020-01999-x PMID: 32632244

Nardi, B. A., & O'Day, L. (1999). Information Ecology.

NAREIT. (2023). ESG reporting guidelines for REITs. https://www.reit.com

National Geographic. (2023, January). The waste revolution.

Nemhauser, G. L., & Ullmann, Z. (1969). Discrete dynamic programming and capital allocation. *Management Science*, *15*(9), 494–505. DOI: 10.1287/mnsc.15.9.494

Nevatia, V. (2022). Sovereign Green Bonds: Reducing Climate Capital Costs in Emerging Markets. *Available at SSRN* 4983252. DOI: 10.2139/ssrn.4983252

Nielsen, I. B., & Hakala, H. (2022). Circular business strategies and quality of life. *Sustainability (Basel)*, *14*(3), 1782. DOI: 10.3390/su14031782

Nielsen, J. (2003). IM, Not IP (Information Pollution) A steady dose of realtime interruptions is toxic to anyone's health. *ACM Queue; Tomorrow's Computing Today*, *1*(8), 76–75. DOI: 10.1145/966712.966731

Nilashi, M., Yadegaridehkordi, E., Samad, S., Mardani, A., Ahani, A., Aljojo, N., Razali, N. S., & Tajuddin, T. (2020). Decision to adopt neuromarketing techniques for sustainable product marketing: A fuzzy decision-making approach. *Symmetry*, *12*(2), 305. DOI: 10.3390/sym12020305

Nogueira, E., Gomes, S., & Lopes, J. M. (2023). Triple bottom line, sustainability, and economic development: What binds them together? A bibliometric approach. *Sustainability (Basel)*, *15*(8), 6706. DOI: 10.3390/su15086706

Norges Bank Investment Management (NBIM). (2022). Government Pension Fund Global annual report. https://www.nbim.no

Nunden, N., Abbana, S., Marimuthu, F., & Sentoo, N. (2022). An assessment of management skills on capital budgeting planning and practices: Evidence from the small and medium enterprise sector. *Cogent Business & Management*, *9*(1), 2136481. DOI: 10.1080/23311975.2022.2136481

Nyhan, B. (2017). Why the fact-checking at Facebook needs to be checked. *New York Times*.

OECD. (2023). *Green Finance and Investment: Global Taxonomies and ESG Regulation*. https://www.oecd.org/en/publications/green-finance-and-investment_24090344.html

Ogunmakinde, O. E., Egbelakin, T., & Sher, W. (2022). Contributions of the circular economy to the UN sustainable development goals through sustainable construction. *Resources, Conservation and Recycling*, *178*, 106023. DOI: 10.1016/j.resconrec.2021.106023

Oliver, R. L. (1999). Whence consumer loyalty? *Journal of Marketing*, *63*(Special Issue), 33–44. DOI: 10.1177/00222429990634s105

Olson, N., Nolin, J. M., & Nelhans, G. (2015). Semantic web, ubiquitous computing, or internet of things? A macro-analysis of scholarly publications. *The Journal of Documentation*, *71*(5), 884–916. DOI: 10.1108/JD-03-2013-0033

Opferkuch, K., Caeiro, S., Salomone, R., & Ramos, T. B. (2022). Circular economy disclosure in corporate sustainability reports: The case of European companies in sustainability rankings. *Sustainable Production and Consumption*, *32*, 436–456. DOI: 10.1016/j.spc.2022.05.003

Orman, L. (1984). Fighting information pollution with decision support systems. *Journal of Management Information Systems*, *1*(2), 64–71. DOI: 10.1080/07421222.1984.11517704

Ormazabal, M., Prieto-Sandoval, V., Puga-Leal, R., & Jaca, C. (2018). Circular economy in Spanish SMEs: Challenges and opportunities. *Journal of Cleaner Production*, *185*, 157–167. DOI: 10.1016/j.jclepro.2018.03.031

Orth, U. R., & Malkewitz, K. (2008). Holistic package design and consumer brand impressions. *Journal of Marketing*, *72*(3), 64–81. DOI: 10.1509/JMKG.72.3.064

Ortiz-de-Montellano, C. G. S., Samani, P., & van der Meer, Y. (2023). How can the circular economy support the advancement of the Sustainable Development Goals (SDGs)? A comprehensive analysis. *Sustainable Production and Consumption*, *40*, 352–362. DOI: 10.1016/j.spc.2023.07.003

Ostrom, E. (2000). Collective action and the evolution of social norms. *The Journal of Economic Perspectives*, *14*(3), 137–158. DOI: 10.1257/jep.14.3.137

Ozili, P. K. (2021). Circular economy, banks, and other financial institutions: What's in it for them? *Circular Economy and Sustainability*, *1*(3), 787–798. DOI: 10.1007/s43615-021-00043-y

Pagoropoulos, A., Pigosso, D. C., & McAloone, T. C. (2017). The emergent role of digital technologies in the Circular Economy: A review. *Procedia CIRP*, *64*, 19–24. DOI: 10.1016/j.procir.2017.02.047

Palea, V., Santhià, C., & Miazza, A. (2023). Are circular economy strategies economically successful? Evidence from a longitudinal panel. *Journal of Environmental Management*, *337*, 117726. DOI: 10.1016/j.jenvman.2023.117726 PMID: 36933534

Pandita, R. (2014). Information pollution, a mounting threat: Internet a major causality. *Journal of Information Science Theory and Practice*, *2*(4), 49–60. DOI: 10.1633/JISTaP.2014.2.4.4

Pan, S. Y., Du, M. A., Huang, I. T., Liu, I. H., Chang, E. E., & Chiang, P. C. (2015). Strategies on implementation of waste-to-energy (WTE) supply chain for circular economy system: A review. *Journal of Cleaner Production*, *108*, 409–421. DOI: 10.1016/j.jclepro.2015.06.124

Pan, X., Wong, C. W., Wong, C. Y., Boon-itt, S., & Li, C. (2024). The influences of Circular Economy practices on manufacturing firm's performance: A meta-analytic structural equation modeling study. *International Journal of Production Economics*, *273*, 109267. DOI: 10.1016/j.ijpe.2024.109267

Paribas, B. N. P. (2023). Sustainable finance market trends Q2 2023. https://cib.bnpparibas.com

Patagonia. (2022). Built to last: Our design philosophy. https://www.patagonia.com

Pearce, D. W., & Turner, R. K. (1989). *Economics of natural resources and the environment*. Johns Hopkins University Press. DOI: 10.56021/9780801839863

Pennycook, G., & Rand, D. G. (2019). Lazy, not biased: Susceptibility to partisan fake news is better explained by lack of reasoning than by motivated reasoning. *Cognition*, *188*, 39–50. DOI: 10.1016/j.cognition.2018.06.011 PMID: 29935897

Pennycook, G., & Rand, D. G. (2022). Accuracy prompts are a replicable and generalizable approach for reducing the spread of misinformation. *Nature Communications*, *13*(1), 2333. DOI: 10.1038/s41467-022-30073-5 PMID: 35484277

Pialot, O., Millet, D., Bisiaux, J., & Upgradable, P. S. S. (2017). Clarifying a new concept of sustainable consumption/production based on upgradability. *Journal of Cleaner Production*, *141*, 538–550. DOI: 10.1016/j.jclepro.2016.08.161

Pianta, M., & Lucchese, M. (2020). Rethinking the European Green Deal: An Industrial Policy for a Just Transition in Europe. *The Review of Radical Political Economics*, *52*(4), 633–641. DOI: 10.1177/0486613420938207

Pieters, R., Wedel, M., & Batra, R. (2010). The stopping power of advertising: Measures and effects of visual complexity. *Journal of Marketing*, *74*(5), 48–60. DOI: 10.1509/jmkg.74.5.048

Pimenova, E. M. (2021). Specificity of sustainability assessment for industrial enterprise functioning in the digital economy. In *Engineering economics: Decisions and solutions from Eurasian perspective* (pp. 3–10). Springer International Publishing. DOI: 10.1007/978-3-030-53277-2_1

Pinchot, A., & Christianson, G. (2020). *System disruption and sustainable finance: Navigating economic transitions*. Stanford Social Innovation Review. https://ssir.org/articles/entry/system_disruption_and_sustainable_finance

Piscitelli, G., Ferazzoli, A., Petrillo, A., Cioffi, R., Parmentola, A., & Travaglioni, M. (2020). Circular economy models in the industry 4.0 era: A review of the last decade. *Procedia Manufacturing*, *42*, 227–234. DOI: 10.1016/j.promfg.2020.02.074

PitchBook. (2023). Emerging Technologies in Sustainable Transportation Report.

Plassmann, H., Ramsøy, T. Z., & Milosavljevic, M. (2012). Branding the brain: A critical review and outlook. *Journal of Consumer Psychology*, *22*(1), 18–36. DOI: 10.1016/j.jcps.2011.11.010

Podnar, K. (2008). Communicating Corporate Social Responsibility. *Journal of Marketing Communications*, *14*(2), 75–81. DOI: 10.1080/13527260701856350

Polanyi, K. (2001). *The Great Transformation: The Political and Economic Origins of Our Time*. Beacon Press.

Poole, A. (2011). *How-to notes: Political economy assessments at sector and project levels*. Government of Canada, GAC in Projects.

Poulton, C. (2012) Democratisation and the Political Economy of Agricultural Policy in Africa, FAC Working Paper 43, Brighton: Future Agricultures Consortium.

Prause, G., & Atari, S. (2017). On sustainable production networks for Industry 4.0. *Entrepreneurship and Sustainability Issues*, *4*(4), 421–431. DOI: 10.9770/jesi.2017.4.4(2)

Preston, S. H. (2007). The changing relation between mortality and level of economic development. *International Journal of Epidemiology*, *36*(3), 484–490. DOI: 10.1093/ije/dym075

Pretus, C., Servin-Barthet, C., Harris, E., Brady, W., Vilarroya, O., & Van Bavel, J. (2022). The role of political devotion in sharing partisan misinformation.

Pricewaterhouse Coopers Consultants (PWC). (2013). Exploring green finance incentives in China. China: PwC.

Raj, A., & Choudhary, B. (2025). Amalgamation of Corporate Social Responsibility With the Principles of the Circular Economy for Sustainable Growth. In *Driving Business Success Through Eco-Friendly Strategies* (pp. 21–46). IGI Global Scientific Publishing., DOI: 10.4018/979-8-3693-9750-3.ch002

Rajabzadeh, A., Nejadirani, F., Soroodian, R., & Kermani, R. A. (2011). Informational overload; roots and consequences. *Australian Journal of Basic and Applied Sciences*, *5*(12), 353–359.

Ramli, I. M., & Kasih, M. C. (2024). *Integrative Report on Implementation of the Circular Economy in ASEAN*. Economic Research Institute for ASEAN and East Asia (ERIA). Retrieved from www.eria.org/uploads/Integrative-Report-on-Implementation-of-the-Circular-Economy-in-ASEAN.pdf

Rasmussen Pennington, D. (2016). "The most passionate cover I've seen": Emotional information in fan-created U2 music videos. *The Journal of Documentation*, *72*(3), 569–590. DOI: 10.1108/JD-07-2015-0086

Rathje, S., Roozenbeek, J., Traberg, C. S., Van Bavel, J. J., & Svd, L. (2022). Letter to the editors of Psychological Science: Meta-analysis reveals that accuracy nudges have little to no effect for US conservatives: Regarding Pennycook et al.(2020).

Raworth, K. (2017). *Doughnut economics: Seven ways to think like a 21st-century economist*. Chelsea Green Publishing.

Raza, R., & Quaye-Kumah, N. (2024). *People's Republic of China Country strategic opportunities programme 2025–2030*. IFAD.

Reber, R., & Schwarz, N. (1999). Effects of perceptual fluency on judgments of truth. *Consciousness and Cognition*, *8*(3), 338–342. DOI: 10.1006/ccog.1999.0386

Reclaim Finance. (2023). Transition bonds: Greenwashing or genuine progress? https://www.reclaimfinance.org

Reike, D. (2024). *Understanding the circular economy: From synthesized conceptual foundations to system-oriented progress measurement* [Doctoral thesis, Utrecht University].

Reimann, M., Zaichkowsky, J. L., Neuhaus, C., Bender, T., & Weber, B. (2010). Aesthetic package design: A behavioral, neural, and psychological investigation. *Journal of Consumer Psychology*, *20*(4), 431–441. DOI: 10.1016/j.jcps.2010.06.009

Relano, F., Paulet, E., & Mavoori, H. (2024). Addressing the climate–finance interaction in a new light: From green to brown assets disclosure in the banking industry. *Strategic Change*, *33*(5), 399–416. DOI: 10.1002/jsc.2593

Resourcify, (2023, February 16). Find value in your waste: Circularity Benefits in Business. https://www.resourcify.com/blog/circular-economy-benefits-business#:~:text=The%20circular%20economy%20action%20plan,for%20as%20long%20as%20possible

Rezayi, S., Balakrishnan, V., Arabnia, S., & Arabnia, H. R. (2018, December). Fake news and cyberbullying in the modern era. In *2018 International Conference on Computational Science and Computational Intelligence (CSCI)* (pp. 7-12). IEEE. DOI: 10.1109/CSCI46756.2018.00010

Riedl, A., & Smeets, P. (2017). Why do investors hold socially responsible mutual funds? *The Journal of Finance*, *72*(6), 2505–2550. DOI: 10.1111/jofi.12547

Riedl, A., & Smeets, P. (2021). Social preferences and portfolio choice: Evidence from ESG ETFs. *The Journal of Finance*, *76*(6), 1–42.

Rieh, S. Y., & Danielson, D. R. (2007). Credibility: A multidisciplinary framework.

Ristoski, P., & Paulheim, H. (2016). Semantic Web in data mining and knowledge discovery: A comprehensive survey. *Journal of Web Semantics*, *36*, 1–22. DOI: 10.1016/j.websem.2016.01.001

Ritzén, S., & Sandström, G. Ö. (2017). Barriers to the Circular Economy–integration of perspectives and domains. *Procedia CIRP*, *64*, 7–12. DOI: 10.1016/j.procir.2017.03.005

Rizos, V., Behrens, A., Van der Gaast, W., Hofman, E., Ioannou, A., Kafyeke, T., Flamos, A., Rinaldi, R., Papadelis, S., Hirschnitz-Garbers, M., & Topi, C. (2016). Implementation of circular economy business models by small and medium-sized enterprises (SMEs): Barriers and enablers. *Sustainability (Basel)*, *8*(11), 1212. DOI: 10.3390/su8111212

Robertson, R. (1995). Glocalization: Time-space and homogeneity-heterogeneity. In Featherstone, M., Lash, S., & Robertson, R. (Eds.), *Global modernities* (pp. 25–44). SAGE. DOI: 10.4135/9781446250563.n2

Rockström, J., Steffen, W., Noone, K., Persson, Å., Chapin, F. S.III, Lambin, E. F., Lenton, T. M., Scheffer, M., Folke, C., Schellnhuber, H. J., Nykvist, B., de Wit, C. A., Hughes, T., van der Leeuw, S., Rodhe, H., Sörlin, S., Snyder, P. K., Costanza, R., Svedin, U., & Foley, J. A. (2009). A safe operating space for humanity. *Nature*, *461*(7263), 472–475. DOI: 10.1038/461472a

Rocky Mountain Institute. (2023). Lowering clean energy financing costs. https://rmi.org

Rodin, J., & Brandenburg, M. (2021). *The Power of Impact Investing*. Wharton School Press.

Rodríguez-Antón, J. M., Rubio-Andrada, L., Celemín-Pedroche, M. S., & Ruíz-Peñalver, S. M. (2022). From the circular economy to the sustainable development goals in the European Union: An empirical comparison. *International Environmental Agreement: Politics, Law and Economics*, *22*(1), 67–95. DOI: 10.1007/s10784-021-09553-4 PMID: 34744532

Rojas, J.-C., Contero, M., Vergara, M., & Higuera-Trujillo, J. L. (2024). Using event-related potentials to evidence the visual and semantic impact: A pilot study with N400 effect and food packaging. *Foods*, *13*(12), 1876. DOI: 10.3390/foods13121876

Roozenbeek, J., Freeman, A. L., & Van Der Linden, S. (2021). How accurate are accuracy-nudge interventions? A preregistered direct replication of Pennycook et al.(2020). *Psychological Science*, *32*(7), 1169–1178. DOI: 10.1177/09567976211024535 PMID: 34114521

Roozenbeek, J., Van Der Linden, S., Goldberg, B., Rathje, S., & Lewandowsky, S. (2022). Psychological inoculation improves resilience against misinformation on social media. *Science Advances*, *8*(34), eabo6254. DOI: 10.1126/sciadv.abo6254 PMID: 36001675

Roy, M. (2021). Chapter 7-circular economy: a new sustainable management paradigm. *Sustainable development strategies*, 189-214.

Saad, M. (2023). How a Novel Stock Valuation Model Outperforms Traditional Models in Information Efficiency: Implications for Shareholders and Regulators. *Journal of Financial Economics*, *11*(2), 113–130. DOI: 10.12691/jfe-11-2-5

Saad, M., Bajalan, S., & Tehrani, R. (2025). Integrating and updating the stock market regulation: A significant approach to enhance the information efficiency of the stock market. *Interdisciplinary Journal of Management Studies, 18*(4), 669-684. DOI: 10.22059/ijms.2025.379692.676885

Saarinen, A., & Aarikka-Stenroos, L. (2023). Financing-related drivers and barriers for circular economy business: Developing a conceptual model from a field study. *Circular Economy and Sustainability*, *3*(3), 1187–1211. DOI: 10.1007/s43615-022-00222-5

Sabeeh, Z. A., & Ismail, Z. (2013, November). Effects of information overload on productivity in enterprises: a literature review. In *2013 International Conference on Research and Innovation in Information Systems (ICRIIS)* (pp. 210-214). IEEE. DOI: 10.1109/ICRIIS.2013.6716710

Safdie, S. (2024, March 28). Circular Economy: Definition and Principles. https://greenly.earth/en-us/blog/company-guide/circular-economy-definition-and-principles

Samson, K., & Kostyszyn, P. (2015). Effects of cognitive load on trusting behavior–an experiment using the trust game. *PLoS One*, *10*(5), e0127680. DOI: 10.1371/journal.pone.0127680 PMID: 26010489

Sanchez, B., & Haas, C. (2018). Capital project planning for a circular economy. *Construction Management and Economics*, *36*(6), 303–312. DOI: 10.1080/01446193.2018.1435895

Sarkhoshkalat, M. M., Afkham, A., Bonyadi Manesh, M., & Sarkhosh, M. (2024). Circular Economy and the Recycling of E-Waste. In *New Technologies for Energy Transition Based on Sustainable Development Goals: Factors Contributing to Global Warming* (pp. 319-354). Singapore: Springer Nature. DOI: 10.1007/978-981-97-2527-4_16

Sarra, J. (2020). Sustainable Finance and the Move to a Circular Economy. *From Ideas to Action*, 249-294. https://doi.org/DOI: 10.1093/oso/9780198852308.003.0008

Schmitt, J. B., Debbelt, C. A., & Schneider, F. M. (2018). Too much information? Predictors of information overload in the context of online news exposure. *Information Communication and Society*, *21*(8), 1151–1167. DOI: 10.1080/1369118X.2017.1305427

Schöggl, J. P., Stumpf, L., & Baumgartner, R. J. (2020). The narrative of sustainability and circular economy-A longitudinal review of two decades of research. *Resources, Conservation and Recycling*, *163*, 105073. DOI: 10.1016/j.resconrec.2020.105073

Schröder, P., & Barrie, J. (2024). How the circular economy can revive the Sustainable Development Goals. *Chatham House*. https://www.chathamhouse.org/2024/09/how-circular-economy-can-revive-sustainable-development-goals

Schroeder, P., Anggraeni, K., & Weber, U. (2019). The relevance of circular economy practices to the sustainable development goals. *Journal of Industrial Ecology*, *23*(1), 77–95. DOI: 10.1111/jiec.12732

Schumacher, K. A., & Green, M. L. (2023). Circular economy in a high-tech world. *Circular Economy and Sustainability*, *3*(2), 619–642. DOI: 10.1007/s43615-022-00220-7

Scorrano, P., Borin, E., Thrassou, A., Cavallo, F., & Mastroleo, G. (2025). Knowledge sharing between businesses and stakeholders for systemic and sustainable regional development. Insights in the agri-food sector. *Journal of Knowledge Management*, *29*(4), 1278–1300. DOI: 10.1108/JKM-05-2024-0517

Securities and Exchange Commission. (2023). ABS disclosure and reporting requirements. https://www.sec.gov

Sen, A. (1987). *The standard of living – The Tanner lecture 1985*. Cambridge University Press.

Serrat, O. (2011). *Political economy analysis for development effectiveness*. Asian Development Bank. http://digitalcommons.ilr.cornell.edu/intl/186/

Serrat, O. (2017). Political Economy Analysis for Development Effectiveness. In *Knowledge Solutions* (pp. 207–222). Springer. DOI: 10.1007/978-981-10-0983-9_21

Setyowati, A. B. (2020). Governing sustainable finance: Insights from Indonesia's peer emulation strategies. *Climate Policy*, *20*(8), 1015–1030. DOI: 10.1080/14693062.2020.1795321

Shah, I. H., Dong, L., & Park, H. S. (2020). Tracking urban sustainability transition: An eco-efficiency analysis on eco-industrial development in Ulsan, Korea. *Journal of Cleaner Production*, *262*, 121286. DOI: 10.1016/j.jclepro.2020.121286

Shams, L., & Seitz, A. R. (2008). Benefits of multisensory learning. *Trends in Cognitive Sciences*, *12*(11), 411–417. DOI: 10.1016/j.tics.2008.07.006

Sharma, H. B., Vanapalli, K. R., Samal, B., Cheela, V. S., Dubey, B. K., & Bhattacharya, J. (2021). Circular economy approach in solid waste management system to achieve UN-SDGs: Solutions for post-COVID recovery. *The Science of the Total Environment*, *800*, 149605. DOI: 10.1016/j.scitotenv.2021.149605 PMID: 34426367

Shavkatov, N., Abdurakhimova, D., Sherkuziyeva, N., Omonov, S., & Rakhmedova, M. (2024). *Circular economy practices and their effect on corporate financial performance*. Economic Annals-XXI., DOI: 10.21003/ea.V207-01

Shierholz, H., & Zipperer, B. (2017). Here is what's at stake with the conflict of interest ('fiduciary') rule.

Siddi, M. (2020). The European Green Deal: Asseasing its current state and future implementation. Upi Report, 114.

Sinanoglu, S., & Breuer, A. (2024). *Countering information pollution to protect democracy* (No. 29/2024). IDOS Policy Brief.

Singer, P. (2015). Are you ready for Industry 4.0? *Solid State Technology, 58*(8), 2–2.

Smol, M., Kulczycka, J., & Avdiushchenko, A. (2017). Circular economy indicators in relation to eco-innovation in European regions. *Clean Technologies and Environmental Policy, 19*(3), 669–678. DOI: 10.1007/s10098-016-1323-8

Smol, M., Kulczycka, J., Henclik, A., Gorazda, K., & Wzorek, Z. (2015). The possible use of sewage sludge ash (SSA) in the construction industry as a way towards a circular economy. *Journal of Cleaner Production, 95*, 45–54. DOI: 10.1016/j.jclepro.2015.02.051

Solar Energy Industries Association. (2023). Solar loan performance metrics. https://www.seia.org

Soucek, R., & Moser, K. (2010). Coping with information overload in email communication: Evaluation of a training intervention. *Computers in Human Behavior, 26*(6), 1458–1466. DOI: 10.1016/j.chb.2010.04.024

Spry, A., Pappu, R., & Cornwell, T. B. (2011). Celebrity endorsement, brand credibility and brand equity. *European Journal of Marketing, 45*(6), 882–909. DOI: 10.1108/03090561111119958

Spunt, R. P. (2015). Dual-Process Theories in Social Cognitive Neuroscience. In Toga, A. W. (Ed.), *Brain Mapping: An Encyclopedic Reference* (Vol. 3, pp. 211–215). Academic Press: Elsevier. DOI: 10.1016/B978-0-12-397025-1.00181-0

Stahel, W. R. (2016). The circular economy. *Nature, 531*(7595), 435–438. DOI: 10.1038/531435a PMID: 27008952

Stahel, W. R., & Reday-Mulvey, G. (1981). *Jobs for tomorrow: The potential for substituting manpower for energy*. Vantage Press.

Stanford Social Innovation Review. (2021). "When Grants Outperform Investments."

Stanley, O. E. (2021). Information overload: Causes, symptoms, consequences and solutions. *Asian Journal of Information Science and Technology, 11*(2), 1–6. DOI: 10.51983/ajist-2021.11.2.2887

Stanton, S. J., Sinnott-Armstrong, W., & Huettel, S. A. (2017). Neuromarketing: Ethical implications of its use and potential misuse. *Journal of Business Ethics*, *144*(4), 799–811. DOI: 10.1007/s10551-016-3059-0

Stasiuk-Piekarska, A., Hordyńska, M., & Michalska, M. (2024). The Usefulness of Cleaner Production Projects as an Element of the Initial Assessment of the Circularity of SMEs in the Context of Obtaining Funds Supporting the Implementation of the Circular Economy. *Sustainability (Basel)*, *16*(12), 4951. DOI: 10.3390/su16124951

Stavins, R. N. (2023). *The future of carbon pricing*. Harvard Environmental Economics Program.

Stewart, R., & Niero, M. (2018). Circular economy in corporate sustainability strategies: A review of corporate sustainability reports in the fast-moving consumer goods sector. *Business Strategy and the Environment*, *27*(7), 1005–1022. DOI: 10.1002/bse.2048

Stiglitz, J. E., Sen, A., & Fitoussi, J. P. (2009). *Report by the Commission on the Measurement of Economic Performance and Social Progress*. https://ec.europa.eu/eurostat/documents/8131721/8131772/Stiglitz-Sen-Fitoussi-Commission-report.pdf

Stirling, A. (2006). Precaution, foresight and sustainability: reflection and reflexivity in the governance of science and technology. In *Reflexive governance for sustainable development*. Edward Elgar Publishing. DOI: 10.4337/9781847200266.00020

Strange, S. (1970). International economics and international relations: A case of mutual neglect. *International Affairs*, *46*(2), 304–315. DOI: 10.2307/2613829

Sturgeon, T. J. (2021). Upgrading strategies for the digital economy. *Global Strategy Journal*, *11*(1), 34–57. DOI: 10.1002/gsj.1364

Suárez-Eiroa, B., Fernández, E., Méndez-Martínez, G., & Soto-Oñate, D. (2019). Operational principles of circular economy for sustainable development: Linking theory and practice. *Journal of Cleaner Production*, *214*, 952–961. DOI: 10.1016/j.jclepro.2018.12.271

Su, B., Heshmati, A., Geng, Y., & Yu, X. (2013). A review of the circular economy in China: Moving from rhetoric to implementation. *Journal of Cleaner Production*, *42*, 215–227. DOI: 10.1016/j.jclepro.2012.11.020

Sun, M., Li, J., Yang, C., Schmidt, G. A., Bambacus, M., Cahalan, R., Huang, Q., Xu, C., Noble, E., & Li, Z. (2012). A web-based geovisual analytical system for climate studies. *Future Internet*, *4*(4), 1069–1085. DOI: 10.3390/fi4041069

Surla, S. M. (2007). An information architecture approach to building a much better digital library. *Bulletin of the American Society for Information Science, 33*(6), 41–43. DOI: 10.1002/bult.2007.1720330612

Sustainability Directory. (2025, April 24). What Are the Key Barriers to Circular Economy Adoption? URL: https://climate.sustainability-directory.com/question/what-are-the-key-barriers-to-circular-economy-adoption/

Swar, B., Hameed, T., & Reychav, I. (2017). Information overload, psychological ill-being, and behavioral intention to continue online healthcare information search. *Computers in Human Behavior, 70*, 416–425. DOI: 10.1016/j.chb.2016.12.068

Sweeney, L., & Coughlan, J. (2008). Do Different Industries Report Corporate Social Responsibility Differently? An Investigation Through the Lens of Stakeholder Theory. *Journal of Marketing Communications, 14*(2), 113–124. DOI: 10.1080/13527260701856657

Sweller, J. (1988). Cognitive load during problem solving: Effects on learning. *Cognitive Science, 12*(2), 257–285. DOI: 10.1207/s15516709cog1202_4

Sweller, J. (1994). Cognitive load theory, learning difficulty, and instructional design. *Learning and Instruction, 4*(4), 295–312. DOI: 10.1016/0959-4752(94)90003-5

Sweller, J. (2011). Cognitive load theory. []. Academic Press.]. *Psychology of Learning and Motivation, 55*, 37–76. DOI: 10.1016/B978-0-12-387691-1.00002-8

Swire-Thompson, B., DeGutis, J., & Lazer, D. (2020). Searching for the backfire effect: Measurement and design considerations. *Journal of Applied Research in Memory and Cognition, 9*(3), 286–299. DOI: 10.1016/j.jarmac.2020.06.006 PMID: 32905023

Sylvain, F. R. A. C. C. O. L. A. (2021). OECD Science, Technology and Innovation Outlook 2021-Perspectivas de la OCDE sobre.

Tabas, A. M., Rehman, M. A., Khitous, F., & Urbinati, A. (2025). Stakeholder and customer engagement in circular economy ecosystems: A systematic literature review and research agenda. *Business Strategy and the Environment, 34*(1), 402–416. DOI: 10.1002/bse.3989

Taera, E. G., & Lakner, Z. (2025). Sustainable Finance: Bridging Circular Economy Goals and Financial Inclusion in Developing Economies. *WORLD (Oakland, Calif.), 6*(2), 44. DOI: 10.3390/world6020044

Takacs, F., Brunner, D., & Frankenberger, K. (2022). Barriers to a circular economy in small-and medium-sized enterprises and their integration in a sustainable strategic management framework. *Journal of Cleaner Production*, *362*, 132227. DOI: 10.1016/j.jclepro.2022.132227

Talwar, S., Dhir, A., Kaur, P., Zafar, N., & Alrasheedy, M. (2019). Why do people share fake news? Associations between the dark side of social media use and fake news sharing behavior. *Journal of Retailing and Consumer Services*, *51*, 72–82. DOI: 10.1016/j.jretconser.2019.05.026

Tan, W. K., & Kuo, P. C. (2019). The consequences of online information overload confusion in tourism.

Tantia, V., & Sukanya, R. (2024). Reinventing the Business Model to Navigate the Evolving Business Landscape. In *ESG and Ecosystem Services for Sustainability* (pp. 259–282). IGI Global. DOI: 10.4018/979-8-3693-3771-4.ch010

Taxonomy, E. U. (2020). EU taxonomy for sustainable activities. *Available at: EU taxonomy for sustainable activities–European Commission (europa. eu).*

TechCrunch. (2023, May 15). Fairphone's $90M funding round signals shift toward repairable tech. https://techcrunch.com

Teixeira, A. A., Jabbour, C. J. C., de Sousa Jabbour, A. B. L., Latan, H., & De Oliveira, J. H. C. (2016). Green training and green supply chain management: Evidence from Brazilian firms. *Journal of Cleaner Production*, *116*, 170–176. DOI: 10.1016/j.jclepro.2015.12.061

Teixeira, T., Wedel, M., & Pieters, R. (2012). Emotion-induced engagement in Internet video advertisements. *JMR, Journal of Marketing Research*, *49*(2), 144–159. DOI: 10.1509/jmr.10.0207

Thaler, R. H., & Sunstein, C. R. (2009). *Nudge: Improving decisions about health, wealth, and happiness*. Penguin.

The World Bank. (2012). *Operationalizing political economy: Urban bus operations in Dhaka*. https://documents.worldbank.org/en/publication/documents-reports/documentdetail/693780BRI0P1080Bus0Operations0final

Thorne, J., & Vlachos, A. (2018). Automated fact checking: Task formulations, methods and future directions. *arXiv preprint arXiv:1806.07687*.

Tian, H. (2018). Establishing green finance system to support the circular economy. In *Industry 4.0* (pp. 203–210). Empowering ASEAN for the Circular Economy.

Todaro, D. L., & Torelli, R. (2024). From greenwashing to ESG-washing: A focus on the circular economy field. *Corporate Social Responsibility and Environmental Management*, *31*(5), 4034–4046. DOI: 10.1002/csr.2786

To, M. H., Uisan, K., Ok, Y. S., Pleissner, D., & Lin, C. S. K. (2019). Recent trends in green and sustainable chemistry: Rethinking textile waste in a circular economy. *Current Opinion in Green and Sustainable Chemistry*, *20*, 1–10. DOI: 10.1016/j.cogsc.2019.06.002

Tóth, G. (2019). Circular economy and its comparison with 14 other business sustainability movements. *Resources*, *8*(4), 159. DOI: 10.3390/resources8040159

Toxopeus, H., Achterberg, E., & Polzin, F. (2021). How can firms access bank finance for circular business model innovation? *Business Strategy and the Environment*, *30*(6), 2773–2795. DOI: 10.1002/bse.2893

Traberg, C. S., Roozenbeek, J., & van der Linden, S. (2022). Psychological inoculation against misinformation: Current evidence and future

Trevisan, A. H., Lobo, A., Guzzo, D., de Vasconcelos Gomes, L. A., & Mascarenhas, J. (2023). Barriers to employing digital technologies for a circular economy: A multi-level perspective. *Journal of Environmental Management*, *332*, 117437. DOI: 10.1016/j.jenvman.2023.117437 PMID: 36801533

Tseng, M. L., Chiu, A. S., & Liang, D. (2018). Sustainable consumption and production in business decision-making models. *Resources, Conservation and Recycling*, *128*, 118–121. DOI: 10.1016/j.resconrec.2017.02.014

Tuboalabo, A., Buinwi, U., Okatta, C. G., Johnson, E., & Buinwi, J. A. (2024). Circular economy integration in traditional business models: Strategies and outcomes. *Finance & Accounting Research Journal*, *6*(6), 1105–1123. DOI: 10.51594/farj.v6i6.1245

Tukker, A. (2015). Product services for a resource-efficient and circular economy–a review. *Journal of Cleaner Production*, *97*, 76–91. DOI: 10.1016/j.jclepro.2013.11.049

U.S. Department of Energy. (2023). Technology readiness levels handbook. https://www.energy.gov

U.S. Environmental Protection Agency. (2023). Green buildings and investment opportunities. https://www.epa.gov

Ugli, R. D. J., & Ugli, K. A. M. (2020). The Concept of Digital Economy in Modern Life and Its Application to Life. *JournalNX*, *6*(05), 118–121.

Uğraş, T. (2015). Bilgi tüketicileri ve üreticileri. In Gülseçen, S. (Ed.), *Bilgi yönetimi, Bilgi Türeticileri, Büyük Veri, İnovasyon ve Kurumsal Zeka* (pp. 17–29). Papatya Bilim Üniversite Yayıncılığı.

Underhill, G. R. D. (2000). State, market, and global political economy: Genealogy of an (inter) discipline. *International Affairs*, *76*(4), 805–824. DOI: 10.1111/1468-2346.00166

Underwood, R. L. (2003). The communicative power of product packaging: Creating brand identity via lived and mediated experience. *Journal of Marketing Theory and Practice*, *11*(1), 62–76. DOI: 10.1080/10696679.2003.11501933

UNEP. (2021). *The circularity transition: leaving no one behind.* Retrieved April 2025, from https://www.unep.org/news-and-stories/speech/circularity-transition-leaving-no-one-behind

UNEP. (2023). *Unlocking Circular Economy Finance in Latin America and the Caribbean: The Catalyst for a Positive Change.* Retrieved from https://www.unepfi.org/publications/unlocking-circular-economy-finance-in-latin-america-and-the-caribbean-the-catalyst-for-a-positive-change/

UNEP. (2024). *Circular Economy as an Enabler for Responsible Banking.* Retrieved April 2025, from https://www.unepfi.org/wordpress/wp-content/uploads/2024/07/PRB_CE-Climate-Nexus_Guidance-Doc.pdf

UNEP. (2024). *Circular Economy as an Enabler for Responsible Banking:Leveraging the Nexus between Circularity and Sustainability Impact.* UNEP. Retrieved April 2025, from https://www.unepfi.org/wordpress/wp-content/uploads/2024/07/PRB_CE-Nexus_Guidance-Doc.pdf

United Nations Environment Programme Finance Initiative (UNEP FI). (2007). *'Green Financial Products & Services: Current State of Play and Future Opportunities', A Report of the North American Task Force (NATF) of the UNEP*. UNEP FI.

United Nations Principles for Responsible Investment (UNPRI). (2023). Global trends in sustainable investing. https://www.unpri.org

Unsworth, S., & Williams, G. (2011). *Using Political Economy Analysis to improve EU Development Effectiveness*. URL: https://thepolicypractice.com/using-political-economy-analysis-improve-development-effectiveness-unsworth-and-williams-2011

Unver, A. (2020). *Fact-checkers and fact-checking in Turkey*. EDAM Research Reports.

Upadhyay, A., Mukhuty, S., Kumar, V., & Kazancoglu, Y. (2021). Blockchain technology and the circular economy: Implications for sustainability and social responsibility. *Journal of Cleaner Production, 293*, 126130. DOI: 10.1016/j.jclepro.2021.126130

Urban Green Council. (2023). New York City building emissions law impact study. https://www.urbangreencouncil.org

Urugo, M. M., Teka, T. A., Gemede, H. F., Mersha, S., Tessema, A., Woldemariam, H. W., & Admassu, H. (2024). A comprehensive review of current approaches on food waste reduction strategies. *Comprehensive Reviews in Food Science and Food Safety*, *23*(5), e70011. DOI: 10.1111/1541-4337.70011

Van Bavel, J. J., Harris, E. A., Pärnamets, P., Rathje, S., Doell, K. C., & Tucker, J. A. (2021). Political psychology in the digital (mis) information age: A model of news belief and sharing. *Social Issues and Policy Review*, *15*(1), 84–113. DOI: 10.1111/sipr.12077

Van der Linden, S., Leiserowitz, A., Rosenthal, S., & Maibach, E. (2017). Inoculating the public against misinformation about climate change. *Global Challenges (Hoboken, NJ)*, *1*(2), 1600008. DOI: 10.1002/gch2.201600008 PMID: 31565263

Van Opstal, W., Borms, L., Brusselaers, J., Bocken, N., Pals, E., & Dams, Y. (2024). Towards sustainable growth paths for work integration social enterprises in the circular economy. *Journal of Cleaner Production, 470*, 143296. DOI: 10.1016/j.jclepro.2024.143296

Vangeri, A., Bathrinath, S., Anand, M., Shanmugathai, M., Meenatchi, N., & Boopathi, S. (2024). Green Supply Chain Management in Eco-Friendly Sustainable Manufacturing Industries. In *Environmental Applications of Carbon-Based Materials* (pp. 253–287). IGI Global., DOI: 10.4018/979-8-3693-3625-0.ch010

Vanham, P. (2025). A brief history of GDP – and what could come next. *World Economic Forum*. https://www.weforum.org/stories/2021/12/stakeholder-capitalism-episode-1-a-brief-history-of-gdp/

Varela, P., Antúnez, L., Cadena, R. S., Giménez, A., and Ares, G. (2014). Attentional capture and importance of package attributes for consumers' perceived similarities and differences among products: A case study with breakfast cereal packages. Food Res. Int. 64, 701–710. doi: . foodres.2014.08.015DOI: 10.1016/j

Vecchiato, G., Astolfi, L., De Vico Fallani, F., Cincotti, F., Mattia, D., Salinari, S., & Babiloni, F. (2011). EEG correlates of sensorimotor integration and embodiment during the appreciation of virtual architectural environments. *Brain Research Bulletin, 85*(5), 253–260. DOI: 10.1016/j.brainresbull.2010.12.003

Vecchiato, G., Astolfi, L., De Vico Fallani, F., Cincotti, F., Mattia, D., Salinari, S., Soranzo, R., & Babiloni, F. (2010). Changes in brain activity during the observation of TV commercials by using EEG, GSR and HR measurements. *Brain Topography, 23*(2), 165–179. DOI: 10.1007/s10548-009-0127-0

Velenturf, A. P., & Purnell, P. (2021). Principles for a sustainable circular economy. *Sustainable Production and Consumption, 27*, 1437–1457. DOI: 10.1016/j.spc.2021.02.018

Venkatraman, V., Dimoka, A., Pavlou, P. A., Vo, K., Hampton, W., Bollinger, B., Hershfield, H. E., Ishihara, M., & Winer, R. S. (2015). Predicting advertising success beyond traditional measures: New insights from neurophysiological methods and market response modeling. *JMR, Journal of Marketing Research, 52*(4), 436–452. DOI: 10.1509/jmr.13.0593

Vernon, R. (1966). International investment and international trade in the product cycle. *The Quarterly Journal of Economics, 80*(2), 190–207. DOI: 10.2307/1880689

Vidal-Raméntol, S. (2020). Neuromarketing and sustainability. *Advances in Social Sciences Research Journal, 7*(12), 364–377. DOI: 10.14738/assrj.712.9360

Vraga, E. K., & Bode, L. (2020). Defining misinformation and understanding its bounded nature: Using expertise and evidence for describing misinformation. *Political Communication, 37*(1), 136–144. DOI: 10.1080/10584609.2020.1716500

Wang, R. Y., & Strong, D. M. (1996). Beyond accuracy: What data quality means to data consumers. *Journal of Management Information Systems, 12*(4), 5–33. DOI: 10.1080/07421222.1996.11518099

Wang, Y., Ren, H., Dong, L., Park, H. S., Zhang, Y., & Xu, Y. (2019). Smart solutions shape for sustainable low-carbon future: A review on smart cities and industrial parks in China. *Technological Forecasting and Social Change, 144*, 103–117. DOI: 10.1016/j.techfore.2019.04.014

Wang, Y., & Zhi, Q. (2016). The role of green finance in environmental protection: A global perspective. *Energy Economics, 58*, 123–134. DOI: 10.1016/j.eneco.2016.07.012

Wardle, C., & Derakhshan, H. (2017). *Information disorder: Toward an interdisciplinary framework for research and policymaking* (Vol. 27). Council of Europe.

Waste Dive. (2023). CEO interviews: The new economics of trash

Whelan, E., Islam, A. N., & Brooks, S. (2020). Applying the SOBC paradigm to explain how social media overload affects academic performance. *Computers & Education*, *143*, 103692. DOI: 10.1016/j.compedu.2019.103692

Whysall, P. (2005). Retailers' Press Release Activity: Market Signals for Stakeholder Engagement? *European Journal of Marketing*, *39*(9/10), 1118–1131. DOI: 10.1108/03090560510610752

Wild, U., Laumer, S., & Kroenke, A. (2012). The bipartite influence of information overload on user resistance to knowledge management systems.

Wilson, C. (2010). Prioritizing sustainability: Economic agents and the pursuit of green finance. *Journal of Sustainable Finance & Investment*, *1*(2), 95–110. DOI: 10.1080/20430791003780485

Wood, T., & Porter, E. (2019). The elusive backfire effect: Mass attitudes' steadfast factual adherence. *Political Behavior*, *41*(1), 135–163. DOI: 10.1007/s11109-018-9443-y

World Bank. (2022). State and trends of carbon pricing 2022. https://www.worldbank.org/carbonpricing

World Bank. (2023). Global waste management outlook. https://www.worldbank.org

World Business Council for Sustainable Development (WBCSD). (2020). *Circular Transition Indicators v2.0.*

World Economic Forum. (2020, Jan 22). https://www.weforum.org/stories/2020/01/the-world-needs-a-circular-economy-lets-make-it-happen. (F. v. Houten, & N. Ishii, Eds.) Retrieved April 2025, from https://www.weforum.org/: https://www.weforum.org/stories/2020/01/the-world-needs-a-circular-economy-lets-make-it-happen

World Economic Forum. (2022). The Green Venture Capital Playbook. https://www.weforum.org

World Economic Forum. (2023). Circular economy economic potential. https://www.weforum.org

World Economic Forum. (2023). Digital platforms for resource efficiency. https://www.weforum.org

Wu, T. (2018). Blind spot: The attention economy and the Law. *Antitrust Law Journal*, *82*, 771.

Xavier, L. H., Giese, E. C., Ribeiro-Duthie, A. C., & Lins, F. A. F. (2021). Sustainability and the circular economy: A theoretical approach focused on e-waste urban mining. *Resources Policy*, *74*, 101467. DOI: 10.1016/j.resourpol.2019.101467

Xavier, L. H., Ottoni, M., & Lepawsky, J. (2021). Circular economy and e-waste management in the Americas: Brazilian and Canadian frameworks. *Journal of Cleaner Production*, *297*, 126570. DOI: 10.1016/j.jclepro.2021.126570

Xiao, L., & Mou, J. (2019). Social media fatigue-Technological antecedents and the moderating roles of personality traits: The case of WeChat. *Computers in Human Behavior*, *101*, 297–310. DOI: 10.1016/j.chb.2019.08.001

Yadav, G., Luthra, S., Jakhar, S. K., Mangla, S. K., & Rai, D. P. (2020). A framework to overcome sustainable supply chain challenges through solution measures of industry 4.0 and circular economy: An automotive case. *Journal of Cleaner Production*, *254*, 120112. DOI: 10.1016/j.jclepro.2020.120112

Yap, N. T. (2005). Towards a Circular Economy. Greener Management International, (50).

Zahid, M., Hayat, M., Rahman, H. U., & Ali, W. (2024). Is the financial industry ready for circular economy and sustainable development goals? A case of a developing country. *Qualitative Research in Financial Markets*, *16*(5), 962–992. DOI: 10.1108/QRFM-06-2023-0135

Zhang, C., Hu, M., Dong, L., Gebremariam, A., Miranda-Xicotencatl, B., Di Maio, F., & Tukker, A. (2019). Eco-efficiency assessment of technological innovations in high-grade concrete recycling. *Resources, Conservation and Recycling*, *149*, 649–663. DOI: 10.1016/j.resconrec.2019.06.023

Zha, X., Liu, K., Yan, Y., Yan, G., Guo, J., Cao, F., & Wang, Y. (2019). Comparing digital libraries with social media from the dual route perspective. *Online Information Review*, *43*(4), 617–634. DOI: 10.1108/OIR-11-2017-0344

Zhen, Z., Yousaf, Z., Radulescu, M., & Yasir, M. (2021). Nexus of digital organizational culture, capabilities, organizational readiness, and innovation: Investigation of SMEs operating in the digital economy. *Sustainability (Basel)*, *13*(2), 720. DOI: 10.3390/su13020720

Zlotnik, M. (2021). Circular economy as a part of the organizational corporate strategy. *Management and Entrepreneurship in Ukraine: the stages of formation and problems of development*, 183-192. https://doi.org/DOI: 10.23939/smeu2021.01.183

Zollo, F., Bessi, A., Del Vicario, M., Scala, A., Caldarelli, G., Shekhtman, L., Havlin, S., & Quattrociocchi, W. (2017). Debunking in a world of tribes. *PLoS One*, *12*(7), e0181821. DOI: 10.1371/journal.pone.0181821 PMID: 28742163

About the Contributors

Mohamad Saad El Dine Knio holds a PhD in Economics from Cardiff University in the United Kingdom. Currently, Dr. Knio serves as an Assistant Professor of Economics at the Lebanese International University. With a career in academia that began in 2011, Dr. Knio has taught at several well-reputed universities. Notably, he previously worked as an Assistant Professor and Head of Sustainability at City University Ajman in the UAE. Dr. Knio has made significant contributions to academic research and student mentorship. They have supervised numerous DBA students, guiding them to successfully complete their theses. His research primarily focuses on macroeconomics and sustainability, producing applied research aimed at addressing real-world problems. In addition to their academic endeavors, Dr. Knio was actively involved in an Erasmus project and has been a member of AACSB, where they contributed to strategic planning initiatives for their school. They have an extensive publication record in the areas of sustainability and macroeconomic variables, solidifying their reputation as a scholar committed to impactful research.

***

Ahmad Ashaal Finance professor with a doctorate degree from Rennes School of Business, bringing over a decade of experience in teaching accounting and finance to undergraduates and graduates. Currently serving as the finance department research leader and MBA finance coordinator. Demonstrated leadership and competence in academia and over six years of managerial experience in various industries. Proven commitment to community service, collaborating with civil societies to enhance social, economic, and legal capacities. Recognized for organizational skills, ability to thrive under pressure, effective communication, and proficiency in MS Office and Stata. *Peer reviewer for International Review of Financial Analysis (IRFA). *Peer reviewer for the Journal of Cleaner Production (JCLP). *Peer reviewer for Finance Research Letters. *Peer reviewer for Management of Environmental Quality (MEQ).

Ali Eren Balıkel completed his primary, secondary, and high school education in Mersin. To gain international experience, explore job opportunities, and enhance his foreign language skills, he pursued higher education abroad. He studied Business Administration at the London School of Commerce (LSC) through a program affiliated with the University of Wales Institute, Cardiff (UWIC). Following his undergraduate studies, Dr. Balıkel completed an MBA at the University of Gloucestershire, where his thesis on branding and entrepreneurship earned an honorary award and was placed among the university's most valuable theses. Translating theory into practice, he opened his first restaurant, "Kilikyas," in London. Continuing his academic journey, Dr. Balıkel obtained a master's degree in Politics from Queen Mary University of London and earned a PhD from the University of Wales Trinity Saint David. He currently serves as a lecturer at Istanbul Kent University, Faculty of Economics, Administrative and Social Sciences, Department of International Trade and Logistics. His research focuses on the intersections of politics, economy, entrepreneurship, and sustainability. Ali Eren Balıkel is the author of two books: Turkish Foreign Policy from Past to Present in a Theoretical Framework, which has been translated into eight languages, and A Sustainable World is Possible, which was distributed free of charge to libraries across Turkey to promote sustainability awareness. In addition to his books, he has published numerous articles in various international peer-reviewed journals.

Fatma Gülşah Dizar Karadağ is an expert with 17 years of experience in neuromarketing, brand management, and biometric technologies. She has contributed to award-winning campaigns for brands such as Bingo, Molfix, and Molped by working on 100 neuro-research projects involving over 2,500 consumers. Currently serving as the Neuromarketing Lead at Hayat Kimya, she has previously held managerial positions in marketing and neuromarketing at companies like ETB and Neuroscience ABS. She has participated in events such as the International Neuroscience Symposium organized in collaboration with Istanbul Aydın University and has conducted academic research exploring the impact of neuroscience on consumer behavior. DİZAR KARADAĞ holds an MBA from Istanbul Aydın University and a second master's degree in Neuroscience from Üsküdar University. She is currently pursuing her PhD at İstinye University, specializing in neuromarketing, biometric analysis, and consumer behavior. She effectively utilizes professional tools such as Power BI, Atlassian Jira, iMotions, Emotiv, Tobii, and Shimmer to develop data-driven marketing strategies. Combining academic and industry expertise, she offers scientific approaches to understanding consumers and measuring their conscious and subconscious responses, shaping marketing strategies for leading brands.

Fadi Ghosn is a researcher in finance and economics and a dedicated educator committed to advancing knowledge in these fields. Dr. Ghosn holds a PhD in Business Administration, providing a comprehensive understanding of financial theory and research methodologies, which they bring into the classroom. Dr. Ghosn currently serves as a full-time Assistant Professor of Finance at the Lebanese International University. In addition to their teaching responsibilities, Dr. Ghosn is involved in coordination, administrative, and research activities within the university. Beyond academia, Dr. Ghosn is the CEO and co-founder of Success Gate International, a consultancy firm specializing in financial and strategic advisory services. Dr. Ghosn's research interests span both finance and economics. This blend of academic expertise, research work, practical experience, and entrepreneurial work makes Dr. Ghosn a vital member of the academic community and a respected authority in their field. Their expertise is regularly sought by prestigious media outlets to discuss domestic and international trends in financial markets.

Mohamad Hijazi is a researcher and lecturer at the School of Business, Lebanese International University, Lebanon. His academic interests span financial management, financial economics, and business administration. Dr. Hijazi has contributed to several research initiatives in these areas and is actively engaged in peer review, serving as a reviewer for journals such as Cogent Business & Management. He is committed to advancing knowledge in financial and economic disciplines through both teaching and scholarly work.

Hassan Houmani is a seasoned mathematician and academic strategist with over 14 years of experience in higher education, specializing in Statistics, Business Mathematics, and research coordination. Currently serving as Assistant Professor and Assistant Dean at the Lebanese International University's School of Business, Dr. Houmani has played a pivotal role in academic leadership, curriculum development, and student advising across nine campuses. His academic journey spans multiple countries and disciplines. He earned his PhD in Mathematics from the Politehnica University of Bucharest, Romania, where he investigated nonlinear operators and best proximity point theory. Previously, he completed a Master's degree in Statistics at Lund University, Sweden, graduating with high honors, and a Bachelor's degree in Mathematics from LIU Lebanon. His work reflects a rigorous blend of theoretical insight and practical application—ranging from proximity point theorems in gauge spaces to econometric modeling and process monitoring using truncated gamma distributions. Throughout his career, Dr. Houmani has championed the integration of statistical computing tools—including MATLAB, SPSS, Eviews, and STATA—into academic research and classroom instruction. He has taught and coordinated a wide array of undergraduate and graduate courses, including Business Research

Methods, Econometrics, Time Series Analysis, and Statistical Computation. His publication record spans internationally indexed journals and conferences, notably in the areas of proximal contractions, gauge spaces, and statistical modeling. He is also a recipient of the Erasmus Mundus Josyleen Scholarship and has contributed to interdisciplinary statistical projects in ecology, historical biology, and educational behavior. Outside academia, Dr. Houmani brings managerial experience from Lebanon's private sector, adding a practical lens to his pedagogical approach. Fluent in Arabic and English, and highly proficient in French, he actively bridges cross-cultural perspectives in education and policy. With a passion for advancing analytical frameworks and promoting academic resilience in complex regional contexts, Dr. Houmani continues to mentor students, develop research initiatives, and explore the frontiers of mathematical logic and statistical innovation.

Nada Mallah Boustani is a full professor in the Faculty of Business & Management at Saint-Joseph University- Beirut, holding a PhD in Business Finance and an HDR in business (innovation and finance) from France. She is an active member in different international research associations such as AIS, LEFMI, POLYTECH, and an engaged researcher with published papers related to Innovation in Finance and in Business . In addition to her academic and research performances, She is President and co-founder of AXISSED, Board member in several business groups and NGOs in Lebanon and EMENA region and a prominent business consultant for several businesses.

Fatih Ölçekciler holds a strong academic background and extensive professional experience, with two MBA degrees from distinguished universities in the United Kingdom (University of East London / International Business and UWIC / Marketing) and a doctorate from Switzerland (Swiss Management Center University / International Marketing). In addition to International Business and Marketing, he has specialized in Human Resource Management (Dokuz Eylül University / Labor Economics and Industrial Relations). He has also received academic training in various fields, including statistical analysis. Over the years, he has served as a manager at two UK-based research companies. Currently, he is the General Manager of Neuroscience Ltd., responsible for Turkey and the Middle East, while simultaneously holding the position of Research Department Director at one of the leading research companies in the United Kingdom and serving as the Turkey Representative of a Switzerland-based international writing and research company. With more than 20 years of academic and professional experience, he has participated in over 1,000 international research projects and has been honored with numerous national and international awards for his contributions.

Gizem Ölçekciler is an accomplished researcher and operations manager with extensive experience in international business, data analysis, and academic research. She currently serves as Head of Research Center Operations at Neuroscience ABS, where she leads neuroscience-based projects focusing on human behavior and decision-making. She holds an MBA in International Business from Cardiff Metropolitan University and is pursuing a Ph.D. in Business Administration at Istinye University, specializing in data-driven decision-making and operational efficiency. Proficient in advanced statistical tools such as SPSS, AMOS, and LISREL, as well as neuroscience technologies including EEG, eye-tracking, and GSR, she integrates scientific insights into strategic business practices. With a strong background in research management, statistical analysis, and sustainable business growth, she has contributed to internationally published books and articles and continues to bridge the gap between academia and industry through innovative, evidence-based approaches.

Mohamad Saad is a lecturer at the School of Business at Lebanese International University, Lebanon, where he currently serves as the chairperson of the Finance department. His recent research works focused on the stock market and asset valuation.

Suha Tahan is the Chairperson of the Economics Department at the Lebanese International University. With around 14 years of professional and academic experience, her research mainly focuses on sustainability and green practices.

Bassam Tarhini Assistant Professor in Marketing, holding a PHD in Service Marketing earned from Bucharest University of Economic Studies in Romania in November 2021. Earned his Masters degree in Marketing and Management Information Systems from Oklahoma City University, USA in December 2004. The BS degree in Marketing was obtained from the Lebanese University in 1998. Currently, holding the role of Assistant dean at the Lebanese International University since 2011. Also, claimed the role of Chairman for the Marketing Department at the Lebanese International University from Fall 2011 till 2019 simultaneously with the role of Assistant Dean which currently still claiming. Acquired 15 years of teaching experience at both the graduate and undergraduate levels while providing high standards and quality education. Prior to teaching, had several years of corporate experience in the field of Marketing Management including 5 years of marketing management for the daily operations of Intercontinental Hotel Groups IHG in the USA, and prior to that was a corporate account manager and sales trainer for 3 years at Dell Inc. in the USA.

Caner Yazıcıoğlu was born in Istanbul in 1989. He completed his primary and secondary education in the city where he was born. After graduating from Zonguldak Karaelmas University (now Bülent Ecevit University) Department of Economics, he completed his master's degree in Human Resources. Yazicioglu, who conducts research on generational differences, he wrote his thesis on career planning Generation Y Scholars in Turkey. Yazıcıoğlu has gained professional experience in various structures and positions of the education sector. He has 11 years of professional university experience by working as an expert, coordinator, manager, director etc. in administrative and academic units of various foundation universities. In this experience, he participated in intertwined with the sector and took interactively responsibleness in university-sector cooperation. Yazıcıoğlu, who also works as a Asst. Prof., was a lecturer in the Department of Public Relations and Advertising. Yazıcıoğlu graduated from PhD in Marmara University. He studied at Interpersonal Communication department and writed a thesis about "Narcissism at Academicians". Be on the point of being corporate level, he has been presenting trainings of managing, conflict management, motivation, persuasive skill, performance management which are focused on communication, human resources and generation gap.

Index

B

C

D

E

F

G

I

L

M

N

P

R

S

www.ingramcontent.com/pod-product-compliance
Lightning Source LLC
LaVergne TN
LVHW081540300926
849161LV00006B/1497